To Caroline
with best wishes from

Thirty Men & a Girl   7/7/2016

For my cousins Rosemary and Tim Skipper and their sons Andrew and Peter, who brought me a ready-made family.

Thirty Men & a Girl

*A singer's memories of war, mountains, travel,
and always music*

Elisabeth Parry

ALLEGRA

Copyright © Elisabeth Parry 2010
First published in 2010 by Allegra
Broadmeade Copse, Westwood Lane, Wanborough, Guildford,
Surrey, GU3 2JN
www.elisabethparry.com

Reprinted in paperback 2011
Reprinted 2014

Distributed by Lightning Source worldwide
The right of Elisabeth Parry to be identified as the author of the work
has been asserted herein in accordance with the Copyright, Designs and
Patents Act 1988.

British Library Cataloguing in Publication Data
A catalogue record for this book is available from the British Library

ISBN 978-0-9564538-1-5
Typeset by Amolibros, Milverton, Somerset
www.amolibros.com
This book production has been managed by Amolibros
Printed and bound by Lightning Source, UK

Contents

List of Illustrations

Facing page 106

1 My first public appearance aged four and a half singing "Little Jack Horner".
2 With my mother and father.
3 Learning to read with my mother.
4 With my step-father in the Pyrenees, August 1939.
5 Singing with the Staff Band of the Royal Army Medical Corps conducted by Harry Johnson.
6 Granny Forbes at Broadmeade Copse.
7 Dancing with Michael Lyndon.
8 Making tea in the Sinai Desert, New Year's Eve 1943.
9 The Band in the desert near Baghdad, January 1944.
10 Our ambulance train in the Persian mountains.
11 Opera stars on tour in Paiforce.
12 The Nairn buses, Baghdad.
13 Baalbec, the Temple of Bacchus.
14 The Luncheon in Cairo in honour of Lily Pons and André Kostelanetz.
15 Our "theatre" with the 5th Armoured Division in the desert by the Red Sea.
16 Benjamin Britten with Joan Cross and Peter Pears in the garden, Glyndebourne 1947.
17 Benjamin Britten with Eric Crozier and Frederick Ashton.
18 Norman del Mar rehearsing *Let's make an Opera*.
19 *La Bohème* by Puccini, last Act. The Opera Players' 1951 production.
20 *Don Pasquale* by Donizetti, 1951 production, showing the convertible couch used as a bed in La Bohème in all its glory.
21 Loading Phyllis's car for Hänsel and Gretel in a London Junior School.

Facing page 330

About the book

Elisabeth Parry was born in Aberdeen on 3rd September 1921. She had just left school, planning to study French and German literature at Oxford, when war was declared on her eighteenth birthday, 3rd September 1939. She was already having singing lessons with Mark Raphael in London, and a chance audition with the Staff Band of the Royal Army Medical Corps led to her becoming soprano soloist with them and singing in hundreds of variety shows and classical concerts until the war ended. They toured Britain and the Middle East as "Thirty men and a Girl", and Elisabeth was voted Forces sweetheart for Paiforce (Persia and Iraq Force).

In 1947 she launched and ran the Wigmore Hall Lunch Hour Concerts for young musicians returning from the war. She also auditioned for Benjamin Britten's newly formed English Opera Group, was taken on as an understudy, and found herself unexpectedly singing a principal role, Lucia in Britten's *The Rape of Lucretia* when the Viennese soprano she was covering had a row and departed for Vienna in a cloud of dust. She found herself singing for a Glyndebourne First Night and Third Programme Broadcast, working with great artists like Kathleen Ferrier, Peter Pears, Joan Cross and Ottakar Kraus, and of course Britten himself, a wonderful if daunting experience.

She left the EOG to start up her own small touring company along with a pianist friend in 1950. They survived a bitter struggle with the Arts Council to establish themselves successfully, and toured for fifty-six years, the first company in England to take classical opera on a reduced scale, fully costumed and produced and sung in English, all over Britain to audiences and schools who otherwise had no chance of hearing opera live.

She started to climb at the age of forty, and became a passionate mountaineer and traveller during her holidays, which led to a second career as a successful lecturer In 1973 she was awarded a Diploma of Commendation for Distinguished Achievement in *The World Who's Who of Women* – she is still uncertain what for! She retired when her company, the London Opera Players, closed in 2006, and now enjoys her big garden, U3A classes, practising the piano, reading, and writing the occasional poem.

Some reviews

"Six generations of young singers have been inspired and nurtured at a crucial stage of their careers by Elisabeth Parry and the London Opera Players. Her artistic integrity, indomitable energy and sound common sense made her greatly loved as well as respected." *Tom Hawkes*

"Thank you so much for your very interesting book. People's experiences during the War can only add to the history of our country. May I wish you every success." *Dame Vera Lynn*

"Some of my happiest musical memories are of the days I would be involved with the London Opera Players. Elisabeth Parry always managed to assemble such delightful teams – co-operative, compatible and talented, a pleasure to work with." *Antony Hopkins CBE FRCM*

"Elisabeth Parry's book should make fascinating reading for anyone interested in music, mountains, the second World War, and especially her life work, London Opera Players, which for 56 years gave invaluable performing experience to so many rising young singers." *Josephine Veasey CBE, HonRAM*

"Elisabeth Parry is a marvel. In venues spread country-wide, against all odds, with her enthusiasm and inspiration we somehow managed to play operas to audiences who would otherwise maybe never have had the opportunity. They don't make them like that any more!" *Richard Balcombe, conductor, London Opera Players*

"A wonderfully entertaining account of an indomitable spirit and a uniquely full life, including more than half a century during which Elisabeth Parry nurtured the grass roots of English opera through a drought, enabled the careers of hundreds of young singers, and brought the very best of live performances to thousands who would otherwise never have heard a note of opera, and who will now love reading about it all." *Edwin Glasgow (QC, CBE)*

"Elisabeth Parry's fascinating memoir fills an important gap in British operatic history. In it she tells the story of Opera Players, a small touring company which she founded in 1950, and led for fifty years. Surviving on a shoestring and mostly without Arts Council subsidy, it brought live opera in English to the schools and theatres of provincial Britain, creating an audience for opera which it had never had and giving scores of young singers experience of leading roles which led them to national and international careers: an unsung story which has belatedly found its authentic voice." *Robert Skidelsky*

Some of Elisabeth Parry's press notices:

WIGMORE HALL, LONDON. MARCH 1947

"Elisabeth Parry, a soprano of much promise, performed arias by Bellini and Verdi." Scott Godard. *News Chronicle*

GLYNDEBOURNE, 1947, *THE RAPE OF LUCRETIA*

"Elisabeth Parry, coming late to the role of Lucia, was stiff on the stage, but not in her high-lying vocal line, which she sang prettily in a voice not unlike Miss Margaret Ritchie, who had the part last year". *The Times*

"…Lucretia's women, Flora Nielsen and Elisabeth Parry, sang their delicate and difficult music well." *The Manchester Guardian*

THE ENGLISH OPERA GROUP. AUTUMN 1947

"Miss Elisabeth Parry, a young singer with a Welsh background…has her feet firmly planted on the first rungs of the ladder to fame. A soprano, her voice has already something more than promise, and it is likely that in the near future she will be received with great acclaim… her voice, pure and rich, held us spellbound." *Northern Echo*

Some Italian and other Press. 1950 onwards

GENOA. THE PARRY CONCERT AT THE ITALO- BRITANNIC ASSOCIATION, PALAZZO DURAZZO

"…The programme was of the greatest interest, presenting a wide selection of English songs, extending from the brilliant period of Purcell and Arne to the romanticism of Quilter and Armstrong Gibbs. It also included a short series of traditional English, Irish and Scottish songs…Elisabeth Parry attacked this arduous interpretative task with secure ability and a pure and convincing musicianship. Gifted with a voice of extremely sweet timbre and a technique which allows her to bend it with inimitable grace to all the exigencies of the lyric genre, she gave a display of great versatility and rare good taste, knowing how to change the accent of her expression from the linear plasticity of the classics to the more free and nostalgic poetic vein of the romantics, and achieving supreme moments, especially in the traditional songs…" Capocaccia. *Il Corriere Mercantile*

"The young singer opened her programme with a group of English songs of the 17th and 18th centuries, executed with admirable grace and refined style; a true model of graceful singing which recalled to us with nostalgia the most noble traditions of our own bel canto, so often neglected, particularly amongst ourselves…" Borselli. *Corriere del Popolo*

SIENA CONCERT

"The English soprano Elisabeth Parry sang with a beautiful voice (especially the high notes) and with a very fine style, early English songs, and a big aria from Mozart's *Die Entfuhrung aus dem Serail*, brilliantly overcoming all the technical difficulties, and displaying a rare vocal virtuosity." *Il Mattino*

Home Press

"…A young soprano with a pleasing voice that is both pure and rich in quality." *The Times*

"…A fresh and agreeable voice which gave evidence of careful training, definite ideas of interpretation, and a pleasing platform manner. The Mozart section was dominated by the Masonic Cantata, a notable work, rarely to be heard, which was finely sung." *The Scotsman*

"…Miss Elisabeth Parry, who broadcast a recital of songs by Debussy yesterday evening, has been widely acclaimed for the purity and richness in quality of her voice." *Western Mail*

"…in particular Constanze (Elisabeth Parry) managed her two very difficult arias, which come almost on top of one another, with extraordinary success." Rathcol. *The Belfast Telegraph*

ROSSINI'S STABAT MATER. BIRMINGHAM

"…It was thrillingly well done. All four voice parts held firmly and fervently. In view of the fact that the solo parts were originally written for Grisi, Tamburini and Co., they were astonishingly well tackled… Miss Parry and Miss Hughes blended sweetly and tenderly in "Quis est Homo", and Miss Parry's top Cs were as safe as houses in the great "Inflammatus". J F Waterhouse. *Birmingham Post*

MUSIC IN MINIATURE

"…Elisabeth Parry sang two groups of songs, including Mozart's triumphant "Alleluia" and Strauss's delicate "Serenade". Her voice was a joy, full, round, flexible and beautifully controlled. She achieved some exquisite pianissimi in Mozart's tender "Cradle Song", and made the technical difficulties of Schubert's "Shepherd on the Rock" seem negligible". *Folkestone Herald*

"…In her groups of songs Elisabeth Parry revealed a fine voice. She sang with artistry and finish throughout" *Western Mail*

DON PASQUALE. FESTIVAL OPERA COMPANY. ARTS THEATRE. CAMBRIDGE

"...Possessor of a superbly and beautifully produced soprano voice is Elisabeth Parry, who as Norina the masquerading widow entered spiritedly into the fun of the thing."

"Elisabeth Parry's lovely voice, grace and good looks, charmed everyone... . Truly delightful singing, clear diction, and the polished mannered acting which is an essential ingredient of operas of this sort."

THE BARBER OF SEVILLE. ROSSINI

"...Elisabeth Parry gave an excellent presentation of Rosina. She looks well, and her singing ability is equal to the exacting demands of her role." *Eastern Daily Press*

"...Elisabeth Parry was a golden-toned Rosina whose looks were as charming as her sweet soprano voice." *Surrey Mirror*

"...Elisabeth Parry as Rosina held the audience breathless on several occasions with her magnificent voice, notably in the singing lesson scene." *Lincolnshire Free Press*

Acknowledgements

The Company

I am very sorry that it has been impossible in this book to mention all the many kind people who helped us on our way during our fifty-six years on the road. Our directors gave their time voluntarily and unstintingly, amongst them James Dewar, who did our accounts for free during all our early years, and later Mary Glasgow, Chair Person supreme, whose wisdom and enthusiasm were boundless. Both are no longer with us, but they are remembered with much gratitude. Following the retirement of Margarita Ferriday, Jane Mackinnon gave me invaluable book-keeping and secretarial help for ten years while I was running the company from home. During our last somewhat troubled years I owed many thanks to Bob Clarke (Chair of our small Board) and Peter Andrews (promotions and general office help), who together with Helen Lawrence, Brenda Stanley and Clive Simmonds helped steer the company to a wise closure in 2006. Grateful thanks also to our late President Philip Langridge, whose untimely death has been announced as I write. We are all proud that he sang his first operas with us, and his loyalty and enthusiasm cheered me through some dark days.

Mountains

I owe much joy to my "mountain men" as I call them, Sidney Nowill who first pointed my faltering footsteps uphill, and guides Willi Truffer (Switzerland), Celso Degasper (Italy) and Gilles Josserand (France). I thank them for their patience and forbearance, and for all the fun and adventures we had together.

Wales

I discovered my Welsh heritage in middle age, and it is through the hard work of Mansel Richards, Head of History, with his Cyfarthfa School pupils, the Heritage Trust, and Carl Llewellyn with his carefully researched biography of Joseph Parry, that much of my father's family history was revealed to me. An English version of the excellent biography by Dr Dulais Rhys has also just been released. Through the initiative of my cousin Rosemary, contact has been made with the National Library of Wales, which kindly supplied me with a photo copy of my great-grandfather's hand-written draft autobiography, a rare document which is held in their archives. And finally thanks to the enthusiasm of John Fisher, Chief Executive and Artistic Director of the Welsh NationalOpera, and his staff, a Parry Family annual Bursary for a rising young singer has been established.

Home

At home so many people have smoothed my path, amongst them George Chant, who has done every sort of thing from making and painting odd props and bits of furniture for the operas to helping me with the final awful clearing up and disposing of fifty-six years of costumes and scenery, plus tons of paper work from my office.   My cousin Rosemary has also helped me in many ways these last years, amongst other things by sorting through hundreds of old programmes, press notices and photographs to form an archive for the London Opera Players. My friend and neighbour Rocky has helped me greatly in my battle with computers and printers during the writing of these memoirs, and Mike Logan, my computer and photographic guru, has provided invaluable help in preparing the illustrations. Grateful thanks to you all.

Amolibros

Finally, I am greatly indebted to Amolibros and Jane Tatam, without whose expertise and kind assistance this book would never have come into existence.

The Arts Council

I would like to put the record straight about our relationship, sometimes stormy, with the Arts Council. After all, they did launch us before they decided to get rid of us! Years later, on the occasion of the Company's twenty–first birthday, we were taken back into the fold and they helped us financially towards the cost of the first children's opera we commissioned, "Dr.Musikus" by Antony Hopkins. During the 1970s I resigned from the Board of the Opera Players, as we were then called, and was paid a salary of £600 p.a. by the Arts Council to manage the company. During this time they sent a representative to all our Board meetings to oversee our doings. This arrangement ceased when they withdrew all support from us (and two other companies) without notice in 1979. However, when we commissioned our second children's opera, *The Pig Organ*, from Richard Blackford. with libretto by Ted Hughes, they paid the commission fee for us. After that we had no further dealings with them, apart from for our Lottery Appeal, which had to be made under their auspices, and from which we got a grant towards a new van.

Apologies

Wherever possible all dates and names in these memoirs have been checked in my diaries. I would like to apologise for any errors I may inadvertently have made, and will be happy to correct them.

The reader may find some Middle East names spelt in unfamiliar ways or even in two different versions. Spellings varied from signpost to signpost and from map to map, as they still do to this day, so I have used the versions which were in common use when I was there.

Lastly, I am very ashamed by the racist tone of some of my remarks in my Middle East letters, and I apologise for them. Those diaries were written when I was twenty-two and reflect the thinking of the time; and they come to you warts and all!

Acknowledgements: Illustrations & Quotations

Photographs 10, 11, 12, 13, 14, 15, 21, 23, 25, 29, 40, 42,43, 44, 45, 46, 47,48, 49, 50, 51, 52, 53, 54 and 58 were taken by me.

Photos 22 and 24 were by kind permission of the *Jersey Evening Post*.

Photo 31 is reproduced thanks to the Merthyr Heritage Trust and photos 32 and 33 are courtesy of the Merthyr Express.

Photos 37 and 38 were by Amanda Scope (only contact a twenty-year-old London telephone number – I think she was Viennese and may have gone back to Vienna).

Photos 60 and 62 are by kind permission of Robert Carpenter Turner.

Of the remaining twenty-seven photos, many were taken by friends or Army personnel, and there are some the source of which I have been unable to trace.

Virginia Graham's poem "Zut!" reproduced with permission of Punch Ltd.

Bishop Tom Butler's words quoted by courtesy of the BBC.

Ernest Newman's poem appears by kind permission of his son Mr Peter Newman.

The quotation by Stephen Hawking is from: *A Brief History of Time* by Stephen Hawking, published by Bantam Press. Reproduced by permission of The Random House Group Ltd.

The author has made every effort to contact the copyright holders for Einstein and Teilhard de Chardin, without success. She would be pleased to hear from them so that the matter may be cleared up.

The limericks (by Monsignor Ronald Knox) are reproduced by kind permission of A P Watt on behalf of the Earl of Oxford and Asquith, but the limericks have been written from memory and are not necessarily correct.

Prologue

To write, or not to write,
That is the question…
(with apologies to Hamlet)

How to begin? From the advanced perspective of eighty-seven years I look back on my life and see a tangled skein of many coloured threads. They interweave, disappear, reappear for no apparent reason and in no special order, full of richness and diversity, a jumble of light and dark, to create a kaleidoscope of memories into which I must plunge. I think I shall try following through the individual threads one by one in the hope at the end of discovering a pattern – if there is one. So here goes, to start at the beginning – as all good stories should – with childhood. You asked for it, my friends!

Chapter One

1921–39

The first seven years

> Our birth is but a sleep and a forgetting;
> The Soul that rises with us, our life's Star,
> Hath had elsewhere its setting and cometh from afar.
>
> Wordsworth, 'Ode: Intimations of Immortality from
> Recollections of Early Childhood'

I was born on 3rd September 1921 in an Aberdeen nursing home. My father, Arthur Haydn Parry, was Welsh, and my mother, Mhari Margaret Forbes, was Scottish with a dash of French. She was a true romantic and had been staying during the end of her pregnancy at one of the old Forbes houses, Druminor, which she loved greatly and where it was intended I should be born. However, she became unwell with a kidney infection, which caused her to have a rigor during my birth. I had already been named John, all my new clothes were blue, and when the old family doctor handed me to my mother, saying with some distaste in broad Aberdeenshire dialect, 'It's a queenie,' my mother muttered 'Put it back. I want another one.' As a result, I expect, of the difficult birth I had a major operation when ten weeks old to remove a damaged ovary, during which I also lost the use of one kidney. Despite these early events, about which I remember nothing, I have had a healthy active life.

My earliest memory is of lying on my back in my pram being pushed in Kensington Gardens. My nurse was chattering, probably with other nannies, and I was filled with frustration at being unable to communicate. Later, when words had come, I can remember toddling up to a large swan that was sitting on its nest, and being seized back by Nanny who told me it could break my arm with one sweep of its wings…probably why to this day I run from a flock of farmyard geese. I remember when sheep came to graze in Kensington Gardens every summer, and also feeding the tame red squirrels. If you had the control to stand quite still they would climb up you and along your arm to eat nuts out of your hand.

Another memory, the first of a lifetime in thrall to natural beauty, must have been on my third birthday, a picnic on Loch Linnhe in the West Highlands, with what seemed to me an immense expanse of sand, paddling into little ripples edging a glassy mirror of water and blowing soap bubbles on my clay pipe, which floated magically away into the distance. I didn't see the mountains beyond – they were outside my still limited perception. But they would come later. It was at this time that the postman reported he had just seen in the loch 'Mary, Mother of God, going up to heaven in a cloud'. Enquiry revealed that this was my old Irish nanny bathing fully clad in a voluminous white flannel nightie.

I can't have been more than four when it hit me with traumatic suddenness that the two suns in my small firmament, my mother and father, were hurting each other. Not physically, for they never shouted at each other or had rows in my presence. One of them, I think my mother, was halfway up the stairs in our tall London house; my father was at the bottom and I was in the hall. I have no memory of what was said but I was suddenly vividly aware of their bitterness and pain. The whisperings of Nurse and the maids – 'He said this' and 'She did that' –which had passed over my head before – now all made sense. My parents stayed together for another three years but from then on my loyalties were divided and I never forgot the scene on the stairs, which I can still picture today. Nor the sick feeling inside: for years my tummy would turn over if there was any hint of a family row brewing.

At that time I loved my father most. He took me to the Malcolm Sargent children's concerts at the Queen's Hall every Saturday morning and introduced me to the great man, whom he knew slightly and whom I found hilarious. My memories of the concerts are definitely not intellectual. A highlight was when Sargent called out the trombone player to demonstrate to us, and made him play higher and higher – or was it lower and lower? – until his instrument came in two. My father was a brilliant pianist who was occasionally asked to accompany singer friends professionally. He used to get me singing bits from *Hänsel and Gretel*, or, more exciting, the young prince in his favourite opera, Musorgsky's *Boris Godunov*. He had a score with Rimsky-Korsakov's pencil-written alterations in the margin. Another favourite piece of his, which used to haunt my dreams was the 'Ritual Fire Dance' from de Falla's *El Amor brujo, Love, the Magician*. For my seventh birthday I was given a wind-up gramophone and my very own records of Yehudi and Hepzibah Menuhin playing the César Franck Violin and Piano Sonata.

Words were always as important as music to me, and I was lucky that when I was four my mother taught me to read from the good old-fashioned *Reading Without Tears*. 'C-A-T, cat; M-A-T, mat. The CAT sat on the MAT.' I still remember the pictures of that cat and that mat! I was soon racing through *The Jungle Book* and the *Just So Stories* and *Kim*, and I dreamed myself as Mowgli night after night, if I wasn't flying off to join Peter Pan in Kensington Gardens (which were only a stone's throw away). I think I must have had a sense of theatre because, the first time I was taken to church, after the first hymn, I asked loudly 'Do we clap now?' But my first play was not a success. After being taken to see *Peter Pan* I was so terrified by Captain Hook that for days I refused to go to the lavatory, which was on a half-landing in our old London house, unaccompanied. Years and years later I took a French godson to see it during its annual Christmas run at – I think – Drury Lane. His reaction was to remark coldly, 'I can see the wires.' Perhaps they do these things better in Paris. One of my mother's brothers, Mansfield Forbes, was a distinguished don of English literature at Clare College, Cambridge. He was always giving me wonderful books, and one I remember, which became a special treasure, was by a Dutch writer called Van Loon. It was an imaginative and beautifully illustrated sort of world geography – I wish I could remember its name – which triggered what is to this day an insatiable wanderlust.

My mother was a great Francophile and spoke fluent French. We had French cousins on her side of the family and somewhere I knew there was a château called Varennes with vineyards. The story goes that a Forbes forebear from Aberdeenshire married a French heiress, hired a ship, embarked his entire household, maids, animals, children, the lot, and set sail from Aberdeen never to return. We also had Huguenot cousins called Duval, refugees to this country in the bad old days of the persecution. A French governess, a sturdy no-nonsense Breton woman who couldn't speak a word of English, was imported round about my fourth birthday, and soon I was speaking fluent French, reading the wonderful Bibliothèque Rose children's books of Madame de Segur and even dreaming in French. I have no memory of actually learning anything – it just happened. All languages should be learned before the age of five!

I was probably very spoiled when this first governess arrived, and I remember being well slapped – what she called *soufflets*, administered with the flat of the hand on the cheek and ear. I can't say that I feel in any way warped by this experience! She also had a firm belief that children who were feverish should not be allowed to drink water, and this was much more serious as I caught whooping cough, at that time a serious illness with no vaccine, and I was very ill – and sometimes very thirsty – for three months. When I was at last allowed up I shot out of bed and fell flat on the floor, to be told I would have to learn to walk again. There was one invaluable and long-lasting result of this illness. The doctor advised my mother to take me to the South of France to convalesce, but that was not at all my mother's scene so off we went to Switzerland, which was to become a second home. My mother had been one of an intrepid band of Scots who pioneered 'sheeing', as it was then pronounced, before the First World War, and she was among the first women to race downhill. When the opportunity of my convalescence arose she joyfully took me back to Villars, where it had all begun.

For three happy years this was an annual event. Several Scottish families, friends of ours, the Formans, the Haldanes, the Steeles, all went together plus one or two governesses. We children did lessons in the mornings and skated, luged or skied in the afternoons. There was a children's luge club, called the Gang Warily Club, run needless to say by a Scotsman, which had a splendid run with built-up corners every bit as menacing as the Cresta to us. On one never-to-be-forgotten day our least favourite governess lost control of her luge, shot over the big corner and disappeared in an enormous snowdrift. 'Health and Safety' hadn't been invented, and the Steele boys made us all peashooters from sections of brass curtain rod. The 'barrels' were all that could be desired, shooting dead straight, and we made Plasticine holders for various missiles including ink, which made an awful mess. Disaster struck when someone racing round a corner had a collision and rammed the brass rod into the back of his mouth. It was a nasty injury and the peashooters were confiscated.

The first year we were at Villars I managed to fall while learning to skate, and crushed my right thumb in a folding iron chair I was hanging on to. My poor mother had to rush me by taxi to Lausanne, where I had an operation and we spent two nights in hospital. I remember us both getting the giggles because we were issued with hospital nighties split right up the back. When I got back to England the pad part of my thumb went hard and black and became a great object of interest to my small friends. Eventually it had to be removed with another minor op. I hated the old-fashioned anaesthetics and always fought like a tiger when the chloroform mask was put over my face. I was left with a rather short right thumb, which did not help my piano technique but gave me a good excuse to be clumsy with needle and thread. I remember having to write left-handed for a year.

Undismayed we were back in Villars next winter, and this time I was allowed to start skiing, which had been forbidden during the convalescence year. Every Saturday there were children's races on the nursery slopes. Patient ski instructors used to hold us round the middles pointing downhill from the top of the slope, and on the word 'Go!' they let us loose. He or she still standing at the bottom got a prize. I have two small silver cups on my mantelpiece to this day to prove it – though I seem to remember much preferring the consolation prizes, which were bars of chocolate.

We spent three months in Villars the last time we went out, and I knew the magic of skiing down onto patches of grass full of crocus and soldanella and snowdrops. And oh the mouth-watering smells wafting on the cold evening air from Robert's patisserie, where we called in for hot chocolate and cakes after our afternoons of hard exercise!

I was by now the youngest member of the Ski Club of Great Britain and the youngest to have passed my third-class test. My small ash skis had been found with some difficulty in London and came from a stage play called *Autumn Crocus*, which was set partly in Switzerland. My poor father never came on these trips; I was told he had to work.

Emotional and financial storm clouds were massing over my parents' heads by now. It would be years before my mother and I got back to Switzerland, and by the time we did so I would have a new stepfather. I have just one happy holiday memory with my father, when we stayed on Iona, at that time undiscovered and unspoilt. We walked from shore to shore and up the little hill from which St Columba is supposed to have looked yearningly back towards his beloved Ireland. It is not visible from Iona, which is why the saint is said to have decided to stop there – he could not bear to be within sight of his homeland. I remember the whitest of white sands and vivid turquoise and blue water, and the thrill of finding a real orange-coloured cornelian on the beach. It was put in a matchbox for safety, but on the way home I opened the box once too often to look at it and it jumped out and was lost in long heather. One fine day we went in a small boat to Staffa and walked in to Fingal's Cave, where great green swells rose majestically almost to the level of the ledge we walked on. We were a group of friends including the distinguished Scottish artist William Peploe, fondly known as Peppers.

I still return in dreams to that tall old London house of my early years. There was a basement with kitchen and staff bedrooms, where the London cockroaches refused to be exterminated despite many visits from the authorities. On the ground floor was a handsome dining room and a servery where food came up from the kitchen below on a noisy old lift. This was masked by a fine triple screen designed by my mother and covered by a single ox hide. I have it still in my dining room, the same dull golden colour, but the ox hide gave place to leatherette long ago. The big first-floor drawing room had a parquet floor and my father's grand piano, where I used to sing with him when I was allowed down, dressed in my best frock, for about an hour after tea. The nursery was right at the very top, together with bedrooms for my nurse or governess and me.

I can remember looking down and seeing the lamplighter come along on his bicycle to light the gas street lamps, which glowed greenish on winter evenings. The muffin man would come by too ringing a bell with his hot muffins on a tray on his head. The gas stove puttered cheerfully, it was warm and cosy, and later on my mother would come up, beautifully dressed and sweet-scented, to kiss me goodnight. I had a considerable repertoire of nursery rhymes, which I sang most nights to anyone who would listen, or to myself. In fact my first public appearance was a performance of 'Little Jack Horner' when I was three or four. I went to dancing class, not with the great Madame Vacani, who taught royalty, but with a lady next down on the social scale, I think Miss Jackson was her name, who was a lot less expensive. Every year she presented a charity show with her pupils in a London theatre. I had to run on and sit on a large pouf centre-stage, and squeak with appropriate gestures,

> Little Jack Horner
> Sat in a corner
> Eating his Christmas pie.
> He put in his thumb
> And pulled out a plum
> And said, 'What a good boy am I!'

I am told I shot to my feet, bobbed my little curtsey and bolted into the wings before I had finished the last line.

Our house was beautiful. My mother was what would be called now a minimalist, preferring pure-white walls, lots of empty space and just the odd very special vase or picture. She and my father had lots of interesting friends, musicians, poets, artists, and she kept what she called her Visitor Books with programmes of all the shows they saw, press cuttings, letters of interest, her own photographs, a fascinating picture of young London society in the 1920s, a brittle and somewhat feverish scene that did not quite conceal the haunting horror left by the Great War. Our house, 5 Westbourne Street, indeed the whole street, no longer exists. It was blown away by a landmine in the Second World War and never rebuilt. One of my special treats when I was small was to ask my father to take out his glass eye for me. This leads me on to his story, and as we are about to lose him from my memories I want to vindicate his unhappy life without delay.

He was one of a whole generation who left their universities and colleges in their early twenties in 1914 to go to war. He had a brilliant career at Cambridge where he got a degree – I think it was maths – and had the unusual distinction of being President of both the Music Club and the Music Society concurrently. He was severely wounded, losing an eye and having to live the rest of his life with a brain full of shrapnel, which the surgeons of those days were unable to remove. When he was well enough he got the job of junior personal secretary to Winston Churchill, working under the great Sir Edward Marsh. It was during this time that he married my mother at the Guards' Chapel in London. Winston was there, and went into the vestry to sign their marriage certificate. He is reported to have said that my father was one of the most brilliant young men he had known.

The marriage was a failure from the start. My mother was on the rebound from losing the love of her life, who had been killed in Africa. My father adored her and as far as I know never looked at another woman. By the time I came on the scene times had changed. Winston was no longer in office, and my father had moved on to a job at the Stock Exchange. When he came home in the evenings even I noticed at the age of six that his face was hot and sweaty, his breath smelled strange and his words were slurred – all of which I found repugnant. If only I had understood. The great slump was looming and when the final collapse came his firm went bust and he lost every penny of his and my mother's money. Just up the road the husband of my mother's greatest friend and father of *my* friend, with whom I shared music lessons, committed suicide for shame when his firm went bankrupt owing many people money. I came to realise what a dreadful time this must have been for my parents, particularly for my father, who should never have drunk at all because of his injury.

My mind is blank as to how it all came about, but when I was seven my life changed completely. No more beautiful house and staff of four, and no more Swiss holidays. My mother and I, with no money, went to live with her mother, my very dear Granny Forbes, in Folkestone. She welcomed us into her gentle and kindly arms, though her husband had developed premature senility and they had a male nurse living in the house. Life was about to begin again.

The second seven years

Another tall house and another room at the top with a puttering gas stove for me. At the back our own small garden and a little apple tree I could climb, opening onto public gardens with sooty laurel bushes where we played hide and seek, and a big church into which we did not go. In front Earl's Avenue lined by flower beds surrounded by low railings that we could jump into and out of all the way up and down, to the fury of the municipal gardeners who could never catch us. At the sea end was the Leas where old men with suspiciously red noses pushed people up and down in big creaky old bath chairs. And a wonderful lift – or rather a pair of lifts – powered only by water, which ran up and down the chalky cliff face passing each other slowly halfway. For the young and energetic – or those without the pennies for lift fare – there was an exciting cliff path looping its way down to the promenade, the pebble beach and the cold waters of the English Channel. Here despite the unwelcoming shingle I discovered the joys of sea bathing, and better still of rock pooling, because at low tide there was a wide stretch of rocks and pools to explore. I had learned to swim in London, I think at the Marylebone Baths, taught by an old man who looked as if he hadn't been in the water for years, who shoved a sort of wicker basket on the end of a long pole under our chins and simply lugged us up and down from the side of the baths until we could stay afloat on our own. At Folkestone he was replaced by a boatman who had to keep a heavy old rowing boat in position, often in quite a heavy swell while yelling at us unruly kids, who were always going out too far or getting stuck out on the rocks as the tide came in. The tides rise and fall a lot at Folkestone and a frighteningly powerful undertow could develop. This was quite a different ball game from the Marylebone Baths.

In those early days came two new friends whose kindness was invaluable to a rather confused little girl, our dear house parlour maid Ethel, who did everything that had to be done in the house and found time to be a second mother to me (it was to her I ran when I had my first period); and my grandfather's male nurse Geoffrey Clinton. As I write I have by me a small book called *Birthdays* and inscribed 'To Elisabeth with all good wishes and love. Geo. Clinton. Xmas 1936'.

It must have been shortly after this that my grandfather died, and Mr Clinton, as I always called him, went out of our lives forever, to be greatly missed by me. I wish he could know that I still use his gift to list birthdays, and enjoy the quotations at the top of each page – words of wisdom from Shakespeare, the Bible, Omar Khayyám, Milton and many more. He was the fairy godfather who built me a superb two-up and two-down mansion for my guinea pigs. In London attempts to keep pets, which I longed for, all ended in tragedy, a goldfish disappearing down the plughole when an over-zealous governess changed its water, and my adored fluffy grey Persian kitten Llewellen dying from cat 'flu – for which there was at that time no vaccine. Now my long-suffering grandmother tolerated the arrival of a pair of guinea pigs, Hänsel and Gretel, who soon turned out to be both Hänsel. We never changed their names. I just got them a wife each, and before long Mr Clinton was having to build the new mansion for the thriving families. The facts of life held no mysteries for me and before long I was doing excellent business selling the cavies, as the baby guinea pigs are called, for 2/6 each to the local pet shop.

My mother must have had a very sad time when we first came to Folkestone. Any married woman who was separated from her husband for whatever reason was not nice to know in those days, and several respectable families discouraged their children from playing with me. So when I was nine my mother sent me to a local girls' school as a daygirl to make new friends. It was a horrid school, run by two – or was it three? – spinster sisters, the Misses de la Mare, the oldest of whom was the headmistress. I was bullied at first by a bigger girl, whose name and face I remember to this day. When I reported home tearfully to my mother she just said 'Fight her back!' which I proceeded to do with disastrous results, as she got me down and sat on me in the locker room. But I must have landed the odd punch or scratch because she never bullied me again. The school had a lot of very sad little boarders whose fathers planted tea or coffee or rubber in remote lands. They were sent home much as my mother and her two brothers had been, aged about five or six, to be cared for by distant relatives during the holidays. Parents could rarely afford to get home more than once in two years, and the journey took weeks. One child while I was there was cruelly treated because she 'made a fuss' when her mother was leaving. The headmistress refused to give her her mother's last letter, whereupon she ran and locked herself in a lavatory. When she eventually emerged, instead of being cuddled and loved she was severely punished. The history teacher was called Miss Conquest. English history apparently began in 1066, and flushed with patriotism she assured us that in all the years since we British had never done any wrong thing. I could stand this no longer so I put my hand up and reminded her of one of the more shameful episodes in our past, which delighted the class but did me no good at all! Most dreaded of all was a teacher called Miss Gilbert, who bullied us remorselessly through various subjects including gym. I can see us still, lined up in our black wool bloomers and white blouses. But in that class were two sisters, Pam and Elizabeth Flint, who were to become my lifelong dearest friends. We were so miserable at the school that our respective parents took us away after one term and Mrs Flint decided to educate her daughters at home, as was quite often done with girls in those days. I was asked to join in with one or two others, and there began a happy interlude of four years when we did lessons with a plump lady called Miss Tolputt at the Flints' house. I am afraid we teased her unmercifully and often told her what we wanted to learn, but it worked, because when four years on we were all sent together to boarding school we found ourselves a year ahead of our class in most subjects. During Miss Tolputt's era we all got bicycles. My career as a cyclist had had an unfortunate start as I rode my fairy bicycle in Kensington Gardens between the legs of an elderly gent, who was not amused. Now we quickly became demon cyclists and terrorised the local residents by tearing around the public gardens in our school breaks.

We also started our lifelong interest in gardening, dazzled by lurid penny packets of seeds from Woolworth's. I remember a really nasty plant we had a passion for called Burning Bush — unfortunately it never turned out like the magnificent picture on the packet. Pam and I were squeamish about squashing slugs and snails, but Elizabeth was made of sterner stuff. She was appointed Executioner-in-Chief and we had a slaughter stone on which she dispatched her victims.

Way back in the London days my mother had seen me looking longingly at children riding in the Rotten Row. Bless her, she sold a good picture, which paid for me to have lessons with the Carter brothers, well-known children's teachers who had stables across the park in Knightsbridge. On my first day she came to see me off, and

saw me lifted into the saddle of a pretty little grey pony and led away
for my first ride. I turned round in my saddle to wave goodbye to her
and promptly fell off. My small foot went through the stirrup and I
found myself dangling ignominiously upside down beneath the pony,
which luckily was placid and experienced. Mr Carter leapt off and
soon had me right side up, quite unfazed by the experience, because
before long riding and ponies became the passion of my life. And in
a scruffy little stable yard at Hythe I discovered a new and important
friend who is gratefully remembered among my happiest Folkestone
days. Dear Miss Twyman – I can see her still with her ruddy face, wide
gappy smile and black beret rammed firmly onto untidy fair hair. She
made many children's lives with her long, generous rides and her
charge of 10/- for a full day's hunting. She put me on a young New
Forest pony called Tarzan – a gutsy little 12.2 hand bay who became
the love of my life. We must have been a menace out hunting. Tarzan
and I could tackle most obstacles but I remember one day when we
were considering something that really was beyond his short legs. A
rider behind, who was trying to get past us, shouted, 'Little girl, will
you please make up your mind and either go over or under it.' Another
time I collided with a very large horse and rider as we all tried to get
through a gate together. When we were disentangled the man doffed
his hat courteously to me and said, 'Would you kindly sound your
horn next time you are coming.' I first became interested in astronomy
in Folkestone and saved for several years to buy a telescope. The fund
reached £4, then I realised one day that it would not buy a telescope
but it would get me eight days' hunting. Years later I went back to try
to find Miss Twyman and thank her for all the joy she had given me,
but the whole place, little stable yard and all, had been flattened to
make way for a big new road.

I was lucky to find another riding friend in those early Folkestone
days, a friend of my parents who was Master of the West Street Harriers,
which in fact hunted foxes. He had a son and daughter, neither of
whom liked horses, so I became a sort of adopted daughter to him,
and rode his horses for hunting in winter and Pony Club meets and
shows in the summer. I also began showing ponies for the Maslins,
who had a riding establishment at Street. Jumping was my thing. I
was crazy about it, and as I hadn't got my own pony I even trained
my guinea pigs over a miniature show jumping course at home. They

could achieve astonishing heights, taking off from all four legs at once by a surprising sort of direct levitation. In those safer times my friends and I used to go off riding for whole days on end, with picnic lunches in our saddlebags. I can remember when I was ten and a small friend and I were halfway across a very large field. We suddenly spotted a big red bull near us snorting and pawing the ground menacingly (bulls and ponies do not get on). We leapt off and bolted for the nearest gate leaving our ponies to their fate, but at that moment a little girl much smaller than we were emerged from a farm building carrying a stick. She marched up to the bull, smacked him hard on the behind, seized hold of his nose ring and led him away. Covered with shame we crept back and retrieved our ponies.

Evenings were often spent with my cousins singing round the piano with Granny playing Scottish songs and sea shanties for us. Other happy childhood memories of Kent are of the amazing bluebell woods where lilies of the valley also grew if you knew where to look, and the wild salty smell of the Romney Marshes and the lonely beaches at Dungeness.

For my mother the early Folkestone days must have been very unhappy. After some three years she and my father agreed to divorce, which was far from easy as there had been no infidelity on either side. In those days the man, if he was a true gentleman, would agree to become the 'guilty party', and to achieve this status he would have to hire a woman from a special agency, take her to a Brighton hotel, and be discovered in bed with her next morning by the chambermaid bringing the early morning tea. By the time my father had sorted all this out it had been done once too often. I of course knew nothing, except that one day my mother had to go to London, and was obviously unhappy. She had to appear in court, which must have been agony for her as she was a very shy and private person. The judge threw the case out as obviously rigged, and my mother came home and cried all night. I know because at that stage I was sharing a room with her and was only pretending to be asleep when she got back from London in tears and told Granny all about it. I lay awake with no idea how to comfort her. Help came most unexpectedly through A P Herbert, who at that time was campaigning for modernisation of our ridiculous divorce laws. He wrote a book called *Holy Deadlock* about a couple seeking to separate, who both committed adultery only to find that they could

15

not then obtain a divorce because by law only one guilty party was allowed. This stalemate situation was sorted out by new legislation that allowed for automatic divorce if an absentee husband had failed to pay maintenance to his wife and family for three years. So my mother got her decree nisi without having the trauma and expense of another court appearance She was also granted custody of me. My last contact with my father was an Easter egg, which arrived broken with no name or address, though we knew it was from him. I remember crying a lot as I found that broken egg unbearably poignant.

While all this was going on my mother had by a strange chance re-met the man who eventually became her second husband. This was a wonderful happening and a truly romantic story. He was an officer in the Royal Artillery and it transpired that he had been in love with her many years before, when he was a young officer stationed at Shornecliffe Barracks near Folkestone before the First World War. Granny's hospitable house in Earl's Avenue hosted many parties for my mother and her two brothers, and there he met and fell in love with my mother. They played Ernest and Geraldine opposite each other in an amateur performance of *The Importance of Being Ernest*, but he did not propose to her because a subaltern's pay was not enough money to support a wife suitably by the standards of that time. The war came, he was away fighting, and when war ended he stayed on to serve with his regiment in Egypt and the Sudan. When he finally came home my mother was married. Years later, posted back to Shornecliffe again, he called to see if Granny, whom he remembered with much affection, still lived at 32 Earl's Avenue, where he remembered they tied cushions round the legs of the grand piano and played hockey in the drawing room. And there he found not only my grandmother, but Mummy and me. This miracle led to a second marriage founded on true love, but he was a very diffident person and kept on not proposing, though I did my level best to leave them alone together whenever possible. My mother told me she eventually proposed to him in the bluebell woods. They were married at St Ethelburga's Church in the City of London – the only church they could find where the vicar, an enlightened Scotsman called the Reverend Geike Cobb, would marry couples including a divorced person; and I was their bridesmaid. No one could have had a dearer stepfather. They were forty-four and forty-six when they married, and they had forty years of devoted life together.

I refused to call my stepfather Father as I felt this would be disloyal to my real father and also to some extent living a lie. So, as he was Stuart Ferguson, we settled on Uncle Stuart. He was in no way hurt or offended, as many men might have been, nor did he reproach me for being rather a goody-goody little prig. Over the years Mummy and I found the most delightful wise and humorous being under his rather conventional army façade. One of the happiest days of my mother's life, she told me, was when she discovered that he too loved poetry. They shared a great love of nature, mountain flowers, animals, and later on, when he retired, gardening. And he made my day when he offered me the chance to join the children's riding classes taken by an army roughrider sergeant in the riding school at Shorncliffe. I was in heaven! I fell off a lot, but it was a stern school and all I got for sympathy was, 'What do you think you're doing down there again?' It *was* 'down there' too – I was mounted on an enormous battery hairy, as the horses that pulled the guns were called, who was misnamed Fairyfoot, and who was much too wide for me. But she was a gentle soul and would stand gazing sadly at me until I was hoisted up onto her back again, trying hard to keep back the tears. If you didn't keep your horse going, Sergeant Woodford could throw his cane, twirling like a boomerang, right across the riding school to hit the rump of your horse – or you if you were one of the cocky big boys. He came to treat me like an extra daughter, and taught me all I know about horses and riding. When I could ride he chose for me a chestnut mare called Hotpot, smaller than the average troop horse, high-spirited and sensitive, who regularly bucked off the raw recruits but who was an angel with me because my light hands suited her tender mouth. She and I shared a great love of jumping and when out on rides we would deviate to go over anything jumpable. She and Sergeant Woodford were the loves of my life. But the idyll couldn't last, and after three years the regiment was posted to Edinburgh. Hotpot, always nervous, panicked and hurt herself badly on the long train journey, and had to be destroyed. When Sergeant Woodford's letter came I was heartbroken.

It was about this time that my mother's favourite brother, Mansfield Forbes, died at the early age of forty-seven, in Cambridge. He was a brilliant, eccentric but much-loved don of English literature, whose lectures his students described as never-to-be-forgotten. He was a talented amateur artist, and one year he was so fed up with what he considered the pomposity of the judges at the annual art exhibition that he painted a special picture and deliberately framed it upside down. It was duly hung and stimulated much deep intellectual discussion among the adjudicators, who were not amused when the truth of the situation was revealed to them. Manny had a show house, Finella, which was renovated and done up for him by a rising young Irish architect and interior designer Raymond McGrath. It had two beautiful drawing rooms, North and South Pink, which could be opened up to produce one large space. Here he showed Epstein's masterpiece of a woman giving birth, the *Genesis*, which had been refused space by all the local galleries as indecent. Various aged dons were heard to mutter 'Disgusting!' as they wandered round. Among Manny's friends were Maynard Keynes and his ballerina wife Lydia Lopokova. Manny became a keen supporter of the Hundred New Towns scheme on which Keynes was currently working. He was a great lover of his native Scotland and used to disappear up north on digs during the holidays as he was a keen archaeologist. One of his most delightful watercolours was of a small church set against a grey stormy sky with a solemn procession of black pinmen emerging from it, much in the style of the later Lowry. It was entitled *Les Wee Frees sortant d'église*. Anyone who has spent a Sunday in the Outer Hebrides will not fail to recognise it. Finella became an open house to many brilliant people from every possible social background, and Manny's parties were famous. I am sad that he died before I was able to appreciate him properly.

My mother was not into horses, though she encouraged me, but she was a passionate lover of ballet. She told me that she had just twice in her life queued all night at the Royal Opera House with my father; once was to hear Chaliapin in *Boris Godunov*, and once to see Nijinsky dance *Spectre de la Rose*. I can just remember being taken by her to see Diaghilev's baby ballerinas in *The Firebird* – pure magic. My father wanted me to be a concert pianist; my mother dreamed of me as a ballerina. In Folkestone she heard of a very good teacher who came from London several times a week to take classes at the Grand Hotel.

I was duly enrolled in Miss Oliver's school of dancing, and began to dream of being a ballet dancer as well as teaching riding. I had three or four happy years with Miss Oliver, ending up in what she called her professional class, girls who hoped to graduate as ballet teachers. Alas, I grew and grew. My back was long and stiff so that I could never achieve a good arabesque, my feet had long big toes quite unsuited to point work, and in short I was a gangly sort of child who struggled with Miss Oliver's strictly classical training. My moment of glory came when she put on a show with her pupils at the Folkestone Theatre. It was a ballet to the music of Mendelssohn's Hebrides Overture, including the Fingal's Cave section, which I adored, and I was perfectly cast as the Octopus. Perfect – not a single classical arabesque or *jeté* – just lots of lovely imaginative dancing, and music that took me back to Staffa and the magical cave with the great green Atlantic swells rising and falling around us.

I can't leave Folkestone without noting an event that had a vital effect on the most important of the threads woven into these recollections, the one thread which is constant as life itself because it is the spiritual journey on which I have always believed myself to be travelling.

I got into trouble at school when I upset the history mistress, Miss Conquest, by suggesting that the behaviour of England over the centuries had not been quite so lilywhite as she led us to think. The same thing happened in a divinity lesson taken by the school chaplain, when I upset him by querying certain miraculous happenings that I didn't understand and was reluctant to believe in. I was reprimanded in front of the whole class and came home in tears. My dear Scottish grandmother comforted me and said, 'I have some books which may help you.' She gave me her copies of *Esoteric Buddhism* and *Mystic Christianity* by Yogi Ramacharaka. I was not much more than eleven years old at the time, but I most vividly remember that reading those books was like coming home. I felt I knew what was coming over the pages, and I was totally absorbed by this new approach to the divine. From then on I refused to put C of E in my passport and described myself rather grandiloquently as a free thinker!

By the time we were thirteen Pam, Elizabeth and I had outgrown Miss Tolputt. We went first as daygirls, then after a year as boarders, to a school which moved from Folkestone to Lymington in Hampshire. At the same time my parents moved into army quarters at Farnborough where my stepfather was now stationed. I was fourteen, and life was about to begin again.

The uneasy interlude

The years when Pam, Elizabeth and I were at boarding school I now see as an interlude of uneasy peace during which our elders did their best to ignore the growing Nazi threat. We seemed to be in a sort of state of denial as reports of the Hitler regime's growing arrogance and inhumanity towards the Jews filtered through. It couldn't possibly be as bad as rumour would have us believe – or could it? Our headmistress tried to make us politically aware without being alarmist. Several of us joined a movement called – I think – Federal Union, which advocated a European union and was backed by Winston Churchill, then hardly a name to us. I also remember having fun standing as a communist when we had a mock general election.

Our school, Eversley, was then the smallest girls' public school in England. We had been there for a year as daygirls when it moved from a cramped Folkestone site to Elmer's Court in Lymington. This had been the home of a great yachtsman, Andrea by name, who owned the famous racing yachts *Candida* and *Endeavour*. He had employed twenty-seven gardeners, which was quite beyond the reach of a small school, and it grieved our hearts to see the place gradually deteriorating.

The main lawn running down to the muddy reed beds of the Solent was called the Queen Mary because it was the exact length of the liner's main deck. Boarding school is linked for me to the scent of the yellow azaleas that filled the grounds in spring, to be followed by an intoxicating perfume from a huge old wisteria which covered the south side of the house. On Saturday mornings we would sit gazing enviously out of our classroom windows at the lucky people racing yachts and dinghies out on the Solent. Yes, in those days we worked all Saturday mornings and did prep every weekday evening.

My friends and I were not particularly happy at school. The regime was strict and very old-fashioned. Even when we were in the sixth form we were not allowed to go outside the drive gates unattended. Each year as summer arrived our headmistress, Miss McCall, would make the same little speech at assembly telling us that the time had come to put on our lightweight 'intimate garments'. She could not bring herself to say 'knickers'. The arrival of any male – even a father or brother – was a great excitement, and when the headmistress took on a sort of general factotum who was a good-looking youngish man the whole school was agog. She doted on him; he could do no wrong, until one morning he was missing together with all the weekly wages. It turned out that he was a well-known conman. At one stage a young accountant was hired to teach the sixth form bookkeeping. This was a great thrill, but the wretched young man was so embarrassed that he became positively incoherent, which may explain why I never mastered double entry. However, Miss McCall atoned for many things as a brilliant teacher of English literature. Every evening a different form would go to her drawing room after supper to be read to – every sort of thing from Bernard Shaw's *St Joan* to *Winnie-the-Pooh*, which was an all-time favourite with every age group. The only fly in the ointment was her large very spoilt golden retriever, who used to let off the most appalling smells from time to time, reducing an otherwise rapt audience to uncontrollable giggles. She had been a leading light in the Oxford University Dramatic Society (OUDS) while up at Oxford, and we were continually doing plays – form plays, house plays, which we often had to write ourselves, and of course school plays for the parents every summer. For some unknown reason Miss McCall lighted on me in my very first year as a daygirl to play a lead, and I discovered when we put on *Daddy Long-Legs* that I could make people cry. I think it was only my histrionic talent, but it was a great thrill to have the whole school, staff and children, in tears. This ability stayed with me into my operatic years, and one of my greatest joys was singing the last two acts of *La Bohème*. Yet I longed all my life to be funny – and to have that miraculous gift of making people helpless with laughter.

A strange thing happened during my first year as a boarder. We slept in small dormitories of about six girls headed by a prefect or sixth former. The senior in my room was our head girl Rosemary Sandilands, for whom I had a great crush at the time. One night of brilliant moonlight we were all asleep when we were woken by a voice saying, 'I've just seen a ghost.' It was Rosemary, sitting up in bed smiling. It turned out that she had woken to see a young man standing at the end of her bed, dressed in khaki army officer's uniform but with wings on it like that of the R.A.F. She said she hadn't been a bit frightened because he smiled at her then just faded away into the moonlight. She knew she was a bit psychic from other experiences. Incidentally she grew up to become Rosemary Verey, a brilliant gardener and writer of gardening books who knew Prince Charles. I forget about this exciting event until several years later when I was introduced at a party to a young man who was a descendant of the family who had owned Elmer's Court during the Great War. When he heard that I had been at school there he said, 'Did you see our ghost?' I said that I hadn't but someone in my dormitory had, and described the young man Rosemary had seen in the puzzling mixture of army and RAF uniforms. 'That was ghostie!' he said and went on to explain he was the ghost of a young army officer who had joined the Flying Corps in the First World War, when it was still part of the army, and had been killed in action.

One of the highlights of school was my music teacher, Eileen Walmesley, to whom I was devoted. She was a brilliant and sensitive piano teacher, and she helped me to recover from unhappy days in Folkestone, when I was completely turned off the piano by an older sister of our nice Miss Tolputt, who sat beside me rapping my knuckles at frequent intervals. She appeared to be totally unmusical and indeed I never heard her play the piano. I have a shrewd suspicion she couldn't. With Miss Walmesley I progressed rapidly through the exam grades and also started singing lessons. After some months she told me very definitely that I would go farther as a singer than a pianist, and at the same time I saw my first opera, when we were taken to the Carl Rosa at Bournemouth. The operas were *Carmen* and *Samson and Delilah*, and to this day I remember the name of the mezzo-soprano who starred in both. She was Pauline Maunder, and I thought she was the most marvellous thing in the world. I was utterly under the spell of those operas. Out of the window went all aspirations to teach riding or become a ballerina; from now on it was to become a *prima donna* for me. The artistic highlight of school, equalling in importance the magic of the Octopus in the Hebridean ballet, came when Miss Walmesley gave me the soprano solo in a cantata called *The Lady of Shalott* by Wilfrid Bendall, accompanied by the school's small but very acceptable string orchestra.

It was about this time that my nerves got the better of me. I had always been a nervous performer, and now I seemed to be doing piano or singing exams, or dancing or acting, all the time, with the added stress of preparing for a university entrance exam to study French and German literature at Oxford. We were all thinking about our careers, and I vowed that whatever I did would have nothing to do with any sort of public performance. I lighted upon translating books, which seemed to me the most tranquil and inconspicuous sort of work. In July 1937 my class was confirmed in Winchester Cathedral, which was a very lovely occasion. Although I refused to put 'C of E' in my passport and liked to look on myself as a free thinker, the tolerant approach of *Esoteric Buddhism* that had so deeply impressed me as a twelve-year-old made it no problem to accept the basic principles of Christianity. My parents and granny from Folkestone all came down for the service and were put up for the night at the school so that they could come to my first communion the following day.

My mother and stepfather had just moved into Broadmeade Copse, where I live to this day, and I went home to a very happy summer holiday. Having a stepfather in the army meant that I met lots of young people of my own age, and we rode, swam, played tennis and squash and went to the cinema together with boundless energy. We also took my stepfather to Davos two winters running. He learnt to ski very quickly, inspired by a beautiful young Austrian girl who taught the beginners' class, and was soon able to come for runs with us in the afternoons. What he lacked in experience he made up for in daring, and I remember one horrendous occasion when he slid from top to bottom of a very icy slope wearing ski pants he had borrowed from his commanding officer. My mother could only moan, 'Henry's trousers!' as she watched helpless. Luckily both trousers and wearer came to rest undamaged at the bottom.

In the autumn of 1938 Mummy took me away from school for a term and sent me to Paris to study. This was a brilliant move, but it upset Miss McCall who thought it implied a criticism of her establishment. I had a magical three months at a girls' finishing school run by Mlle Vincent at Rue la Fontaine in the 16th arrondissement. She took about ten *jeunes filles* of mixed nationality, and prided herself that both the du Maurier and the Mitford young had been with her. She was a very literate and intelligent woman who took us every week to the Louvre and taught us how to look at pictures and sculpture.

This opened my eyes to the visual arts and a whole new world of appreciation. I travelled most days sixteen stops on the Métro to the British Institute, attached to the Sorbonne, to attend lectures. In the evenings we bought roast chestnuts from the brazier men who plied their trade on every corner. Paris was a revelation to me, architecturally so grand and with the feeling of years of culture and history behind it giving it that special distinctive ambiance of a great city. We had elocution lessons from one of the leading actresses of the Comédie Française, a beautiful young woman who was I believe as much esteemed for the fact that she was the current mistress of a leading member of the government as for her histrionic talent. Sometimes we had appalling parties, to which a gaggle of wretched French boys of impeccable background, all dressed in dark suits and stiff collars and ties, were invited. We put on our party dresses, and they hovered at the far end of our large salon trying to pluck up the courage to invite us to dance. The great excitement was an end-of-term visit to – of all places – the Folies Bergère! Mlle Vincent was nothing if not broadminded. Our parents were asked to give their permission for us to go, and the Anglo-Saxon ones all agreed, but two Spanish girls were refused permission and had to be left behind in tears. In the end about eight of us went, dressed in our best frocks and escorted by a chaperone dressed in a sort of Dickensian black bombazine outfit. What the audience at the Folies-Bergère – mostly middle-aged businessmen out to enjoy the nudity for which the theatre was famous – thought of our self-conscious procession headed by the chaperone, I hardly dare imagine! The show was beautiful, highly polished and sophisticated, with lovely girls and very good dancing. If there was anything dirty about it, that must have been in the words, not all of which we understood – we certainly didn't dare to laugh!

I went back to school in January 1939, hating it after Paris, but allowed to have a room to myself and wear my own clothes, to do final studies for the university entrance exam in March. I was so nervous that I had been running a temperature for some days and all I can remember is that I blanked out completely for what was usually my best subject, English essay. The subject was 'miracles' but certainly one didn't happen for me on that day.

In the summer we went for a family holiday to the Pyrenees, an area that was to become a favourite in my later mountaineering days.

We drove down through France, stopping off to see many lovely places and eat and drink deliciously in vine-shaded courtyards of little inns, and we ended up staying at a tiny village called Gourette above Eaux Bonnes. In those days it was all delightfully undeveloped, but our small Hotel Edelweiss high in the mountains was comfy and full of a multi-national crowd of walkers and climbers, Belgians, Germans, French, Dutch, Brits, all reassuring each other '*Il n'y aura pas de guerre!*' The walks and the little ice-green lakes filled with trout and the mountain flowers were glorious. We were out all day with picnic lunches, and the only hazard I can remember was the large and rather aggressive Pyrenean sheep and goats, which would do their best to push us off the paths. But as August drew on the subterranean unease grew and grew. My parents and I were lucky to get back to England without a problem, crossing the Channel on the evening of 21st August. A few days later the Channel ports were crowded with panic-stricken holidaymakers all trying to get cars onto the last boats. Soon the car ferries stopped altogether, and it would be six long sad years before they ran again.

Chapter Two

The War Years, 1939–43

The war years are such a vast subject that I have been considering how best to record them. And as I thought back and re-read my diaries, I realised that it was the early days that were still the most vivid to me because of the life-changing events that were unrolling, and so deserved the most detailed recollection. Somehow later on even such a tremendous thing as war became routine, a grey and depressing sort of existence, particularly to those of us who were left at home often not knowing about the great battles, the failures, the successes, that were going on elsewhere. We had our war duties, we grew vegetables, we salted down crocks of runner beans and preserved eggs in a nasty-smelling sulphurous liquid, as rationing grew ever more stringent, people's brothers, fathers and sons continued to die, while there seemed to be no end to it.

But to go back to how it all started, I find that the day after we got home from our magical holiday in the Pyrenees I was very busy arranging for my eighteenth birthday party, which was to be held on Saturday 2nd September. I was also re-packing for a visit to my friends Pam and Elizabeth in their Folkestone home where we had done lessons together. Despite the worrying news from Europe my mother said I could go there on 24th August. Gasmasks had already been issued, and I left mine behind, so it had to be posted on by first-class post. In Folkestone we played tennis and went deep-sea fishing and saw *The Corn is Green* at the local theatre. But a dance and a tennis tournament were cancelled and my friends had to begin packing up, as their father decided to evacuate the family to Devon, Folkestone being within reach of German shells from across the Channel. Rumours flew around, 3,000,000 people were to be evacuated, and the trains were packed with young men recalled to the forces and civilians moving away from the coast.

I got home on 30th August to continue preparations for my party and a trip to Scotland in a week's time. On Friday 31st August Germany invaded Poland and the big shutdown began. My mother and I went to London that day and I wrote in my diary 'A terrible quiet all over London, shops empty, people standing about silent and grave… .' On Saturday 2nd September I wrote '…life is very strange now'. Phoning was difficult because all the lines were overloaded, but I put off my small party. We hardly saw my stepfather, who although retired had been called back into the army to an administrative job in Aldershot. We shopped madly for black paint, blackout material, black paper, anything to mask the many windows at Broadmeade Copse, but already the shops were out of many things and petrol was scarce.

On 3rd September 1938 I had written in my diary, 'My 17th birthday. I am thrilled to be so old!' In 1939 I made a very different entry: 'At 11.00 a.m. Mr Chamberlain in a wonderfully restrained speech declares that as Germany has not replied to our ultimatum of 1st September we are now at war with them.' France followed suit, declaring war on Germany at 5.00 p.m. It felt as if a dark and heavy cloud came down over us, not to lift until peace was declared six years later.

We ate my birthday cake and I opened some presents, trying to behave normally, while friends called in, some in tears as husbands or sons had already vanished to join the forces. We were all filled with foreboding. Ironically it was a beautiful sunny autumn, and the 'Bore War', as it was nicknamed, followed: a false lull which nevertheless gave our nation time for some vital if belated preparations. Women were not called up until the age of twenty-one, so I joined the Red Cross as an ambulance driver, having just passed my driving test, and was on duty about three miles from home at Ash First Aid Post. While there we had to do first aid and home nursing training, while wrestling with a horrendous old commandeered van that had belonged to a florist, and was labelled 'Flowers that Last!'. We reckoned nothing would last long bumping around in its noisome interior. It had to be started with a starting handle – a real wrist-breaker – and the great thing was to find a male – they were already thin on the ground – to get it going for us. During the summer I had started having singing lessons in London with

Mark Raphael, and I carried on, going up whenever possible, spending all my spare time practising and playing the piano. I remember doing washing-up in a crowded canteen in Aldershot and later fire-watching, a night-time occupation that involved stumbling around in the dark with a bucket and a stirrup pump. Luckily, our neighbourhood had no firebombs. There was a bitterly cold winter, during which we skated for several weeks. And my three best boyfriends, my Three Musketeers as I called them, kept turning up from France on leave. We danced and played squash and went to the cinema in a sort of frenzy of activity. Then in April Germany invaded Denmark and Norway. What we had all expected but had put to the back of our minds was happening.

> ➢ On 9th May I had a last evening with the youngest Musketeer, Ronnie.
> ➢ Shattering news on 10th May. Germany had invaded Holland, Belgium and Luxembourg. I went to the London Zoo with Tony, another Musketeer, who was on embarkation leave.
> ➢ On 11th May Ronnie rang to say all leave was now cancelled and he was sailing for France in two days.
> ➢ On 15th May Holland surrendered. I was now at the first aid post most of the time, and we were having lectures on what to do in gas attacks, or if you were machine-gunned while driving your ambulance.
> ➢ On 22nd May one of our more elderly Red Cross ladies dashed into the post shouting 'England's been bombed!' We found out later that the casualties were one cow, one pony and some hens, which gave us our first good laugh for some time.
> ➢ On 25th May the Germans reached Boulogne. The next day we got through to Granny in Folkestone who said the gunfire from across the Channel was shaking her house. She reported that refugees were pouring across in a pathetic state and refugee camps were being set up everywhere. Immediate arrangements were made for her to come and live with us.
> ➢ On 28th May Belgium surrendered. According to my diary we were aghast, stupefied, everyone in a daze. We

were warned to expect air raids, and I noted that our air force and British Expeditionary Force (BEF) were being magnificent. We had our first war casualty. A young cousin of my stepfather's was killed. He was an only son and would have become the next Lord Roberts, and now the title was extinct.

➢ On 31st May I heard that Tony had been badly injured in an accident while on his way to the front.

➢ On 1st June came a card from my third Musketeer John to say he was just safely back in England.

➢ On 5th June we heard of the great evacuation going on from the beaches of Dunkirk. But Ronnie was missing. We hoped and hoped as people kept turning up off little boats or crowded trains. But he had disappeared without trace. Not even his identification bracelet was ever found. The song 'A Nightingale Sang in Berkeley Square' epitomises for me that sad spring when Ronnie and I danced so often there at the Café de Paris. Not long after he went missing it was bombed. Bandleader Snakehips Johnson and many of his band and the dancers were killed that night. It was a terrible time, so much heartbreak as the last boats and trains filtered in and still so many had not made it home.

➢ On 10th June Italy declared war on us.

➢ On 14th June the Germans marched into Paris.

➢ On 17th June France surrendered. I wrote, 'We are numbed. It is unthinkable France of all nations to leave us. At present one feels immeasurable pity for the French people, contempt for their rotten leaders, and a strange sort of triumph – now it is up to us alone and we will win!'

During those first weeks on our own I imagine everyone must have felt as vulnerable and afraid as I did. Nights were disturbed. There were raids, and the first stick of bombs fell nearby. My mother, digging for victory in the vegetable garden, got a thorn in her hand which brought on blood poisoning; she was in great pain and ran a high temperature (this was before antibiotics were available); my stepfather was always at HQ in Aldershot, and before long was sent away to command a training regiment. After that we saw him only briefly on leave. As in many households we were just three generations of women left and soon we had land girls billeted on us. We lived for *ITMA* on the wireless, and the very funny daily programmes of Mabel Constanduros, who in the character of Grandma Buggins gave out a series of wartime recipes that grew ever more improbable as rationing got tougher. Grandma's lament, 'Wot I'd give ter clash me teeth in a nice piece of steak!' became a family refrain. The real-life Dad's Army was getting underway, and we civilians were taught over the radio – I beg its pardon, the wireless – how to make Molotov cocktails. 'Take an empty milk bottle. Fill it with petrol. Stuff the neck with rag. Make a short wick of string. Light wick and throw bottle at – or preferably into – an advancing tank.' How the Germans would have laughed!

My comfort was in playing the piano and learning as many new songs and operatic roles as possible. I still went to London as regularly as I could for singing lessons, and my diary has constant references to concerts and music. The proms went on as usual: Bach, Schubert, Brahms, Beethoven, the Germanic names were of no consequence. I copied the following poem into the front of my five-year diary – it may give some idea of the mood during the summer of 1940:

Tell England by Ernest Raymond

For all emotions that are tense and strong,
And utmost knowledge, I have lived for these –
Lived deep, and let the lesser things live long,
The everlasting hills, the lakes, the trees
Who'd give their thousand years to sing this song
Of life, and Man's high sensibilities
Which I into the face of Death can sing –
O Death, thou poor and disappointed thing –
Strike if thou wilt, and soon, strike breast and brow
For I have lived; and thou can'st rob me now
Only of some long life that ne'er has been.

The life that I have lived, so full, so keen,
Is mine! I hold it firm beneath thy blow
And dying, take it with me where I go.

Then, in the autumn of 1940, came another – for me – life-changing event.

I could have gone up to Oxford to read French and German literature at Lady Margaret Hall but I felt I could not immure myself in an ivory tower of university life while all my friends were in the forces. However when I heard that the Staff Band of the Royal Army Medical Corps were looking for a soprano soloist that was another matter. Out of the window went a peaceful future as a translator of books. I had no idea what I was letting myself in for!

My audition was arranged by one Mr Griffiths, who after sixteen years with Sir Oswald Stoll at the Coliseum now found himself running some fifty concert parties round the Aldershot command. His wife was a professional singer, which made me even more nervous, and I was whistled off to sing for them and bandmaster Harry Johnson at the Aldershot Garrison Theatre, a great barn of a place which could seat a lot of troops. It was the first time I had sung in public and on a stage, and I was terrified. I sang 'I'll Follow My Secret Heart' from Noël Coward's *Conversation Piece*, of which I had a delicious recording with Yvonne Printemps and Coward himself, then Arditi's little waltz song 'Il Bacio' in Italian, and finally with the courage of ignorance 'One Fine Day' from *Madam Butterfly*. They were enthusiastic, and next day I had a rehearsal with Mrs Griffiths, who taught me some basic stage technique such as how to make an entrance and an exit. I was to make my debut with the Royal Army Medical Corps (RAMC) Band the following week, so I went to see their variety show, which was a mixture of comedy acts, sketches, jazz, medleys from musicals and popular classics, and was greatly impressed.

Professional musicians who were called up were nearly always drafted into the major forces bands. The RAMC had an excellent classical group from the Welsh BBC Orchestra, including Emanuel Hurwitz, a brilliant young violinist who went on to a great solo career, about half of Geraldo's band, who were top jazz musicians, Oscar Grasso, solo violinist from the Hungaria Restaurant, and Lee Sheridan, a well-known crooner. We were later joined by Michael Lyndon from the Windmill Theatre, a dancer, singer and excellent compère, and impressionist Peter Coates, who as Peter Cavanagh became famous on post-war radio. To be working with such a galaxy of mixed talents was thrilling and stimulating – and nerve-racking!

My debut was delayed as the band was suddenly sent off on tour, and I remember feeling very depressed. Sticks of bombs were falling most nights and we had a friend staying whose house in Farnham had been hit. Nights were disturbed, and I spent most of them at the Ash First Aid Post or doing my stint fire-watching; I got a bad cold and thought I was never going to become a singer. We heard that Taylor's Depositories just outside London, where all Granny's books, furniture, pictures and family silver had been put in store when she left Folkestone, had been totally destroyed in one of the big fire blitzes. We got an adorable kitten that caught cat 'flu, and I had to have it put to sleep. All small things compared to what was going on in the various battle areas, but cumulatively very depressing.

However, eventually it happened. I sang in my first Band Show on 26th November and had an extraordinary experience. I, who had been having sleepless nights with nerves, and who had started on the wrong note at my first band rehearsal out of sheer panic, discovered inside me a completely different person who loved the challenge and the thrill, and who felt an immediate outgoing contact with an audience. It was years later that, when I first discovered my background history on my father's side, I realised where this instinctive response sprang from, and for many years I felt as if I were two people, the performer and the carefully brought-up daughter with a middle-class army background. I think I must have been over thirty when I first felt really at one with myself. I still recollect that first bitterly cold night; I wore a red dress, our little ATS (Auxiliary Territorial Service) girl comedienne Joan Henry showed me how to make up (it was Leichner 5 and 9 in those days), and I sang 'First Music in May' by Ivor Novello, and Deanna Durbin's 'I Love to Whistle' (she was my role model!) with the band, then 'Il Bacio' with piano. Later on Arthur Wilkinson from Geraldo's Band made orchestral arrangements of all my songs for me with the band. Comment in my diary: 'Joan Henry teaches me to make up. What a business! Look pretty odd when I'm finished.'

Our compère Michael Lyndon didn't take long to find out that I loved dancing and had a certain amount of ballet training. His eyes lit up; we would do a Ginger Rogers and Fred Astaire number. I got a very pretty white muslin dress in which I was to float about the stage doing most of the singing while Michael in white tie and tails did a very passable impression of Fred Astaire. I see from my diary that I was struggling to learn tap, with very little success! Eventually we got ambitious and Michael introduced me to lifts, in which I was supposed to float effortlessly in mid-air (this was during a time when I was very light). One day I mistimed the lift more than usual; result, extremely painful torn ribs, several weeks so strapped up that I couldn't sing my more exacting numbers, and a decree from the bandmaster that there was to be no more dancing. Fortunately just before this happened our brilliant young violinist Manny Hurwitz wrote a mad ballet, a sort of crazy war fantasia which was very funny. It had as its refrain 'Hot Sweet Tea!' which was always being drummed into us as the essential cure for everything from mortal injuries to stress. I still like my tea very strong and sweet, made with condensed milk so that the spoon stands up in it, NAAFI-style [Navy, Army and Air Force Institutes].

Towards Christmas life became extremely busy. We had two splendid ladies living in the village, Miss Creagh-Henry who wrote religious plays, and her friend Miss Martin who produced them. They had a small semi-professional group that toured to village halls and small towns, and I was very honoured to be asked to play the Virgin Mary for them in their nativity play in 1941 and '42, with our local grocer as a gentle and dignified Joseph. We had to do a new show every Thursday in the RAMC's own Garrison Theatre, with a classical programme once a month. We would begin rehearsing on the Monday, and it was a good hard lesson in quick study.

It was a bitter winter and I find plenty of entries in my diary about skating; the local lakes and ponds were frozen for over six weeks. My poor mother, coming to London to listen to her favourite French songs, which I was rehearsing, had to be wrapped in blankets with a hot water bottle as the studio where I was working was so freezing.

There were hundreds of Canadians passing through Aldershot, and many of them who we got to know were of Scottish descent. We used to push back the drawing-room furniture and dance reels with Granny tireless at the piano. News from France filtered through rather unreliably. John, one of the Three Musketeers, now down to two since Ronnie's death, was using a skill learnt in our garden, water-divining, to site his gun batteries at the front. To his CO's amazement it worked! Air raids went on relentlessly. I remember one particularly lean period, when the U-boats had taken a heavy toll on our merchant shipping, going to shop at the Aldershot NAAFI where our family was registered. The counter was usually decorated with tins of Spam. On this occasion there were only artistically arranged piles of toilet rolls. 'Are they very nourishing?' murmured a friend.

In the New Year of 1941 the band was sent on tour to Scotland. We travelled across London after a night of particularly heavy bombing, and I remember the piles of debris and the fire hoses snaking their way over the roads with the fire crews still at work, making our progress painfully slow. We got into a blacked-out train in a blacked-out station and sat up all night as the unheated train crawled north through a snowy landscape. We arrived in Edinburgh next day and gave a series of very chilly shows. I can remember my hot water bottle frozen in my bed, and a performance in Edinburgh Castle in a romantic but glacial setting where I was so numbed that I forgot my words and had to sing nonsense – luckily it was in Italian.

The war ground slowly on. The resistance movement in France was doing magnificent work. Little did we know at home that many of the women being trained for the Special Operations Executive (SOE) to be dropped behind the lines in France spent some time training half a mile away at Wanborough Manor. It must have been one of the best-kept secrets of the war. Their amazing courage is commemorated by a simple plaque in our little Saxon church.

The band was touring all over Britain entertaining the forces and giving small shows in hospital wards. I auditioned for the Council for the Encouragement of Music and the Arts – now the Arts Council – and found myself doing concerts in the early hours of the morning for sleepy factory workers who were working round the clock to provide arms and munitions and planes for the forces. Their war effort was truly heroic; four years of long hours each day at a factory bench takes real determination and endurance. Also on the Council for the Encouragement of Music and Art (CEMA) circuit was the great Russian soprano Oda Slobodskaya. She was an old-style *prima donna* of ample proportions who tended to include the song 'Come into the Garden, Maud' in her programme. The sight of a large lady dressed in gold lamé, clutching a chiffon hanky *à la* Pavarotti and adjuring the audience in heavily accented English to 'sleep into my booosom and be lost in me!' always brought the house down, though I am not sure if she knew why. There was one electrifying occasion when she came out onto the platform, wrung the chiffon hanky, said 'Excuse, pliss!' and disappeared. A moment later came the sound of a plug being energetically pulled backstage, the diva reappeared beaming happily, said 'That iss better!' and the show went on to a delighted audience.

I got to know a rich American lady in London who heard me sing and very kindly decided she would like to further my career. She put on a concert in her luxurious apartment for a refugee Polish pianist and myself, and it was for me a horrendous occasion. Chandeliers, heavy velvet curtains, a thick carpet eating up all the sound, an ultra-smart audience perched on gilt chairs, and me almost obliterated by the most enormous violet orchid which waggled about as I sang, perched on my very inadequate bosom.

When I was twenty-one I was called up and went to have my medical. My fate had been decided by my RAMC friends. I was going into the ATS, and would be posted to HQ in Church Crookham, where my principal duty would be to the band. To my great surprise I was turned down, partly because the doctors spotted the scar of my childhood operation and decided it must have involved a hernia, partly because, at seven-and-a-half stone, I was very underweight for my height. I was told to carry on with what I was doing. I remember being very disappointed, as I had braced myself for life in the army, where I felt I would be doing my bit together with most of my friends.

At one stage the Germans took to swooping down and dive-bombing anything that moved on the roads. The ridge of the Hog's Back, now the A31, which is long and straight and which carried a lot of army convoys, was a tempting target, and we all joked about leaping out of our cars and taking cover in the deep ditches full of brambles and nettles. There was one occasion when the bombers struck lucky and hit a loaded ammunition train parked in a siding outside Tongham. Only the heroism of a local porter (yes, the stations did still have porters, mostly very elderly, during the war) prevented a major disaster. He managed to uncouple most of the trucks that had not yet caught fire and pushed them to a safe distance away, for which act of great courage he was awarded the Military Medal (MM).

We had two very happy wartime holidays at Tintagel when my stepfather got leave during the summers of 1942 and '43. We rode shaggy ponies along those magnificent cliffs, and during the second holiday I learned the whole role of Juliet in Gounod's opera *Romeo and Juliet*. I was coaching for opera at the time with conductor Arthur Hammond of the Carl Rosa Company, and he put me forward when a new production was being planned. I did not get the part, and Arthur told me later that it was because the company's leading tenor Francis Russell was aged sixty-plus, and I was twenty and would have 'shown him up'.

The Americans joined the war and we felt less alone. The news that filtered through was good, and I think we all felt that a corner had been turned – we had made it through our period of solitary confinement. But in North Africa things were still bad, and another good friend, an only son in his twenties, was killed there.

I was still going up to St John's Wood for singing lessons with Mark Raphael. He and his wife Ava were Jewish, and they had lost most of their close families in the Holocaust. Mark was one of a trio of Jewish musicians who patrolled St John's Wood as air raid wardens (pianist Harry Isaacs was another), and often when I went for lessons after a night of heavy bombing they would have been out all night working amidst the wreckage of neighbours' houses. I remember once in the early days of my career complaining: 'Mark, I've done fifty performances now and I am still so nervous!' His reply was, 'My dear, it is Calvary every time.'

My diaries for these war years are kaleidoscopic; travel, more and more shows, new music, broadcasts for forces programmes and *Workers' Playtime*, periods of great depression when it seemed the war would never end, grief as friends continued to die (you must remember that when it began we all kept telling each other that it was bound to be a short war); and always the same grim backdrop of killing, killing, which seemed to be spreading all over the world.

During the summer of 1943 I changed singing teachers and went to study with Dino Borgioli, the distinguished Italian tenor who had come to live in London to escape the fascist regime of Mussolini. Dino was a fine if exacting teacher. Although he no longer sang opera he was still recording Italian *arie antiche*, which he sang with perfect style and the amazing breath control of the great singers of the *bel canto* period, who could spin out a crescendo and diminuendo at will – an art almost lost today. Reading between the lines, I seemed to alternate between great depression, as there seemed to be no end to the war in sight and I was despairing about my voice and poor technique, and elation at the many concerts, broadcasts and new opportunities that were opening up.

In the early summer came the invasion of Italy ('Oh, if only everyone would just sing!' wailed poor Dino) and we were thrilled to hear that my first cousin Duncan Forbes had been decorated on the field – or rather, the beach – at Anzio for gallantry. The war had a profound and traumatic effect on him. When it was over he disappeared back to Clare College, Cambridge, and became a distinguished history don. But, in the autumn of 1943, a great change was in store for me.

Earlier in the year Noël Coward had gone on tour to the troops in the Middle East and had reported back that the men in Paiforce (Persia and Iraq Force) had had little or no entertainment. Regiments of men worked in this remote area unnoticed and unrecognised, enduring basic living conditions, bitter winters and burning summers, driving aid to Russia in convoys over unmade mountain roads and high passes, where bandits and landslides were an ever-present danger. A fellow-officer of my stepfather's was at that time Head of Army Welfare at the War Office. His daughter and I were friends, so he knew all about the RAMC band and its varied repertoire of classical and variety shows. I was sent for and asked if I would like to go abroad with them, to which the answer was an enthusiastic 'Yes please!'

So it came about that arrangements were made for us to go on a Middle East tour in the autumn of 1943, and I as the only girl would travel under the auspices of Classical ENSA, with an honorary rank of 2nd lieutenant and a princely salary of £8 a week. What was even more thrilling to me was that I got a generous allowance of clothing coupons to buy glamorous concert dresses!

We left the UK in November 1943. On a cold dark evening my mother was allowed to accompany me to a blacked-out and deserted Waterloo Station. There we said goodbye, and I was handed over to a young army transport officer, who took me across London and put me on a troop train bound for some secret destination to board a ship, going I knew not where. It was all tremendously exciting, but I felt desolate for my gallant mother who went off home alone in the blackout to take up the daily grind of wartime life.

This was the beginning of the most marvellous, exhausting and exhilarating nine months of my life, which I described in detail in a series of letters I wrote home to the family. Much that was exciting and interesting was censored, but I can fill these gaps in from a small five-year diary that went everywhere with me. After I got home I edited the letters for publication, but because of the national shortage of paper they never appeared. They have waited sixty-three years, but now I am using them, because they are fresh and vivid and straight from the horse's mouth – one part of these memoirs for which I cannot be accused of re-inventing myself!

Chapter Three

Middle East Memoirs

November 1943 to August 1944

These letters were written during a nine-month tour of the Middle East, from November 1943, when I was singing with the Concert Orchestra of the Royal Army Medical Corps. I had been their 'resident' soprano for four years, and was, to the best of my knowledge, the only girl permanently attached to an army staff band.

I was the only woman with the party while we were abroad. Our show was the first of its type to visit the Middle East, and we were the first orchestra ever to be heard in Persia and Iraq. The 'Johnny' mentioned so often in the letters is the bandmaster.

These letters have been typed exactly as they were written, in great haste, to my family. Most omissions due to censorship I have filled in.

London to Cairo

On Board SS *Orion* 14th November 1943

My darlings,

I am so thrilled to be able to write to you straight away –
I've been thinking so much of you all three, and wishing you were here to share all the fun and interest of this wonderful experience. So far the conditions have been most luxurious. I

found a complete 1st class carriage reserved for me last night! Next door were three QA[1] nurses, who were introduced and asked to look after me by the kind OC Train who thought I looked lonely, and who were perfectly sweet. We had a picnic meal round about eleven, and then one of them, a very interesting New Zealand girl, came in and took over my unoccupied seat, so that all of us could lie down. We got into slacks, and I got out sleeping bag and rug, and had a most comfortable night, though I was too excited to sleep much. We had enough light to read by, yet the carriages were not blacked out, and the brilliant moonlight gave such a wonderful view of the countryside that we spent a lot of the night peering out of the windows. Today I, as a single and unique phenomenon, was ushered through all the necessary formalities with no difficulty whatsoever. I was the only civilian travelling, so on arrival at our port everyone else lined up and marched away, leaving me on the platform with a vast pile of luggage, including a gramophone of the QA's, which was overweight, and which they'd asked me to take on board for them! However, a sweet OC Station came to my rescue, and between us we got my luggage along the platform. We went on board on lighters and were supposed to have only what baggage we could carry. But the sailors rallied round, of course, and we found no lack by brawny arms to help us. I am now installed most comfortably in a 2-berth cabin with beautiful lighting, very hot running water, a heater, a ventilator for the hot weather, masses of drawer and hanging space, and, best of all, as yet no travelling companion! Have, therefore, pinched the lower berth and all the best drawers. We have 4 mirrors, and your photos are displayed on a very nice dressing-table. I have just had dinner (in a lovely saloon) consisting of soup, fish, roast duck, peas, applesauce and roast potatoes. And plum duff – a meal that is positively pre-war! All the meals are in 3 shifts, and women are always on the middle one. My travelling companions are very assorted. Am sitting at a table with several civilian women (Civil Service?) and 2 charming lady doctors. The friendly QA's sleep nearby, but are at another table. The ship is just now a seething mass of rather bewildered humanity – every sort and type and profession. My zip bag and big suitcase have been swept away to the Baggage Room, but I should be able to get into them soon, and I can do without rug and sleeping bag tonight as I have the blankets off the other berth. How I wish I could feel Johnnie and Co were as comfy as I am – from what I've seen of conditions below I don't envy them their trip.

Today was lovely and sunny (though cold), which added to the interest of the scene, already a never-to-be-forgotten one. We had quite a send-off from civilians and of course the usual masses of small boys. Tomorrow it seems will be spent hurtling up, down and about trying to find our Boat Drill stations and put on our life-jackets all in a very short space of time – no easy job, I can assure you, and one involving much running and climbing. My food you gave me was lovely, and I needed all of it. Am just emptying my thermos in a post-prandial cup o' tea (I got it refilled twice en route). There are loudspeakers all over the ship, and messages and orders are continually being broadcast. Am getting very confused with it all, but luckily my sweet N Zealand QA sister has just been in and told me all sorts of things (she's travelled all over the world both before and during the war) and she has given me a lesson in how to don my Mae West – quite simple really. Am now venturing out to try a (salt water) bath, and will stop. Mums darling, I so loved my days in London with you, and you were so sweet and dear to me, and we had such fun together. It was agony leaving you in dark Waterloo last night, and I worried awfully about you getting home alone in the blackout.

AT SEA. LETTER 1

How I wish I could have you all here breathing the sea breezes and watching the exquisite cloudscapes. I never really believed in Turner before, but now that I have seen sunrise and sunset and moonrise at sea I do. There have been wonderful rainstorms sweeping over, into which we would vanish like grey ghosts, to re-emerge in warm sunlight. And the reds and pinks and golden glows that light up the bleak grey at dawn, until the sea really is red like fire! I could watch it for hours; there is in fact very little else to do, and we lead lives of complete idleness. The programme is roughly: up at 7.30; a refreshing salt-water bath (we have bathroom and lavatory between 3 cabins, which is very lucky); then breakfast; then on deck to see the sunrise, and to speculate vainly on where we are and which way we are going! We walk clockwise round the deck until we've done one or two miles, then we're turfed off for PT and perhaps go below to read, or queue up for Officers' Shop, where one can buy Lux, soap, ink, cold cream, biscuits, sweets etc.; or, as today, we do PT up on A deck ourselves – a very chaotic business involving much screaming, but we'll improve doubtless, as the Instructors take it very seriously! Then probably a long drink before lunch (the ship is 'dry') then lunch, and afterwards a blow on deck, until troops' PT begins again, and we go below to sleep or read till tea-time. Tea is not provided, but we already have a first-class organisation. I have the sweet Argentine QA I travelled up with sharing my cabin now, which is grand, as she's a darling and such fun; she has an electric heater and tea, and the NZ QA who also travelled up with me has tinned milk, and I have my Horlicks and Bovril, and we snaffle bread and butter or biscuits or something and have a good tea. Then say boat drill, at which we try to break our own record every day. Then, round the decks until sunset, always very lovely. Change for dinner (out of trousers into skirt), then after dinner vingt-et-un or Progressive Rummy in the lounge (so crowded that many have to stand), with a very jolly crowd of Air Force officers we've made friends with. Then a last stagger round the decks, falling over hawsers, cables, and other queer nautical obstructions, then bed, or rather berth, and sleep to the rushing water, the murmur and creak of the ship 'talking to herself' (you remember 'The Ship That Found Herself'), and the clump–clump of some unfortunate sentry's feet on the deck just over one's nose. I'm putting on weight rapidly, and will be unrecognisable by the time I get home.

LETTER 2

It's much warmer now, and luckily I have all my luggage in the
cabin, so can get at everything. However I haven't unpacked as
of course there's no room for that, and anyway we knock things
over almost every time we move! Washing of clothes is possible,
but during very limited hours, as we only get fresh water at
certain times of day – morning and evening. Then we rush and
fill glasses, bottles, thermoses, etc. to last us till the next time –
which incidentally I must do at once.

Now, having filled our basin with fresh water, I will resume
and tell you of the burning question:– Have I or have I not been
seasick?? The answer is:– No, and I'm very proud of it as almost
everyone else has. We had rather a grim day our fist day out. It
wasn't rough, but it was what the habitués called 'freshish'. That
meant that things slid about a little, and we progressed very
erratically about the ship. I lasted out (feeling rather queer) till
just before lunch, when I rashly left the deck (where boat-drill
had been a bit of a shambles, with the first to succumb breaking
ranks to fly to the rail!) and went into the crowded and fuggy
lounge and drank an iced Coca-Cola with my Air Force friends.
I left them abruptly, but got to my cabin, lay down flat for a
while, then was able to get to lunch, where there were a few
vacant places already. After lunch I strode manfully round the
decks with Kay Francis, my roommate, Peggy the NZ nurse, a
sweet lady doctor and the RAF crowd, none of whom felt bad,
then we all retired for the afternoon siesta. It got 'fresher' and
'fresher', and was very cold, and at 4.00 p.m. they got us all up
again for boat drill. This for the women involved a long wait
in a crowded anteroom, then a very long wait on deck in lines,
waiting for the wretched troops to get up about 7 decks from
the bottom of the ship. Again I survived, but many poor devils
didn't, and the sweet Navy held us over railings and swabbed
up the decks with incredible forbearance. The ship was a sorry
sight – Tommies laid out in the corridors and on deck, too
green to move, poor wretches, and with nowhere to go anyway.
I had to lie flat with closed eyes, but got to every meal and ate
hard, which I know helps. The danger period was staggering

to and from the Saloon, and undressing, which I had to do in stages! However, I was not sick, and took no medicine, as it was difficult because of not knowing when we'd sail, or being able to fit in with meals. Also everyone says it's no good on a long voyage. Luckily Kay is never sick, but poor Peggy had a cabin with six QA's all laid low. With long hours of blackout, you can imagine what the atmosphere was like, the troops being taken short anywhere and everywhere. The sunset bugle is going – a romantic sound when heard so many miles from anywhere. And we are listening to the evening's announcements on the ship's wireless. [To be continued in letter 3.]

Letter 3

The Navy's organisation is superb. In every corner of the ship there are loudspeakers from which those wretched announcements are hurled at us. At first it went almost non-stop, giving exact instructions as to our conduct and daily programme. Now, however, we have it only twice a day. I am already a really Ancient Mariner. The perpetual shifting and swaying doesn't affect me – in fact I love it. The dining-saloon is full once more, but some people have had a bad couple of days. However, it is wonderfully calm and still again – we are extraordinarily lucky. There are several good pianists (of the swing and light music variety) amongst our 1st class crowd, and generally a sing-song going in our lounge, which is an incredible sight after dinner. There are many charming people, and girls, of course, are in great demand. The Entertainments Officer has already been on to me about singing, and helping to get up a concert, but am being very sticky as I have no music here. At my table for meals are an interesting crowd – 2 sweet lady doctors, a Foreign Office girl and 3 others going out to Government jobs, including Anne Gambier-Parry (daughter of the General) who's charming and most witty. My chief Air Force friend is a very interesting boy called 'Rags' Rabagliate – great-grandson of General Rabagliate of King Emmanuel's court, who led a revolution in 1821 and got kicked out of Italy.

They live in South Africa, and are completely anglicised but more cosmopolitan. Poor Rags has a glass eye and the other all crooked. He was shot up over Trondheim in Norway, his navigator killed and he and his gunner, both badly hit, flew their Blenheim back and landed safely in the Shetlands. He was taken to the local hospital where the doctor did nothing but give him bottles of sherry to drink. When he had lost the sight of both eyes and his hearing, they eventually got worried and flew him to a big man in England. Of course it was too late, but they saved the sight of one eye. He wangled back into active service through his brother, who is a Wing-Commander, shot down a Jerry, then got shot up by one coming on his blind side, was nearly thrown out, wangled his way back, and is now off to do Air-Rescue work overseas, but he swears he'll worm his way back into the active service list somehow! He is so young, like a bigger and better looking (at least he would have been if it hadn't been for his smash-up which has ruined his looks) edition of Dunny, with exactly the same voice and cheerful un-embittered outlook. His friends are a grand crowd, and we have great fun. In the next-door cabin is the ship's gunnery officer, a very nice soul who leads a most monotonous life, poor man.

We are running a concert party! No peace for the wicked. And I am finding myself in the unusual position of being the big noise – being the only pro on board! However in my usual way I've developed a really horrid cold and was unable to sing at our 'first night' last night and am crying off today too. It has all been great fun. We got it up in 3 days – there are several ardent producers on board – 2 Army, and one Air Force padre who is excellent. The Army Entertainments Officer, who is really head, was at Aldershot and had heard the Band and me, and is also a keen admirer of CEMA, and got up the first few CEMA concerts at Clitheroe near Preston, where I went with Lawrence Holmes and Phyllis Spurr this summer! However this man, Mr Davies, had left there by then. He has been very nice to me and most understanding about my not singing with a cold, as it might easily have been taken that I was being 'up-stage' or temperamental. The show is really not too bad. An incredible amount of talent appeared from nowhere – masses

of instrumentalists who we weeded out into a 6-piece band
consisting of tenor and alto saxophone, guitar, violin, swing
trumpeter and pianist – a Wren actress who is very good, an
RAF and an Army Officer who make a wonderful pair of
Western Brothers, sophisticated comedy type, a private who
was a professional tap-dancer and impersonator, a soldier who
does recitations of the old-fashioned 'Green Eye of the Little
Yellow God' variety – in really 'orrid and blood-curdling style!
And various others including a Wren chorus of 7 (so-called)
glamour girls who do their best with great gusto! We run twice
nightly for a week, on one of the lower troop-decks in order
to get most of the lads in once to see the show. Conditions
and acoustics are of course appalling, and heat awful. But the
men love it as they are so bored. I do hope I shall be fit soon.
Everyone has been so nice about my voice. I am writing this
in the lounge listening to a most remarkable man playing the
piano – one Mr Berill, a professional in real life and now a
Ship's Engineering Officer. He plays for me, vamping all and any
accompaniments really beautifully. He was such a relief to me, as
having no music I was very chary about agreeing to sing at all.
[Note: All my music went with the band.]

THREE DAYS LATER

This letter was interrupted in the usual way of on board –
there is no privacy, and one has so many acquaintances who
have nothing to do but talk! We have had three days of calm
and beauty – am in shirts and slacks and bare legs now. The
phosphorescence at night is wonderful. We had another fairly
rough spell, about when I last wrote, but have got out of the big
swell into smaller choppy seas which don't worry our ship. My
cold has been foul, and have been really mouldy for the last days
– but today am well again and have some energy once more.
I got all dressed up to sing last night, then couldn't manage as
the voice was a bit rocky. But tonight it should be alright. We,
or rather the show, are still playing to crowded and enthusiastic
soldiers, sailors and airmen. The big stuff for 1st class passengers

is not till next week, which means I should be quite fit again. There are a grand lot of people in the show – the sweetest RAF padre is one of the leading lights. My Italian is getting on very fast. I've had a lot of time during the trip.

You'd have laughed to see me this morning. We've all reached the stage on board when we simply had to do a bit of washing, and of course we girls have been helping the men. I've just finished 4 people's ironing as well as my own – 1 RAF and 3 Army Officers' – and it took me hours! Never again do I tackle a man's shirt. (Though as a matter of fact, by the time I got to the last, I was quite good.) We have a nice board in the bedroom which I share with 2 other cabins, but of course with no iron-stand, and with the ship moving (it's blowing up just now), it was rather complicated. However, have successfully coped, 'tho I fear the result is not all I would have liked. We have a lot going on board now – PT, film shows, and lectures, boxing, sports, etc., and somehow one always seems to be doing something. I've got all my dresses hanging out now, as I've managed to get all my luggage up into the cabin. So they should arrive in fairly good trim. But I shudder to think what the trunk will be like! I've seen the baggage being hurled ten feet into the hold, and it's a shattering sight. I have had the job of making up the glamour girls for the show every night. Was a little frightened at first never having made anyone else up before, but they all sat round expecting great things, so I got to work, and they didn't look too bad, thank goodness. They wear white shorts and sunbathing tops, which look very sweet.

The Ethel Vance book is very good, and am now reading the Synge plays, which I love. Have read one of the French books – which is excellent, and again all about mountains in the Haute-Savoie. However reading is very difficult as one is constantly interrupted. And I use most of the quiet moments for Italian. Since I last wrote my foul cold has eventually got better – and 'tho I'm still rather noisome and horrid to my fellow creatures, the voice is alright again, and I'm feeling really fit and happy. I sang at the Ship's concert for the first time last night – have missed eight performances, alas, and the day I wrote to you last, when I said I was going to try and sing, I actually got as far as going down to our – well stage would hardly be the word – anyway to the bit of deck (not floor – am now very nautical!) we perform on, and getting myself all changed and made up, before I realised that I had no voice and couldn't possibly sing! Everyone has been very sweet and forbearing, but I'm really glad I made it last night. You see, little me is in the extraordinary position of being the leading light on board! I'm really quite overwhelmed with the compliments I've had, and also with last night's reception, which was terrific. It just makes me laugh to have everyone rushing around saying 'Oh Miss Parry are you really going to sing tonight? How marvellous.' And then being overcome by the definitely rather bunged-up noises I emitted last night.

Then we have troop shows – two tomorrow, and the day after two running concurrently, one in what we call the West End – our 1st Class Lounge where we have not yet played, and one below for the troops again. That will be rather thrilling as one will be racing to and fro from one to t'other. And reaching our troop deck 'theatre' involves going out onto a pitch dark deck – no torches or even cigarettes allowed of course – and groping along until one locates a hatchway, then climbing down two flights of a wooden ladder, all in the dark! This is holding a large life-jacket, an overcoat, evening dress over one's arm, and a bag with make-up etc., and is an exciting proceeding, especially as one is liable to find oneself hugging strange troops in the blackout! However, I usually achieve an escort!

Our show is such fun. We have a charming crowd of people in it, and the WREN chorus are sweet. A lot of them are getting off at the same place as I am, so I hope I may see something of them. The actress WREN is very nice, she knows Sarah Churchill and the Churchill family quite well, and was telling me what a swine Vic Oliver (Sarah's husband) is. She toured with him in 'Idiot's Delight' for some time, and said he is the lowest type of humanity one could imagine. He has a craze for little girls of about seventeen, and he wanted to 'adopt' this girl, Valerie, and gave her the most wonderful presents and was quite frightening and almost savage when she would have nothing to do with him. Poor Sarah Churchill is desperately unhappy and hasn't of course lived with him for ages. The Winston family will have nothing to do with him. The awkward part is that he was a despatch-rider for Germany in the last war. A very nasty affair and no one can think why Sarah married him. I suppose she feels she can't get a divorce, at any rate just now. The operatic tenor whom I discovered on board is very interesting. He's done a great deal and sung all over the place, and it's nice to find one person on board who understands a voice!

THREE DAYS LATER, 4TH DECEMBER. STILL ON BOARD!

We have been rotting in port for 3 days, and are at least allowed to put the date on our letters. I'm going ashore tomorrow, then go by train to Cairo where I report to a certain address. I've discovered that the Band are, or were, in the ship berthed next door, and left yesterday for Cairo. We've not been allowed off the ship and it's been slightly monotonous and hot. But the weather is divine, and the nights too exquisite, and I've had marvellous fun. I made tremendous friends with Dick Kauffman – his history and life are so interesting; he's travelled all over the world and sung at the Metropolitan and the Scala and toured with Lily Pons, and yet is the most modest and retiring person. Have met more charming people in the last 3 weeks than in years, and it has been lovely being frivolous and gay again. My darlings – how I wish you were here to enjoy it with me. The sunsets and sunrises are incredible – orange and green. Am hoping to go by camel to see the pyramids on Tuesday, with a party of friends from on board, led by the very interesting archaeologist Mr Whittemore, which should be marvellous. Have sent all my luggage ahead and am living in about 1 shirt which I wash and dry frequently – we wear no undies at all, it's so hot.

7TH DECEMBER. HELMIEH, NEAR CAIRO

Imagine me at 7.30 a.m. – blue sky and bright sun, but cold – sitting up in bed in a cubicle in a long Army hut just having had breakfast, and with an hour's leisure, before getting up for rehearsal. How lovely, as I have so much to tell that I hardly know where to begin. The real thrill is that we are off to Baghdad for Christmas! What a travelled person I shall feel! We will be in Iraq (can't spell) for a while (Col Foote is there as DDMS – he was on my ship, and, by curious coincidence he had been Commanding Officer of the RAMC at Church Crookham where the Band was based and where I sang weekly!). Then we are visiting Persia, and then Syria, Palestine, etc. then coming back here before going off in another direction. Will give you all the addresses very soon. Am thrilled I brought warm as well as cool things – The Canal Zone is hot, but Persia is icy in winter.

Well, well! I must be coherent, and think I will start at where I left off before, as it will be clearer. I was on our ship (which I can now safely say was a large luxury liner) for three weeks, and fear you will be very worried at not having heard from me sooner, darlings. I have sent off 2 cables to you. We had a marvellous journey as to weather – only for one day was the sea just fresh; the rest of the time one might have been on shore. However there were other events, as I fear you will have gathered from wireless and papers. We are very lucky that we are all here safe and sound. We arrived at Port Said, where the weather was heaven – very hot during the day and glorious nights of moon and stars, with incredible sunsets of orange and green. We lay there just near the canal entrance for 4 days and were not allowed on shore. But it was very interesting. The flatness was what struck me most. Approaching Port Said from the sea is extraordinary – it rises from the water like a city built on piles, and there appears not to be any land at all. Closer inspection reveals it to be a dirty-looking place, but I should have liked to go ashore. We were not allowed to buy fruit or goods so didn't have the usual crowd of native boats, though a few crept up to tempt us, laden with bananas, grapefruit, oranges etc. And there were plenty of feluccas and queer craft chugging and paddling up and down, all blowing funny hooters hard, and swearing at each other. I had a gloriously happy last few days – no shows and time to get to know all my new friends. I've made several very valuable ones whom I do hope I shall be able to keep in touch with – my room-mate Kay Francis, the singer Dick Kauffman, and Walter Newlyn – all three very deep-thinking people – and Maj Philip Holbrooke, going out to join the 3rd Hussars, a skier and sailor and terrific fun, with whom I've fixed up a skiing party after the war!

The last days on board were very sad, as people were disembarking every day to go off to all corners of the world. I was one of the last to go, but luckily had three Air Force friends and Philip travelling with me. We went ashore on lighters, and there whom should I go off in an Army truck to have a drink with but Pimmy! [Note: my mother's godson.] He had appeared on board in the morning, to my great surprise, and is O/C Army Signals at Port Said. It was very lucky I was left on board so late as he had only heard the night before from Aunt Billie that I was coming out East, and had dashed straight off to see passenger lists, etc. He rushed me off for ½ an hour to his tent where he and I and two sergeants drank gin and green chartreuse! He looks flourishing – is in a tented camp which he is in sole charge of, with 4 sergeants for company and his CO 50 miles away down the Canal. He says he is very happy, and looks it. How strange to find Pimmy in that dreary spot of dirty sand, with just a tent as home and 4 sergeants to drink with! He was too sweet, and said he would cable you [I had already sent one from the ship] and also took all my letters to post. We are hoping to meet again some time. Well, then I got into the train, which in the usual Egyptian way had stood around for hours before starting. Pimmy, who knew the RTO there, had arranged for it not to leave without me! The trains are most amusing – long grey affairs with huge windows, which of course are wide open all day and which are the most usual way of getting in and out of the train, as the steps up into the carriages (which are very high off the track) are usually crowded with soldiers and Egyptians who do the whole journey sitting on them with legs dangling. This is not as dangerous as it sounds, as the train seems to average 15 MPH and never exceeds 25 MPH in its greatest bursts of velocity. Of course the hooter goes nonstop, as the line is covered with Arabs and children selling oranges etc. who dive at you the moment you stop anywhere. We were quite comfy – 6 in a first class carriage, and I with Philip Holbrook who looked after me most sweetly. I had discovered at the last moment that the Band had been on a smaller ship berthed next door the whole time. She was quite comfortable and carried masses of women so there was absolutely no reason why I shouldn't have been on her too. The Band I discovered had gone to Cairo the day before, so I expected everything to be cleared up ready for me when I arrived. We travelled from 2 o'clock till getting on for 11 p.m., which will give you some idea of the rate we went at, as I believe it's about 90 miles. The trip was very interesting – down the Canal to Ismailia, then across country. The Canal Zone is most strange – acres and acres of salt lakes like the sea stretching on every side, with odd clumps of trees like pines or larches, and of course the palm – now a very beautiful vivid green. Sunset was almost unbelievable with its blue and violet shadows. We were very merry, and ate bananas, chocolate, etc., and drank iced lemonade hard, and bought new supplies (actually it was forbidden to buy fruit, but we all did as it is alright if it has peel on it) at every frequent halt. We had of course changed our money to Egyptian piastres on board.

Later. I left off at night in the desert, with our funny train chugging along in the moonlight while I talked religion with my sweet RAF padre friend, and skiing with Philip. We arrived in Cairo round about 10.30 p.m. and I was very surprised to find nobody to meet me. However it was a long time before the baggage was all unloaded, and I had to wait about for three quarters of an hour, all the time expecting someone to turn up from the Band or ENSA. I had been given a Movement Order on board, which told me an address to report to, but I was feeling terribly lost and knew only two words of Arabic – 'Impshi!' ('go away') and 'Yalla!' ('go away!' really rudely!). Two signal officers who were meeting their draft of men found out my plight and were horrified that I was all on my own, as even soldiers are not allowed out singly after dark here now. They took me in hand, and I was thankful, as all my friends were busy seeing to their men or being rushed off in Army transport. My big worry was that my big blue globetrotter case, which should have been with my small one and the brown zip in the van, had completely disappeared. However we had to leave that for the night as it was already 11.30 p.m., so the two signal officers who were really good Samaritans took me out and got a taxi, and set off for the address I had been given. We had great difficulty finding it and I'd have been lost alone, as the driver knew no English. When we eventually got there, we went upstairs and found that it was merely an office and all looked up. There was a large Negro porter on the door, but he also spoke no English and couldn't help us. We debated for a second or two what to do. The hotels are packed, and anyway one can't arrive there at midnight. So eventually we decided on the YWCA, and had another long drive there. It was locked up too, but we roused a Negro porter, and literally dragged a wretched woman out of bed, and I begged her to give me a bed for the night. She said she had just one left, in their big rest room, so I bade a very grateful farewell to the officers, who had been too sweet for words and who refused even to let me pay for the taxi, and then I fell into bed in a huge room with seven other little beds full of service girls, most of them on leave in Cairo. I was very empty, having had lunch at 11.15 a.m., on board, and it was 12.30 a.m. by the time we got to the YWCA, and too late for them to give me anything. What a day! I have never felt more lost or really in a foreign country, with everyone jabbering a completely strange language, and crowding around for tips which anyway I could never work out in piastres! However the whole thing was too exciting and interesting for words. And the kind signals people found out at the station that the Band had arrived and were here, so I wasn't a bit worried as I knew I wasn't stranded.

Next morning I woke up early in a huge room – red and gold walls, immense black furniture, and great arched windows covered the carved wooden sunscreens, in real harem style. I was brought a delicious breakfast in bed, starting with what I think were cape gooseberries – a divine fruit. I got up slowly and washed inches of filth off myself, then, feeling clean and tidy once more, explored our large palace. It had a cool marble staircase, a wide terrace, and a garden where poinsettias and many to me unknown flowers and trees grew, sunk deep in the shade between ours and other tall cream painted buildings. It was very peaceful and everyone so kind and helpful. At about

09:00 I rang up the RAMC Base Depot, and got straight through to Johnny, and were we glad to hear each other's voices! He'd been quite frantic for two days trying to find me, and had had all the ENSA people trying to trace me – they got on to hotels, etc., and were just going to call the police. He had my blue case, heaven knows how, so knew I was in the country.

8TH DECEMBER. HELMIEH

Yesterday (when I had written the first three letters) I discovered I had committed the most appalling breaches of security. So have been through them and blocked out all names, and do hope they will get to you alright.

I had got to where I contacted a frantic Johnny the morning after my arrival here. Well he arranged to come round straight away in a truck and collect me and my luggage and bring me here. We spent most of the day in town first, seeing the ENSA officials, getting photos taken for my pass, etc. etc., then drove out here and were met by the charming RAMC Colonel, who brought me along to the Mess I am living in, which is that of the most charming lot of girls I've ever stayed with – South African volunteer ambulance drivers. In our long stone huts, where about twelve of us live in cubicles, the doors and windows are never shut and umpteen dogs, cats, kittens and a very cross parrot walk in and out at leisure. The trouble is noise, as we are only divided off by half-walls on two sides with completely transparent sacking across the front, and people have to get up at all hours. However am getting used to it, and blessing my Quies. Of course there are nets over all doors and windows. Just sand in between huts, so I wear proper shoes, not sandals, as a rule. We are waited on by young Arab girls and a few men. They are excellent servants and very sweet, with a colossal sense of humour, but I have awful difficulty with my limited vocabulary! They stand round chattering at me, or seize on things to tidy away, and I feel quite helpless. The girls mostly sleep outside, but I dare not risk that as it's very cold at night, though hot enough for frocks and aertex undies by day. Have

nowhere to hang or put anything, and as I am now completely
unpacked, my cubicle is festooned, which causes amusement and
consternation to my little maid, Susie, who is very tidy-minded!
I'm ironing in slow instalments – alas, I will have to pack up
again very soon, however. I am leaving some stuff behind when
we go off on this tour, as we will need mainly warm clothes for
it. We have to walk miles to our bathrooms here, which makes
washing rather hard work, but the little girls and the dhobies can
cope, luckily, so I'll be able to start clean. The Mess is very free
and easy – one can ask people in for dinner and drinks every
day. We will be here a lot between tours, I gather. We are very
busy already – first concert on Saturday, and all large classical
affairs here, which am delighted about. ENSA are routing us, not
the army, thank God, and are most efficient and quite charming.
The Straight Music Section have seized on us firmly, and we
hope to do a lot of broadcasting. They are thrilled with the
Band's versatility. We have a nice hut for rehearsal here, and I
can practise in town. Unfortunately am not allowed out alone,
which complicates things, but is safer. The poor Band's had a
very uncomfortable trip over, under troop conditions, but are all
fit now.

8TH DECEMBER. HELMIEH

On reading through the last four letters, I have decided I must
write one more as there's still such piles to say, 'tho shall be late
for going into town with J. Rehearsal yesterday went well, and
with a few days of real practice the voice should be alright. Our
concerts here are really big affairs, and am singing 'Caro Nome'
and such like. The first is for Lady Russell's 'Music for All' club –
you'll remember the archaeologist Mr Whittemore whom I met
on board ship who wanted to introduce me to her. The publicity
departments are interviewing us, and today I have to go to some
well-known photographer to get photos taken. This will be the
first time that ENSA here have routed an Army Band and they
are getting right down to it and will see we get really good
publicity. [Author's note: we didn't!] It was all a muddle between

ENSA and the RTO about my arrival – I did not appear on any list as ever having left England apparently, so of course nobody knew I was due to arrive. We are some way out of town, and either hitch-hike (which is done quite officially from proper Halts here) or catch an incredible tram packed with people, which fairly hurtles along. The traffic is much worse than Paris and all on the wrong side of the road!

Darling, it is now next morning, Dec 9th as had to break off. Had a most interesting day yesterday. A nice sergeant in ENSA (one of the concert organisers, and a singer himself), who has been here several years, took us out to lunch at two real Egyptian restaurants. Their food is superb – first we had sort of hors d'oeuvres, with a huge round of soft bread which one breaks and dips in tahina – an oily sauce of sesame seed. Then we had Kebab, a Turkish dish of lumps of very tender lamb grilled on skewers over charcoal, and Kofti, also Turkish, a sort of rissole, and very delicious, both lying on chopped green stuff that tasted something between parsley and celery. With them we ate divine pink coloured rice tasting of cheese. We then went on to a restaurant celebrated for sweet meats, and had a famous Arabian one called 'Bread of the Palace'. It is bread soaked in a sort of molasses with whipped goat's cream on top of it, rather like Devonshire cream. Then we had Turkish coffee, which I love. The whole thing was very cheap – about 6/- for three people, and we ate under half the portion the normal Egyptian gets through. Then this sergeant took us round some of the best native sweetmeat shops. Their cakes and sweets here are quite fantastic. There is absolutely no rationing. Have bought you a tin of rose petal jam, some dates, and some crystallised dates, which will send off as soon as possible. Did some hard rehearsing and practising yesterday, and must get up for the same now. I had a divine party last night – the kind Signal officers and Rags, the charming CO of the Depot and one of the South African drivers, and we went over to the local club where there's a heavenly outdoor dance place. The nights are exquisite but it was very cold.

13TH DECEMBER. HELMIEH

Am scribbling in my little cubicle in bed, resting before tonight's
show – a local variety one out of doors, which should be rather
lovely, as it is full moon and gloriously warm. I'm so happy
and fit, darlings. We did our big classical concert in Cairo on
Saturday, and thank heaven I was absolutely on top form. I sang
'Caro Nome' (really well for once – shan't do it again for years!)
and 'Vissi d'Arte', 'Filles de Cadiz' and two with piano. It was a
lovely hall in Lady Russell's 'Music for All' Club – a magnificent
place with reading and rest rooms, outdoor tea-garden, restaurant
etc. all for the troops and officers. We had a big audience,
sitting right out into the foyer, and the concert went down
marvellously. Old Professor Whittemore (whom I met on the
boat) and Lady Russell and all the ENSA Classical music people
were there, so I'm very happy that it was so successful. Yesterday
morning we went to Alex by train for one night and did a light
classical concert in a small theatre there – again very successful.
The train journeys are quite fantastic – I am supposed to go 1st,
Johnnie 2nd, the men 3rd, but we try to all stick together, as it is
much easier for luggage etc. Anyway it's not at all pleasant for a
girl to travel alone. (Johnnie is going tomorrow to fix that we all
go together 2nd class always.) Imagine a milling throng of Arabs,
Sudanese, Egyptians, and soldiers, most of the former complete
with household goods, bedding and innumerable babies, and all
swearing and cursing and fighting and laughing. When the train
arrives, they leap on as it draws in and go headfirst through the
windows, babies, grandmothers, bundles and all! The train is
packed before it leaves, yet hundreds more get on at each stop.
They travel clinging to the running boards and perched on the
roof and on the bumpers between carriages – quite fantastic.
The country is flat and dull: oxen turning water wheels every
few hundred yards – camels and tiny donkeys padding patiently
under immense burdens – women in flowing black with huge
bundles on their heads. There are great red poinsettias in the
gardens and hedges of purple bougainvillea – very lovely. And
oranges ripe and tall date palms. Johnnie and I were driven
round Alex by a very nice ENSA Captain – the sea and sailing

look lovely, but the town rather horrid – like a Hollywood set
of cheap luxuriousness, with awful squalor beside it. The poverty
out here is unbelievable, and the villages look to me like bomb
debris – piles of brick hovels, or filthy tattered tents. Am busy
preparing for our Persian tour – it's very difficult to keep clothes
nice as everything is so dirty. I step out of my door into sand,
and it gets everywhere. Also no ironing board or hot water in
the basins. However am very happy here. An adorable Persian
kitten, Scarlett O'Hara, is sleeping right under my rug with me,
purring hard. Wear trousers nearly all the time, as do all the girls.
Since I last wrote we have done several shows – one in the open
air here, on a nice stage with our audience sitting in the skating
rink! (Roller-skating is funnily enough the big sport here, and
most of the rinks are converted into outdoor theatres for the
summer.) Then we did one at Mena under the pyramids. When
that was over, our driver took us up the steep hill on which they
stand, and we spent an hour walking round pyramids and Sphinx
in brilliant moonlight – a most thrilling and awe-inspiring
spectacle. There is nothing very beautiful in them except for
the vastness, which one can hardly take in. I think they must be
at their best by moonlight, with the stone gleaming white and
deep dark shadows, and their tops soaring up into the depths
of the heavens whose riddle they are supposed to solve. The
remains of temple buildings all around are very interesting, but
I'd like to go there with an archaeologist. Next morning one
did actually materialise – do you remember my mentioning
Professor Whittemore – the charming and interesting old man I
met on board? Well, I had a wonderful morning with him, seeing
mosques, which are much more beautiful than the pyramids,
though of course they are not of such great antiquity. It was a
lovely day, with brilliant sun making strange shadows, and the
first thing he explained to me is that oriental architecture of the
periods we were going to see (C15 back to C10 or even earlier)
used light as an element in the design of their buildings. By a
marvellous play of shadow and double shadow, and the recessing
of some parts, and throwing forward of others, the lovely pearly
grey stone they use is made to seem luminous and living and
ever changing. The trained eye can apparently see the complete

spectrum in the gradations of light and shade, which was what the architects aimed for. The buildings are on a very vast scale – huge and airy, with sunlight coming through exquisitely carved windows or unroofed parts. The most wonderful thing is the ornamentation. It is of a beauty I have never seen in Europe. There is much of it, but it is so lightly and delicately done, so harmonious and above all so varied, and un-stylised, that there is never the slightest feeling of it being too much. Besides, the buildings are vast and empty; it is just the walls that are so beautifully worked. They are carved more exquisitely than any stonework I've seen yet, and the whole effect, in the lovely silver grey, is of something insubstantial as a tracery of cloud or foam, thrown upwards and held poised.

18TH DECEMBER. HELMIEH

The first mosques I saw were two that stand on either side of a steep hill climbing up to the old citadel of crusading fame. The vista looking up between those two vast buildings is one of the greatest in the world. Imagine on the right the Mosque of Hassan – a very masculine and stern affair like a fortress, with a wall rising straight from the road to a terrific height, almost unbroken, then on the other side its female complement – I can't remember its name but I think it's the present Imperial Mosque, generally called the Blue Mosque, and was probably built for Hassan's wife – a much lighter and more delicate structure with lovely minarets soaring up. Between these two, the narrow road plunges into dark shadow, climbing up to the crumbling yellow walls of the citadel, above which rise a multitude of spires and minarets and mosques of all sorts. The Imperial Mosque is carpeted in the most exquisite soft green, for which the Persian name is 'Moss under Melting Snow' – the effect is of walking in a forest. Then we saw another lovely mosque which has the most beautiful C10 stained glass – plum colour and dark green and pearl, such as I've never seen elsewhere. Then there was a little tiny single-chamber one right in the slums of the native quarters – the only place in the world, so Prof Whittemore says, where the name of God is written in light made by clear glass set into a coloured background. We also saw the City of the Dead – a strange sight, with its acres of deserted unroofed houses where each family has its burial place. It is very unsafe to go there at night as it is all supposed to be haunted and is actually infested by thieves. During the day whole families go there with food and bedding to be with their dead – rather a nice reverent idea.

Then we went back through the bazaars (gold bazaar, silver bazaar, copper bazaar, jewellery, food, fruit, each in their separate departments, divided by narrow alleys teeming with donkeys, horse-drawn garries and the odd taxi such as ours) to the Continental-Savoy Hotel, rival of Shepherd's, and had a marvellous lunch specially ordered by the dear Professor. When I thanked him, he told me the story of Melba and Sir Edward Lutyens. Melba went to dine with Lutyens, who said, 'Do you know, Dame Nellie, I have never heard you sing.' 'Well, Sir Edward,' said she, 'that is easily remedied.' And she sang for him. Afterwards he thanked her, and she said, 'Now, Sir Edward, you build me a house.' 'You sang for me,' said Professor Whittemore. 'I try to build you a house.' Wasn't that charming? He is a very celebrated personage out here, and is much beloved by all the native priests and keepers of the Mosques. I'm hoping to go out again with him when it can be fitted in, as he's offered to take me any day. That afternoon my friend Walter Newlyn arrived for a few hours, having escaped from his Transit Camp at Suez. He came to our show that night and I was presented with a huge basket of red roses from him. He's a dear, and I admire him and his outlook on life enormously. He's deeply interested in the occult and mystic, and so well read, and is going into politics on the Social Science side. You'll meet him someday if he survives India.

We should have left for Persia and Iraq yesterday but the tour has been postponed – only temporarily. We'll be here over Xmas, which should be fun, though. Have heard from many of my friends on board, and one of them, Flying Officer Bramer, alias 'Ginger' or Cad No 1 of our Western Brother's show on board, came over yesterday, and came to our concert, which was great fun. Have been rehearsing all sorts of things – much classical stuff such as the Bell Song, the Villanelle of Eva dell'Acque, 'Lo here the gentle lark!' etc. as we seem to be doing more of that type of work. Am delighted. Also am very happy as the voice really going well – Johnnie is quite surprised and overcome by how much better I'm singing! It's really very lucky, and I can't think why it is. I get in some practising, as the sweet OC Ambulance driver here, who is a pianist herself, lets me use her private sitting-room, but of course I can't do half as much as at home. Am hard at work with Tithy (the Band's pianist) on a recital programme which am hoping to do at 'Music for All' sometime! A group of French (Duparc, Debussy, Chausson and Fourdrain), a group of Rachmaninoff, Rimsky-Korsakov, and the two Richard Strauss songs, 'Morgen' and 'Ständchen', and a group of modern English. Am also getting well settled in here, and adore the informal life. Have acquired a hurricane lamp for my cubicle, so now can read in bed, and have permission to use the OC's ironing board, and have all my clothes ironed, including the white muslin. Am paying one of our little Arab maids 50 piastres (10/-) a month, which means she does my laundry, shoes etc.; but I do anything at all tricky myself, as though she's the sweetest and most willing thing out, she might spoil the more delicate things. At present my whole cubicle is scented by Walter's roses – the flowers here are exquisite and very cheap, and we all have masses. Two of the cats, Scollops and her very beautiful Persian daughter, Scarlett O'Hara, have attached themselves to me and generally sleep on my bed – welcome hot bottles as we've had three days' rain (unusual for here) and it's quite chilly. Rain is so unexpected that the lack of drainage becomes very apparent, and there are huge puddles everywhere! Am getting hold of a suit of battle dress for our trip, as it's very cold in Persia. I have official Army Rank here – a 2nd Lt! and am on active service with regard to all facilities of transport, army post office, free letters, etc., as are all ENSA artists. You won't recognise me when I come home – I'll be fat! The food is marvellous, masses of very tender veal, lamb, and steak. Vegetables of every sort (hardly any fresh potatoes though, and the sweet ones become very monotonous), and incredible cakes and pastries, éclairs, meringues, ices, sweets etc. also of course tangerines, bananas and peanuts galore. I had indigestion for days, but am now acclimatised! The price of things in Cairo is fantastic – it is possible to pay £2.10.0. for a pair of stockings. And could you send me some toothpaste? It's 5/- a tube here! Have sent off three small parcels to you – rose petal jam, crystallised dates, and dried dates. Very dull I'm afraid, but if you could send me the toothpaste in a large tin, I could send you more. Tins are very difficult to obtain, and I need mine for our journeys. Am in jumpers and skirts and mainly trousers now.

22ND DECEMBER. HELMIEH

Our tour which I told you was cancelled is now, I am very glad to say, on again. We leave soon after Christmas, which is all very nice as it will be lovely being here over the 'festive season'; they have a big tree laid on, with lots of decorations, and a party and all sorts of fun in the Mess. However I don't expect we'll have terribly much time, as partly why they are not sending us off sooner is that they need us to do shows round about. We've been very slack for a few days, while all sorts of things to do with who really was responsible for us were thrashed out. It has all turned out very well, as ENSA have got complete charge of our routing, and we much prefer this as they send one to big places with good stages, have a very active publicity department so that one is well advertised, and also have much more comfortable transport than the army. For our long journey (we have 2,000 miles to go – a very thrilling thought!) we have to have camp kit, and I am getting a bed and bedding from ENSA. Also they are supplying another primus stove, so that we will have two cooking outfits, and tea, sugar, milk, and big water tins, all things we'd probably have had to go without if we'd gone under the army. Also the men get 3/6 a day pay, or rather allowance, from ENSA, and Johnnie gets £1 a day. It is all great fun and very exciting. Am taking sleeping bag, rug, and all the woollies I possess, as I believe there are, or soon will be, feet of snow where we are going! We are all going to have typhus inoculations, but they have no reaction luckily. Tomorrow we are doing another concert at 'Music for All'. Am singing the Jewel Song, 'L'Été' by Chaminade, and 'Morgen!' (Richard Strauss, with a really exquisite arrangement for muted strings and woodwind made for me by Johnnie, who has fallen in love with the song) and the Mozart 'Alleluia'. Also we are doing 'Peter and the Wolf' with self as narrator – this is its 1st performance in Cairo. Wish you could hear 'Morgen!'. Am strangely enough really singing it, which could not have done a few months ago. Darlings, am thinking so much of you all happily together. I sent you off a box of chocolates and 2 Turkish Delights yesterday – there is a marvellous YMCA in Cairo where one just goes and chooses what one likes and they do all the wrapping and labelling etc. As I'm now officially in the army I'm able to use it, and you'll be tickled to see 'Soldier's Gift' on the label! Also my rank (2nd Lt)! Tonight we have a show nearby. And we're hoping to broadcast 'ere we leave for the wilds. Have rung up Lady Coates (who was a Spink) and am waiting to hear from her as she was out when I rang. But it is difficult seeing people from out here. One can't go about by day alone, and Cairo at night even with a man is rather horrid.

25TH DECEMBER. HELMIEH

Here am I sitting up in bed on a lovely sunny morning, being thoroughly lazy as we have a day off. I am very happy to be here over Christmas as they are all so sweet to me. I've bought a lovely big Christmas cake (£1 at Groppi's, which is the best place as a restaurant, and for cakes and sweets) for the Mess, and also three smaller cakes as my present to the Band. Today we have a Christmas tree in the Mess, all beautifully decorated, and an official ceremony for distributing the parcels off it this morning. Then Christmas lunch. Then I'm hoping to play tennis (have had two good games with Johnnie – we have very good singles together). Then we have tea and running buffet party in the Mess, with many guests invited, including Colonel of the Depot, who is a most charming person and has been very kind – he is, I think, Irish, and has spent summer after summer sailing all up and down the west coast of Scotland, and knows every nook and cranny of it. As a family they are mad on riding, and his brother is MFH of the Armagh. Altogether we are terribly lucky in our 'home from home' here. We've just completed a busy few days. At the last moment we did a return visit to the 'Music for All' Club on Thursday, and am glad to say it was very successful. Everything went wrong – I felt awful, fighting 'flu which everyone is having here just now; then after our dinner party with Col Keating we failed to get a taxi (Cairo is almost as bad as London) and had to walk a long way to the concert, arriving at ten to nine, when we were due to start at nine (everything is very late here). Then we found the microphone was bust, and I had to do 'Peter and the Wolf'. However it all went well once we were started. 'Peter and the Wolf' was much appreciated, and I sang two groups as well – the Jewel Song and 'L'Été' then 'Morgen!' with Johnnie's heavenly new arrangement and the Mozart 'Alleluia', which got a terrific hand. Various friends came, including Professor Whittemore, who left an important dinner party after the soup to come and hear the Alleluia! You would laugh at my dressing room; it is generally cluttered up with several 'fans'! I have a charming but rather pompous new one – a young Lt in the 4th Hussars who is mad on music, ballet, French literature, climbing etc., and was at Oxford. His name is Arculus, for future reference. The following day – i.e. yesterday – we did our first broadcast from Egyptian State Broadcasting, for its European Dept, which is run by the British. They were thrilled with us, and we are to do an enormous amount of it while we are here and when we return. Of course it is all terribly one-horse out here – we could only take Salon orchestra as they have no studio bigger than about your bedroom, Mum! But we can do outside broadcasting for full orchestra or variety shows.

25TH DECEMBER

I left you at ESB or Egyptian State Broadcasting, an imposing edifice with the usual Muddle East confusion and Egyptian inefficiency inside. There is another broadcast programme out here – our own Military Station, and we hope to do a lot for them too. We are finding ourselves rather 'big stuff' out here and the Band really are playing beautifully. We are doing such a variety of shows – dance-band, salon orchestra, full orchestra and variety, and everyone is amazed at our versatility. Yesterday was very amusing, as we were shown round the other studios where Arabian programmes were in progress – incredible sounds issuing forth from orchestras of prehistoric instruments, and Egyptian film-stars being exotic in intense melodrama, Greek patriarchs in black tall hats preaching to Greece over the air, and a rowdy party of French kids doing a 'Children's Corner' programme to Free France. This is the most cosmopolitan place in the world – the population is Egyptian, Arab, Sudanese, Armenian, Jewish, Greek, French, and Italian. Then there are troops of every nationality under the sun. The traffic is shattering – electric trams rush about with people clinging on to the sides by their eyebrows, and jumping on and off all the time; the rich Egyptians have huge cars which they drive very fast. There are convoys of Army traffic; then there are old 'buses of incredible antiquity which boil perpetually, lorries which are generally broken-down, taxis dating back almost pre-Great War, garries drawn by two Arab horses which will stop for nothing, and the usual rabble of small donkey carts trundling along under vast burdens, and street vendors pushing barrows and women walking with great bundles on their heads, and babies in their arms. How millions aren't killed a day beats me; of course nothing ever stops hooting, whistling, or ringing its bell. Johnnie and I got out very early last night as the town was already a shambles, with most people drunk. There's a lot of street fighting still in the lower and darker districts – it is really a very unpleasant town at night.

We are off on our trip fairly soon, darlings, and I may not have too much time to write. It is a marvellous thought that our first destination is about 2,000 miles away. I have been issued with camp bed and bedding, and have acquired a spirit stove and mess-tin for cooking and boiling water in; the Band have 2 Primuses, and we carry big tins of water and fuel, and food, tea, tinned milk, etc., as at times we will have to be completely self-supporting. How thrilling! I believe there are feet of snow in some parts, so I might even get some skiing! By the way, don't worry about the 'flu – I've successfully avoided it with quinine, and am flourishing now. The trouble was that when we first arrived it was boiling – the summer went on very late, and I was in aertex undies or even none at all, and open cotton shirts. Then it suddenly turned cold, and we've had one of the wettest spells ever. The Band have been down with bad colds, and Gyppy Tummy, poor dears, but I've been quite fit. It's really funny here – most of the theatres and cinemas are bug-ridden, and one gets awfully bitten. However our huts are quite clean, fortunately. One feels so well with this dry climate and I find I don't need so much sleep. Reveille is 5.30 a.m. ('tho I don't get up!) and we start rehearsal at 8.30 a.m., and concerts or shows generally don't begin till 8 or 9 at night, so we generally try to sleep in the afternoon. But it's difficult in a hut with people coming in and out, and talking, and the dogs, cat, and parrot all frolicking about, and the latter talking nineteen to the dozen.

Appendix to Chapter Three

The following is from my secret diary and could not be written home.

21st November 1943

We are all wondering where we are! We reckon we went West-North-West for three days and South for three days (including today), and then (inside info – probably wrong!) altered course as we thought we had been spotted. We should turn East soon.

23RD NOVEMBER

We did turn East, then North-East (we had been sure we were going to America or round Cape Horn!).

24TH NOVEMBER, EVENING

We are now passing Africa and Spain – lights everywhere – ships in line astern going very slowly – native boats out – warm and lovely.

25TH NOVEMBER

Last night was thrilling. The Padre and I under cover of the blackout climbed up into one of the high gun turrets on A Deck and had an incredible view of Spain, Africa and Gib. No moon, but bright starlight. We had sighted Africa in the afternoon and been met by a submarine from Gib, which is now in convoy. Have left several ships at Gib. Today no land in sight. The native boats out with flares last night were apparently measuring the length of each ship in the convoy and passing the info to the enemy.

26TH NOVEMBER

Land in sight again. We pass Algiers in the morning. Leave 3 large transports, pick up a new one and escort, also Aerocobra fighters (French planes). Have our first air attack at sunset (just after 4.30 p.m.). Our Action Station on B Deck just under the guns is awfully noisy. We are there 2½ hours while Junkers 88's (?) and new Heinkel 77's attack with torpedoes and bombs. We bring down a Junkers and hit 2 or 3 others – 2 or 3 of our fighters lost, also one transport which joined us this morning and was full of American troops. It was hit amidships and left burning. We did community singing to keep up morale. After v late dinner we did the second house of our show and got a big ovation.

27TH NOVEMBER

Yesterday really was very thrilling though was frightened as we are terribly cooped up – our ship is now much the biggest in the convoy and gets all the attention! The girls are very good; the WRNS led by Lieut Mervyn Jones the rugger international who also sings in our show, sang silly songs hard. We were just missed by several bombs and two torpedoes (a new aerial type). Tea with Guns (the Gunnery Officer), as usual he is very interesting. Sunset and sunrise are our danger times – next danger point is when we pass Crete. Pass Sicily today – get a warning but no action.

29TH NOVEMBER

Air attack at 5.00 p.m. – quite sharp and we are just missed several times and glass broken. Impromptu concert on F Deck at 8.30 p.m. Always conscious that if the ship is hit it takes twenty minutes to get on deck from down here.

30TH NOVEMBER

We passed our nearest to Crete at midnight. Today we are nearer the African coast. Were expecting the attack yesterday. Two very successful shows in the 1st Class Lounge. Submarine attack during the second but show carries on. Had a very narrow escape yesterday – we were attacked by 14 bombers.

1ST DECEMBER

Last night a depth charge dropped between us and the [ship's name illegible] and damaged her plates – she put into Alex and we are now the Commodore Ship.

2ND DECEMBER

Up before 6.30 a.m. and on deck to a perfect sunrise and our
destination, Port Said, climbing out of the sea.

Chapter Four

Middle East Memoirs

Cairo to Baghdad

1ST JANUARY 1944. ST JULIAN HOTEL, JERUSALEM

I am lying on my bed, having just arrived after a very
adventurous journey, and last night spent on the sand in the
middle of the Sinai desert! What a queer and exciting New
Year's Eve! I will begin at the beginning. I left off last Saturday
when we were still in Cairo awaiting orders, I think. In fact
it was Christmas Day. I can't remember if I told you that we
were suddenly rushed off to do some shows for an American
hospital some way out in the desert. We missed the Xmas lunch,
which was to have been rather fun in my Mess, but Johnnie
and I were lucky as we got a special bit of very delicious turkey
served early for us. We had our first taste of desert scenery on
the way out, and saw a mirage – only water. The shows were
very disappointing – half-tight, lethargic and blasé Americans
for our first audience (who anyway hadn't expected us) and
mental patients in a small ward after that. Then we were taken
to a big RAF Ferry Station (also USA) where we had coffee
and hamburgers in a most super restaurant with perfect daylight lighting and every labour-saving device. The Yanks do their
troops in grand style. We watched an exquisite desert sunset of

flame and gold and deep violet, and came home in the afterglow.

Then we had a terrific Christmas party in our Mess, to which Johnnie was invited. He and the charming Colonel of the RAMC Depot and a very nice Englishman and two of the S African drivers who have been looking after me, Danny and Christine (both lovely and of tiptop colonial family) formed a party. We had a buffet supper that would have made your eyes pop out! Then we cleared part of the mess and danced to a radiogram. Dear Danny and Christine had hung two presents for me on the tree, and also one for Johnnie, inscribed 'To our Bandmaster with love'. I retired early as we had a busy time ahead, but most people had a real thick night. The streets of Cairo were awful over Xmas. Next morning we rehearsed for a broadcast, and did a show locally in the afternoon, and it was very funny as the Band nearly all had fearful hangovers and looked too awful. In the evening we went into Cairo and I met my 4th Hussars fan for dinner and to hear a recorded version of 'The Messiah' at 'Music for All'. The place was packed right to the foyer with Service people who sat breathless during the 3 hours of the programme – really a very wonderful sight. On Monday we went miles for a show in the desert to the RAF. It was a huge success, and funnily enough I met various people who had been on the 'Orion' with me. We got back at 1.30 a.m. and were up early next morning as usual rehearsing. Then another show at night, and we heard that we were to leave the morning after next for this tour. It meant cutting 3 broadcasts – rather a pity as we were doing one home to you, and a big classical one from 'Music for All' on New Year's Eve. Wednesday was hectic – Tuesday night's show ended very late as they all do here, and Wed I was on the go non-stop, packing, arranging things so as to leave a trunk-full of stuff behind, dashing into Cairo to collect camp-kit and my khaki shirts for my battledress, and finally doing a show at night again. However I somehow managed to get straight in time.

1ST JANUARY 1944. ST JULIAN HOTEL

Am just recovering from a fearful attack of heat bumps due to overeating, and also a lot of bites from sand-fly, and I'm afraid a bug, which I have successfully destroyed.

We left each other at the end of letter 1, with me all packed to set off early on Thurs morning for our tour. I was up at 6.15 a.m., said farewell, and gave my present (a hideous sham gold brooch!) to my sweet little bint, Susie, who was almost in tears at her 'Miss Biss' (her nearest to my name!) going, and finally was picked up by our convoy of buses and a lorry, and set off, waved away by the sweet Wazzis, who have been so kind to me. I may say here and now that the big hold-up over our getting off on tour had been the transport; the 2 buses and lorry we were getting were straight out of the garage, having been overhauled and made perfect for our use, so we were assured. Well, we set off for Ismailia, on the Suez canal, which we were supposed to reach in 2 hrs, and which was to be our 1st halt on the way to Jerusalem, where we were due to arrive round about 7 p.m. that night. Our bus turned out to have the most appalling steering which made it almost uncontrollable, and, what was worse, all three of our vehicles were loaded to the roof with baggage, campkit, four days' food etc. My own kit consists of 2 suitcases, a zip bag, a bundle of rug, sleeping-bag, canvas folding chair etc.; a valise with complete camp kit, bed, pillows, sheets, etc; my small zip bag; an ironing board in with the Band kit; a large box with 4 days' tinned food, a small spirit cooker, a large bottle of meths, and a mess-tin for cooking in. So you can imagine how much we had all told! We parted company from the lorry early on, as the roads were crowded. Our two buses got to Ismailia at lunch time, and we went straight to a garage, where the local Transport Officer arranged to have the bus J and I were in overhauled. No lorry turned up, and we spent the afternoon frantically trying to trace it, with awful visions of it having overturned as it was terribly heavily loaded.

We arranged of course to stay the night there, as it was impossible to reach Jerusalem. Eventually we got news of the lorry, which had broken down completely early on due to

overloading. It was a huge thing quite incapable of carrying
the load it was constructed for. A repair lorry was sent off,
which fixed it up, but it broke down again on the way in, and
eventually arrived at about 6 o'clock at night, the men on it
having had no food for twelve hours. When it first broke down,
Fredericks set off to get help on a tangerine cart pulled by a
donkey! Meanwhile the garage had found that our bus's steering
was dangerous as a vital nut had been forgotten, and they said
it was a miracle we had got there at all. The journey certainly
was rather a nightmare, and J and I had front seats so could see
what we missed! We had Palestinian and Egyptian drivers –
anyone who has driven with them will know what that means!
We all got fixed up for the night, I at a big YWCA with lovely
rooms and excellent food (the YWs out here are like very good
clubs), the men partly at a YMCA and partly at a Holiday Camp
on Lake Timsah. The lake is very lovely – half way down the
canal, with Ismailia as the holiday resort on it, and all beautifully
green after the desert. I saw an amazing sunset of black palm
trees against lemon sky, reflected in the water. Then to bed very
early, to sleep like a log – the other occupant of my room was a
sweet ATS girl – native of Alexandria. I even had a huge private
bathroom with shower, bath, bidet, and basin, but no hot water
– typically Egyptian. These YWs are run mainly by charming
Colonial and American women. Was called at 7 a.m. yesterday
morning with a delicious breakfast in bed, and was all set to
leave again at eight o'clock, clad in my battledress, which is a
boon as it's so practical for this rough travelling, and very warm
for the cold nights. Will stop – yesterday's adventure demand a
complete letter!

1ST JANUARY 1944. ST JULIAN HOTEL

Next morning we left Ismailia on a beautiful morning like the
best English summer. The steering of the bus was supposed to
have been repaired, and we'd been loaned another 3 ton lorry,
so had been able to thin out the baggage. Our original lorry had
been repaired during the night too, so our convoy was now 4

vehicles. First of all the new 3-tonner punctured and held us up 2 hrs. However we spent that time crossing the canal – a slow business as it is ferry between ships going through. Also we had customs, passports etc. before crossing, though one does not actually leave Egypt there, but over a hundred miles on in the desert. The views of the lake, with shipping and sailing yachts, the pleasant green of trees, and parks, and the vivid blue water and background of glowing sand, was very lovely. Eventually we were all across, and set off into the Sinai desert on our long crossing. At first it is wind-swept sand-dunes, very fascinating in their shading of sun and shadow and symmetrical curves; here and there patches of funny grey shrubs, now in full flower with small papery yellow petals and red centres on silver-grey stems; occasional stray camels or a few Bedouin tents half drifted over with sand. We stopped after about an hour – and, lo and behold, right in the middle of nothing, a tin lavatory!! The stop of course was made for my benefit – our driver has not driven ENSA parties around for nothing, and knows exactly where modern conveniences are to be found, or where the lie of the land is accommodating. Desert is apt to be a bit flat! It really was very funny; dear J had been very worried about how I was to 'spend a penny', and had had a special lavatory made for me back at the Depot. It consisted of a petrol tin with the top off it and a wooden seat affixed all correct, and a two sided canvas screen. However, we were so overloaded that it had to be jettisoned – a great pity. It was designed by Johnnie, Les Marsh, and a sweet RAMC Staff Sgt who was very worried about me, for, as he put it, 'She'll have to walk a bloody long way if she wants to walk out of sight!' However there has been no difficulty so far – the men simply go off into one half of the desert, and I have all the other, and there are convenient dunes in most places. To continue, the steering of our bus was quite appalling still, so at about lunch-time we halted at a REME Rescue Point – a small party of intrepid engineers who live miles from anywhere, and work miracles on all the vehicles that break down crossing the desert. We got out primuses and brewed tea and ate sandwiches and waited 2 hrs while they had our bus out on test and under repair.

Eventually the REME Sergeant said he could do nothing about it – it was quite unfit to be on the road at all, and he refused to allow us to continue in it. He had it out on test and came in saying 'My God, I daren't do over twenty (MPH) in this.' We had been doing 60k an hour, loaded to the roof with men and luggage, all the way from Ismailia – horrific thought. The Sgt would not even allow the bus to be driven to a proper garage (of course some 200 miles away), but sent it on tow. He also warned us that we shouldn't drive after dark, which falls promptly at about six o'clock here. It was by then getting on for three.... We hastily reloaded ourselves and most of our kit into the other vehicles and set off. One of the lorries refused to start, and had to be left behind, with some of the men and much baggage. 1 bus and 1 lorry carried on. The bus, which J and I were in, drew ahead of the lorry and we passed the Palestinian frontier (where there are few formalities, but the most attractive Frontier Police in astrakhan hats) with no difficulties. Again they warned us of the road ahead; about eight or ten miles on our bus punctured, and the driver found that though he had a spare tyre he hadn't the tools to remove the wheel. No sign of the lorry, so we all got out and settled down to a picnic. There was glorious sun, and warm lovely sand and hills, and we brewed tea and lay about very happily waiting for something to turn up.

1ST JANUARY 1944. ST JULIAN HOTEL

Have been speaking much French in Cairo and here, am getting practice in German too. One of our drivers is a very nice German Jew – the others are Palestinians – all very good but rather on the reckless side! The last instalment left us with a small portion of the RAMC Orchestra, including self and J picnicking happily in the desert with a punctured bus, no tools and the rest of the convoy lost. The sun set in quite incredible beauty. Colouring here by day is matt and monotonous. At dawn and dusk it became incandescent. Flame and gold and orange (real genuine theatrical orange), and violet and periwinkle blue and black that has to be seen to be believed. Then the sun is down and the sky is lemon with the hills black and rimmed by that strange aura of light one gets in the West Highlands.

We were feeling thoroughly New Year's Eve-ish, and as the sun vanished and the air grew chill we got two fires burning (tins full of sand soaked with petrol), and set alight a full tar-barrel we found by the road, which caused a huge conflagration and clouds of black smoke, but kept us warm. The bus limped back to the frontier post, and got its wheel changed, but of course it was by then dark, and we were frantic about the 2 lorries, which should have been with us long ago. Eventually the first one, which had been left behind with carburettor trouble, turned up. Just as it was ready to leave the REME post it had met the other one, which had set off behind us, being towed back by a break-down lorry! The first one came on and joined us, and we were very glad, as we'd run out of water and hadn't all got our blankets, and it was getting cold. However, the 2nd one had had to stay at the REME place with several men and the baggage. We decided to go on, as the lorry with us had to get through to Jerusalem quickly. It led off, and we followed. You can imagine how crowded we were, as the bus that had had wonky steering had had to be completely evacuated. The bus we moved into turned out to have almost as bad steering, and we were coming to the worst parts of the road – up and down hill with hairpin bends round wadis, and drops often on either side, and only a few stones to mark the edge of the road. It was terrifying – Johnnie and I sat side by side in front, 'driving' for all we were worth. We all joked desperately amongst ourselves, as one does during bad Air Raids, but it was one of the most nervous two hours I've ever spent, though a calm appearance was essential to general morale!

The lorry got on fairly well as its steering was alright and its lights good. Our lights were bad, and when we arrived at a little outpost called Asloodj (phonetically spelt!), Johnnie and I agreed that it would be suicide to try and do the odd 90 miles to Jerusalem that night. We sent off the lorry, and parked our bus in the car-park. Asloodj is a petrol and repair station for desert traffic, and it boasts a NAAFI – a filthy spot lit by erratic naphtha lamps. We flocked in there, to find it full of Arabs,

Palestinians, Poles, etc., all in advanced stages of their New Year's Eve celebrations! However, they served us fried egg sandwiches and tea, and we made a good meal. Then we settled in for the night. Of course no sleeping accommodation at all, and not a woman in the place; in fact my entrance into the NAAFI caused quite a sensation! Drivers in transit sleep in, under, or alongside their vehicles. Thank goodness instinct had prompted me to transfer my bedding during our various change-overs, and I had it with me. I had to choose between inside or outside the bus and I decided on outside, so Johnnie, myself and three or four of the Band camped on the sand, I had my Mac underneath, my rug, and my sleeping-bag and my camelhair and fur coats, so between them I made a very comfy sleeping-place. The others all had blankets and coats. The stars were exquisite – but in the middle of the night it was jolly cold, with an icy wind blowing sand over us. The sleeping-bag was marvellous – I got right into it, even my head, and kept quite warm, except for the tip of my nose and actually slept very happily, feeling so thrilled with it all. Next door to us a whole lot of camels were parked, each hobbled out of biting or kicking distance of the other. Imagine me slumbering, guarded by Johnnie on one side and the Band on the other, with vivid stars overhead, and the sands of the desert growing exceedingly cold underneath!

1ST JANUARY 1944. ST JULIAN HOTEL

Meanwhile, the small crowds of local troops were trying to forget what an awful dump it was, miles from anywhere, by getting very drunk and singing lustily and disturbingly into the night. I blessed my battledress, which is both inconspicuous, and a great protection, as a girl in uniform is looked upon differently from a civilian here, and is less likely to be molested or worried. Also it is lovely and warm, and one just doesn't care how dirty it gets. We were awake at dawn (Johnnie had actually been up since 3 a.m., unable to sleep for the cold), collected up our bedding, ate a couple of doughnuts and a foul cup of tea produced by a drunken Sergeant from the NAAFI, and set off. Our first bus that was on tow had arrived and was going on to a big garage, but the lorry that had been left behind at the REME post had not turned up. However, we set off, and had a wonderful drive to Jerusalem. It began with sunrise, and the greyness warming magically from red to gold, like a vast electric fire. Then we left the sand-dunes, and reached real hills. The basic colouring here is completely different from home; imagine cream-coloured rock, veined with blue and red, and interspersed with patches of very red soil, so that one's background is cream and stone all speckled with the red-brown like a bind's egg. Against this, greens are amazingly vital; a tree or a cabbage positively glows. There are copper-coloured trees, and silver-blue cypresses, and vivid evergreens, but they are few against the general stone effect. The country is terraced, and seamed by watercourses, and every foot is laboriously ploughed, and the stones cleared – donkeys, camels, and oxen all yoked together. We passed through Bethlehem and arrived just after 10 a.m. in Jerusalem – a very steep up and down town but clean and bright after the mellow dirt of Cairo. The lorry which had gone on the last night had arrived at 2.30 a.m. after taking the wrong road. The bus on tow had had to go to a garage nearby, and the driver absolutely refused to drive as it was. The 2nd lorry still hadn't arrived. Our own bus we also refused to go further in, as the steering was so bad it wasn't fit to be on the road either. The 2nd lorry has now turned up – they all slept the night at an out-post and came on by daylight. They had four breakdowns en route – nothing nasty, only carburettor trouble. However they were all done in, and unfortunately two of them are in a bad state of nerves. They had a very nasty experience – being towed on a 6ft rope by two mad Australians in a thing that usually pulls tanks – so that they swayed all over the road and nearly went over the edge rounding bends. They were literally kicking the sides of the lorry and shouting for it to stop, and one man almost had to be laid out, he was upsetting the rest so. This last run had been difficult – some of the party objected to carrying on, with the vehicles in such a bad state, but of course we simply had to. All so worrying for Johnnie. However, here I am safely installed in this hotel, which is very dirty, but run by nice people. The

Band, except for the few who can afford a YMCA, will be in the Transit Camp. Am so sorry, as it looks grim. I slept heavily all this afternoon, and am feeling fine. We are broadcasting tomorrow – with Carol Levis, the Discoveries man, who has done shows with the Band at home, and thinks very highly of them. We did two performances with him back in Cairo, and he has been thinking out terrific posters for us headed '30 Men and a Girl'. The title stuck, and we were known as that during our whole time abroad! We do not continue our journey till Monday, and they have promised us new transport. Certainly it would be impossible to carry on as we are, as the nervous strain and responsibility for Johnnie is just too much.

8TH JANUARY 1944. SEMIRAMIS HOTEL, BAGHDAD

I stopped my saga in Jerusalem a week ago. We had a very interesting two nights there. The day we arrived we had a much-needed rest. Unfortunately Les Gilbert went into hospital suffering from acute shock due to the journey, and Glan Spiller followed him with tummy trouble, so we are without them and will be so for some days. On Sunday morning we did a grand broadcast with Carol Levis, who plugged the Band like anything – Johnnie and I had interviews with him during the programme, in which he asked how long I'd been with them, and so forth – The official name of our show now is '30 Men and a Girl'! Carol drew up rough prints for our posters, which are being printed by ENSA right away. The broadcast was hectic, as we had one hour in which to decide on programme, write a complicated script with interviews etc. and get balanced. We had no chance to run through it but thanks to Johnnie's brilliant sense of timing, it ran for half an hour to the second. While we were on the air a telephone call came through asking who the lady was who was singing, but we have not yet been able to trace it. I sang 'Spring in my Heart' (a medley of Strauss Waltzes) and our Walt Disney Fantasy. After lunch I dragged Johnnie out sightseeing – we luckily got a hold of a first-class official guide, who took us about all afternoon, for the sum of 10/-. We went through the Jaffa Gate into the Old City, which is just exactly as it must have been in the days of Christ – narrow steep alleyways with worn steps, up which pour and jostle crowds of Arabs and Jews with side-curls and Greek Orthodox priests and children and cripples and beggars, and donkeys clopping in and out of the crowd buried under loads of merchandise.

On either side are houses dating back to crusading days and earlier, with shops on the ground-floor where all kinds of colourful wares are sold – oranges, pumpkins, melons, bananas, sweets, spices which smell delicious, queer sweetmeats and cakes cooking over oil-stoves, exquisite silver filigree work, and gold, copper and tinsmiths plying their trade, silks and brocades and Persian rugs, all huddled together amidst filth and smells such as one has never dreamed of. We saw the beautiful Mosque of Omar (outside only as it is closed to Christians and other infidels in the afternoons) which is all mosaic from the floor of its great courtyard to the tip of its minarets. It has a huge dome that was completely encrusted with diamonds and precious stones, but someone or other removed them some six hundred years ago and leaded it over. It must have been unbelievable before. We saw the Moslem and Algerian quarters (the Old City is four complete towns clearly defined and segregated – Jewish, Moslem, Greek Orthodox, and Christian – the Algerian quarter is just a colony). Then we followed the fourteen Stations of the Cross, from the House of Justice where Christ was condemned, throughout His journey to the Holy Sepulchre. The latter is interesting but very disappointing – incredibly over-ornate, with every religion vying to establish itself and outshine the others. I can't describe it – it is a chaotic jumble of *objets d'art* and relics of genuine antiquity and different styles – the wealth must be fabulous.

8TH JANUARY 1944. SEMIRAMIS HOTEL, BAGHDAD (CITY OF A THOUSAND SMELLS)

I left off in the midst of trying to describe to you the Holy Sepulchre – a well-nigh impossible feat after one hurried visit. It is all very dark – one lights a taper at the entrance and proceeds to climb up and down stone steps through churches of all denominations – now one for the Greek Orthodox, now a Jewish Synagogue, now a Moslem temple, all jostling each other to be on the Holy spot. The mount or hillock, on which Christ is said to have been crucified, is completely built over and under – only odd bits of the rock are preserved here and there. A huge crowd of Polish soldiers and officers and ATS were going round while we were there, and they continually knelt down and prayed and kissed the stone floor – their reverence in the light of those little flickering tapers, was an extraordinarily moving sight – I was glad they were there to counteract the commercialism. Then I had my first experience of shopping in the Far East – your birthday present, Mummy darling, which I bought in a little shop near the Holy Sepulchre. I nearly bought all sorts of other things too – I am not a good haggler yet, and after partaking of a tiny cup of coffee, felt in honour bound to buy something. The shop is owned by a family of craftsmen from Bethlehem – there were some lovely things and I eventually chose for you a silver bracelet set with jade. That evening we did a troop show to a nice audience at Allenby Barracks. The new town is clean and bright – grey stone houses and wide steep streets, and a most cosmopolitan and intellectual population; flourishing opera, ballet, drama, art, etc., a first-class orchestra, and many excellent artists who have had to leave Europe. I spoke German to the hotel servants and most shopkeepers while we were there, and bought German and French books.

Next day, we left for our long journey here. We had been given two different buses and one new 3-ton lorry, as our own transport was in such a shocking state, and our old lorry had been thoroughly overhauled. I got in a good practice before we left – ENSA have studios and pianos wherever one goes, luckily. We left after early lunch, and had a wonderfully interesting run. Jerusalem is two and a half thousand feet up, and we ran down to the Dead Sea 1,300 feet below sea-level in about an hour. It had been cold and windy with rain, but the temperature became quite mild as we dropped down and down, curling round hairpin bends with our cheerful Palestinian driver accelerating furiously until the last moment, then breaking and swinging round on half a wheel. We passed the Good Samaritan Inn, and the place where Christ gave sight to the Blind, and ran on down through creamy-brown stony hills terraced with vine and fig trees, with square mud houses clinging to the slopes. Then we saw the Dead Sea very blue on our right, with the Mountains of Moab rising to over 5,000ft beyond, and on our left the hills where Christ fasted, and the pointed mountain-top where, legend has it, he was tempted of the Devil. Below lies Jericho – winter resort for the rich of Jerusalem – where we drove through an oasis of trees, and banana and orange groves, and lovely flowers. Then across a mud plain seamed with watercourses and dotted with queer mounds and hillocks, often with burial urns perched on them; this must have been the bottom of an infinitely larger Dead Sea billions of years ago. There is no vegetation to speak of – just mud. On the far side of this curious and age-old plain the mountains of Moab rise quite sharply, and we hurled ourselves at them and found a way over what looked like an impassable barrier by a marvellously constructed road that loops to and fro and doubles over itself up the mountain side, and takes one from 1,300ft below to 4,000ft above sea level in about 2 hours' (slow) climbing time. It follows the course of a mountain torrent, where vivid green vegetation and tall bulrushes make a curious and tropical contrast with the bare rocky brown of the mountain. Herds of goats and camels graze on the sparse dry grasses – the former amazingly sure-footed.

8TH JANUARY 1944. SEMIRAMIS HOTEL

Halfway up one of the lorries' brakes started to burn out, so we stopped and waited while the driver repaired it. We were in a little village clambering up the mountain – one mud hut's roof the doorstep of its neighbour above – and I got out the camera and photographed the picturesque locals – a family consisting of a most beautiful and dignified Arab mother, and masses of children who all emerged plus a donkey from a mud hovel. The

Band grouped themselves amongst them and violinist John Tollis
seized a kaftan from an Arab and put it on – I hope the snaps
come out. The brakes loosened, we set off upwards, and emerged
4,000ft up on the great plateau across which we were to run for
four days. We stopped for tea on the top, and it was a panorama
such as I've never seen – one felt oneself to be on the top of the
world, with those mellowed and prehistoric hills rolling away
for thousands of miles and never a sign of humanity. We had
a jolly picnic up there with several fires going, then drove on,
passing through Aman, capital of Transjordan, where the Emir
Abdullah Ibn Hussein – elder brother of late King Faisal of Iraq,
lives. The town was built by the Romans for trade – one of ten
they set up – what a vast civilisation was theirs. After dark we
arrived at a camp and small village called Mafraq, where we
struck the Haifa-Kirkuk oil pipeline which we were to follow
for the next few hundred miles. There the Band were in tents,
and I had a room in a hut, where I set up my camp bed. It was
cold, but I've luckily been given oil-stoves wherever I've been.
The lighting was oil lamps, as usual, and sanitary arrangements
very primitive, but am now well used to that! The tin lavatories
had no roof, which was a pity as it started pouring with rain! As
it is a fair sized camp, there is a small garrison cinema, and there,
after a hasty supper, and changing in pitch darkness owing to a
complete lack of curtains, we did a show to a very enthusiastic
crowd. We had a lot of Indians in the audience – this part of the
world is full of Indian troops – and they seemed to enjoy it, I
can't think why! Up at 6 a.m. next day – awful rush repacking,
stowing camp-kit in valise, etc., then off in pouring rain, with
forked lightning playing around, and thunderstorms passing over
the plateau – a scene of most primeval desolation. We ran into
a lava belt – black stone stretching for hundreds of miles, north
and south, with small extinct volcanoes here and there – the
whole thought to be 2,000,000 years old – and we travelled
for 85 miles through it. We had about a 250 mile run before us,
but the rain was torrential, and our buses had no windscreen
wipers, and the roads were becoming flooded. So when we
arrived at the small outpost where we were due to lunch (a
tiny camp of Engineers and RASC, a NAAFI for convoys, and

one of the pipeline pumping stations with about 10 British Staff and a doctor – the whole known as H4) we decided on the advice of the OC there to stay the night with them. It was a real oasis in the wilderness, metaphorically speaking – there was no vegetation to speak of, and they were marvellous to us. The men there seemed happy and were noticeably of a superior and intellectual type, who read, and liked good music. They had no room to put up such a large party so they took us along to the pipeline people, and the Chief Engineer rallied round nobly. Most of the British families are still evacuated because of the troubles in 1940, when the pipeline stations were nearly all captured by the Iraqis. So the Band were given two complete cottages to themselves, and Johnnie, Pop, the Band Sergeant Major, and I were put up by the Chief Engineer in person – his family being still away. We did a show that night in a tiny hut – no electricity, just flaring Aladdin lamps, and a fearful atmosphere. No mike possible of course, and awful acoustics! There were all the white people on the place here – some 60 all told – and they adored it. Their last entertainment of any kind was a year ago. It poured all night, and we were thankful we hadn't gone on; a convoy which crossed us going to Mafraq got stranded and the lorries were nearly swept away by water. [Inserted later because I did not want to alarm my family: a car going the other way with Polish officers and an Indian driver carried on against the advice of people at H4, went over the edge of a bend, and one or two of the occupants were killed. We heard this next morning from the doctor of the station who looked after them.] It is so dry here that when the rains come the water can't sink in at first and what they call the 'Irish Bridges', where the road dips into wadis, get flooded. Next morning dawned fine and bitterly cold with icy wind. We were not allowed to proceed till a road patrol had gone along the route on motorbikes to make sure all was clear. So the Chief Engineer took us all round the pumping-station. These are dotted all along the pipelines about 100 miles apart – tiny self-supporting colonies of about ten families with carefully grown trees and gardens in the midst of the desert. Each station has a fort, with doctor, food, wireless transmitter etc. where they can support a siege if attacked, as happened in 1940. The CE was very musical and had heavenly records of opera etc. which we played by the hour.

8TH JANUARY 1944

We left H4 in the middle of the morning, much rested after a comfy night and hot baths. I washed masses of clothes, dried them on the hot pipes, and wore them next morning! Laundry is a fearful problem here; thank God for battledress. We had run out of the black lava belt just before we reached H4, and were on real billiard-table sand. The roads have been quite incredibly bumpy all the way, and the poor men in the back of the 3-ton lorries have a fearful time with the piano and big crates sliding to and fro. I haven't mentioned odd hold-ups such as punctures etc. of which we have had at least 2 a day. The funniest thing was Mafraq, where we had a slow puncture and, of course, no spare, and they took it to the Indian REME post – the only repair place there – where there was nothing bigger than a motorcycle foot-pump, and believe it or not that tyre took 40 minutes to blow up! The Indians had it all taped – they did a continuous jogtrot on the pump. We reached another outpost called Rutbah just in time to unload, change and put on a show in the 'Rutbah Pavilion' (a leaky matting-roofed hut!) at 8 o'clock. We'd snatched a hasty picnic lunch, having been held up by dynamo trouble on one bus and carburettor trouble on a lorry, and hadn't arrived till dusk, which comes early and swiftly here. Rutbah was our first station in Paiforce, as Persia and Iraq Command is called. Incidentally, the Transjordan-Iraq Frontier consists of a line of empty oil cans! Rutbah people were grand to us again. It was bigger than H4, and actually had an Officers' Mess, with RASC, REME etc., luckily all British and therefore efficient. REME spent all night servicing and overhauling our rickety vehicles. I had a bunk in the Officers' hut – the poor men were as usual on a concrete floor, but most of them now have camp-beds, and J and I lend them ours as we are usually well catered for. Next morning we were up betimes and on our way, and they sent us an escort of lorry, REME officer and Sergeant in case we had trouble en route. We reached a little spot called Wadi Mohamedi for lunch; there are just a handful of British troops, one Officer and a crowd of Indians there, and they have never had a show at all. We couldn't stay to give them one, but had to push on as one lorry had already had brake trouble and we were behind time. It was funny there; we had been told there was a NAAFI where we could get lunch, but when we drove in and asked where the canteen was, they said 'eighty miles down the road' and quite seriously thought nothing of it! We were going through rolling sand-hills – very pretty in the sun, with blue sky, and great herds of camels wandering around. Gradually we came into sparse pasture land, with Bedouin camps of black tents, and sheep and goats and donkeys feeding. Then into irrigated cultivation of a sort, and across the Euphrates (I think) and at sundown we ran into RAF HQ for Paiforce, a huge station called Habbaniya. We did no shows that night – they'd arranged two, but our lorries didn't get in till late owing to brake trouble. I was put up in the most sumptuous Officers' Club – Indian servants rushing around doing everything and calling me 'Memsahib', and perfect food, etc. I met some RAF Sisters who had had the opposite cabin to mine on the 'Orion', strangely enough. There are just 38 of them there, and they have a marvellous time – riding, sailing on the lake, games, and a party every night. The climate now is lovely – dry and bracing, but in summer they get 120°–140° in the shade, which isn't so good. Johnnie and I went to the cinema that night – and the following day we did 2 shows there. It is a magnificent place, that seats 1,200, has beautiful lighting and curtains and perfect amplification and a huge stage – very strange to find it miles from anywhere, but there are 4,000 RAF and troops there, and the RAF always do themselves well. We spent all the day rehearsing, practising, and organising lighting with an ex-London Hippodrome electrician, and I dug out dresses and ironed hard. Our two shows were a colossal success, and everyone thinks ours is the best they have seen in the ME. My difficulty was avoiding very fast and hard-drinking Offices. They were rather nasty to Johnnie at first and he wasn't able to

come into the Club, which was ridiculous and very hurtful, as
everywhere else, of course, he is received into the Officers' Mess
as he should be. However we had two good nights' rest there,
and the men felt better for it.

9TH JANUARY 1944. SEMIRAMIS HOTEL, BAGHDAD

Herewith letter No 5 of the series – scene Habbaniya, self
consuming excellent breakfast of two or three eggs scrambled
in masses of butter (one never eats one egg in the Middle East –
always at least two) with the Indian Club Secretary, Head Waiter,
and my table waiter all standing round anxiously awaiting my
approval of the food! Before I left I had a special request from
the Sergeants' Mess to go and write my autograph on the wall
of their bar. They had been thrilled as I had gone and had a
drink and chat with them after the show the night before, and
I was the first woman ever to go into their Mess. We had a very
easy drive to Baghdad, and arrived here yesterday (Saturday) at
midday and went straight to ENSA HQ for Paiforce. There we
found a very nice and helpful crowd of people, who had heard
from Carol Levis and from Brig Foote (both of whom are here)
about the Band's versatility, and had been overjoyed as they were
expecting a very military brass affair and had had no details from
Cairo at all. We have an incredibly interesting couple of months
here. I can't mention place names on ahead, but we are going
to travel a tremendous lot, and will be amongst snow and hills
part of the time. We are going to have all sorts of fun such as
travelling with all our transport on a train – lorries, buses and all,
and actually living in a railway carriage on the line, and living
on a launch somewhere else. Also we have an armed guard part
of the way! There are still many bandits around, and we were
warned to keep our vehicles together on the road latterly. We
are staying here a good ten days, which gives time to repack and
get laundry done. Johnnie and I are living in the best hotel – a
very nice place full of British Officers. It is on the Tigris, and
I have a large room with a balcony overlooking the river and
the hotel garden. The hotel is very Continental – every room

has its own comfortable bathroom. The food is excellent and plentiful – Jerusalem was terrible as the country is overflowing with refugees and rationing is almost worse than in England. The city of Baghdad is the most squalid, filthy and unpleasant town in the world, according to most people. Apart from one or two mosques, there is little to see in it, and its best street is like the slums of Cairo. Troops go out in threes and fours at night, and I don't move a yard without Johnnie. In Cairo there are large numbers of Colonials and white troops, and Jerusalem has a European civilian population in the New City, but here the natives and Indian troops are in a great majority, and people who know consider the Iraqis and Persians the scum of the earth.[2] Prices everywhere are fantastic – beer is 10/- a bottle, and a decent meal £1 a head. Luckily we are all very well provided for. Next week we are playing six nights running at the King Faisal Hall – rather an honour as parties generally play at the Garrison Cinema. The hall is lovely, I am told. We are doing five nights of variety for the troops, then a big orchestral concert on Saturday. Then on Monday a charity concert for the Lord Mayor of Baghdad, for the Iraqi civil population to come to (heaven knows what we will do to entertain them!). We are broadcasting variety on Thursday, part of the classical concert on Saturday, and dance band on Sunday. On Wednesday, the Ambassador and wife, Sir Kinahan and Lady Cornwallis, and the Prince Regent, Emir Abdul Illah, etc., etc., have all been invited, and they will probably come on Monday too, which will be rather fun. Our shows here don't begin till 9.15 at night! The broadcasting is very one-horse, owing to lack of equipment, but is run by a grand Army Captain who does wonders with the means at his disposal. Besides these shows every night, we are playing in hospitals etc., by day. Spiller and Gilbert luckily rejoin us on Wednesday. We then get issued with masses of leather jackets, warm socks, blankets, etc., and set off on our travels on Tuesday week, calling back here for odd nights, then setting off again. The ENSA and Welfare Officers here are charming and helpful. Had a hair wash and set in a Mohammedan shop to-day – the usual audience of admiring natives! We've changed currency three times now, and Persia is different again – I can't cope at all

– or with the different languages. Must stop and get to bed now darlings. Am feeling marvellously fit – probably due to masses of good food and dry healthy climate!

12TH JANUARY 1944. SEMIRAMIS HOTEL

Am seizing a few minutes between shows to scribble this – we are very busy indeed, and having a really marvellous time. Our show which is at 9.15 every night at the very nice King Faisal Hall is absolutely the biggest hit they've had here, which is very thrilling. We had an excellent newspaper write-up after our first night, and were honoured by being the only show ever to have been photographed, caricatured by a brilliant ex-newspaper man who is now in the Publicity Dept here, interviewed etc., etc., and are in fact in the unusual position of finding ourselves local celebrities. The title of the show, '30 Men and a Girl', has tickled people's imagination very much, and they are full of curiosity about 'the girl'! My battledress is unique here, and I wear it everywhere. Tonight we have the Prince Regent (Uncle of little King Faisal), and the Ambassador and Ambassadress, Sir Kinahan and Lady Cornwallis, and all the C in Cs, GOCs etc. coming to the show.

13TH JANUARY 1944. SEMIRAMIS HOTEL

I'm so glad the letters from on board ship turned up at last, so that you could have the full picture of the trip. It was great fun. Yes, it was air attack that we had – two quite nasty days of it. Our ship, as biggest in the convoy, was singled out for special attention, and lived up to her reputation as the 'Lucky Orion'. It was quite frightening 'tho also very exciting, but of course I was always worried about the Band, especially when one ship was hit and left blazing away, and we heard reports of many casualties. Women's Action Stations were in the Lounges under the Gun Deck – the best position for getting into the boats if we were torpedoed, but the worst for bombing as we were right at the top, and directly under the guns. The armament on our ship was terrific; I have never heard anything like the noise when they all went off at once. It was mostly dive bombing, but we also had aerial torpedoes and the new magnetic bombs which are dropped from some miles away. We had many incredible near misses, and had portholes blown in by explosions. During the alerts we all did Community Singing and really had great fun. We also had a submarine attack at night, while we were doing a show, and depth charges were being dropped, but we were allowed to go on with the show as usual.

Last night was our Command Performance – my first! It was very thrilling and interesting, but I was tired as we'd done one show for a hospital in the afternoon, and rehearsed in the morning. Also I suddenly came over very nervous with all the formalities and etiquette that have to be observed even for the Regent of Iraq, Emir Abdul Illah! And I didn't sing as well as I might have done in the 1st part of the programme, and felt terribly upset after, because of being strung-up. However it was all very successful. Johnnie, myself and five of the Band were presented to the Regent, who is very shy and quiet, and I also met the Ambassador and wife, Sir Kinahan and Lady Cornwallis, who are charming, the Area Commander, General Bright, and etc. Today I hear from the charming journalist, Berwick Holt, who is a Captain in the army here and on the (British controlled) Iraq Times, that I have been elected official Paiforce Sweetheart!

I now have a fearful lot of publicity to go through, and have to write letters to 'the boys' in the local papers, and be photographed from all angles, and have masses of small photos autographed to give away, etc. I feel it is all very undeserved, but they are all being so sweet to me here, and there are some very interesting people, including Beric Holt, a good press-photographer, and a really brilliant caricaturist who has done caricatures of self, Johnnie and one or two of the Band, all of whom worked together in Fleet Street. Also there is an ex-manager for Jack Hylton, and one of the most helpful men I've ever met, Lt Bill Whittle, who is 2nd in command at ENSA, and who was with George Black before the war. All these people really know a lot about the stage, and have been so sweet to me. Darlings, I'm going to rest now – we have a broadcast this evening (am singing 'One Fine Day'), then our usual 9.15.

13TH JANUARY 1944. SEMIRAMIS HOTEL

Everything is very continental here – one goes and has drinks, tea, etc., in each other's bedrooms, and in fact we have a small party after the show every night, as there are two ENSA Officers, Major Williams, and Mr Whittle, and Capt Holt, all living in the hotel. Imagine the scene – I have a nice room with French windows and a balcony overlooking a narrow strip of garden and the Tigris – a broad coffee-coloured river with a very swift current, I'm told, though it seems flat and still from here. My room is rather cold now – it is tiled with stone walls, built to keep out the heat, as they get 140° in the shade in the summer, and, of course, it has no heating at all. It has been really very cold these last few days, but we've had bright sun until today, which is foggy and raining, just like home. At midday it has still been gloriously hot on the balcony. In front of me is a huge bunch of pink roses – a bouquet I received last night from the Area Commander, General Bright, 'A tribute in admiration and with grateful thanks.' Very charming of him.

The day before yesterday a young Welfare Officer took J and myself on a tour of Baghdad. It is on the whole the dirtiest and most sordid town, but there are one or two interesting things to be seen. The first place we visited was the one and only park, made by the 1st Prime Minister under the Mandate, who committed suicide as a result of his uphill task. The soil of Iraq is very fertile, and the country would be extremely rich if it were properly worked and irrigated; it is going to be one of the countries of the future, many people seem to think. Then we visited a 12th century mosque – tomb of the great Arabian poet, Abdul Qadir Gailani. Gailani is a name that has been important all through this country's history – do you remember the troubles in 1941 when the traitor Rashid Ali tried to form a dictatorship and eventually fled to Germany? He was a Gailani. The present family was put on the throne by Lawrence of course. Faisal I was made King of Syria first, then the French walked in and he had to abdicate, and we gave him this job as a sop. It was letting him down that was one of Lawrence's big sorrows. He was a very fine man, an Arabian from real or Saudi Arabia, and had a very hard time here. The political life is very complicated and bitter still. There are two sects of Moslems – the Sunnis, who wear green hat bands and are progressive, educated (relatively) and pro-government, and the Shias who wear white bands, and are mainly the poor and anti-government element. They still knife each other frequently! Gailani's tomb was most interesting and had a fine mosaic dome and minarets, done in the usual blue and white used for religious buildings, with lovely turquoise colours too. We saw the War Graves from the last war – most of them were demolished by the Iraqis in 1941, but have been mended. Also we saw the only remaining old gate of Baghdad, which was nearly blown up by the Turks when Allenby advanced to throw them out in, I think, 1917. We went also to Kadhimain – only really well known place in Baghdad – which is called the Golden Mosque, or the Golden Domes, as it has I think, 2 big domes and 6 minarets covered in solid gold. We saw it in evening sunlight – a fantastic sight. No infidels may go inside, so we climbed onto the roof of a nearby mud house, and looked over into the courtyards. They have just finished 'Maharam' – the religious ceremony at which the Moslems bewail the murder of Caliph Hussain in the 6th or 7th Century. A week ago no one could go to Kadhimain as there were great processions of pilgrims going to the shrine, and secret ceremonies going on. All the sects concerned are flagellants, and were beating and stabbing themselves. Kadhimain is 4th Holy City after Mecca – it is a tomb of two Caliphs (religious heads of the Moslem world) and very old and sacred.

14TH JANUARY. SEMIRAMIS HOTEL

Am writing this from the DNSE office (DNSE = ENSA out here). We have just had a balance test and rehearsal for the classical broadcast tomorrow, at which am singing 'Caro Nome', and it went very well, luckily. This morning I firmly slept until 9.15, and feel grand in consequence. We are going out to lunch with two very interesting people in a few minutes – Mr and Mrs Sinderson Pasha. He is a sort of film character – the power behind the throne here and a very influential person, and Court Doctor into the bargain. They have a lovely house with some interesting furniture, pictures, etc., and it should be very pleasant. He is Scots – one of these personalities that Bonnie Scotland seems to strew over the globe in important positions – a huge great man, handsome and I should say brilliantly if unscrupulously clever. He holds every decoration in the world except a knighthood, and is flat out for that. We are doing a Charity Concert for him on Monday, to which all the Iraqi high-ups will come, in aid of the Lord Mayor of London's Air Raid Relief Fund; hence our invitation to lunch.

Last night's broadcast and show went very well. Today we do a show in a big hospital at 4.30 – then our usual do at the King Faisal in the evening. We had the American Embassy in strength last night, and the American Ambassador comes tonight. Can't remember if I told you the programme we are doing at the Faisal – it is the same every night. I'm singing two groups – the Bach-Gounod 'Ave' and 'My Hero', then 'Vespers' and 'Funiculi-Funicula', and doing our Viennese Medley, Christmas Memories in which I just sing a verse of 'Oh come all ye faithful'! And we end up every night with the Noël Coward, in which I now do most of the talking and speak the famous toast. The latter is the *pièce de résistance* of the evening, and the toast manages to move the audience almost to tears.

On Sunday we have a free day, and am riding in the morning! There are some lovely horses here, polo ponies, race horses and chargers, and am getting one from the Iraqi Army, also an escorting officer. The Press photographer is coming along to get a photo of Paiforce Sweetheart on horseback!

19TH JANUARY. BAGHDAD

We are off this evening on a rather exciting part of our trip,
which will last about 6 weeks, as far as I can see, and will take us
from quite hot climate to snow and – possibly – a day's skiing!
We have a 16- hour train journey, but the local ENSA people
have been quite marvellous and have got us all sleeping berths –
12 first-class and the rest second, so we will be very comfortable.
From now on we have an ENSA 'escorting ECO' with us – a
sweet and most capable young Sgt who knows exactly where
we are going, the roads, the people, etc., and will take charge
of all our movements. That will be a great relief to Johnnie, as
the responsibility was proving just too much for someone who
didn't know the country. Also we are taking a stage-carpenter-
cum-electrician from ENSA, 2 comfortable buses, 2 3-ton
lorries and a special 15 cwt truck entirely for Johnnie and myself
to run about in (which never materialised). And 5 drivers. So
you can imagine what a huge caravan we now are. The ENSA
people here have christened us 'the Brigade'. We are all being
issued with special clothes – I have a 'pushteen' or sheepskin
jacket which was given me by the OC Signals here, and which
I've lived in as it's been very cold here latterly. It is a sleeveless
affair that slips over battledress or coats, and is worn with the
wool inside, very dirty looking but extremely warm. Also have
had a marvellous Army greatcoat made for me (the tailor insisted
upon doing it free) and have also a sort of quilted British Warm
affair which has to be lifted onto me, it is so heavy. However, am
writing this to you sitting on my balcony overlooking the Tigris,
in hot sun, as today is fine again. Our broadcast on Thursday
night went off all right. Then we rushed back to the hotel and
had dinner, and went back to the Hall for our usual 9.15 show.
We had a packed house and the same again on Friday, which was
our last Variety programme. I've been so busy that I just can't
describe to you all I've done. On Friday morning we rehearsed
for the following day's orchestral concert – luckily Spiller is
now well and arrived just in time for it. During the rehearsal,
Beric Holt was taking down my life story for a terrific article in
the Iraq Times, which appeared on Saturday, acclaiming me as

'Paiforce Sweetheart', plus photo and life history, etc. Publicity
is the most exhausting thing in the world, and merely very hard
work, as I shall in future assure all young aspirants to fame! Well,
the concert on Saturday evening was rather nerve-racking, as
we broadcast the first ¾ hour, and I was singing 'Caro Nome'.
I didn't sing it so well as at 'Music for ALL', but it might have
been worse, and reports say that it came over well which is a
relief to us, as there are only two broadcasting mikes in Baghdad
and no proper control system, and it is a terrible job balancing a
big orchestra and a soloist. In the 2nd half I sang 'Vissi d'Arte',
the Mozart 'Alleluia', and 'Filles de Cadiz'. We had a speech at
the end, made by Bill Whittle in which he announced that I
was now Paiforce Sweetheart (which thank God, got a good
round of applause!) and then I was given two lovely bouquets
of roses. It was a very tense evening as we were all extremely
overtired. We had done 8 shows and 2 broadcasts in 6 days, and
much rehearsing, and hadn't got to bed till after one o'clock
every night. We had a row with sweet Bill Whittle, the ENSA
officer (it was all his fault as he was very strung up too – all
about nothing at all) and I was in tears at the interval, but we
made it all up after the concert, and ended up with a champagne
party in Bill's room at the hotel – he had produced a bottle of
Heidsiek, especially to toast me!

19TH JANUARY. BAGHDAD

We have broken all records by filling the Faisal Hall for a week.
It is not very big, but it is a long way for people to come, and
it is normally in an out-of-bounds area. Bounds were lifted
especially for us. And I must tell you that after our first night,
which was only half-full owing to lack of sufficient notification
of our arrival, we've had mounted police out to control our
queue! On Sunday morning I slept fairly late, then a very
charming Capt Rawes, who is also on Public Relations and
is ex-BBC, took me out to meet two of the British residents
here, Judge and Mrs Campbell. The idea was for me to ride
one of their ponies, and be photographed on it. Of course I

was hoping for a ride – the photo idea had cropped up quite by the way. But when I arrived out there, I found that they had thought it was all a publicity stunt, and that I was only going to be held onto the pony, photographed, and then hop off. I soon disillusioned them, though I was unable to ride that day as I had to get home for lunch and the photographing took some time, and they luckily asked me over to ride the following day. The photographing was quite frightening. They produced a really lovely Arab stallion, a typical grey pony with a lovely head and tail. But he was very fresh as he hadn't been out for five days, and I had the awful job of getting on in front of a small crowd, and then trying to get a very highly-strung, 3-year-old racing pony to pose for a photograph. I thought the new Paiforce Sweetheart would be seen vanishing through the hedge to an untimely end at any moment! The Syce was rather nervous at first and didn't want to let go of the pony, but I made him, and we got one or two good pictures, though none is perfect. That afternoon a whole crowd of us went to Baghdad races, and I lost ¾ dinar (15/–) in a very short space of time, and came home early! People bet fantastically high here, and one of the ENSA Sergeants has made between £800 and £1,000 already this season. It was bitter on the race-course – a wind that came from the Arctic Circle, I feel sure. The ponies are very fast and lovely, but the riding is pretty foul. I wrote a letter to Paiforce (pronounced Pyforce, incidentally) that day, to be published in the special Troops' Newspaper. Then we had the CC Signals and his Adjt to dinner. He has been very sweet and got my lovely new greatcoat made, and given me his 'pushteen' – he is a vast man, ex-army Heavyweight Champ of India who has christened me Tich and written in large letters inside the coat, 'To Tich, as one soldier to another, keep your hands out of the pockets!' He brought bottles of drink to the hotel (smuggled in a suitcase to avoid corkage!) including a bottle of sherry for me. Everyone here drinks an enormous amount, and I have a hard job avoiding it. On Monday morning we rehearsed for the night's charity show, which was a new programme. I had to have a studio photo done, and was rushed around Baghdad in full evening dress in the back of a truck – a sight which aroused no curiosity in this extraordinary town! The photos aren't too good, which is a pity as 500 have been printed for 'hand-outs' – i.e. to give to future fans who, I am convinced, will never materialise! Have just signed 30 – a very boring job.

19TH JANUARY. BAGHDAD

I am OK for money as yet, but living is terribly expensive – as an example, Johnny's and my hotel bill here for two single rooms for 10 days minus extras was £32! But ENSA are wonderful, and pay for everything, including extras for meals in bed and an electric fire in my room, laundry, etc. On Monday afternoon I went riding with Judge Campbell, who is charming. Capt Rawes came out with a cine-camera, and filmed us going over a couple of tiny jumps. The ride was great fun, but I found it very tiring as I find these Arab ponies have horribly uncomfortable paces – they throw one right out of the saddle when cantering – they are so bouncy. Judge Campbell told me the Arabs won't ride stallions because of that – they always ride mares. But the English use mainly stallions. There seem to be no geldings here, and the stallions are all perfectly well behaved though pretty full of beans. Our show in the evening went off very well – we had been nervous as it was really for Iraqi civilians who were charged £1 each. However, they were a very good audience, and to our surprise a lot of soldiers had stumped up 10/- each to come in, and of course they were splendid, and saved the situation when the comedy was not quite understood. We had the two Princesses, the Queen Mother, and the women of the Royal Household there – all black-hooded of course! – a very rare event as they don't go to mixed gatherings as a rule. When we return we may do a special afternoon concert for Ladies only, as many of the Iraqi women won't come to mixed shows, and then possibly little King Faisal may come. He has been very curious about me, and asked all sorts of questions as to where I came from, what I did before the war, etc. He has been brought up very English – I have met his governess several times, and she's taken back the details about me that he wanted to know!

He's only nine, and very sweet and unspoiled, I'm told. Mrs Sinderson has a nice story about him. A year ago she wanted to know if he realised who he was at all, so one day when he was playing in the garden, she called him up and said: 'Well, Faisal, I want to see how you're getting on with your Geography. Tell me how many names of Kings you know.' Faisal thought for a minute, and then said 'King George of England, King Carol of Rumania, the Shah of Persia, King Farouk of Egypt…' then he stopped. 'That's all,' he said. 'But what about Iraq – who is King of Iraq?' said Mrs Sinderson. Faisal looked bewildered. 'I don't know,' he said, 'I don't think there is one.' He is very naughty just now – he has several unfortunate ministers who can't speak English, and he refuses to speak Arabic to them! Apparently the Royal Family enjoyed the show very much – the thing that tickled all the Iraqis was 'Mad dogs and Englishmen'! I got another heavenly bunch of roses – all the British residents' gardens in Baghdad must have been scoured for my benefit! There have been some good stage photos taken during shows – am getting copies of them all. Also we have been lent a cine-camera to take on this tour – isn't that fun? [This never materialised!]

19TH JANUARY 1944. BAGHDAD

Yesterday I again lay in bed late. Then we had a day off – very much needed. I practised hard and have got some more in today luckily. In the afternoon Johnnie and I wandered around the bazaar – it is terribly squalid here, and unutterably smelly and filthy. But the bazaars are fascinating – lined with tiny shops in which one can watch the silver- and gold-smiths work. The goods are terribly costly – lovely wrought-gold necklaces which used to be £5 are now £25. There are also cameras and films to be had, but I was asked 10/- for a film the other day, and developing and printing is very expensive, and shockingly bad. The clothes shops are on the whole awful. The streets are crowded – one winds in and out between incredible old buses, very erratic Arabs on bicycles, families sleeping or begging on the pavement, people peddling fruit, cut-throat Iraqi soldiers, and police in German grey and pickelhaube hats, with donkeys and even fiery Arab ponies with dashing Sheiks on them, coming along the pavements. We have the richest Sheik in Iraq in the hotel – he was here for the Pan-Arab conference. He owns thousands of people and many tribes, has 16 wives (not here of course!) is hugely fat, wears Arab head-dress and a robe of Gent's suiting and has a seven-foot black eunuch as bodyguard. There are a lot of Arabs in the hotel – many look very fine, but it is odd to see them playing billiards somehow! They all drive huge cars most dangerously. The Tigris is rising owing to the rainy season, and by March will be right up to the top of the hotel garden wall, I'm told. It is tremendously swift-flowing – the little boats which are always flying across it get swept right down-stream, as at Corran Narrows. By the way, in case you were worrying, we have had our typhus injections. Am trying to think of the million interesting things I have to tell you, sweethearts, so excuse incoherence. Have met so many nice people here – Prof Henz, Professor of Music here – Chafoo – Iraqi Bandmaster of the Royal Band (he was through Kneller Hall) – a charming Dr Hans Hoff (who sent me some divine dates stuffed with almonds, a local specialty of which am having a box sent off to you) – and a nice young Englishman over to form a Youth Movement here to counter the one the Nazis started – amongst others. My dressing-room has been crowded before, during and after shows – a little trying sometimes! Funnily enough, several people who were on the 'Orion' have come up to me here. Dear Johnnie has been so sweet – have cried on his shoulder twice this week, due mainly to being tired, and he has been most understanding and kind. We are quite glad to be leaving the dizzy whirl of Baghdad for a bit! Am hoping to get some more riding – there are ponies everywhere in this part of the world, and can go to the Campbells anytime we are here.

Letter from Johnnie to my parents

RAMC Base Depot
MEF
21st January 1944

Dear Mrs Ferguson,

I do hope you won't mind my inflicting this on you, but I feel it may help to ease the pain you must have being parted from Elisabeth, if you receive a second opinion on how marvellously she is doing, and, to a non-medical eye, how well she is keeping. A Major we have here said, in all good faith, that she seems five years younger than when he last saw her at Netley, well over two years ago. This is all the more remarkable, as this trip has most certainly, had more than its fair share of excitement. I know that her letters to you have given fairly vivid descriptions of some of our more hectic adventures, and I'm afraid I can't hope to compete, but the thing that gratifies me most, is the calm way she has taken everything as it comes, even when I, and most of the boys, have been scared stiff. Her complete acceptance of the rough with the smooth (and at times it has been very rough indeed), has rather spiked the guns of some of our feather-bed soldiers in the Band. This all reads like a testimonial to a faithful employee, although this most certainly is not my intention – what I'm trying to say, with my limited command of the language, is she is doing a grand piece of work in a dignified way, admired by everyone she meets, from Generals to Privates, and at least one Bandmaster.

You would love to see the way she freezes up fresh young officers, who give her what she calls the 'ENSA look'. At the same time it is lovely to see her melting crusty old male and female 'Grundy's' who have already made up their minds that one lone girl with so many men, must obviously be living in sin. She has had a lot of publicity (no more than she deserves), which you will eventually receive, showing just how the bells are ringing in her favour, and I feel proud to think that I have had some part in producing all this. I can assure you that I am doing, and will continue to do, everything possible to ensure that she gets back home no worse for her trip to the Middle East, and for my own part, I am extremely grateful to have had such a charming and sensible companion for my off duty hours. Having had the opportunity to see her under all conditions here, I feel honoured to know that she counts me as one of her dearest friends. I must apologise once more for the stilted tone of this letter, but if I have succeeded in letting you know that she is, in herself, in first class form, and is receiving her due as she seldom did at home, then that is what I set out to do. Please don't trouble to answer, as I know you are very busy.

Yours most sincerely,

Harry Johnson

Chapter Five

Middle East Memoirs

Shaibah to Khanakin

22ND JANUARY 1944. SHAIBAH, IRAQ

My three darlings,

How I wish you were here with me enjoying this glorious sunshine. We have come some way south, and it is much warmer. I'm writing this on a terrace outside the bungalow I am living in here, with an overlapping roof keeping the sun off my head, and the good old Crooks lenses keeping the glare out of my eyes. The view is not inspiring – just desert all round, and not the nice yellow sand-dunes that have lovely shadows, but rather stony muddy stuff. I'm in a huge scattered camp that straggles over many square miles, and we are actually living in the hospital wards that are sunk about six feet to keep them cool. They have big eaves and windows recessed several feet, and the glass is of a type we use to cover up seed-boxes – finely wired so that it keeps out the glare. I'm being looked after in the Sisters' Mess, and am next door to a sweet Matron, who has been so kind – I've a very comfy room and everything is spotlessly clean. We have Indian soldier servants, and they are excellent, but unfortunately most of them speak no English, and I don't know a word of Urdu, so sometimes things are a little difficult! Just in front of the terrace Matron is doing her best to have a garden, which she has Italian prisoners to cultivate. There's not a thing in it yet except some very sad grass, and a few bulby things, probably gladioli, struggling up. However she has had a pigeon house made, and there are about a dozen pigeons of all types, including a black tumbler who turns over in the air in most rakish fashion. There were no birds here before, but now desert sparrows, wagtails, and larks have all gathered round a little oasis, and are bathing in the pool as I write.

Yesterday we went and saw a bit of pure Rudyard Kipling – the opposite camp, which is an Indian RASC Cy where one young English officer and an Indian officer with Indian other ranks have the handling of 149 mules, most of them untrained. The Englishman is a very nice Captain Padbury, a shy type of person who lives for animals. He has twelve lovely saddle horses, and I'm going riding with him any day I can fit it in. He also has a farm entirely home-made from desert mud, where live in various carefully tented and spotless pens a bitch with two puppies; three rabbits, about to become many more; various ducks, geese, turkeys, chickens, and their several young; an aviary of pigeons, all laying hard; a sheep and lamb; two lovely little Iraqi cows, with calves about a week old; and – the *pièce de résistance* – a father and mother goat with a six-day-old curly-coated kid that is pure Walt Disney. He's sweeter than Bambi even. You can't think how lovely it is finding this in the middle of nothing – one misses animals enormously here, and camels just don't count – they are horrid even when young! Dogs are not allowed here, but there are masses of pie-dogs which the officers are always trying to shoot. At present the weather is perfect – warm sun and cool breeze, and the dust laid by the late rains. It is strange to see water lying in pools at every dip of the road – the ground is so baked that it just cannot absorb.

We came here on the Mail train or Express – which averages the stupendous speed of about 23 MPH taking 16 hours to do 350 odd miles! The other train, the Baghdad Belle, takes 24 hours to do the same journey, so we were lucky! We travelled overnight, and all had sleeping berths, thanks to the splendid work of our friends in Baghdad. Johnnie and I shared a 1st class carriage in the air-conditioned coach – always much in demand. We had a lovely dinner and breakfast on board – a most comfy train for this part of the world. How it stays upright on its funny little narrow-gauge track, I don't know. It just couldn't go very fast or it would tip over.

22ND JANUARY 1944. SHAIBAH

We are here in this particular spot for another week, then we move about 16 miles for another nine days. Then we start climbing. I can always tell you afterwards where we have been, but am not supposed to say so ahead, and have to be a little careful here as am censoring my own letters. We did our first show last night in a huge RAF hangar that seats 2,500. They have a first-class stage, lighting and amplification there, and we were able to put on a really nice show. They were a marvellous audience – I got an ovation after each of my group solos, and they fairly cheered us to the end. We were very pleased, as they have the reputation of being critical and tough there, and have booed two unfortunate ENSA parties off the stage. Also we have had such a lot of publicity that we're afraid of disappointing people. However, there seems to be no fear of that, as we are the first big show to have got to this part of the world. The hospital is delighted to be having us – we are doing our orchestral concert in the dining-hall, where they're rigged us a very nice stage – acoustics will be bad as it is a long low hut, but it is stone, or rather mud-blocks, which give a certain amount of resonance. Tomorrow we are doing a Church Service with orchestral in-and-out-going Voluntaries and interlude, and I am singing the old 'Alleluia', and 'Morgen!' (in German) with Johnnie's beautiful arrangement. People who have heard about the Service are coming from miles to it and the Area Commander and Lady Cornwallis (the Ambassador's wife – a dear person) are coming over too. Afterwards, Johnnie is doing a Military Band programme on the outdoor stage they have here.

The outdoor theatres are often better than the indoor ones in this part of the world as they are used more. To-night we are going to the original port of Sinbad the Sailor – now many miles from the sea. I always thought Sinbad was a legend, but it appears he was very real, and where we are going was his home town. It is a very bad village, still Out-of-Bounds to all troops, because it was the last headquarters of the Ali Raschid revolt in 1941. Anyone who goes through it is always well armed. Of course we will be at a camp outside it, so will be quite all right, and anyway we are such a large party now.

All hospitals in this part of the world have 'refrigerator rooms' for people suffering from heatstroke. In the summer one has to drink 20 pints of water a day here and always take a tablespoon of salt. Anyone who can't or won't put away the minimum of 16 pints becomes dehydrated! And goes down with what they call 'heat-exhaustion'. The first sign is ceasing to sweat, which is a very serious thing. Then the blood temperature whizzes up to terrific heights, and people die unless they can be whipped off and shoved into the refrigerator and artificially cooled. There is a great deal of smallpox here too – the people are about 80% pockmarked, some terribly so – and the Indian troops are the same. It ruins the women, who might be beautiful otherwise. Freya Stark lives in Baghdad – am hoping to meet her some time.

27TH JANUARY 1944. SHAIBAH

I am sending you off by Surface mail a few more press-cuttings, etc. from the troops' paper in Paiforce – 'Trunk Call'. Don't hold me responsible for all that is therein said – I've never been in the clutches of journalists before, and find the results of my interviews rather embarrassing! We will have moved again when I next write, but only about twenty miles. We have had a very happy time at this desert hospital, and our shows every night have been really a huge success. We've played at lovely big places, luckily, and it has all gone off very well. Tomorrow we are playing actually in the hospital, and it will be our first bad spot – it is a long low dining-hall – but they have a nice big stage and have done splendidly over putting up curtains and lights. On Monday I had a very nice ride – five of us went out, three officers and a Sister, and I had a large comfortable horse and wasn't one scrap stiff despite quite an energetic ride. I could have ridden every day but of course have been unable – which was very annoying! However am going again tomorrow. And I think I shall be able to get a lot all round this part of the world, as there are horses everywhere, and people are very glad to mount one. When I rode from Baghdad I borrowed my hostess's jodhpurs, but here I wore battledress, and found it excellent, if worn with long socks over the leg part to keep it from working up. This morning we were issued with our warm kit for Teheran – 2prs natural wool socks, thick black Persian-lamb-lined gloves, rubber knee boots, and I have a huge coat beautifully lined with sheepskin – and – breathe it not – I believe I may be able to bring them home! The CO announced casually, as we were leaving, that the whole lot (the men's too) had been unaccountably eaten by white ants!

PS No, don't address me as 2nd Lt. It is a courtesy rank. Have been promoted – the Indian bearers at Shaibah would insist upon referring to me as the 'Colonel Memsahib'! Must have been my battledress that did the trick!

30th January 1944. YWCA, Basrah, Iraq

We have now moved some miles, and are slightly more civilised again – when I say civilised, this is definitely the most back-of-beyondish spot I've ever been in – really very fascinating, it is so completely Eastern and squalid. This is the hottest area in the world, except for Death Valley in Arizona, and the climate is worse than Arizona, because it is damp. In the summer the humidity will quite suddenly rise to 84; this means nothing to me, but I am told that if it were to remain at that height for more than a couple of days, all life would be extinct. Luckily it only stays up for about six hours, but those hours are sheer hell, when one is just wringing wet from sweat and outside moisture.

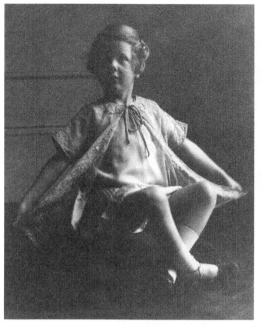

1 Above: My first public appearance aged four and a half singing "Little Jack Horner".

2 Above right: With my mother and father.

3 Right: Learning to read with my mother.

4 With my step-father in the Pyrenees, August 1939.

5 Singing with the Staff Band of the Royal Army Medical Corps conducted by Harry Johnson.

6 Granny Forbes at Broadmeade Copse.

7 *Above: Dancing with Michael Lyndon.*

8 *Right: Making tea in the Sinai Desert, New Year's Eve 1943.*

9 *Below: The Band in the desert near Baghdad, January 1944.*

10 Our ambulance train in the Persian mountains.

11 Opera stars on tour in Paiforce. Back L. to R: Ivor Newton (pianist), Walter Widdop (tenor), Johnny. Front: Alfred Cave (violin), Dennis Noble (baritone), Nancy Evans (mezzosoprano), Miriam Licette (soprano).

12 The Nairn buses, Baghdad. These were the first-class ones with air-conditioning.

13 *Above left: Baalbec, the Temple of Bacchus.*

14 *Above right: The Luncheon in Cairo in honour of Lily Pons and André Kostelanetz. He is leaning forward centre with Johnny on his left.*

15 *Below: Our "theatre" with the 5th Armoured Division in the desert by the Red Sea. The vehicle on the left was converted into a Rest Room for me for the day. Troops were under special orders to wear trunks when bathing. I was given a ride in a Sherman tank and allowed to fire the guns. The Sergeants' Mess reported that if I sang as well as I shot I would be OK!*

*16 Benjamin
Britten with Joan
Cross and Peter
Pears in the garden,
Glyndebourne 1947.*

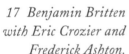

*17 Benjamin Britten
with Eric Crozier and
Frederick Ashton.*

18 Norman del Mar rehearsing
Let's make an Opera. *Onstage
right, Elisabeth Parry (Rowan)
with Gladys Parr, 2nd from right,
and Anne Sharpe, 2nd from left,
with local schoolchildren.*

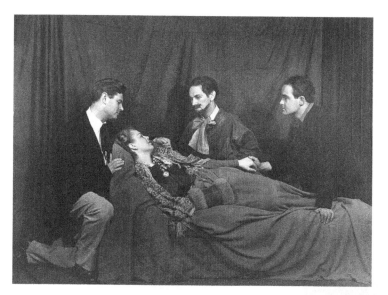

19 Above: La Bohème *by Puccini, last Act. The Opera Players' 1951 production with cast L. to R: Leslie Andrews (Rudolph), Elisabeth Parry (Mimi), Norman Platt (Marcel), Thomas Hemsley (Schaunard).*

20 Right: Don Pasquale *by Donizetti, 1951 production, showing the convertible couch used as a bed in La Bohème in all its glory. Cast: Elisabeth Parry (Norina) Thomas Hemsley (Don Pasquale).*

21 Below: Loading Phyllis's car for Hänsel and Gretel *in a London Junior School. L.to R: Stanley Pine (Father), Marian Hughes (Hänsel), Phyllis Thorold (Pianist).*

22 Above: Die Fledermaus *by Strauss at the Jersey Opera House, Lorna Windsor as Rosalinda.*

23 Right: Die Fledermaus *with Philip Langridge (Alfredo) and Madge Stephens (Rosalinda).*

24 Below: Die Fledermaus *at the Jersey Opera House. Eric Shilling as Colonel Frank and David Fieldsend as Eisenstein.*

There are no hot water taps at all here; in the afternoons during
the hot weather, you scald yourself if you turn the cold tap
on, and it is impossible to have showers during the daytime!
Doesn't that seem incredible? Sun temperature of 187° F has
been registered. Johnnie and I are living in this rambling and
oriental building for the next week. It is all very amusing, but
we are missing our last place, the big desert station of Shaibah,
where we were so spoiled and well looked after at the hospital,
very much. They are being very good to us here though, and
it is no one's fault that there just aren't the amenities that we
luxurious home livers are used to. The house is the usual mud
brick and carved wooden affair, with courtyards, balconies and
huge high rooms and corridors, and funny bits of roof that one
has to cross over. My room isn't really a room, but the end part
of a corridor partitioned off, with a partition that doesn't reach
the roof, which means it is very noisy. But I am lucky as I have
it to myself, and most other people are in big dormitories. I have
a bow window with no glass, just fly-netting, which is a little
chilly at night; but the outlook is fun – I can see the Shatt-al-
Arab, which is the big river that the Tigris and Euphrates form
when they're joined together, and I can watch the native sailing
and row-boats plying up and down. (Point of interest re the
river – there is such an under-tow, due to thousands of miles
of weight of water, that hardly anyone who falls in is rescued
– one just goes straight under.) We are still 18 miles from the
sea here, but the river is slightly salty and tidal when it is not
in full flood. At present it is rising rapidly, and the tides are not
noticeable. Actually we are living at a place called Maquil or
Ma'qil, pronounced Margil. Basrah doesn't really exist now,
except as a squalid native village – the sea having receded, and
the river shifted its course considerably; so Basrah is the name
given to all this area. It is pleasant to see rows of palm-trees and
apologies for gardens after the complete desolation of Shaibah,
where there isn't a tree to be seen.[3] But the climate here isn't
nice – we are actually a foot below sea-level, I believe, and it
is rather enervating and damp. We had such a happy last few
days in Shaibah. The Matron, Miss Hill, just mothered me, and
completely spoilt me, and the CO and a dear Major Hickey

(who had bought my gold RAMC brooch for me at Netley
2½ years ago!) looked after us marvellously. We left there
laden with presents – grapefruit, oranges, sweets, drink, and a
lovely leather baby camel, made for me by the patients in the
Occupational Therapy ward. He is a really Walt Disney camel, of
great character – I adore him already, and have christened him
'Shaibah'. You would laugh – I have been issued gumboots for
Teheran, and they are full of grapefruit and, well hidden in this
strict institution! a bottle of sherry – J has a bottle of whisky
cached too, so we are likely to be discovered and thrown out
at any moment! You can't think what a nightmare my packing
is becoming – people are so sweet out here that one only has
to admire something to be given it, and I'm just laden with
extras already. The whole band are the same, and we can hardly
cram into our vehicles – the trouble is the winter clothes, the
sheepskin 'pushteens' are so huge that they can't be packed or
even rolled up. However they will be marvellous when we get
up to Teheran – I heard today of someone just down from that
part of the world who reported 42° of frost! All the railways
in Persia are American-run now, and very good, and I believe
we are in for a thrilling 24hr journey up into the mountains,
through over 100 tunnels. A convoy went in at the bottom at a
temp of 115° F and came out at the top in 15° F! Well darlings, I
must stop describing this fantastic country.

30TH JANUARY 1944. YWCA, BASRAH

My most beloved and darling Mum,

I feel it is all such a jumble of the personal and impersonal as to
be neither travel-story nor personal reminiscences. However, I'm
so happy that it all interests you – I know you will read between
the lines all that I fail to say. I had a last ride before leaving
Shaibah, with the nice young Capt Padbury who took me out
before. He is OC an Indian Mule Company – pure Rudyard
Kipling still in these modern days – and he has 429 mules under
him, with an Indian officer and Indian syces looking after them.

They looked lovely all picketed in rows, and one was taken right back to the old 'Barrack room Ballad' days. We rode out to 'Sinbad's Tower' – a queer crumbling old affair reputed to have been a lighthouse, standing where the original Basrah used to be, but now many miles from the river. Sinbad is supposed to have sailed on his adventures from there. Our last shows at Sahibah were a little disappointing – the first ones were a huge success, but we did two days in a horrible cold bleak place, which wasn't full either night (we are still trying to find out why), and it was a bit of an anticlimax. Then our very last of all was in the hospital, where they had been so good to us, and it was a great success from everyone's point of view but mine – I was miserable as the acoustics were so bad that I just couldn't justify myself – we were in a very long narrow low building like two Nissen huts put together, sunk about eight feet, as are most of the hospital buildings, for coolness. However, everyone was very sweet, and we had a great party after. Whenever anyone has a show in this part of the world, it is made a great occasion and COs for miles around are invited, so one always has to go and be very social afterwards. Everyone is marvellously kind, but it is most tiring. We did our first show here last night – and had a marvellous audience despite the fact that sudden torrential rain beating on the tin roof of the huge hangar affair we were playing in, and lasting for the whole show, must have prevented them from hearing more that the fff's and my top notes! We were up early this morning, for a big Church Service and March Past. Then J and I went to a grand sherry party in the HQ Mess, then on to lunch in another Mess. This evening, thank goodness, is free and we are off to bed early. Have not been to bed before 1 a.m. for nights now, but am very fit, 'tho tired.

3RD FEBRUARY 1944. YWCA, BASRAH

I see now why the people in this part of the world make brilliant rugs and have their best clothes in vivid pinks and oranges and reds – one gets starved of colour here. The houses are of mud, with overhanging upper storeys, and much carved

woodwork on windows, shutters, eaves and balconies. The ones
on the river look as if they'd crumble into it at any moment,
especially when one sees a projecting 1st floor restaurant, packed
to capacity, and the whole leaning out over the water. The local
boats are fascinating – there are the dhows, things the size of a
launch, but with carved poops and square bows, made entirely
of wood, even to the pins nailing the planks together and all
most beautifully fitted. They carry the incredible weight of 147
tons, and actually go the whole way to India. They have pivoting
masts, which lean forward when they are at rest, but swing over
and slope backwards when they set sail. Of course everything is
sail here – engines are unknown to the natives. The dhows go to
India during the N West monsoon when the sea is beaten pretty
flat. Then there are mohailas or flat sort of barges, with only
about a foot of wood above the water, which get sunk rather
too easily by the wash of our motor craft. And lastly the little
pleasure and fishing boats, canoe-shaped affairs with high curling
prows, generally carved and painted, which are called bellams,
and sail or are rowed with funny oars like spoons. On Tuesday
we were taken for a trip on the river in a British speedboat, and
had great fun taking photographs of the queer craft we passed.
I can't tell you very much about what we saw, unfortunately,
but there is much of interest here. Tomorrow J and I have been
invited to lunch with the Manager of the Imperial Airways hotel
here; he is a man called Hoffman – I think ex-German cavalry
officer probably – and he and I made friends immediately on
the subject of horses. He has had to give all his up but one – a
marvellous chestnut Arab stallion, quite the loveliest horse I've
seen – which he allows no one to ride but himself. It is very
fiery, but beautifully schooled – he brought it out and showed
it off to me on the lunging rein. In the YW there is a v old
HMV box gramophone, and a precious store of classical records,
to which all the music lovers in the neighbourhood come and
listen. There are heavenly singing ones – Gallicurci, Gigli etc.,
and I listen to them with such heartaches. Opera is my dream
out here – I will achieve that ideal if I wait years and years.
Though I get very depressed occasionally, I do think that my
singing has improved, in that my worst, when I'm tired and out

of practice, is better than it would have been. In fact this is all
giving me confidence – do you remember how worried I used
to get if I had to sing if I was at all tired or had had a late night?
Well, now I don't worry a bit as every night is a late night, and I
know I can do it all right – invaluable experience. Also tiredness
is not affecting my voice at all as it used to, which means I must
be singing better. So don't worry about me vocally my darlings!
Today a Welsh soldier came along with a book of hymns of Dr
Joseph Parry, and his photo and signature in the front of it, and
asked me to autograph it – rather interesting. He had seen in
the paper about my being his great-granddaughter. The band
are rehearsing Scheherezade so beautifully. Glan[4] is playing
exquisitely out here, and has been doing a lot of solo work. He's
doing the Mendelssohn Concerto tonight.

SUNDAY 6TH FEBRUARY 1944. BASRAH

We cross into Persia tomorrow, and are doing a week or ten days
in the Gulf area, then playing our way north to Teheran. There is
only one road to where we are going, and it has been impassable
owing to heavy rain, so unless it is pronounced OK we go down
river on launches and a barge – the latter to carry our two
buses and two lorries. I am rather hoping the road is impassable,
though the river route is very much longer! I last wrote on
Thursday morning, during the rehearsal for the night's orchestral
show. That afternoon we did a concert for a hospital here – it is
mainly Indian troops, but has of course British Staff. Then the
evening's affair, which was for the Red Cross, and was the first
orchestral concert ever to have been given in Basrah, according
to the memories of the residents of 25 years' standing. We had a
full house, and they loved it – we even had Iraqis there. We made
over 100 dinars (1 dinar = £1), which isn't bad, considering that
the troops only paid 100 fils, or 2/-. I sang the 'Jewel Song', 'On
Wings of Song', 'Vissi d'Arte', 'L'été' (Chaminade) then 'Comin'
through the Rye' as an encore. The C in C Paiforce, General
Selby, was there – he's a dear, in fact all the Senior Officers
here are grand. Then on Friday Johnnie and I had the most

exquisite lunch with Mr Hoffman, the manager of the luxurious Airport Hotel that I was telling you about. He turns out to be a Swiss, and very charming. Also there were the Town Major, a nice Scots Major Bell, and the Chief Intelligence Officer here, Squadron-Leader Scott. The latter job is no sinecure in this part of the world, where life is hardly worth living for the enormous majority of the population, who will therefore cheerfully risk knifing somebody for a very little money. To revert to the lunch though! It started with real Amontillado Sherry; then delicious hors d'oeuvre, including lobster; soup with sherry in it; a dish of Mr Hoffman's own invention, sliced fillets of beef, stuffed with truffles and pâté de foie gras, served with asparagus dipped in bread crumbs and braised green peas, sliced tomatoes with cream and mushrooms in them, and puff-balls of potato; then Bombe Hoffman, a marvellous ice, standing on a block of ice hollowed out and with a candle burning inside it; with all this a most excellent Palestinian hock; then to top up, coffee and cream and Benedictine! Johnnie and I reeled into the YWCA and went to bed for about three hours after it! I'm so sorry to make your mouths water, darlings – I feel so horribly lucky getting all these good things to eat. However, as a very small compensation – a box of dates stuffed with almonds is on its way to you, and today or tomorrow am sending off a parcel which will consist, I hope, of 1 tin butter, 1 tin jam, 1 tin Kraft cheese, and some blocks of dates stuffed with walnut – the latter are divine – cut the blocks up and serve in a little silver dish. There is some tobacco for Uncs too – do tell me what brand you like, darling. One of our Palestinian drivers has given me a lovely wrought silver dagger in a scabbard – the sort of thing the locals knife each other with!

6TH FEBRUARY 1944. BASRAH

I left you just where J and I were sleeping off the effects of Mr Hoffman's divine lunch. Mr H has had some interesting times, and I should say has done a good deal of espionage for us. During the trouble in 1941, this part of the world was all in the hands of the rebels, as the British only had about 50 RAF here.

The hotel, which is officially controlled by the Iraq government, was allowed to continue, under strict guard, and thousands of British and Jewish women and children passed through it being evacuated down to safer areas. They were unmolested, except at one place where the rebels deliberately shelled them; however, the Iraqis can't do anything well, luckily, so there were no casualties! Besides these refugees the Italian Legation were there – a curious situation – also many very questionable people, as the hotel acted as a sort of clearing ground. One night the present Regent (who was of course being looked for by the rebels as they wanted him out of the way) was smuggled in, and they managed to smuggle him out into a plane next morning, and fly him to England. When Raschid Ali had been defeated and forced to fly to Germany, the Regent was flown back and reinstated, with us very much 'the power behind the throne' though of course it all has to be done v carefully, as there is no official mandate now. There are incredibly interesting things going on in this part of the world – I don't wonder Lawrence was fascinated by it all. I think most of these Eurasians are the scum of the earth, though the pure bred Arab is quite different, I believe. There are so many minorities, such as Assyrians and Armenians, living in little colonies everywhere. The latter still get a very rough time, and they and the Jews get massacred every now and again, poor devils.

I wrote last on Sunday, I think. Just after I'd finished my letter, J and I were dragged away from our respective packings and persuaded to go over to drinks at the local English Club, where there was a small party going on, and an Indian Band playing. I went very reluctantly, but when we got there it was terrific fun. We sat in the sunshine listening to the Indians playing Strauss, Lehár, etc. with great concentration, but many wrong notes (I'm sure our music conveys nothing to them!) and talked to Col Hinchcliffe, the charming area Commander I've told you about, the sweet and jolly Senior Padre, appropriately called Beer, and the Senior Naval Officer of the Persian Gulf, Commodore Hamill, and various others. They are a grand crowd, and have looked after us marvellously. After lunch the CE here, Major Holman, fetched J and me by car and took us out to tea with

Matron and the CO at the hospital at Shaibah. We had a tyre
burst on the way over, and were stuck for an hour in the desert,
waiting for help as we had no spare. Tyres go in no time here, as
the roads are so appalling and one drives often on desert tracks.
A tyre is worth £200 or £300 second hand on the black market
here – they are pretty well unobtainable for civilians. Hence a
spare tyre lasts no time unless it is padlocked on, and even then
it will probably be pinched. There is the classic instance of a
British Army car parked outside one of the cinemas here under
the gaze of an Iraqi and two British policemen. When the owner
came out of the cinema it was resting on four blocks of wood
with not a wheel left! To get back to our delay – I enjoyed it as
Major Holman is most interesting and has been here three years
so knows his country backwards. He was telling us all about the
port of Kuwait, right down in Saudi Arabia, which is a little tiny
sort of principality of its own, under a hereditary sheik who
wields supreme power. It is a sort of British sphere of influence
– we keep a political agent there – and the Americans have
about two families of oil people. Otherwise the place is most
strictly ruled, and British people have to get special permission
to go there. Women have to have arms, legs and head covered.
The place is spotlessly clean and pretty well flyless, and the Sheik
will allow no innovations such as cinema, etc. The Kuwaitis
are very proud of their town; they build most of the beautiful
wooden boats used round here, and their port is the only good
one for Saudi Arabia. How I'd love to go there.

Tuesday 8th February 1944. Persia. Khorramshar

We had got as far as Major Holman, J and myself awaiting a new
tyre on the desert between Basrah and Shaibah. Imagine the sun
setting and the generally very monotonous landscape becoming
almost beautiful in the red glow. We are on a high-level road,
as the desert around is about 4ft below sea-level, and becomes
completely flooded later on in the spring when there are South
winds and flood waters from the melting snows combined. At
present there are big pools of water lying everywhere, from

the other day's rain, with the odd pelican, stork, crane, or little kingfisher fishing in them. Otherwise nothing but grey muddy sand (all this is old sea-bed) with a crusting of white salt, which comes to the surface always after rain. We got out to Shaibah rather late to find that dear Matron had a marvellous tea laid on for us, with all our favourite things, including an Indian sweet called 'jalaties' (can't spell) sort of whorls of very light gauffre stuff that are in some wonderful way hollow with a kind of treacle inside. Major Holman came back and dined with us at the YW and presented Johnny with a bottle of champagne (our store of bootleg is growing, and is cached, appropriately enough, in my gumboots!). We were supposed to be coming here by bus yesterday morning, but Major H offered to take us down in the RE launch, which is much slower but rather fun, and better than bumping over awful roads in our old vehicles, which just haven't a spring or shock-absorber between them. So we didn't have to rush off early yesterday, but had a peaceful morning doing up your parcels and strolling down to the church, where I practised; then we had early lunch, and at one o'clock a lovely white launch drew up at the jetty opposite the YW with an Indian driver and mechanic on board and Major Holman and a Sapper Captain armed with shotguns for duck-shooting. We loaded ourselves and luggage onto it, and set off – it was a glorious warm sunny day, and we had a very pleasant 3 hrs' trip down river passing every sort of native craft, from stately dhows with big sails to tiny rafts with a square of sackcloth rigged onto a pole. The scenery is monotonous – just an unending line of date palms, which stretch back for about a mile on either bank, and are owned by different millionaire date-kings. The only breaks are the latter's palaces – most sumptuous affairs usually distempered yellow, with much carved and painted woodwork on window-frames, balconies etc. The most amazing sight was the duck, though, Uncs darling, your mouth would have watered, there were hundreds and hundreds. Unfortunately we had to keep the engine going as we had the tide against us, and only got one as they wouldn't let us get close enough. But on the way back Major Holman and friends were going to cut off the engine and drift, and they should have had marvellous sport, because they left here after tea and wouldn't have got home till after dark, and there was a full moon to see by after the sun had set. We took 3 hrs to get here, and thoroughly enjoyed it.

Here I am for the first time in my life living in a wardroom! There are no women at all so J and I are being put up by the Navy, and have very comfortable cabins in a bungalow with two Senior Officers – we have our meals in a private ante-room, which is nicer than having to face a crowd of strangers. We are only here two nights more and are doing two shows in a small cinema – then we move a short way off to an oil town, which one can smell from here! This particular place is very nice, as it was the HQ of the Persian Navy which consisted of some five gunboats, I believe!

We beat them in the Battle of Khorramshar in about 1941, and took over here. There are quite pretty gardens, and I have a lovely vase of jonquils, stocks, petunias, marigolds and roses in front of me. The views of the river, which is very wide here, with tributaries and creeks off it, and a big island, are lovely. I had a very early night last night and feel marvellous in consequence. In fact have just staggered an audience of Ratings and Petty Officers by doing rather well on the rifle range! J and I have been firing 303's and awful things called 'Perishing Persians' which they captured from the Persians here, and which kick pretty hard. It was 100 yards, and though I didn't get a bull, I was pretty close the whole time, and only missed one when sighting was quite wrong.

14TH FEBRUARY 1944. PERSIA. TEMPORARY, ABADAN

We are probably working our way up to Teheran by road, playing all the way and arriving in March. The spring flowers should be perfect, and I believe there are many almost unknown varieties. However, J is very worried about our going by road, as we now have 1 bus and 3 lorries, the bus very rickety, and it will be bitterly cold. Bill Whittle, sweet ENSA officer, from Baghdad, is travelling with Nancy Evans and Co, though, so we will have a chance to lodge all our complaints with him today. By the way,

Uncs darling, I fired again with a 303 the other day and got 4 bulls! Also a black and blue shoulder! Am possibly to be in the band team if they have another match, but don't feel I could cope with the 'Rapid' yet!

17TH FEBRUARY 1944. PERSIA, AHWAZ

We left Abadan on Tuesday, after a very pleasant stay there. It was a most interesting little community. They make themselves as comfortable as possible, with well designed bungalows and carefully watered hedges and gardens creating an illusion of suburban England. They are fairly strictly rationed now for butter, sugar, etc., and local produce is wickedly expensive. As an example of prices out here – a second-hand wireless is £150, a frightful old upright piano £250, and Johnny's host had just sold his car with 7 wheels, purchased for £168 some years ago, for £2,000. The purchaser, a wealthy Persian, really only wanted the tyres, and offered to leave the rest behind! Lipstick is 150 reals, or about £1 5s 0d a stick – am running out of that too, but it's cheap in Cairo luckily. The Oil people here have to be completely self-supporting. When we saw over the Refinery on Sunday (by the way it is the largest single one in the world), we saw every sort of thing being made, from small boats and railway engines and vehicles of all kinds, to furniture etc., for their bungalows. They also have a huge watch-repairing department, and I managed to get my watch cleaned there – it had stopped and they found it was completely clogged up with sand and dust which gets in everything. Oh, and I don't think I've yet mentioned the Smell! One gets it at Basrah, which is about forty miles away when the wind is right, and of course at Abadan one lives in it. It is rather sickening at first, but you soon get used to it.

NEXT DAY. TEATIME

I had to stop writing, as I had rather a lot of bobbing on and off to do last night. However, here I am just back from a good practice in the big NAAFI we play in here, and clean after a lovely bath. I hadn't intended to have one at this hour, but my sweet Indian bearer came up beaming all over his face and said 'Memsahib gussal gurram,' and then went on to say that the gussal (water) was very gurram (hot), and as it only is for a few hours a day I took his advice! There are only two baths in this hospital – the Sappers have just put them up for the Sisters, and they are extraordinary affairs – deep square things made of very rough and prickly cement. The water we use for drinking and washing here is just river water, full of 50% each mud and chlorine. It tastes foul, smells pretty bad, and looks very dirty – in fact I can't think why one bothers to bath! The natives stand in the mud washing themselves and their clothes carefully with precious cakes of soap – a pathetic sight!

18TH FEBRUARY 1944. 21 COMBINED GENERAL HOSPITAL, AHWAZ, IRAN

Abadan is on an island, with the Shatt-Al-Arab on two sides of it, and the Karun river, which is a big tributary flowing from the Persian hills, at its Northern end, with Khorramshar where the two rivers join. We brought our vehicles over the Khorramshar Ferry, but a ridiculous and officious Transport Officer discovered, after we had crossed onto the island, that they were just too long, or just too heavy, or something, and refused to allow us to cross back that way. The other Ferry which we had to use brought us to a desert track over which we had an awful journey. Ahwaz lies some eighty miles up the Kuran river, and if we had crossed at Khorramshar, we would have got there in 2½ hours up a beautiful American road. As it was, we were on the Southern bank, and had to go across the desert following a track which the pipe-line people use, but which is quite unsuitable for our bus and lorries – you just can't imagine the bumps! Our bus broke its third spring since Baghdad ten miles out, but we carried on. The dust was awful, but the men in the lorries were even worse off. We have only one bus now, which means that most of them have to go on the lorries, and we have what is called a troop-carrying lorry with seats round the sides in place of the bus. However, the sand gets all into them, and the poor men arrived at Ahwaz coated with dust. The journey took seven hours, and we had no lunch with us as we'd been expecting to arrive in time to get it. The jolting was really terrific, and Johnny, who had the worst side of our seat, with no springs at all, arrived here quite numb in the nether regions! The worst of it was that we had to play that night too. My voice went half way through the show, and J hastily changed all the programme so as to leave me out altogether. There was nothing at all wrong with my throat or vocal chords, it was just plain being clogged up with dust and muck! Yesterday it was quite all right, and I practised and sang a heavy programme — this climate which is terribly dry, actually suits the voice if one can only keep clear of sand; unfortunately it blows about in great clouds here. They are being sweet to us in the hospital: it is an old Persian building, and terribly primitive — no drainage at all and lavatories are just little tin pots with wooden rims, not even the large pail with wooden seat affixed, commonly known as a 'thunder-box'! The men use 'desert lilies' — Uncs darling, you will know these! — a funnel on top of a pipe like this: Y. These are dotted all over the camps in the open, and I have several times caught people performing as they don't expect women to be about! My sleeping place reminds me very much of a barn. It is a big high room, with open doors either end, a central passage, and cubicles on each side of it. Unfortunately it is very noisy, as it opens to the four winds always, and all stone, and people clump up and down from 6.30 a.m. onwards. I'm sleeping on a charpoy, the wide Indian beds of webbing slung between wooden frames. They are very comfortable and cool in the hot weather. The most disturbing sounds here at first are the trains (huge long fellows, carrying 'Aid to Russia' stuff), which hoot for minutes on end most of the night, and the dogs. In every place I've been to in the East so far, the pye-dogs seem to bark all night. There are jackals too, and they all go to it in chorus. Am quite hardened to it now though, and have even got to the stage when I can sleep in the bus between bumps! Ahwaz is a ghastly dump — incredibly poor mud hovels, cripples and dropsical children everywhere, and people dying of starvation. Typhus has been very bad too. In contrast, there is a huge German suspension bridge over the Karun, which is very wide here, and a Grain Silo, also German, and the American-built and -controlled railway line. We are going most of the way to Teheran by Ambulance Train, which will be very comfortable. We have been routed to go by road, but J refused to do it with our vehicles as they are. Three of them had to go into workshops on arrival here. We have our first sight of purplish sandy hills to the N East from here. Tomorrow we go by road to Andimeshk, nearer them still. Then we start climbing by train. There is a huge Polish refugee camp here – I met a sweet Polish girl while I was practising. She had been arrested by the Russians three days before an important piano exam, and taken to a labour camp where she went through absolute hell. She is very young still, and has heard nothing of her people for five years almost. She says the Russian treatment of the Poles was appalling, and swears our next war will be with them.

SATURDAY 19TH FEBRUARY 1944. ANDIMESHK, PERSIA

A special letter to you on your birthday. Johnny and I and the Matron of the hospital we are at drank your health at tea-time today, in whisky, which was the only thing we could lay hands on. My sweetheart, you would, I think, love to be where I am now – at least not perhaps exactly where I am because I'm in a rather uncomfortable tent, where one can only stand upright in about one spot, writing to you by naphtha lamp during a show; we are playing in about four marquees run together – awful for sound and no mike possible as there is no current available. However, there's a grand crowd listening, and they are miles from any entertainment, so they are appreciating our efforts! We are at a place called Pay-i-Pul, 20 odd miles from Andimeshk; it is simply a big camp dumped down here because, one feels, somebody at HQ stuck a pin into a map and hit this spot. No, it isn't the immediate entourage that would appeal – it's the farther vistas; we are on a plateau some 5,000ft up, with the Persian hills rising in a huge semi-circle in the distance, violet blues and

queer greys, and golden gleams of sunlight catching the high
snows, and mist and clouds making the whole a mysterious
realm of faery into which we are to plunge soon – thrilling
thought! The plain we are on is covered with short vivid green
grass just now, with flocks of long-eared sheep and goats,
and cows and donkeys and horses (all watched by mounted
tribesmen), grazing over it. Soon it will be covered with poppies;
and then the million stony water courses with which it is
seamed will be full of green snow water from the mountains.
Then the heat comes, and everything dies – flies, mosquitoes,
fleas, and even body-lice die in this part of the world, it is so hot.
Andimeshk is actually one of the two hottest inhabited places
in the world, and even now the sun is very hot at mid-day. The
hospital here is nice; from the Sisters' Mess we look over a wide
and deep-sunk riverbed, with vivid turquoise water bowling
over the stones, to the native town of Disful, unfortunately out
of bounds. There are no trees up here, but one gets a lovely top-
of-the-world feeling, and the hills melting into the heat-haze
look exquisitely mysterious. The day we arrived, there was a
thunderstorm on, and as we drove to our concert at dusk there
was the most wonderful forked lightning, pink against purple
clouds. We had a very good run from Ahwaz – 90 miles of 1st
class American road. Our 3 shows there went well – The Area
Commander came to the first and reappeared every night! The
last was to an American camp – the most deluxe affair compared
to ours (the Sisters' quarters where I stayed at the hospital are
actually ex-stables for Persian Cavalry horses!). Anyway, the
Americans enjoyed the show, 'tho I didn't; first I was demoralised
by being told that the complete opera party, who had just
arrived in Ahwaz and had a free night, were coming, so J let me
put on 'Fillies de Cadiz' instead of a more popular thing. The
party never turned up, and the Americans didn't like the song!
Then Arthur was taken ill and we had to cut 'Noël Coward', our
Pièce de Résistance and finale, as he plays the piano for it. We have
three casualties now – one left in Abadan, one at Ahwaz, one
here. Nothing serious – sand fly fever and such like – but very
upsetting to programmes and worrying for Johnny. However,
we do the next part of our trip in two coaches of an ambulance

train, which I think we will live on for four days, being shunted off at our destination each time. The vehicles come with us on flats. We do the lovely 11hr trip up into the mountains by day, starting at 7 a.m. – perfect. It must have snowed yesterday – how I wish you could enjoy it with me, my darling – Perhaps another day... . Must stop – show over and very successful despite terrific heat and bad conditions. We have a day off tomorrow, and am going to take photos – have quite a lot already.

21ST FEBRUARY 1944. ANDIMESHK, PERSIA

Here I am writing to you in the same little tent at Pay-i-Pul camp from which I wrote your birthday letter two nights ago, mum sweetheart. The show is on again, and again the audience is grand, despite the heat, fug, bad acoustics, and lack of microphone (due to there being no suitable current available). Yesterday was a day of rest. In the morning J and I had a lovely walk along the cliffs that border the river. The hospital looks across it to the Persian town of Disful and a very fine 'pineapple tomb' (of a type common I believe only to this part of the world), which stands on a cliff overhanging the river. On the wide beach there are always scores of native women washing their clothes, their children and themselves, while herds of donkeys, horses and buffaloes splash all around, the latter just an ecstatic nose appearing above water. The cliffs are full of caves and deep rifts and blowholes; there is a coating of fine vivid grass just now. We lay in the sun (75° in the shade already!) and listened to the slap-slap of the women beating their washing – very peaceful – and the rush of the water below. In the afternoon a very sweet old Indian Cavalry Colonel took us some fifteen miles in a jeep to visit one of the five accredited Tombs of Daniel – very improbable but quite interesting! A tomb and mosque with the usual courtyard surrounded by little rooms where huge families live. And above it, on a hill, a castle, built by a French archaeologist who excavated the place, out of the old bricks of the town, which was a capital called Shush many hundreds of years ago. There were lots of Yanks sight-

seeing, and doing the usual mad things in the way of climbing
rickety minarets to be photographed at the top. We were all
besieged by the usual crowd of baksheesh-wallahs; one small
boy so persistent and with such a naughty and winning grin
that of course we fell! Then tea with the very charming young
CO here – then very early bed and a divine night's sleep. Mum
darling, your penny whistle would be very popular here – the
Indians all play them, and the camp during the afternoon rest-
period sounds like an aviary. I started to play one once when we
were on the river in a launch, but one of the Indian crew seized
it from me, told me I was no good, and proceeded to curl up in
a ball in a hole under the bows and play sad little Indian tunes
to himself by the hour. All these hospitals we've been to lately
have had mainly Indian doctors and staff and sisters – all very
pleasant to get on with, but it must be rather a difficult situation
working with them, I feel. Tomorrow afternoon we are doing a
salon orchestra concert for the hospital patients – we gave them
a variety show on Saturday before coming out here so they've
not done too badly. Then we get into our Ambulance coaches,
sleep the night in them, and draw out early in the morning.
When we saw the RTO this morning there was some doubt as
to whether they could get the coaches for us, and we were to go
by night 3rd class – not so good. However, all is now well, and
we go up the mountains on the end of a freight train. They have
been lost in a heat haze ever since we arrived, so I am longing to
see them near. My clothes are getting very dirty and un-ironed
– no chance to do any washing for ages, as there is no running
water anywhere here, and we often don't have time to get things
to the dhobie. Teheran will be my first bath for many days.
Practice has been difficult too – I eventually got going with
a funny little portable harmonium which I pinched from the
Troops' Recreation Room, and had moved to an uninhabited
block! Oh – have forgotten my main item! You remember our
journey across Transjordan – picnicking happily everywhere en
route! Well, we met some troops here who crossed the desert
two days after us. They were attacked by bandits all one night at
H4 (where we stopped), and fired on with rifles! And a couple
of RE lorries crossing at the same time were burnt out and

the crews killed! A real case of 'Ignorance is Bliss' as we were unarmed, except for J's tiny 6-shooter!

24TH FEBRUARY 1944. DOROUD, PERSIA

I am writing this to you in such amusing circumstances. The scene is 5,400ft up in the mountains between Andimeshk and Teheran, at a tiny bleak place called Doroud where we have spent the night. A blizzard is blowing outside – fine driving snow which despite the cold is not lying here – and the surrounding peaks, which are blotted out just now, will be whiter than ever when they re-appear. Our temporary home is in two coaches of an Ambulance train, and we are having a big picnic, as conditions are all fairly primitive. The band moved in on Tuesday morning, and found the coaches in a filthy condition, having been used by Indian troops. However, the boys all got down to it, and when Johnny and I came along in the evening (after a last salon orchestra concert for the hospital patients at Andimeshk), we found that they had scrubbed and swept the place into a very good state. There is one long ward-coach where about 28 of the men sleep in two-tiered bunks, then in our coach there are two smaller rooms, a kitchen, a lavatory and wash place, and a nice compartment with a top and bottom bunk and a cupboard, which J and I have. It is all terrific fun, and the men are doing wonders in the cooking line. The kitchen, as you can imagine is like the Black Hole of Calcutta, and an added difficulty is that we have no hot water. We have 100 gallon tanks on each coach, which have to be filled generally by hand, every day, and which provide very chlorinated water for lavatory, basin etc. However, J and I are very lucky. We belong to a 'swindle-gang' (as our small cliques of primus-owners are called!) run by Rossiter, one of the double-bass players, and he on one tiny primus produces excellent food and tea for seven of us all told. Then there is Lee Sheridan, who runs a large-scale swindle for about eighteen, and is a very good cook. The others struggle for themselves on a couple of little spirit stoves, poor devils! However, Les Marsh and Buddy

Woods and one or two other of our most practical people, have
just rigged up an old oven in the kitchen as a first-rate oil-drip
stove. I can't begin to describe the oil-drip principle, which
is used to make marvellous fires out of old petrol tins etc., all
over this part of the world. But it is a system whereby drips of
oil and water falling upon shavings of wick or a stone, ignite,
and give off a gas, and produce an incredibly hot fire for very
little fuel consumption. It can be improvised out of a couple
of empty tins quite easily, and of course oil out here flows like
water. The train is very cold, as the Indians removed most of
the glass, and we only have open-work steel shutters, which
keep out the view, and let in the wind in many places. Luckily
the big ward-coach is OK, but we have only 1 pane of glass
left in our compartment, so I'm clad in scarf, cardigan, battle
blouse, and sheepskin pushteen over all! Another difficulty is
that we have 6 small hurricane lamps and a few candles between
us! There is no electricity – but it's all such fun and such a
marvellous experience that I'm enjoying every moment. We
slept Tuesday night on the train at Andimeshk – very disturbed
as the American Aid to Russia trains were shunting and hooting
round us all night – then they shunted us about a good deal, and
eventually tied us onto a freight train which drew out around
5 a.m. It was terribly hot there – the change of temperature in
24 hours was quite startling, as we awoke to find ourselves in
foothills, and we came straight up to the snowline. The railway
is American-built and -staffed, and the great freight trains go up
pulled by several powerful diesel engines. We spent more time
in tunnels than in the open, curling to and fro up incredible
gorges, with amazing larva structures all round – columns like
Staffa, regular striations, whorls, curves, jagged toothed edges
and pinnacles and overhangs, like the scenes in Walt Disney's
conception of the 'Sacre du Printemps'. We followed a river
which ran the colour of red Devonshire earth for a long way,
and it was fascinating to watch green ice-torrents flowing into
it and mingling. As we got higher there were exquisite vistas of
high snow-peaks. I saw white broom flowering, and I think pink
broom, but have seen no alpines yet. There are gazelle, cheetahs,
panthers, bears and wolves in quite large quantities, and I saw a

black heron, rather like a cormorant, and a buzzard. Each tunnel is guarded at either end by a few Indian troops who live in tiny huts perched on ledges in the rocks. We did a show here last night in a small tin hut, bitterly cold with wind and the odd snow-flake whistling through large chinks. The only available dressing space was, as usual, partitioned off by an army blanket, with me on one side, and Les and Lee on the other. The oil-stove provided flickered and died during the early part of the show, and was it cold! In the front row, sat, or rather huddled, two Brigadiers, with only the tips of their noses visible outside enormous pushteens. I sang my solos, with chattering teeth, in the net dress, then fled and changed into the old red taffeta and warm quilted jacket. At dinner in the Officers' Mess, J and I had gazelle – a lovely tender meat. Strangely enough the CO of the tiny garrison was on the Orion with me! Must stop – have just started on 5 hours climb to Sultanabad – our halt for tonight. We are a 'special train' this time, just our two coaches and the four flats with the vehicles on them. Manny Hurwitz, who is an expert photographer and is sharing my camera, has taken many photos, and I have too, in fact we spent yesterday hurtling from window to window! I let him do most of it as he's so good, and he despairs of teaching un-mathematical me to cope with stops, lens, apertures, etc! Snowing hard now!

PS I heard later that the Officers' Mess were bitterly disappointed when I appeared for dinner in battle-dress! How typically male! The poor dears really imagined that I would paddle around in the snow in evening dress and sandals!

24TH FEBRUARY 1944. SULTANABAD, PERSIA

Here we are safely in Sultanabad, and in the middle of our show, and I find myself with a long wait, so am starting a second letter to you to tell you a few odd things I hadn't room for this morning.

It has snowed hard here; when we arrived we were taken to a dinner in the very nice Officers' Mess, and we drove back after in a positive blizzard, and got snowed up trying to find

our coaches, which were shunted onto a siding. I am wearing
my big pushteen – a vast garment which I laughed to scorn
when I first saw it, but which I fell into gladly today! Also long
rubber boots with thick socks over stockings and trousers, and
a few odd scarves, gloves, hoods, etc., thrown in. Johnny says he
must photograph me, as it would make you laugh so! Everyone
here is dressed very much Russian style – fur caps and coats
etc., and there are droschkes (can't spell!) in the streets. But in
my room, or rather in the few square feet which J and I are
inhabiting at present, I have (on the floor, as there's nowhere else
for them) three tins full of heavenly sweet smelling jonquils –
the white and yellow ones. Yesterday morning when we awoke
in the foothills we halted at a tiny village, and children came
along selling bunches of them – they must grow wild there,
but I couldn't see any. Anyway before I could say hey presto,
I had acquired four big bunches, from dear Oscar Grasso and
Bill Hyde, our young ENSA 'Conducting NCO' – very sweet
of them, and it makes all the difference to our little room. The
band are all so sweet to me – Lee Sheridan has been hard at
work trying to fix a lock on the door of the lavatory that has
been allocated to me, and eventually succeeded; I extended the
hospitality of it to the band for washing and shaving, as it has the
only washbasin.

25TH FEBRUARY 1944. EN ROUTE FROM SULTANABAD TO QUM

Am writing this during a halt – still very cold and windy,
but we are dropping down a bit, and it has stopped snowing.
Excuse scribble – the train is swaying and my compartment
is a social centre for all the boys, who come in and sit on my
bunk and chat. You can't think how amusing they all are; the
kitchen is next door, and I sit in here and listen to Les Marsh,
Lee Sheridan, Tommy Hopkins, Freddy Clements and other of
our wits trying to cope with the cooking in there, and almost
setting the train on fire with their various Heath Robinson
stoves, and it is as good as any skit or farce. They are the most
ingenious crowd, and as Les says, the RTO won't recognise their

train when they get it back. We have acquired some nice things en route too – a couple of hurricane lamps, and two American heaters amongst others! Marvellous ranges of hills passing now – the big one above Teheran is 18,559ft high!

You will notice I haven't written for some days. I think I last wrote on the way to Qum on Friday – I had a relaxed throat that day, and my voice gave out in the middle of the show 'tho I got through a group of songs and the Noël Coward, and I arrived in Teheran with mild laryngitis. I saw a doctor on Friday night after the concert at the American camp we were at. He was very nice and said it was nothing serious. And the moment we arrived here our English Army one came along from the local military hospital, and gave me cough mixtures, inhalations etc. I was in bed from when we arrived on Saturday morning till Tuesday – nothing but this croaky voice and a cough – no temperature at all – and luckily was able to appear at our 1st show here on Tues – a Gala Charity affair – vast sums charged for seats, advertised in 5 languages – Russian, Persian, French, Polish and English! The idea being to make enough money from the rich Iranians to pay for the next 2 nights of free troop shows! As I say, I just made that, which was a great relief as I'd been extensively advertised, but it was a bit nerve-racking as the old voice was still rocky! However, I managed to do all right – I sang 'Filles de Cadiz', 'L'été', 'I give my heart', 'My Hero', and our Viennese 'Fantasy'. Poor J has had a worrying time as we seem to have some casualty in the band every night, and have had 3 trombone players ill – all very difficult.

2ND MARCH 1944. TEHERAN, PERSIA

Lovely to be writing to you again – the first few days we were here I have just felt too limp, but now I've come to life and am revelling in this interesting town, and the mountains, and the shops and all the cosmopolitan life of it, and our most comfortable hotel. I think I stopped writing at Qum, which is a most fascinating old city – one of the holy ones in Persia, with a marvellous golden mosque where Fatima is supposed to be buried. Otherwise filthy and insanitary, with incredible clouds of dust blowing along the streets and getting into everything. It is much warmer there – we had come down about 2½ thousand feet. But overnight it became very cold again, and when we arrived here at about 8.30 a.m. next morning, it was bitter with new snow down on all the mountains. They had managed with some difficulty to get J and me rooms at the best hotel here – the Park, and I found myself in a really Swiss-hotel bedroom – clean linoleum floor, duck-egg blue walls, cream-enamel-painted wooden beds and furniture, a big stove with a pipe (shades of Kühtai!) and French windows opening onto a big balcony facing South. The mountains are to the North, so I only see them round one side, but I can just see the big fellow, Demavend, 18,550, who rises behind some trees in a perfect cone rather like Fujiyama. They all lie some way back, and are not half so imminent and overpowering as Innsbruck, but more like a rather unreal back-cloth, and they have been veiled in mist most of the time we've been here, which adds to the effect of the illusion. The snows have receded a lot and cannot be very near now. Strong winds have done a lot to blow them away, but there is a chance that there may be more. The temperature here reaches 110° in summer, and from photos I've seen, even the big Demavend only keeps snow in his deepest gullies in midsummer – strange, as we are fairly far North by now.

3RD MARCH 1944

My darlings – was interrupted yesterday by the nice editor of the Teheran Daily News, one Capt Duff, who has written a marvellous article about the show and wanted a little more information, photos, and also a letter from me to the Persia troops. Then we had to go off to our nightly performance, and I took this meaning to go on with it there, but the little time I had, had to be given up to composing a letter to the local Sapper paper. Am getting quite good at jotting down hasty messages to the 'dear boys'! So here we are, next day arrived, and I'm sitting in my dressing room during a show in a nice hall for the Americans. General Conolly is here, I believe. In the afternoon we are recording ½ hour variety programme to be played over the air here, and then sent home we hope for the BBC to use. The Yanks are lending us their studio and gear as the British have nothing of that sort up here. I'm singing 'I Give my Heart' and we are doing a rather shortened version of the Noël Coward I think.

4TH MARCH 1944

My darlings – impossible to get my usual letter written! The show went very well last night, despite a very tough audience of American railway-men, whom I had expected not to like me! It is again a glorious morning – warm sun, cool air, and the mountains still all white-capped. Have just returned from having my hair done at the Teheran Club by a nice French woman who is married to a Persian professor and who 'coiffes' the English population two mornings a week for her own amusement. She's done me very well too – such a relief after the efforts of Iraqis and Persians! Last night we went on after the show to a small party given by Matron at the hospital – all the band invited, lovely eats, and an informal dance after. All the Sub-Area HQ Officers were there, and I had a long talk with the Area Commander, a nice Brigadier Douglas. After early lunch, we are rushing off to the Americans to record. Then to the hospital again for the short concert, followed by a dance, to which I shall have to go for a bit. Tonight is our last show here. Tomorrow is free – Capt Duff is possibly taking J and me up to Darband, the lovely skiing and holiday resort in the mountains, and if there is any snow left I may ski! Have an introduction to the Secretary of the Ski Club, Major Watkinson. Am so longing for it. Must stop – will write another letter from here, as have not yet done justice to it!

4TH MARCH 1944. TEHERAN

This last of the Teheran series will be an attempt to tell you something of the Franco-Russo-Iranian cosmopolitania that is this town. I still haven't got used to seeing dusky faces and veiled women and oriental bazaar scenes against a background of snow mountains – mosque and peaks silhouetted side by side against an evening sky – luxurious cars winding in and out of long caravans of camels tied head to tail and buried under huge bales of merchandise – donkeys and dangerous Persians on bicycles – Russian droshkies pulled by scraggy Arab ponies with hand beaten bells (like a Davos sleigh or a Pyrenean sheep) round their necks – mad Americans in jeeps, and erratic Indian drivers in lorries, going through to Russia – all bumping over wide and, for the East, clean, cobbled streets, with two-foot-wide runnels of swift mountain water on either side, in which the natives drink, water their animals, wash themselves and their clothes and relieve their every need!

We went on Thursday to see the Gulistan Palace, where the treasures and presents of the Shahs are collected. A fantastic affair which has to be seen to be believed; imagine the Salle des Glaces at Versailles, only a thousand times vulgarised and exaggerated and turned into the nightmare mock Crystal Palace of some blatant tripe-king millionaire – not a ceiling but is mirrored or silvered and glistening with cut-glass and unbelievable chandeliers, walls moulded and ornamented in every conceivable way, huge gilt banisters, enormous china and inlaid vases on stands in the corners, priceless carpets all overlapping and two deep on the floor and, round the walls, case after case of the presents of different nations. Some exquisite things there, and we spent a couple of hours amidst the welter of stuff. The *coup de grâce* was given by the famous 'Peacock Throne' which the old Shah used – a massive affair that is solid with gold, mosaic and precious stones, and encrusted with writhing lions, peacocks, etc. After that we retired overwhelmed! The gardens and outside aspect are much nicer – beautiful mosaic inlay round walls and pillars, and a great big throne, more like a bed carved out of solid alabaster, but again ruined by being in a loggia inlaid with tarnished mirrors like a cheap version of the good old Criterion! I believe the late Shah Reza Pahlevi was a marvellous man, who did a terrific lot for Persia – abolishing the veil (which the women still persist in using though), and building the Trans-Iranian railway (which we came here on and which goes through to Russia), and doing much for the poor. His son, Mohammed Reza Pahlevi, is not so good – he insists on being called the Shah in Shah, or King of Kings, as if one wasn't enough. (Excuse pencil – alas have lost my precious fountain pen.)

5TH MARCH 1944

Was again interrupted yesterday, my darlings. But today is a free day and I really will get this off to you, as we leave tomorrow for our 2½ day journey to Baghdad. The recording yesterday afternoon was rather trying – things seemed to just keep going wrong and a very patronising Yank Sergeant rather irritated us! They have very poor mikes at their Broadcasting Station, and seemed to have more difficulty than anywhere else in balancing my voice. We eventually got finished, though it is not as good a programme as it might have been. Poor Lee Sheridan wrecked the Noël Coward by getting tongue-tied and stopping just at the end, and we had to break off and do it all again, which involved putting off their Radio Programme five minutes, and worried me as my voice was giving out. (Too much work too soon after laryngitis.) However, the nice part is that they have masses of equipment there, and when we went along this morning to hear our playbacks, they made us some records for ourselves – I have 'I Give my Heart', the talking and 'Zigeuner' and the Cavalcade Toast, self and Lee singing 'I'll See You Again' (the usual finale of our shows) and the announcer signing off as from Radio Teheran. They are not good records, but will interest you – I will be very careful of them – they are glass, not wax, very breakable and play from inside out, but am told that is OK on a radiogram as the needle will follow the thread either way. We did a short concert at the hospital last night. In a converted operating theatre, with the audience rising steeply to the very high roof and almost within handshaking distance of the tiny stage – most disconcerting. Then I went to bed fairly early – have a silly tickly cough which tends to keep me awake still. Alas no snow for skiing today – the mountains are almost bare – they are brown and treeless, and I think can't compare with the Alps.

The shops here! – one can buy marvellous cosmetics, scent, cameras and all sorts of things unobtainable at home, but at huge prices – have fallen for some toys – a Persian Policeman doll with typical Russian fur trousers and hat, and a white and maroon kid baby elephant, a real Dumbo, which I thought Jane or Hermione's babe might like. Also have got a few cosmetics, otherwise nothing – furs are now prohibitive, and the lovely silver work and bracelets of hand-painted mother of pearl are ridiculous prices. I took Johnny and Bill Hyde, our nice young ENSA Sgt, for coffee and cakes to one of the best cafés here. We had nice coffee in big glasses and delicious cakes, and it cost me 70 reals, or about 12/6! The café was very amusing – hardly any women, and those that were there were Polish, French or Russian. And everyone turning to literally gape at the sight of a girl bare-headed and in battle dress in a public place! I don't like the Persians – sinister looking people on the whole. Much of even this town is still out of bounds, and troops are advised to go down the bazaars in groups of five or six, as there is still much hostility to us. The other day one of the boys walking in an out-of-the-way part of the bazaar, came round a corner to find a wretched doughboy running like the wind, pursued by a crowd of natives. He didn't stay to help, but fled himself, and we never heard what happened to the American! How the Poles loathe the Russians. When Russia freed the Polish prisoners they had taken, after several years of keeping them in labour-camps, they came through here, and were looked after by the British, as usual. There were many of them in an appalling state. On the whole one finds the Russians getting on very well with the Americans (who of course are here entirely for Aid to Russia, and I must say are making a marvellous job of it), and not so well with ourselves. There is a certain amount of soreness between us and America, just because they seem to have everything. Their camps are perfect – lovely recreation rooms, a theatre in each, radios and gramophones for the men, a shop where they can buy marvellous food and every sort of thing, full-time radio stations on the go while we broadcast two half-hours a week etc., etc. It's the old story – money, money, money. They do have lovely things, though – portable typewriters that weigh nothing and are tiny, hundreds of little gramophones arriving in crates, masses of electrical equipment such as excellent stage-mikes which poor ENSA cannot achieve, and so on. And the Area Commander tells me he has 140 isolated posts up and down the railway, and cannot get a gramophone or radio between them. However, the Yanks have handed it to us over our show – they used to think a lot of their own USO parties which are touring here, but they have all agreed that they've never heard anything to touch ours! And they have been very nice about giving us the records and letting us buy some of the delicious foodstuffs at their shops – also lending us a mike all this week as ours (ENSA's) is hopeless. I think our little party of drivers and Bill Hyde will be splitting up and leaving us soon, as we expect to go to Syria and Palestine from Baghdad. I'm sorry, as we have some grand characters – Palestinian driver David Hassan, 18 years old, and one of the best (and most reckless!) drivers in the ME, a square short red-haired and freckled lad exactly like a Swiss Guide in his solid strength and nerves of steel, doesn't drink, doesn't smoke, loves dancing and has a girl in Alex whom he is rushing back to on leave now: Joe Shapiro, Jewish ex-Berlin actor, a grand and intelligent and charming person, great friend of Charles Goldner (do you remember him at Garrison Theatre, and of course in 'Watch on the Rhine'), has a sister who is, or was, a concert pianist in Vienna, and plays very well himself, the only really reliable driver we have – Miserahi No 2, again Palestinian and presumably mad, who succeeded Miserahi No 1 (no relation!) who was quite undoubtedly mental and known to all as 'Misery' or 'The Dope', and who caused Johnny's and Bill Hyde's hairs to go grey! – Mohamet, Arab, and very nice, a Baghdad man with wife and family – and lastly Ruben our little carpenter, also from Baghdad, and very sweet though fairly incompetent. Our vehicles and baggage are all going (in fact the lorries have left already) back to Baghdad over the Paytac Pass that you've read so much about, quite a different route from us, and I believe exquisite. Johnny won't hear of me going that way, though he'd have loved it himself, but he's allowing some of the band to go. They will be 4 or 5 days on the road, lucky things. You can't think how sweet J was while I was ill – you should have seen him trying to explain to our Persian room-boys that I wanted boiling water for inhalations every 2 hours! Then rushing round every time to get it as no Persian has any sense of time at all! Also giving me different medicines at the right times, and even reading to me!

6TH MARCH 1944. MAIL TRAIN, TEHERAN, AHWAZ

Here we are, the time only 9.45 a.m., and already well on our way, and I felt I must write a bit to give you my last impressions of Teheran and its surroundings – we left fairly early this morning, and the town and mountains in the first sunlight were lovely – the latter more clear-cut than I've seen them yet. While we were waiting outside the hotel in very nippy morning air, I took a couple of photographs looking up the wide street our hotel was in to the mountain barrier which rises to the North – I hope they will be good. But the extraordinary thing is that the mountains from Teheran itself do not look at all impressive. I think it is because they are so big and rise so gradually that from the town which is close in under them, one sees only the foot-hills. Now, however, the view is quite fascinating. We have crossed the plain on which Teheran stands, and are beginning the long climb over the Southern mountains – the old engine chugging away furiously, and we doing, I suppose, 20 mph, if as much. We are running over hillocky red desert – no vegetation, but here and there sunken watercourses with clear greenish streams bowling along them. The colouring deepens to the peculiar purple-brown that all desert seems to become at a distance, with dry card-boardy hills and blue-shadowy corrugations. Then behind them tower the mountains – I am sitting at a window looking back North-East, and I see the massif behind Teheran in all its glory. Demavend shoots up above the others in a perfect symmetrical cone – his base is in haze, and he is floating like a mysterious faery peak in the blue sky. We have just passed a tiny outpost called Roude-Chour – half a dozen tents with a little company of fine-looking Sikhs in spotless puggarees, a few doughboys in the usual appalling Yankee déshabillé of squash linen hat and dungarees (railway staff), and the usual village belle with hennaed hands and hair and a baby at the breast. Also an imposing station building looking a little bleak in the middle of nothing. We are on this train for 26 hours or more during which time we re-pass Qum, Sultanabad, Durud and Andimeshk, stopping at the first two for lunch and dinner respectively, and then reaching Andimeshk for early breakfast. The band have a whole 2nd class coach – only 14 sleeping berths unfortunately, but they are not too crowded as there are only 28 of them, the rest having gone by road. Johnny and I have a compartment in the 1st class coach which is 'Reserved for Allied Military'. I am the only female and there seem to be officers of many nationalities – American, Indian, British, Russian and Persian. Food of a sort is brought to us 1st class passengers, and there is a NAAFI on the train, at which the troops can buy cigarettes, tea, cakes, etc.; the chauffage is terrific, and we shall need it as by tonight we'll be up over 6,000ft again. Yes, the altitude has affected all of our breath-controls a bit. Also have not felt hungry or slept very well – we will be better when we get down to the plains, I think. We have only one casualty in the band now – our base trombone who has been in hospital since Abadan with a bad septic finger. We all iodine the slightest cut here, as infection sets in rather easily. Arthur Wilkinson had acute bronchitis and Wolfe Phillips has had a sort of nervous collapse due to the conditions and tiredness and also very much lack of guts we all think! However, they are both with us – also John Tollis, who had a bad attack of your trouble, sciatica, mum darling, in Teheran. We've had one or two with eye-troubles too – many people cannot stand the light and the dust out here. I still flourish, though, and have had a marvellous night's sleep with no cough, thank goodness. Another little station – these halts are so convenient for writing! The usual crowd of natives have appeared from nowhere – absolutely no habitation except the railway building visible! The Persian soldier is a most ruffianly individual – they are still impressed into Service as in England in the press-gang days, I'm told. One of the interesting characteristics of Teheran was the street cries – quite long musical phrases, all oriental twiddles and quarter tones. The engine has just let off steam preparatory to its next effort, upsetting a rather nice Arab pony, and sending a little donkey with heavy panniers frisking unheeded into the wilderness. It will come back – no animal is ever tethered here, and the shepherds do literally lead their flocks. Have just heard we are not leaving Paiforce yet, but are going up to play the oilfield area – Mosul and Kirkuk – after a few days in Baghdad.

6TH MARCH 1944. MAIL TRAIN, TEHERAN–AHWAZ

The saga continues – keep finding new things to say to you. Johnny has just been inspecting the sanitary arrangements and finds they are of the usual Persian type – two footplates and a hole in the floor! Our hotel was, I am told, the only one in Teheran where one can have a bath. And even there I found live red worms in the cold water – only discovered these after I'd been drinking it all week. The bill for two rooms and three meals a day for 10 days came to about 6,400 reals, or £56, minus extras such as tea, elevenses, shoes cleaned, laundry etc., for which we each paid nearly £6 – the band have made a lot of money this week, as the Teheran night-clubs and cafés have been competing for their services, and they have been working at two or three different places a night. They were well paid, and treated as guests of honour – free food and drinks etc. The clients pay terrific prices, but the rich Iranians seem to have money to burn. One asked for 'Begin the Beguine' and when the boys had played it he handed them a 1,000 rial note, and at another place Les Marsh, who had just done his act, happened to say that he had never tasted champagne; a Persian immediately ordered a bottle for him – £15!

8TH MARCH 1944

Here we are back at Basrah – or rather at the Airport Hotel,
Margil, which is some 5 miles from where we stayed before
at the YWCA, Ashar. We had quite a comfortable journey on
Monday night, despite slight difficulties caused by the choice
of either suffocating through overheating with the windows
closed or through fumes coming in from the tunnels in which
one spends two thirds of the journey! By nine o'clock in the
evening we had reached snow again; there was bright moonlight
coming through woolly clouds, and lighting up stray snowfields
or summits; and our train was not blacked out, so I spent most
of my time with nose pressed to the windows, or rushing from
left to right as the view kept reappearing on opposite sides as
we twisted and turned. Nothing like a real snowfield even at
the highest point we reached – over 7,000ft – just patches and
streaks of it, rapidly melting. I got a photo of the Golden Dome
at Qum as the train drew out, with the evening sun lighting
it up, and in the foreground an orchard of plum and almond
and cherry trees sprinkled with blossom. We all slept like logs,
and have done since we came down to lower altitudes. I had
a short spell of earache as we rushed downwards during the
night, but woke feeling very peaceful and relaxed, as we used to
when returning from Switzerland. We arrived at Ahwaz to find
a fearful journey before us; we had to hang around all day, catch
a train at 11.30 p.m., change during the night, and arrive here
at about 6 a.m., hang around here all day, and catch the night
train to Baghdad. Johnny immediately got going and managed
to arrange for the two of us to get a lift here yesterday, though
the band had to do the night journey. We were brought in an
open 15cwt truck, and had quite a nice run – the first half on
a lovely new American road, then onto a desert track and over
miles and miles of completely flat mud, naked, except for a few
tufts of a heathy plant. The horizon was an unbroken circle, and
one felt as if one was crawling round the surface of a large grey
billiard ball. South Persia is definitely the Land that God forgot!
We arrived here to find that arrangements had been made for us
to stay the night at this very deluxe hotel, and we are catching

the fast mail train tonight, arriving Baghdad tomorrow morning. The band have now arrived – they had an awful journey, and are getting a slow train tonight, taking 24 hours, poor dears. The first people we met as we walked into the hotel were our great friend Lt Whittle, who has been fetching a girl from a South African concert party, who, poor thing, got pneumonia at Durud and was very ill indeed, and Sgt Patterson, always know as Pat, who is a great personality and was our stage manager at the King Faisal Hall, and who is here with an ENSA party. We had a great reunion for a few moments, before we all had to disperse in our various directions again. This morning have been practising at the Port Club Cinema, where we played. Had a long talk with Col Hinchcliffe, the sweet area Commander, last night, and have met various other old friends here – all talking about our show still!

13TH MARCH 1944. KIRKUK, IRAQ

I've borrowed Johnny's fountain pen, and here I am all set to continue my saga to you. Am feeling miles better this morning – last night I still felt a bit seedy, and our 5½ hrs bus journey didn't help. I left off just after we'd arrived in Basrah, when we were staying at the Airport Hotel, Margil. We had two nights there eventually as our berths on the mail-train on Wednesday were taken over by GHQ suddenly, and we didn't leave for Baghdad till Thursday night. However, it was lovely there. The first day I practised twice – in the Port Club Cinema (where we played for four nights) in the morning, then in the church in Ashar after lunch. After that, we wandered round the fascinating old bazaar and waterfront, and shopped. I bought Lux, 2 Super XX films (of which there seem to be unlimited supplies here at a price) and 4lb of dates, 2lb stuffed with walnuts and 2 with almonds, which I posted off to you. Then tea at the YMCA, then as we weren't leaving after all, we went to see the show of the ENSA party who were staying at the hotel with us – 'By the Way' is the name of their company. It was excellent – far and away the best ENSA show I've seen yet and beautifully dressed. They are a very nice crowd too, and so disgusted at the behaviour of some of the other parties out here. I was feeling rather rotten by then, having been violently sick, and had a poor night, and kept very quiet next day. We had the sweet chief sapper there, Major Holman, to lunch with us, and he and Squadron-Leader Scott, the head Intelligence Officer, to tea. They are a really charming lot, the senior officers of that Area. Then Capt Fox, the Welfare Officer, saw us off on the mail-train, in which we had a very comfy air-conditioned compartment. I love the Basrah area – it is still very untouched by civilisation and the town of Ashar is purely native. There are date palms stretching inland from the river, with cool little irrigation canals between each row, and vivid blue kingfishers flitting about in the green shade; funny little creeks with curly-prowed bellams gliding up them; and a picturesque waterfront with crazy buildings leaning over it, and every sort of craft plying to and fro, usually gunwale under with people and cargo. We arrived in Baghdad at about ten o'clock, to find dear Bill Whittle to greet us. I still feel very sick and generally upset inside, and unfortunately we had to leave for this tour that same night. However, rooms had been booked at the Semiramis, and we were able to go there and wash and rest. I practised in the morning – while all the arrangements were being made about this trip and Johnny was discussing with Maj Williams (head of ENSA for Paiforce) how our tour had gone. They have had wonderful reports of the show, and all thanked us for what we had done, I suppose in the way of propaganda to the Americans, Persians, Russians, etc., and for the good name of ENSA. Our lorries and bus arrived in on Wednesday, after a wonderful run over the Paytac; the band got in the night before us after awful journeys on terrible slow trains, poor dears. We left that evening for Mosul, and travelled all night – again very comfy sleeping berths for us all. We were on the Orient Express that goes to Istanbul, a very good train. At Mosul, J and I stayed at the Station Hotel, best in the Middle East, and run of course by a Swiss. We did a very successful show that night – I was still upset inside, but sang OK luckily! We stayed the night there and came here yesterday.

13th March 1944. Kirkuk

Here we are just setting out from Mosul – 2nd largest town
in Iraq, and a very interesting old one – on the Tigris, and
with the craziest skyline of mosques, minarets and spires, all
leaning different ways, as do all the buildings out here after
being up a few years. We drove out of the maze of little streets,
and embarked upon the vast plain of Central Iraq that rolls for
hundreds of miles like a great ocean – at present it is soggy with
the winter rains, and covered with acres of ploughed land, young
corn, and short grass. But it is so huge and infinite that one
has no feeling of an inhabited country, and I wondered where
the people came from who had cultivated those great tracts.
Never a hedge or tree to break the monotony, just the foothills
rising very blue to the North, and cloud shadows racing across
continually. Here and there a little black Berber tent, just like a
tiny ship. And then little mud towns, each a fortress, close behind
high walls. This must have been a very wild part of the world,
as one sees no isolated houses – I suppose Kurdish tribesman
drove all the people behind the village walls. There were big
flocks of sheep and goats and cattle, all very fat and healthy with
the good feeding – the sheep, skewbald and piebald and spotted
fellows, the goats big black long-coated ones, with heavy plus
fours and short tails standing up in the air in a very gay manner;
all surrounded by young, frolicking and playing about. I thought
the first shepherd I saw was a scarecrow. They wear funny coats
of a whole animal skin, with the legs standing at right angles,
and they keep their arms inside, so the effect is very amusing
– the sheepdogs are lovely – like Aunt Nora's 'Peter' – (wasn't
he a Samoyed?). The natives here wear a most picturesque kilt
– very full baggy trousers, Russian blouse, heavy dark turban,
embroidered leather cartridge belt, and rifle or dagger. We passed
one most romantic little group – a man who must have been a
Sheik or some high-up Chieftain, on the most beautiful Arab
stallion I've seen, a henchman riding one lovely fat horse and
leading another (the natives' horses are usually half-starved-
looking) and, striding along in step behind, three retainers – we
passed them three times, once when they'd halted, once when

we'd halted, then we overtook them again, and each time the old man who was riding on a marvellous embroidered saddle of purple leather, showed off his pony to us and made it curvet and prance. But the biggest thrill was catching a fleeting glimpse of red in the short turf, and then another and another, and finally we halted because 'Nature had intervened', discovering, on my usual lonely little walk over the horizon, scarlet St Bridgid anemones studding the earth – the only exciting wild flower I've found here yet. We had a lovely halt – warm damp air smelling of earth, and desert larks singing fit to burst (they are big light-brown crested fellows) and a sweet Persian driver called Hatton, who has just joined us in place of Joe Shapiro, digging a great clump of anemones out of the soil for me. I may try and send you the corms. We stopped again outside a very famous fortress town called Erbil, which stands on a hill plateau with a steep drop all round, and manages to look like a big Christmas cake. It has a marvellous cobbled drive up to a huge drop-gate – we all photographed hard, and managed to get some natives to pose too, all in their baggy trousers. The drive seemed to go on forever and was pretty bumpy. We left at 9.30 and arrived in at about 3.30, feeling quite dazed and queer in the head – however, we are marvellously comfy here.

13TH MARCH 1944. KIRKUK

It is evening now, and the band have just struck up the first notes of our first show here. I am sitting all ready dressed in the ENSA blue crêpe dress (which is lovely on the stage) and made up, and nothing to do but write to you and give you a few odd bits of information that I couldn't get into No 3 this morning. I think I told you everything about our trip here from Mosul. This is of course a huge oil-field – one of the biggest, if not the biggest, in the world – Johnny and I are being put up by the Oil Company in their guest house, a most comfortable bungalow inside their huge compound, which is all planted with avenues of olive and gum and other attractive trees, and borders of stocks, marigolds, anchusa, tulips, verbena, etc. etc.

The chef is a piratical-looking individual who is generally clad all in scarlet, with a little cap on his head; however, he produces exquisite food at whatever hour one feels like it. And every morning the Head boy comes into my bedroom and says, 'I have soup, fish, beefsteak, and tart for lunch, and hors d'oeuvre, fish, roast mutton, and custard and fruit for dinner. Is that what madam requires, or would you prefer...?' whereupon I hastily say 'Excellent,' and he fades away. What a way to housekeep! Today we had a marvellous high-tea – 2 poached eggs each on toast (it is rare to find an Iraqi who can do anything but fry, but this man scrambles beautifully too), cheese-toast, and newly-made jam tarts and cakes that melted in the mouth, and of course, masses of fruit. How I wish you were all here to enjoy it, my darling ones. We are here until Wednesday evening, when we catch the night train to Khanakin (can't spell) where we stay I think 5 nights. Then back to Baghdad, 1 night at Kut, 1 night at Habbaniya, then nearly a week of rest at Baghdad e'er we leave Paiforce for good.

Re health, you will notice from the above descriptions of food that I am now quite fit again! I really was rather rotten for a few days. Johnny took me to the MI Room at Ashar, but there was an Indian doctor who didn't seem to know much, so we poured his medicine down the drain! When we got to Baghdad on Friday I went to the MI Room there, and saw a very nice Captain Barton of the RAMC who gave me a thorough overhaul, and said there was nothing much wrong, but I might just be sickening for jaundice, which however has fortunately not developed. He just told me to stick to the treatment I'd been having – Maclean's Tablets – It is really very funny as Mrs Johnny sent them out for J, imagining he would live on them as he has rather a delicate tummy, and I have eaten them all!

14TH MARCH 1944

Time has flown, and here we are starting our night show, having already done one this afternoon. Last night was a big success, and the Brigadier who filled in our Completion Form, wrote 'We have heard much about our Paiforce Sweetheart and were not disappointed...'. I sang the Bach-Gounod Ave, 'My Hero', our Scotland medley, 'Vespers', 'The Kerry Dance', and the Viennese medley, and ended up with the Noël Coward. That afternoon sang the Schubert Serenade, 'My Hero', 'Invitation to the Waltz', Scotland, 'Tzigane', and Noël Coward, and tonight 'One Fine Day', the 'Alleluia', the Walt Disney 'Bird Songs at Eventide', 'Amapola', and 'Motherland'. The climate here is very odd – a hot damp gale, very enervating, and the humidity has given us all relaxed throats. However am now marvellously fit again, and rested by our comfortable life here. Tomorrow is free, and shall practise hard – do some every day, and the voice is working pretty well. We have two big concerts at the Faisal Hall when we get back to Baghdad – the King just may come to the matinee.[5] Must stop, my darlings – a storm is brewing – the air thick with dust and yellowish and hazy and one sweats the whole time. It thundered hard last night, with terrific lightning.

17TH MARCH 1944. KHANAQIN OIL COMPANY, KHANAQIN, IRAQ

Friday. Good morning to you – how are you all today? I do hope it's fine and sunny with you, and not too horribly bitter and English-spring-ish? I feel so disgustingly lucky. Here am I, shirt sleeves rolled up, sitting writing to you in the shade on a terrace in front of the Oil Company's Guest House, where Johnny and I are staying with the charming and interesting Manager, Mr Dix. His garden is lovely – mulberry and lilac trees just budding, and beds of stocks, larkspur, Gerbera (African Daisy), alyssum, antirrhinums, pansies, and big sweet scented violets, all giving out a sweetness which manages to overpower the oil smell. Beyond the garden the ground slopes down to the river-bed, then beyond that is bare desert. On the right are the mountains – we are only 5 miles from Persia here, and I can see distant snow peaks to the North East. This actually was Persia until after the last war; now the Oil Company have their wells in Persia, and their refinery here is in Iraq, thanks to the readjustment. However, nobody seems to mind very much what country it is! We left Kirkuk on Wednesday night, and had a very comfortable journey here; our last two shows there went off very well. We had Wednesday free, and I practised hard. Also made a rather interesting discovery during a walk – the ground, which is bare hard gravel, was covered with tiny dwarf irises about 4ins high – Mr Dix, who knows all about the local flora and fauna, tells me they are simply wild onions; anyway they are very pretty! I saw a lovely lurid sunset too – the gravel goes all flame-coloured as the sun sinks behind the belt of dusty air just above the earth, and the mountains in the distance are genuinely purple. Heavy Kitehawks soaring about add to the effect. This place is much the same, though a little nearer to the mountains. Our host is so nice; his house is full of really beautiful things – Isfahan silverwork of amazing delicacy, Persian woodcarvings and china, Japanese prints, priceless carpets, and some Sumerian stone figures over 3,000 years old that are tremendously valuable. I have learnt a lot about what is the best in native work through talking to him – how to judge carpets and silver etc., as one can be so badly done. Most of the stuff in the bazaars and shops is junk, but for the people who know there are certain craftsmen who do exquisite work. This morning we went to see some big date-gardens – the owner, a Jew, who started life as an illiterate and penniless moneylender (rather a contradiction in terms, but you know what I mean!) and who gradually acquired all his neighbours' lands by usury, and is now fabulously rich. He lives in Baghdad, but the Head Gardener let us in through a big gate in the mud wall and we wandered around in a fairyland of tall palms with apricot trees in cloudy white blossom between them, and orange trees just in bud, tall trellises of vines, roses, violets, banana trees, silver-stemmed plane-trees, dark olives, sweet smelling eucalyptus and blue gums, and short hedges of myrtle, all in glorious confusion, overgrown and unpruned like the enchanted wood of the Sleeping Princess. Then we went through the village – very poor and dirty with flies everywhere, and wailings of Eastern music from the little cafés. Saw a very interesting 600-year-old mud bridge built for pilgrims from Persia to go to Mecca. It was built, I believe, in memory of a rich and noble family who were all drowned fording the river during their pilgrimage. All the arches are different sizes, but it stands firm, and big Army lorries use it.

17TH MARCH 1944. KHANAQIN

We are here until Monday, and it will be a very nice visit with such a pleasant host. Next door to our bungalow is the Oil Company Club where there is a piano, and I can practise in complete solitude morning and afternoon, also a lovely swimming pool, where we are probably going to bathe after lunch if we feel hot enough, and a squash court. We are doing six shows in all here – two each tomorrow and on Sunday, which will be hard work. The NAAFI we are playing in is smallish, but high and over-resonant, which is to the good for me. On Sunday at least one of our concerts is to be classical, for which Johnny and I are thankful, as we get very sick of the Variety. He wants to give it up entirely when we get home, and concentrate on the straight orchestra, which is so much more suited to him and gives more scope for real conducting. However I am afraid that will probably not be allowed.

Later. Here I am at the theatre and I was greeted by a lovely mail, and from Hatchards a lovely copy of the *Arabian Nights*, a present from my friend dear Walter Newlyn, who must have cabled from India for it. Pam had just got the Turkish Delight I sent her – 2½ months! I am sure I am getting all your letters, as there have been no real gaps, but parcels are of course much more risky. We didn't bathe this afternoon – the water in the pool is still too chilly. Mr Dix showed us photos of his little summerhouse 6,000ft up in the Persian mountains, in a gorge with a stream flowing down over waterfalls, where every sort of fruit and tree and flower grows on the limestone soil – it looked a dream place. Somewhere North of Mosul towards Turkey is the place where the mountain-shots in 'Lost Horizon' were filmed – a gorge called, I think, the Rowandas, or some such name, where there is a river with subtropical vegetation, flowing between cliffs that soar up in ledges to 10,000ft. The camps here all look very romantic at night – there are blazing

fires every 50 yards to keep away thieves – Mr Dix keeps the Oil
Company safe by having the head-thief as his Head Chokidar,
subsidising him heavily, and fining him for anything that goes
astray (chokidars are villainous-looking Arabs or Iraqis who
patrol one's domain armed with sticks, ostensibly to keep away
the Kleftiwallahs – usually they just show them the easiest way
through the barbed-wire!). When we get to Damascus am going
to try and get some silk or brocade for a new dress or two – my
own are nearly all going with the hard wear.

21ST MARCH 1944. BAGHDAD

I am so delighted that the Turkish Delight and your bracelet
eventually arrived too, mum darling, and helped to cheer you up
in the middle of your wretched cold. Perhaps the weather will
actually be getting a little warmer by now – funny you should
say that there will probably be a drought at home this summer
– people here are afraid of a famine, as the snow waters which
Lower Iraq and Persia rely on are completely lacking this year. I
am always so interested in all your quotations from books on this
part of the world; I am trying to read a little about it myself. Am
hoping to have time to visit the two excellent museums here,
and am going to see Babylon and Ctesiphon on Sunday. But we
missed out Nineveh, as we had only one day at Mosul and had a
show last night; I was still feeling very rotten after my prolonged
bilious attack, and we were told it was not very interesting there
unless one had expert guidance. Re the awful photo, mum
darling! I knew it was bad, and Johnny knew it was bad, but it
was taken in a fearful rush just before we left Baghdad, by a man
who is a Press-photographer really, and anyway has no studio or
equipment for portraits, it was the best of eight or nine proofs,
and Beric Holt who is the head of publicity and the press here,
and who was tired and rushed himself, more or less insisted on
my taking it. I never thought I'd get rid of two of the darned
things, but they went rapidly, and I am having more hand-outs
done of the nice battledress one. The other had the effect of
making everyone come up and say 'Your photograph doesn't

do you justice,' which is probably nicer than having them whispering 'I say, she's been touched up a lot, hasn't she?'! And the people who had them were poor lonely troops who are only too delighted to have anything that is not a pock-marked Iraqi to gaze at! However, I shall see that future hand-outs are better. Unfortunately I am the sort of person that can photograph very badly. You can't think what the other proofs were like! I hope you have got the Iraq Times by now. You will like the write-ups in that, with their mentions of Uncle Manny and daddy being Winston's Secretary. The latter brought a nice contact – a charming young Capt Harris, whose father was also one of Winston's Secretaries with Eddie Marsh, I think a little later than daddy – He asked J and self to dinner at his Mess where we met a charming lot of officers, between our last two shows at Khanaqin. It is very difficult to get spare copies or back numbers of papers here, so am not risking sending them home in case they get sunk. We have eight rolls of films awaiting developing and printing, but again are waiting till we get to Syria, as the Iraqis often ruin one's photos. Will send home all I can later on. Kut, where we go tomorrow (see letter no 2) is Kut-El-Amara, scene of great siege in the last war.

21ST MARCH 1944. IRAQ

I will now go back to Khanaqin for a short while, and round off my news there. We had a busy last two days – I, unfortunately, feeling not too good for the usual reason. We did two shows each day, and the last of all was classical. Our dear host, Mr Dix, came both on Saturday and Sunday nights, bringing a brace of Colonels the first night and a trio the second. He loved both shows, and was the most enthusiastic audience I've ever seen! He thought a terrific lot of the band, and invited the whole 38 of them up to tea in his garden, and to swim in the Club Pool – very sweet of him. He couldn't do enough for us, and (tho' I say it as shouldn't!) was rather taken with me (in a very fatherly way, of course!). He is quite an influential person, known as the Uncrowned King of Khanaqin, and he entertains everyone from

Royalty to ambassadors and C in C's at his lovely bungalow.
He also extends the courtesy of it to ENSA and has been very
fed up at the behaviour of some of the parties, so I believe we
have done good work in lifting up the prestige a bit! Of course,
the first thing I do always is to tell people that I'm not really
ENSA at all! On our last day at Khanaqin, Capt Williams, head
of ENSA in Paiforce, came and stayed with Mr Dix too and
came to the 2nd show. I sang the Jewel Song, 'Vissi d'Arte', the
Carmen 'Habanera', 'One Fine Day', and the 'Alleluia', and it
went over very well. We played in a big NAAFI, and the sweet
staff, who were all very keen on good music, presented me with
a whip-thong in the form of a bead snake, local work for festive
occasions, and quite an interesting souvenir. Have had a sweet
letter from Mr Dix who has a little home and lovely garden
at Grayshott, and who is coming home on leave at the end of
this year and hopes to see us. He has a wife there, and a son in
the Navy and a small girl, and is a dear – you'd like him. On
Monday Capt Williams brought J and me back here by staff-car.
The band stayed at Khanaqin, had their party with Mr Dix and
caught a night train, arriving here this morning. We are off to
Kut (South of Baghdad – a longish journey) tomorrow, for one
show and one night on Friday, and back here on Saturday for
a few days' rest, then off to Syria. By the way, I can't remember
any scoring out of words or names in my letters – they must
have been censored – will fill in any gaps when I get home.
Re spelling of names, it varies on every signpost and map as
there is no right way; they are all approximations to the Arabic
and Persian. 'Pushteen' is much better than 'Poshteen', I agree!
It is nice to be back in this hotel, with friendly staff – and Bill
Whittle, Beric Holt and Capt Williams all so sweet and helpful.
Am getting Khaki drill – 2prs of slacks and 2 bush shirts, as it's
rather warm for serge now. Am feeling very fit, and looking
forward to a rest (and some regular practice!). Then Syria,
which is lovely, I believe. There are 2 other sopranos here – the
'Bandoliers' one, who had pneumonia and the 'By the Way' one
who is also convalescing. We eye each other suspiciously!!

149

Chapter Six

Baghdad to Beirut

23RD MARCH 1944. BAGHDAD

Here we are just back from our trip to Kut, and I'm feeling a bit fagged as it was a very bad and hot and dusty road-journey. However dear Captain Williams lent us his own staff car for the two days, and Johnny, John Tollis (who has had sciatica) and I went in style, and did the journey in about half the time the poor Band took. All the same, have decided I am definitely not tough enough for desert warfare! My silly back aches so with the jolting – we averaged well over 40 mph all the way on desert track, and did the rather-more-than-100 miles in just over two and a half hours today. I can't think how these cars stand up to it, but they seem to! It is very hot, and I am debating ways and means of getting my summer undies etc. from Cairo. I left everything cool behind, as ENSA HQ told us we'd be away a month to six weeks, silly fatheads. Have no bathing dress, shorts, or even a nightie with me.

We had a lovely time at Kut despite my grumbles. Our hosts were a Mr and Mrs Williams, he head of all the irrigation in S Iraq, she I think Austrian, and both delightful. He was most interesting explaining how they are gradually bringing more and more million acres under cultivation; the trouble is lack of population. At Kut there is an immense barrage across the Tigris completed in 1939 after four years of hard work (with a break every flood season when all labour has to be suspended) and which now feeds a huge area down to the Euphrates. The river was in flood, seething and muddy, with tiny circular wicker boats like large dog-baskets, each containing two natives, bobbing incredibly amidst the eddies but somehow staying right side up as the owner fished. The Tigris salmon are running up the river to spawn, and they have a fish ladder at one side of the barrage where I stood spellbound this morning watching literally hundreds of fish crowding up the narrow shaft and jumping and jumping at the two small falls. The water is hurtling through just now, and they kept falling back, or hitting the concrete sides, but going on trying and trying despite the awful knocks they took, and eventually clearing the fall and vanishing triumphantly upstream. Somehow or other all the thousands of fish in the Tigris fight their way up that small ladder. They are not very large – up to about 20 or 25lb – but very clean and silvery. The flesh is nothing like real salmon.

Another amusing thing just now is the 'storkeries' – colonies of them building their huge nests on the little mud houses, in trees, and even one in Khanaqin on a big chimney stack, surrounded by clankings and steam! The heat should hatch her eggs in no time! The frogs are in full throat too, and the nights are noisy with them and with jackals, which make a really horrid and human sort of maniacal laugh. I thought it was drunken natives the first time I heard them! There are lots of scorpions too, but have not yet met one, touch wood!

24TH MARCH 1944

We had two important Sheiks at our show at Kut, brought by Captain More, the local Political Agent. One of them, a large jolly looking person, is known as Abdul the Murderer as he bumped off several relatives to become Sheik. However nobody minds a bit, and he now has a marvellous palace and entertains the local British at champagne suppers towards the end of which he sings them Arab love-songs – our Political Agent must have interesting jobs. The one at Basrah, Major Dowson, has gone completely native and we never saw him at all.

26TH MARCH 1944

Have just heard that the ship I came out in was sunk on her
next trip through the Mediterranean. I feel so sad, and am
wondering what happened to the Captain and various friends I
made amongst her officers. Her nickname of 'Lucky' has at last
failed her.

I must just take you back to Kut for a while, to try and
describe to you the beauty of our host Mr Williams' garden.
But first of all let me impress on you that the drabness of this
countryside is such as makes the dreariest of Home Counties
flatness and mud look like heaven. I had never realised the value
of colour till I came out here – one craves for it, and hence Mr
Williams' garden was like a priceless jewel. To begin with it had
a real green lawn – tall palms with masses of nasturtiums around
their stems, a twelve-foot hedge of oleander just coming into
fragrant pink flower, spicy-scented myrtle bushes round the
house, a trellis of sweet briar roses that took me right back to
the West Highlands, and clouds of larkspur, nemesia, schizanthus
in great beds, phlox, stocks, gerbera, verbena, Sweet Williams,
sweet peas and all the lovely sweet flowers we have at home,
interspersed with bushes of hibiscus with their tropical-looking
red blooms, and groves of orange and tangerine all in full flower
and smelling unbelievably, mimosa, apricot and peach, and such
a host of lovely things as defy my memory. He and I talked
gardening hard. His vegetables were very good too – we had
new peas and broad beans for lunch while we were there, but he,
like you, prefers flower-gardening!

I think I told you when I last wrote that we were just off to
Habbaniya. Before we went, I saw the film of the riding, and
it was excellent, to my great surprise! Only little bits, but tho'
my grip is not what it should be, I was delighted to see that
I still had rather a nice quiet seat, and the jump was all right.
Then I had a most interesting visit to the Iraq Museum, which
I was taken round by the head YMCA man, Mr Lampard, who
is quite an expert Assyriologist. We saw mostly the stuff which
Sir Leonard Woolley excavated from the great death pits of Ur,
where kings were buried and their complete retinue sacrificed.

Many incredibly interesting things – Sumerian ornaments and pottery, all very beautifully worked, tempered gold daggers (we today do not know how to temper gold – it is a pliable metal), weights in the shape of sleeping ducks carved out of bloodstone, which is harder than steel (Mr Lampard tried to model a piece under a steel drill and failed to make any impression on it), figures of composite gods and goddesses embodying different qualities all most vividly carved and far superior to Egyptian work, skeletons of the men and women from the death pits just as they were found with all their jewellery still scattered amongst the bones, wonderful old harps dating back to 3000 BC, then on to the Assyrian period (the Nazis of olden times) with their huge wall carvings of stern figures, then later still the Greek element, and really natural draped figures and character-studies in stone, just like the Greek section in the Louvre or any big museum. Apparently the way Woolley got the harps out of the ground was this: the centre of the wood was of course completely rotted away. So whenever his workers found a suspicious looking hole in the ground, they used to pour liquid plaster-of-Paris in, and in the case of the harps it ran right through the hollow centre and followed the curves, even filling in a bronze bull's head at the base of one we saw, then they let it set, and when it was hard they gently dug away round it, and were eventually able to lift the whole thing out, with its surface wood held together firmly by the hardened plaster. If it had been dug any other way it would have just fallen to bits.

Back from the Iraq Museum, we lunched and went off to Habbaniya, again in dear Captain Williams' staff car, or rather station wagon (Ford brake). On the way we passed a very big Bedouin tribe on the move, going North to the Mosul-Kirkuk plains for summer pasturage; a single file of camels, horses and donkeys, weaving away as far as the eye could reach into the desert, and probably with herds of cattle and sheep behind. The camels were many of them gay with beautiful carpets, and huge cane howdahs fringed with coloured cloth and big tassels, with the important men and women riding in them. The Euphrates, which had been a trickle when we crossed it in January, was a huge river right up to the balconies of the little houses on its banks.

Bill Whittle is engaged to Doreen Fernley, soprano of the
South African concert party 'The Bandoliers', and we were
celebrating this great event. 'The Bandoliers' have done very
fine work. They were in tents all over the Western Desert last
summer, after having a very unfortunate arrival. They were in a
huge convoy that got into Tewfik harbour a year ago when there
were no facilities for rapid disembarkation. They lay there for
two nights being heavily bombed in full moonlight, but were
untouched. The third night they were ashore in tents, alongside
the harbour, and the biggest ship of all, the 'Georgic', had been
filled with women and children on their way back to England.
She was hit and set on fire, and hundreds of children were
burned to death – a most appalling affair.

2ND APRIL 1944. REGENT HOTEL, BEIRUT, SYRIA

Here we are again in a new world, and I have so many million
things to say that I hardly know where to start – have wanted
to write all the week, but it has been impossible. The old brain
whirls with impressions of Baghdad – a taxi with a bullet hole
through the windscreen, our hotel with swallows nesting on the
capitals of the hall pillars and catching flies unperturbed around
the guests' heads, dust in yellow clouds, flowers everywhere just
now and incredible whiffs of orange blossom above the powerful
effluvium of the East, the Tigris asleep and silver-grey, melting
into the haze as we ride along the river bund, the jumble of
gharries, donkeys, horses and cars in the streets, and at night
the hotel servants sleeping on the passage floors so that one
trips over recumbent figures at every turning when coming in
late – a million more details, but above all personalities. This
has been a week of people, a gloriously happy crowded week,
and Johnny and I find ourselves now with the old familiar
fin-de-saison or end-of-holidays ache in the heart, and a great
sadness at having to leave so many warm friends. Before I tell
you of our doings, I must sort out the main characters so that
they will live a little for you, my darlings. Some you have met
before, others not. Beric Holt, tall, spare and stooping, drinks too

much, charming, intelligent, out-and-out journalist, witty to a degree, and has been marvellously enthusiastic and sweet to us; Peter Ender the caricaturist, a sharp-faced red-haired Peter Pan looking at the world with a most wicked gleam in his narrow eyes; little Captain Grandison, OC Broadcasting, one of the nicest men I've met, quietly and calmly efficient, yet able to sit back and let others do their job without interfering, and such a kindly twinkle in the eye always; Bill Whittle, bad-tempered (partly owing to too long in Paiforce), over-sensitive, lovable, impulsive and most keen on his job, who did everything in his power to help us; Bob Williams his OC and head of DNSE for Paiforce, but actually a queer, whimsical, vague person living in a world quite apart and shockingly forgetful as to arrangements, though most understanding when one could bring him down to earth; Major Trapmore, OC [Officer Commanding] Signals' Training, a huge 6ft 6in man, ex-Army Heavyweight champion, cockney ranker, a marvellous character beloved by all for his big heart and his efficiency, never came to see us or let us leave his Mess empty-handed; and lastly, a new person who really made this week what it was, Major George Bennett, ex-RA and Weedon Instructor, now in the Indian Army because it is the only way he can afford horses, reads first-class books and poetry, loves music and scenery, and has the kind wise eyes of a man who works patiently with animals or on the land. These are the main characters of our last week in Baghdad – there are other subsidiary ones who will crop up en passant.

I last wrote after our Babylon trip on Sunday. Monday began with a hectic rush. First I sent off to you two 2oz tins of tobacco, and a big envelope of odd photos and a Teheran Daily News which I thought you'd like to see. Then practise. Then after lunch Johnny and I went to Major Bennett's place, where J was fitted up with jodhpurs, then on to the riding school, an open mud affair with a jumping field outside it. The 'baby' class, in which Johnny had his first ride, took me right back to Shornecliffe ten years ago. Major B told me to look after J as all the other 'babies' had had five lessons. The instruction was marvellous, all about the saddlery etc., and they only spent about ten minutes in the saddle altogether during which time I ran

round the school holding Johnny's horse while he did his first
trotting! He did marvellously, and trotted alone as I was defeated
by clouds of dust and had to let go! He was thrilled with it and
is now as badly bitten as you were with skiing, darling Uncle
Stuart! It was so sweet and understanding of Major Bennett to
offer to include him in the class (which is Officers only, and
very short of horses) as J had always longed to ride and never
had any opportunity. Well, the Advanced Class followed, and we
did some quite tricky figures of eight, etc., I on a rather spirited
but very fine polo pony that used to belong to one of the
Guinesses. Then we went out and jumped. Major Bennett again
let me ride his lovely Joan, and she jumped beautifully. Then I
did another two clear rounds on a fool-proof old grey rocking-
horse called Bobbie, a really willing jumper. There were many
very interesting people riding – the second Instructor is a pupil
of George's, one Major Plum Warner, who nine months ago had
never set leg across a horse, but who is now a very useful rider.

2ND APRIL 1944

Later. I left off with the evening sun slanting over a dusty
mud-patch in Baghdad, and a crowd of people all in their
seventh heaven at escaping for two hours from the cares and
superficialities of social life into the happy realm of horses –
amongst them one Major James Waller, DSO, MC (this war),
RA, a fine rider, and mountain climber holding a Himalayan
altitude record; and an enigmatic, shy middle-aged spinster, one
Frances Flanagan, who is Foreign Office, and has lived all over
the world, lonely, frail, a most plucky rider despite innumerable
falls, and of whom more anon. Well, we tore ourselves away and
rushed to the Broadcasting Studio, where Captain Grandison
was waiting to let us hear some playbacks of old broadcasts and
recordings. Also there was a young RA Lieutenant Binstead,
editor of 'Trunk Call', and smitten with me, with the result
that he bothered me for interviews at every moment of the
day! The playbacks were fun. 'I hear your voice', which I sang
from a factory last year, OK. And one of the loveliest recordings

I've ever heard, of Johnny conducting a first performance of a modern work, Clive Richardson's 'London Fantasia', with the composer at the piano and 'Orchestra in Khaki', on the same idea as 'Warsaw Concerto', but far superior. You must hear it when I get home – it has made a great hit out here. It is banned at home because the air raid sirens in it are too realistic! From the Studio I tore back to the hotel, bathed, changed into my short duck-egg-blue crêpe dress, and rushed off to a cocktail party at the Embassy to which Lady Cornwallis had bidden me. Was fetched in a huge white and silver Humber with flag-pole complete, and felt most regal! It was very nice – Lady Cornwallis is charming and warm and friendly, he crude and elephantine and, I believe, a very naughty old man. Then back to the hotel, and Trappie (Major Trapmore) to dinner. He arrived, as usual, laden with drink, and he insisted upon giving up his complete issue of 10yds of khaki drill for me to have two pairs of slacks made – I was much too hot in serge battle dress and had no way of getting drill.

The heat was awful that evening – there has been one of the biggest dust and sand-storms ever, from Basrah to Cairo, and though we had only the fringe of it in Baghdad it was blowing a hot wind and the sky was yellow and overcast. After dinner we all went to a rotten ENSA show that had just arrived out, and when we emerged it was raining. During the night it thundered, then poured, and I knew the old agony of wondering if riding would be off! Johnny was going to have done classes every day, and I had a long hack lined up with Major Bennett and a party. It was raining this morning, and everything was off, which was a great disappointment, especially to J who had only six precious days in which to get a groundwork. In the morning I practised, then we went out to Trappie's Mess and his Iraqi tailor fitted me for my new slacks. That was the official day the Army went into drill, and of course there had been a complete change in the weather and it was icy! The poor dears were sloshing around in the mud and rain with blue knees and arms – Baghdad is a most treacherous climate. I had my hair nicely done by a Greek woman, then J and I went out to dinner, our hostess Miss Flanagan, and the other guests Majors

Bennett and Waller and Plum and Mrs Smith (who was very interesting about the exquisite spring flowers here in Syria). We had drinks at the Sinbad Hotel, with a balcony overlooking the Tigris, then dinner, and on to dance at the big nightclub, the 'Scharazad'. Plum proved to be divine dancer, the others bad, but dear Major Bennett and I talked nineteen to the dozen, and quoted Yeats' 'Soldier, scholar, horseman he' etc. to each other with great delight. Next morning J and I went to see Brig Foote – he has been quite charming and I'm sure is a very nice person away from his horrible family – he is delighted with our success, of course. I practised, then Miss Flanagan picked me up, and took me out for late lunch at the Alwiyah Club (local residents) where she lives. After, we went for a quiet hack on her two lovely grey Arab ponies – along the river bank past gardens of date, orange and fruit trees, with everything asleep in the mid-afternoon, and river and sky blended in a silver heat haze – poor Johnny was again disappointed, as the school had not dried up enough for use. That evening he and I went shopping, a fascinating job in Baghdad after dark, and bought a wedding present for Bill and Doreen, a Persian painted and inlaid cigarette box with which they were delighted – J and I fell in love with it, so on our last day in Baghdad we went out again and found much nicer ones at a very good shop, and we have bought a pair each. They are made in Isfahan, which is still the artistic centre of this part of the world, by a well-known artist called Omoomy. He is a pupil of the most famous of all, Imami. Imami works mainly on ivory and mother-of-pearl – exquisite stuff, but these boxes are most beautifully worked too. I do hope you'll like them.

Thursday was a very busy day. In the morning I practised, then rehearsed at the Faisal Hall for our Farewell there that night. Also ironed all my wretched dresses on one of the Iraqi Government's best varnished tables, and ruined its surface, which luckily they did not discover till after I'd gone! Life really is so difficult though, and my ironing board was pinched way back at Shaibah. After lunch we set off for the riding school again. Johnny had a class with Plum in charge, while I went for a very quiet hack with Major Bennett. He let me ride his Joan to whom I have lost my heart. She is a 15.2-hand chestnut lady of extreme sweetness and intelligence, with a mouth like velvet, a very highly-strung temperament, and a tendency to throw light-hearted bucks for sheer *joie de vivre*. Major Bennett had arranged a friendly gymkhana really especially for my benefit, on the following day – too sweet of him. We got back from our ride to find Johnny back from his lesson looking flushed and rather dusty, and strawy in the hair, but triumphant. He had had a terrific hour's grilling from the rather unimaginative Plum, and having been only 10 minutes in the saddle in his life, had had to keep up with a more advanced class, and do trotting without stirrups, touching his toes, and then if you please had had to take off his saddle, vault on, and trot round the school bareback! After two rounds of the latter he rolled off – Major B and I were stupefied at this epic and couldn't understand why he hadn't fallen off long before! I think Plum got a slight rap over the knuckles for cruelty to beginners.

We had tea in Major Bennett's room, and looked at his exquisite photos of the Himalayas and India. Then home and rest, and at 9.15 our 'Gala Farewell Performance' to quote the local press at the King Faisal Hall. At about 6.30 that evening several of us a felt a definite slight earthquake tremor, and we drove to the show through a dust storm, but luckily no rain came. Unfortunately it was not the all-troops audience we had hoped for, who I know would have given us a terrific send-off. Army Welfare had decided to make money out of us, and except for 100 free seats for troops, the charge for entry was 750 phils, or 15/-, and over half of our audience were Iraqis. Doubtless we are good propaganda, and I've heard that they think a lot of the show, but they are an appalling audience and very hard work to play to, so our big farewell which we had looked forward to was from our point of view rather flat. But the show did go extremely well. All our friends came in force, also a Mrs Vernon, head of Welfare for ENSA and on tour from Drury Lane, an influential person who was luckily rather struck with me, and two BBC people also touring the Command, one head of broadcasting in the ME etc. etc. I sang 'One fine day', 'I give my heart', 'Vienna', 'The Kerry Dance', 'The Lord's Prayer', the Walt

Disney two songs, and 'Land of Hope and Glory' in 'Motherland' (mainly requests). Was relieved when it was all over! I wore four dresses, the black and white, my bridesmaid's dress, the old net and the royal blue crêpe. Afterwards stayed up late talking to Bob Williams, who is very sweet when you get him alone, and was so generous about the show and the work we've done. Did I tell you that I calculated that from our first show in Cairo to our last in Khanakin, we had done 82 shows in 100 days, including all the travel from Cairo–Baghdad–Teheran and back. That doesn't include dance-band shows or broadcasts or military band performances, it's just what I've done, excluding broadcasting. Not too bad when you consider distances covered.

On Friday I practised, then elevenses with Beric Holt and a short talk over our final write-up, then out to Trappie's Mess, where the tailor fitted me with two pairs of most beautifully made slacks quite finished in two days and costing £1! They are made sailor-style, with a double flap across the front, which makes a beautiful flat tummy. Also I have acquired a third pair (cut for men, but a very good fit), two bush shirts (short-sleeved) and a lovely pair of brown walking shoes, free! They are all Army issue, and the shoes are ATS. My own were getting very worn as the walking is so stony here. After collecting the trousers, we saw all over Trappie's beautifully run camp, and saw his carrier-pigeons. Signals have hundreds of them, as you know, and we learned a lot about how they breed and train them. One fascinating point – a carrier pigeon has four completely separate eyelids. The first three are transparent. He can close one to keep out bright light, the second to keep out dust, the third to keep out rain and water, and all four are closed when he is asleep. So he can fly quite happily through all weathers. Isn't that marvellous? Trappie gave us his best bird and basket, and we took it back to the hotel, wrote a message and fixed it on (all in a very special way!) and launched it out of my bathroom window, and it flew back to him! Such fun!

3RD APRIL 1944. BEIRUT, SYRIA

Am so enjoying writing this to you – I sit in car, train or bus
when writing is impossible, with phrases and sentences and
things I want to tell you bubbling in my mind, and shaping and
reshaping themselves, and now have taken to making notes on
what I want to say to you so that when eventually I have time
to write, everything is organised. Even then the result is so far
from what I'd like… . However, back to Friday last, afternoon,
fine, and dear George Bennett's 'friendly gymkhana' with a very
good gathering of people and horses (both mainly his pupils).
There was a short class for Beginners first, and Johnny started
rising at the trot quite successfully. Then jumping – six jumps,
brush, post and rails, bar, wall, triple, and small water – not very
high, the biggest 4ft. I rode Joan, and got round with half a fault,
though she was putting on her usual show of temperament, and
not jumping at all freely – she is very excitable, and so clever and
keen that she gets more het up than her rider! Miss Flanagan also
rode her (there were not enough jumpers among the horses, so
each could be entered twice) and she didn't do so well on her as
I did, which I was secretly pleased about! The two people who
rode Bobby tied for first with clear rounds as expected, and I was
third. Before the jumping I forgot that we had Musical Chairs,
with whistles for music and bricks to be picked up instead of
chairs. I did well at first, with dear Joan going like a streak and
stopping almost with her feet on a brick. Then she got too
excited and started bucking, and we were ousted! There was a
race for 'babies' in which they had to lead their horses, saddle up,
mount and trot to a given point. Poor J had a broken girth strap
and couldn't do it up, or he'd have done well, as he was already
riding better than some of the others – very bad luck as he was
so keen. The last event was a galloping-to-your-partner, whistling
a tune, and he galloping-back-to-the-judge-with-the-name-
of-it affair; was second, owing to Loma (the high-spirited polo
pony) getting wild with excitement, and going backwards instead
of forwards for a while! A quiet old nag is the perfect thing for
gymkhanas, but I so prefer the keen horses and of course it was
all most jolly and un-serious so nobody cared who won!

Tea with Major Bennett, then rush home, bath, change into the short pink dress, and a little farewell dinner at our hotel with Beric Holt, George Bennett and Plum Warner as guests, after which we all went on to a very big All Ranks dance organised by Army Welfare, and for which our dance band was playing. That brings in another character, the CC Entertainments & Welfare, one Major Pennington, ex-manager for Jack Hylton, and whom Johnny described as 'a jackal in leopard's clothing', but very suave and nice as far as we were concerned and out to make all he could in the way of honour, glory, and funds, out of us. I must say he was extremely generous about the show, and this dance was a fine affair. It was in the Ahmanah Hall, a huge and luxurious place, with a really lovely ballroom and anterooms, and a great crowd of other ranks and many officers turned up. The Iraqi girls are on a roster for the other ranks' dances, and turn up as part of their war work; they are not allowed to dance with the officers at all at an all-ranks dance, which is a very good idea. I danced an other-ranks Excuse Me, in which I had ninety partners in ten minutes – three steps with each then change over. They were all so sweet and friendly and delighted to have a chance to meet me in person, which shows that our popularity was not just a newspaper affair, and I just loved it, as I felt that those few minutes dancing with them did more good than any number of write-ups.

There was a cabaret with a most lovely Indian dancer – she did European dances with her Polish husband, who is not in her class and kept almost dropping her, to our great anxiety! I'd have loved to see her Indian dances too – she was quite beautiful. Then Oscar played, Lee sang, Les did an act, and at the last moment Johnny and I were called upon. He made a little speech, then introduced me to say goodbye to Paiforce by doing the finale of the Noël Coward sketch, the Mary Clare toast from 'Cavalcade' and 'I'll see you again', which has proved such a triumphant ending to our shows. They fairly lifted the roof after that, and it made up for all the stickiness of the night before! Brigadier Foote was there, and I sat for some time with him and Brigadier Jackson (the MCA, or Major General i/c Administration, Paiforce), who was so nice and has written a

marvellous letter of thanks to Johnny and the Band. We also have
a lovely letter from Major Grandison to the BBC saying how
much our recordings and broadcasts are appreciated, and asking
for more featuring me, as I'm now so well known out here. It
may perhaps do some good![6]

On Saturday morning I packed frantically – a nightmare
job involving posting one parcel on to myself, and doing up
another of breakable dolls, toys etc. to go by lorry, and cadging
some proper record cases from the broadcasting people for our
Teheran records. However eventually all was stowed away, and
J and I went out for a last shopping, during which we bought
the Isfahan cigarette boxes as a souvenir of Paiforce, and I got
lots of films, which are very scarce in the ME but plentiful
in Baghdad. At half past two we left on the Nairn coach for
Damascus. We had very sad partings from the hotel and staff, and
the most wonderful send-off from our friends, who all turned
out in the heat and dust of the afternoon at a time when most
people are sleeping. They turned up one after the other, Beric
Holt, Peter Ender, Bill Whittle, Trappie, our puppy-like but
sweet conducting NCO Bill Hyde, Major Pennington, George
Bennett on a bicycle just before his ride, and two other nice
young officer fans, and we were a most noisy and jolly crowd
while awaiting the Nairn. Even after it arrived, we dived into
somebody's nearby Mess for a quick beer, leaving a guard to
see that it didn't go without us. I got some quite nice group
photos of them all – a marvellous crowd of people, and I was
so sorry Bob Williams couldn't be there as he'd had to go to
Teheran. Eventually we left, and Johnny and I felt very sad as
we sank back in our seats. The place the Nairn leaves from is
called Heartbreak Corner, as so many artists have been seen off
from there. I have never met such a Command as Paiforce for
warm and helpful people. It is as if the isolation and discomfort
of the place made everyone pull together like one unit. George
Bennett pressed a letter into my hand as we left – one of the
loveliest letters of appreciation I've ever had. And I've got some
more copies of the Iraq Times and some very jolly riding photos
for you. But it's the little tit-bits of information like this that
please us the most; a Naval officer from Khorramshar telling me

that his tough ratings were furtively wiping away tears during
'Vespers'; a boy in the Royal Sussex Regiment (which has been
very badly knocked about) frankly crying during the middle
part of 'The Kerry Dance'; and everywhere lumps in throats
and tear-filled eyes during the 'Cavalcade' toast and 'I'll See You
Again' – then again people crying with laughter at Les Marsh's
clowning, and rapt faces listening to the strings playing Strauss,
and hearty voices joining in Oscar Grasso's medleys. All very
simple and unintellectual things, my darlings, but recalling to
me those marvellous lines of Victoria Sackville-West, which I
so wish I could fully remember, about 'Reality down-fluttering
to a bench'. Because life for the men out here is undoubtedly
reality, and emotions become very keen after a couple of years
in Paiforce, where only the very essentials of life can possibly be
important.

We sat back in the Nairn with all these thoughts whirling in
our heads, and before we knew where we were we were halting
beyond Habbaniya for a cup of tea (3/- each!) in a little desert
café under the ground. Our coach was the air-conditioned
Pullman, with seats which tipped back for the night – very
lucky for us as there were two other coaches like ordinary buses.
We even had a WC and washbasin, but they were incredibly
difficult to make use of owing to the lurching and swaying. As
J put it after one effort, 'I was nearly unhorsed several times.'
We had boxes of sandwiches and fruit given us for supper, and
I lay back watching Orion out of the window – have gazed at
him ever since we left England, and used to point him out to
people from the deck of his namesake. All should have been
very pleasant but for an Iraqi just behind us who had TB or
something, because he coughed every few minutes and followed
it up in the fashion of this part of the world by hawking phlegm
with the most revolting noises right 'from the soles of his
feet', to use Johnny's phrase. The passengers in our coach were
mostly Iraqi, and they sat fingering chains of beads; this is done
in Persia and Iraq not as a way of saying prayers, but simply
for something to do and to prevent fidgeting. We stopped at
Rutbah at about 1.30 a.m., and there was foul tea available but
I didn't get out. Then we left the road and set off direct across

the desert, carrying on steadily all night. At about 9.30 a.m. we arrived at a frontier post, Abou-el-Chamad, where a small mud fort said 'Passport and Customs'. However nothing happened at all except a very welcome cup of tea and a leg-stretcher. An Arab lies on the fort roof, and whenever he sees a vehicle coming he rings a gong and someone down below wakes up and has a look-see! All very primitive! Then on to Damascus, through country which became gloriously fertile – every sort of tree, orchards in full blossom, groves of silver-grey olives with young corn, lime-green, beneath them, then Damascus, a fascinating old city climbing up and down hill, with every sort of architecture crumbling and leaning upon each other. We got there in time for an excellent lunch and wash and brush at the huge Orient Palace Hotel. After lunch Johnny and I were picked up from the Orient Palace Hotel by a Nairn taxi to take us through to Beirut. The Band came over by bus and lorry, but we didn't see them as they had left Baghdad long before us. We have two lorries with all the men coming round by road via Mafraq – they will be several days en route. We had a most wonderful run over the Lebanon. My first impression after Paiforce was of the joy of seeing water everywhere – burns gushing down the mountainsides, and waterfalls, and torrents of green water rushing between avenues of poplar and willow trees, the foothills beyond that amazing blend of pastel red, brown, cream and verdigris which I've seen nowhere else but in the lands of the Bible, and higher still the last snow, lying thickly in long symmetrical streaks that show off the curious formation of these mountains. Amazing verdure after poor Iraq with its hard-won acres – and *flowers!*

3RD APRIL 1944

To resume our trip over the Lebanon, we climbed up over one range, then dropped down into a wide, cultivated valley, with a barrier of snow mountains ahead. Then began an amazing ascent, a marvellously engineered road, hair-pinning its way up between little villages where cream houses, bright red-tiled roofs, and

blue shutters and woodwork gave a most continental effect. The
people seem to be pure Arab, but wear much brighter clothes
than in Iraq. There were the same scarlet anemones that I saw in
Kurdistan growing everywhere, and the slopes were thick with
a bright blue-green bulb-like foliage that had the remains of
what I think were freesia flowers amongst them. Also I saw the
leaves of wild tulips, and a sort of crab apple or plum, that made
the lower slopes like an orchard. We wound our way up and up,
and eventually got to the snow line, the road still slushy here
and there, and a funicular alongside completing the Swiss effect.
Then round a corner we came suddenly on an Army ski-schule
in progress! Truck-loads of jolly-looking officers and men being
driven away, and others still laboriously plodding up the 'nursery
slopes' and stemming down! They could only use the large
patches of snow – continuous running would have been out of
the question. Then began a marvellous descent; the mountains
fairly sweep down into the sea, every inch terraced and
cultivated and dark with cedar and fir trees. The lower hills were
buried in a sea of cloud, and we felt like airmen driving along
above it – then gradually down into the shadow, and the sea
emerging through rifts in the cloud a dazzling silver with grey
shadows moving across it; always our road and the little funicular
curling to and fro, to and fro, with drops of thousands of feet to
tiny dolls' houses in the valley below; then another breathtaking
moment when I saw clusters of pink flowers in the shade of the
cedars, and realised the hillside was covered with wild cyclamen
– then gradually into Beirut, a fascinating town where cool
white Turkish mosques crowd upon Moslem minarets and Greek
Orthodox churches, where Roman and Greek remains crumble
next to modern villas, with crowded bazaars selling everything
under the sun, the Mediterranean with its unique blue washing
a craggy shore, and behind the hills, sweeping up to cloud and
snow; a noisy town, jostling and crowded, with overloaded trams,
and frantically tooting horns and yelling street vendors, colourful
Senegalese and Syrian and French soldiers, very much a foreign
country with nothing at all of the British Possession about it,
marvellous patisseries and cafés where Arab sweetmeats blend
with French pastries; lovely materials from Damascus; little boys

in white shorts and black berets; in fact a place that would take many years to explore thoroughly with its many superimposed civilisations and mingled races.

Johnny and I are in an excellent hotel with first-class food. We have several free days, and as we know no one yet have heaps of time to potter about. We are to be five weeks in Syria, and are going right up into the mountains, and to Aleppo and Tripoli. Am trying to get some riding, but this is not the friendly place Baghdad was, with everybody knowing everybody else, and transport is non-existent.

8TH APRIL 1944

Still no mail – we have been three weeks now. There has been the worst sandstorm in living memory everywhere between Basrah and Cairo, and trains in Palestine have been sanded up for four or five days, and have had to have water and food dropped from planes, so that and our move must explain the delay.

This has been a very happy and interesting week here, with plenty of time to potter around the town watching the people and looking at the shops, which are very good. There are whole roads selling nothing but cloth and silks from Damascus, and I am having a very good look round before falling, and am getting all the advice I can on what wears best, etc. Will probably wait to buy till we get to Damascus itself, or Aleppo, as things are supposed to be cheaper there. However they are not too bad here. Silk brocade (not the gold or silver-thread, but pure silk which wears and washes very well and is used for dressing-gowns, house-coats etc., is about £5.10.0 for four and a half yards. There are exquisite patterns of Chinese red on green and cream, etc. The gold and silver thread brocade for coatees is much more expensive, but lasts a lifetime, I'm told. However we'll see – at present I just look with watering mouth.

We have had a broadcast fixed up for next Sunday (it will be from our sixth capital since leaving home!) and I discovered to my joy that I could practise in the studio at certain times morning and afternoon. Then I was pounced on by the local

Welfare Officer, an ex-actor, to read Olivia in 'Twelfth Night' at one of the play-readings he organises for the troops, civilians, and native students of English from the University. This was rather sudden, and not my line of country, but proved to be great fun. I went in to his office, as he later put it '…in quest of a horse (was enquiring about riding) and came out with Shakespeare!' We rehearsed Tuesday night, and performed Wednesday, both at the Beirut British Council rooms. There were some excellent people, several of them professionals. One was Nigel Bruce-Lockhart, husband of Sylvia who I sing for in London. He is head of YMCA's out here – a Shakespearian actor and singer, and he read Sir Andrew Aguecheek marvellously. One Col Sir Gyles Isham, KRR's [King's Royal Rifles], was Malvolio, and first-class. And the Welfare Officer himself, Major Lasbrey, read Sir Toby Belch. The man who is OC British Broadcasting, Staff Sergeant Vickers (ex-BBC) read the Fool. Tho' I says it as shouldn't, I acquitted myself well in the rather difficult part of Olivia, and they couldn't believe I had done no elocution or Shakespeare before, apart of course from school.

On the lighter side, have discovered the most divine 'Patisserie Suisse' here – chocolate with oceans of cream on it and cakes that defy description! Am sending home some of their biscuits, chocolate and sugared almonds – but oh my darlings, how I long to take you there and feed you on the cakes and chocolate!

Johnny is photographing hard with his camera, and studying it seriously. He's got some beauties. Am also very bitten, as have been reading a book about it, and have found out all I was doing wrong. We spend our time in the excellent photo shops we've found, and am spending pounds on prints and enlargements.

On Thursday Johnny and I went out to the Remount Depot here, where, after overcoming formidable difficulties of obstructionism, we found it was perfectly easy for us to ride. The Corporal in charge of horses took us out to show us the way about, and we went into some woods of tall fir trees with sandy rides between them. I was on a chestnut Barb (half-Arab) and while Johnny was trotting quietly along the Corporal told me to take the pony off for a canter and rejoin them later. Well

the darned animal got right away with me when I was on the
way back. I didn't like to turn into the ride they were in as I'd
have upset Johnny's horse (rather too skittish for a beginner
anyway) so I carried on down a broad ride, not knowing where
I was at all and egged on by some very naughty little Arab
jockeys on racing ponies. About five times I thought I was
getting the wretched horse steadied up, but each time it plunged
forward and got the bit between its teeth again. And can these
Arabs sprint! We whizzed out of the wood, across a small wadi,
down a track between two fields, and then, horror of horrors,
across a tarmac road where (perhaps luckily!) I couldn't see
what was coming! However, we were safely over, and tearing
down another track, scattering babies, children, old women
and donkeys in every direction! The pony was going flat out,
and I am convinced quite blindly by then. We rounded a bend
and I saw a car going very slowly along the track, completely
filling it. After a last hopeless effort so stop, I decided the only
thing to do that could save self and pony from a bad crash was
to throw myself off. So I prepared carefully, picked a soft spot,
and jumped, remembering all I'd picked up about parachuting
on our tour to the Airborne Division! All told I didn't do too
badly, considering we were in a flat-out gallop! I landed on
my feet, curled up sideways, and took a lot of the weight on
shoulder and elbow, but managed to bury my head very hard
in the sand, and was effectively sandbagged for a few minutes. I
came to in a Syrian house, with very sweet people dabbing me
with water and disinfectant, and found myself none the worse
except for the odd graze, a bruise worthy of 6d a peep[7] and a
broken back tooth. However I couldn't remember where I was
for some time. Eventually Beirut came back to me, and then the
Corporal arrived, much alarmed, to my great relief. The pony
had got back in its stable quite OK, little devil, and I am still
wondering if I wouldn't have been better to stick on him, but I
am convinced he would have crashed into the car.

They do go sort of blind when bolting sometimes. I
remounted and rode back to where Johnny was waiting, in a
fever of anxiety of course. I must have looked a sight as I was
covered in sand, they'd dabbed Gentian Violet all over my face,

and I was still very dazed! I haven't breathed a word about it to anyone as the Corporal would get told off, and anyway it was unfortunate as the riding had been difficult to fix. It was *not* a good example for Johnny as a beginner, either! We came home and I lay down and took three aspirins, then ate a large lunch, and practised. However I developed a splitting head and slight temperature in the evening so went to bed for dinner. Next day I felt quite all right, except for a stiff jaw that I have had ever since – maddening, as I can't eat all the lovely food here! However, it does not worry me singing luckily! (Not quite true – I had to avoid very high notes, which involved a wide open mouth, for some days!)

8TH APRIL 1944. BEIRUT

My last letter was the sad story of 'Bolted with in Beirut'. However, your tough daughter was perfectly healthy next morning, and hasn't looked back since, which proves what I have always known since childhood days, that my head can take harder knocks than most people's! I kept quiet on Friday morning, and practised a little after lunch. The Studio is the one and only one at Radio-Levant, which is some way up the hillside. It is a French affair, but the British have a couple of hours a day for broadcasting to their troops. The place is an ex-Turkish HQ – a big square with lovely views of the mountains and sea, then a huge courtyard known as 'La Grande Sérail', the whole guarded by fine-looking black troops with red fezzes, who look most warlike, but have the natures of children, and I'm sure could never bayonet anybody.

That evening we did our first show in Syria (you will appreciate my anxiety as to what it was best to do while being bolted with the day before!). It was at the big Transit Camp, and went over very well. The drive there was spectacular – a flame-coloured sunset, and red sands, deep blue sea, and purple hills behind. The Band are now living in a Holiday Camp by the sea – they are very happy, and bathe all day. But we had a sudden gale and thunder and hail the other day, which rather alarmed them as they thought their tents were going to leave them! Our lorries got in on Wednesday, having hit off the sandstorm all one day, poor things. Then yesterday we left after breakfast to go to Sidon, 1½ hours' run down the coast, to a hospital there. The drive was lovely – orange and olive groves, with ripe fruit on the trees in some and blossom smelling sweetly in others, then incredibly blue seas breaking on the sands, and hillsides carpeted with flowers.

We arrived at the hospital to find that their new OC was a nice Col Bruce we'd met at 61 BGH at Shaibah! Also the QM and QMS were old friends from Crookham, so the Band were well cared for. I slept in a ward for sick Sisters (the Sisters' quarters are tents, very damp just now), so I was lucky. I heard news of a riding school every afternoon, so Johnny and I went along and scrounged horses. It was all very primitive and elementary – one or two keen people, who knew very little about it themselves, trying to teach others who knew nothing. There was a big school fenced off, and there various learners disported themselves, while I tried to give Johnny an hour's instruction. But oh! For Major Bennett's beautifully and sternly run classes!

We did two shows, in a large dingy dining-hall, no proper stage, curtains or lights. However, they seemed to enjoy it. Then a nice party in the Officers' Club there, where I met two French Senior officers, one Naval, one Army. Had sung 'Les Filles de Cadiz' for them, and we talked much French. A quick call in at the Sergeants' Mess, then bed. The hospital is a mass of wild flowers between the tents, and very lovely with hills behind and sea in front. The biblical town of Sidon stands nearby, complete with Crusader Castle on a bluff overlooking the sea.

12TH APRIL 1944. BEIRUT

My darlings, I am ensconced under the drier at the best hairdresser in Beirut, having just returned from an hour's riding. I was out alone with Johnny and feeling a little nervous at the responsibility of a beginner, but we got on very well – he had a good quiet horse, and I had a much more sober one today, though no mouth at all. J is getting on very well, and looks so efficient on a horse that people think he's been at it much longer than he really has – today was only his fifth ride. But we go very quietly, as it is difficult for a beginner always having strange horses and strange places. We ride through beautiful woods – tall fir-trees that have had all their branches cut and just a tuft left on top, so that they look like leggy mushrooms; and vistas of mountains, rather blue and misty today, with the snows gleaming out from the distance; and everywhere the most intoxicating smell of orange blossom: little Arab jockeys out on racing ponies; dashing officers of the Syrian Army exercising beautiful Arab stallions; Indians driving mule wagons; and occasionally camels, which our horses loathe and shy away from as they smell so.

We are by now experts at tram-boarding, which is a business requiring no little technique in this town. A tram draws up, so crowded that there just isn't room for another body on it; about twenty people charge forward; one forgets one is British, cuts in in front of them, treads on toes and pushes furiously and – lo and behold, everybody is aboard and all laughing happily. The Conductor worms his way along and says 'Cinq piastres' (about a penny farthing) and you give him a pitying look and say 'Militaire' whereupon he winks broadly and passes on. This is a racket – there is some sort of a bunderbust whereby the Military do not pay if standing, but of course every Conductor asks one for one's fare and the greenhorn pays up, which is just giving so much baksheesh; I find I hardly ever pay now, even when seated. The whole system is gloriously elastic!

On Sunday we are doing a broadcast. The whole show cannot get into the small studio here, so they are doing a quarter of an hour of dance band with Lee and Les Marsh. After that there is a short news, then a programme called 'Evening Star', generally records of some artist. I have been asked to be Sunday's Star, and am doing 10 minutes of singing, accompanied by our small orchestra. Will do 'Les Filles de Cadiz' for one, it being a French station, but haven't yet decided on my other songs. The shows go very well here. Last night we were at the Naval Base, and I met various WRNS who had travelled out with me. After the show some Commander got up, and after I had been given a lovely bunch of roses, he made a long speech telling the ratings to draw three morals from our show – Drill, Dress and Discipline. He proceeded to praise these three things in the Band (while we all nearly burst out laughing, especially as our clothes are much the worse for wear when seen close to, and the men are really rather undisciplined!). He also said the Band were a pretty poor crowd to have collected only one girl, but as she was such a good one would they please take care of her! Then, having given his ratings a fearful ticking off for being slackly dressed, he shook hands with us and departed!

Later. Here we are up the mountains for a show, and I am going to try and write a bit as I have a long time off. Have just done my solos, the Schubert 'Serenade', 'My Hero', and 'Invitation to the Dance', quite successfully. What I want to tell you about, and it will need to be at least one letter to itself, is our Monday's trip to the Mountain Warfare place. It was a marvellous experience. We set off at 9.00 a.m. on a lovely morning, through the crowded streets of Beirut out past the orange groves, then up and up over the first rocky foothills with their groves of pine trees where the pale wild cyclamen grow everywhere, and fields of young corn with daisies, poppies, cornflowers, and a sort of bright magenta gladiolus or montbretia; Beirut getting more and more distant and toy-like, and the sea beyond more translucent as we got higher. Then we stopped at a village called Bik Fayah where we had to await other transport. The Macadam road ceased there, and we left our bus and waited for the vehicles that were being sent. We had quite a long while there, and explored the little town, clambering up and down the rough steps that connect it, and gorging ourselves with bananas and oranges that we haggled for in a little local shop. The orchards are just coming into bloom, and everything grows marvellously on that rich mountain soil. The village people are so friendly and healthy and happy-looking after the wretched Persians and Iraqis – the children brightly dressed and plump and rosy. Little chapels are perched everywhere just like in Austria – its strange how mountain folk tend to be the same the world over. Eventually the Mountain Warfare people arrived, very dashing in their peaked caps and heavy boots. The men who had been in the bus got into two three-tonners, and our own three lorries carried on too. Johnny and I got into a jeep and set off ahead. There followed a run that was really hair-raising, only that I was so enthralled with the views and the flowers that I quite forgot to be frightened. The Mam Rattigan was nothing to it. We came over the spur of a foothill, and had a clear view of the valley we had to go up. The camp was right at the very head of it, high up in the snows at the foot of the last run-up to a great mountain barrier. We had to work our way by devious twists and hairpins, up the gorge on one side, with a river thousands of feet below, then down and across it, and up the other side again, and on up to where the little huts were perched just below the summit. I kept catching glimpses of interesting flowers, but dared not stop the Jeep. The men on the lorries had a most frightening time – the vehicles couldn't make the hairpins in one turn, so had to back right onto crumbly road edges with just nothing below time and time again. And three of our most nerveless types, Lee Sheridan, Oscar and Tommy Hopkins, got out and walked eleven miles uphill rather than stay in their vehicles. J and I were staying seven miles below the camp itself, in a sort of 'Pension' run by an old Syrian woman; it was a most primitive affair re sanitary arrangements, cooking, washing etc., but a nice stone house with bare clean floors, whitewashed walls, and a triple-arched window in the hall-cum-living room looking Southwest away down the valley to the sea. Army rations had been sent down for us to eat, and the old woman turned out to be no cook, so we had a picnic of tinned things heated on a terrifying primus, which I couldn't cope with at all. We kept rushing out to greet the lorries as they struggled past one by one, the men all mopping their brows after the awful run. We had watched them miles away below us, winding to and fro and had counted anxiously to see that our little flock of five were all present. And we watched them on their way toiling up the even worse seven miles to the camp.

13th April 1944. Beirut

And now back to our eyrie – J and I sitting eating horrible
tinned sausage meat and spring onions in our sunny rooms; and
then three lonely little figures appearing, shirt-sleeves rolled
up and sweaty-browed: Lee, Oscar and Tommy, the hikers…we
hailed them in, and broke the sad news to them that they still
had seven miles to go, and to comfort them dived into our store
of tins. Lee, who is no mean chef, got down to it and produced
the usual Army meat and veg, and the old lady made tea – her
only accomplishment in the culinary line. After lunch a young
officer came down in a jeep and fetched J and me up to see the
place we were playing in. They were hard at work converting
a garage for us, and you can't imagine the shambles when we
arrived! The stage was half-built, no lighting yet, and the floor
of wet mud. It looked quite hopeless, but somehow they got it
ready by evening. As you can imagine, it turned bitterly cold at
night, and a wind got up – we had come up for the show in an
open jeep, then I changed in a very cold bedroom, and during
the show the side door had to be left open behind the stage as
our stuff all overflowed, so it was generally very chilly! However,
I wore 2 vests under my dress, and the grey coatee over it, and
they lent me an oil stove, which kept one half of me thawed! We
had no dressing rooms of course, so poor Les had to dress almost
out of doors, while I crouched in a little space behind the stage.
But it was well worth it; our audience (Scotsmen, a well-known
Scots regiment) were terrific. They had had only one all-soldier
party before, and got no cinemas, so our coming was a real event
for them. After the show, J and I went to the Officers' Mess – a
most unintellectual crowd but very interesting on their training.
They learn only very elementary skiing – kick-turns, stemming
and perhaps a stem-christie – but they do terrific climbs and
carry a 50lb pack all the time. The skiing season is now over, and
they are rock climbing. The rock looks to me very dangerous
here – it is soft and brittle – but they seem to enjoy it very
much, and are of course as tough as anything. They were pulled
out of Italy to do this course, and will probably be off again as
soon as their training (five or six months) is over. After a hot

brandy to warm us weaklings up, we were driven down to our village, where J and I brewed tea and heated water by the light of an oil stove. Then to bed. I had one covering, a sort of very warm duvet thing, but had to pinch another off a spare bed before I could warm up. But what a lovely night – bright cold stars, and a full moon lighting the snows, and the little villages gleaming out from the mountainsides so cosily.

Next morning we were up betimes as we wanted to walk part of the way back. I had a longing to pick wild cyclamen, and they are as you know rather choosy little people – they will grow like weeds in one spot, and in another you can walk for miles and see nary a one. The jeep was due to pick us up at a quarter to nine, so we set off before half past eight, missing breakfast. The old lady was heartbroken at our going – she had brought her daughter and countless grandchildren along the afternoon before, to greet us and to finger my dresses, which were hanging up in my bedroom. I was the first British girl to have been to the camp, and all the villagers were very curious about me, and kept stopping us to ask questions. We set off walking in warm sunlight, down the winding road with streams rushing along everywhere, here led on crumbling aqueducts, there broken by a turning wheel so that the force of them shouldn't damage the roads. I was praying that the jeep wouldn't arrive, as we walked and walked through orchards and layers of cultivation, and never a cyclamen could I see. I needn't have worried – two of our vehicles needed their brakes repaired before the run down, and it was an hour and a half before we were picked up. We gradually left the village behind – though everywhere those almost vertical and boulder-strewn slopes were seamed with centuries of patient terracing, where a few square feet of corn straggle among the stones. And suddenly, round a corner, amongst great grey rocks I saw first one, then another, and another! Little pale flowers springing out of clefts in the rock, such delicate things to find at that rugged height – I suddenly developed mountain-goat tendencies, and shattered Johnny by scrambling about trying to reach pinker and larger flowers. I found various other interesting things – orchises, marjoram, queer shrubs, and a dwarf broom; also an ugly flower with big bulb-like leaves, that has a cone of buds on which one pale pink spiky bloom appears at a time. But there was nothing that I could see to touch the alpines.

We had a marvellous walk, with the snowy barrier behind us very beautiful and clear-cut in the morning light, and the camp looking incredibly small and high up, perched on its ledge. They have no avalanches here – I suppose there isn't enough depth of snow. Eventually along came our jeep, and we climbed in and set off down the worst part of the run – the series of hairpin bends called the Seven Sisters, leading down to the bridge across the torrent. We were down well ahead of the lorries and watched them from up the other side winding laboriously down. It's amazing to me how 3-tonners make that road at all. Then into Bik Fayah, and a haggle over oranges and bananas, as we were beginning to feel the lack of breakfast. The Mountain Warfare people left us there, and our bus was waiting.

The drive down into Beirut was most lovely – one has a panorama of the town that is almost a bird's eye view, and the sea is exquisitely purple and green with sailing ships on it. The last two miles through the orange groves are almost overpoweringly fragrant. Many of the trees have ripe fruit on them, and each small owner was wheeling his day's pick into town on a rickety barrow as we drove along. We have two more Mountain Warfare places to visit, one higher than this, so perhaps there might be a chance of some skiing! I dreamt I was doing lovely Christies somehow or other without skis last night! By the way, I took my Ski Year Book and Ski Notes and Queries up the mountain to read in that suitable setting, and the latter died what I somehow feel is an appropriate death – down the lavatory of that primitive cottage!

13TH APRIL 1944, EVENING

Here we are up at Aley again for our second show here – a lousy place and a mouldy audience – like so many HQs no trouble taken at all; we have found infinitely better stages, lighting, dressing-room accommodation etc. right in the wilds. However,

Maleesh! (Arabic for Who cares? or What does it matter? The most frequently used word in their vocabulary.) I haven't told you yet about Sunday – Easter Day, and interesting in many ways. In the morning we saw a big crowd collected outside a church, and waited to see what was doing. It was a Ceremonial Mass, and there was an impressive procession of Bishops, Acolytes, and choir, all in lovely vestments, then a lot of Generals emerged, to be greeted by a fanfare of bugles from the Syrian Band, and a round of applause, according to their popularity, from the crowd. The French got a good hand, the poor British Senior Officer came down the steps in rather a frigid silence. Yet the people of this country prefer us to the French, or so I am told. Beirut is of course more Gallicised than the rest of Syria. Then I went to a dressmaker to whom I had been recommended, and there I made a most astonishing discovery – a girl with a most beautiful soprano voice. It came about thus; there was someone playing the piano when I arrived – a very sweet-looking young girl who jumped up and showed me to an inner room. Then while I was fitting my dress the couturière found out that I was a singer, and said: 'Oh you must meet my young sister – she adores singing and has a most wonderful voice.' Well, I went out and talked to the girl, who was charming and so keen and really seriously wanting to study. She had started at sixteen with a Russian in Beirut, who had nearly ruined her voice, and there was no other teacher in the country to whom they could send her. She is struggling to learn from some book or other on her own. I persuaded her to sing, expecting the usual thing, but it was quite staggering: an amazing full mature voice of beautiful quality, perfect intonation, good control, and a range from contralto low A to top E and F in alt. She has some records of Galli Curci and Tetrazzini and other sopranos, and can sing the full cadenzas from them. Oh to get her to a first-class teacher – it is tragic that there is absolutely nowhere for her here. She is twenty-one and should be at work by now. She was asking me what she should do, and what I thought about her singing, but what can one say about singing in 5 minutes? The only thing I could suggest was that they should send her to Jerusalem, where she could get fairly good teaching. I am really very interested in her and should so love to be able to help. Her voice is so naturally good as to make one who has struggled for five years very envious of such facility!

18TH APRIL 1944. ORIENT PALACE HOTEL, DAMASCUS

I think I last wrote on Thursday during our show at Aley, an awful dump as regards show and audience, tho' an exquisite place, high on the mountainside looking down to the sea. On Friday we played in the Hospital above Beirut, and on Saturday in a big workshop place, both nice, but was tired, strung-up and silly, and in tears during each show, with J being so sweet and understanding. Am quite OK now, and was in good form for the broadcast on Sunday, luckily. I sang the old Schubert Serenade, and 'Filles de Cadiz', and should have done 'Vissi d'Arte' too, but there wasn't time – the little 'Evening Star' programme only has ten minutes. Afterwards J and I had a terrific party with two most interesting and charming people – Tony Vickers, the Staff Sergeant who is OC broadcasting in Beirut (an ex-BBC man, and a real example of how one finds the best people in the ranks these days – he refused a commission) and a most beautiful half-French girl, Nadine Cave, whose English RAF husband was killed not so long ago. She is News Editress for the British section of Radio Levant. Her father has gone pro-Nazi and is Political Editor of 'L'Illustration' – she would not tell me his name, but he must have been someone big in the world of political journalism before the war. Nadine hates him so much that she says she would shoot him if she had a chance. She is of course most interesting politically and knows much inside information. We went to a tiny place called 'L'Excelsior' run by a Viennese or Hungarian refugee, and ate real goulash. I started the evening on 5 Palestinian sherries, then we had vin rouge during dinner, and topped up with Cyprus brandy. It only had the effect of making us talk nineteen to the dozen though, and as Nadine and Tony are both highly intelligent and interesting, it was a memorable evening.

Later. I wish I could have taken down our talk at 'L'Excelsior'

in shorthand – it would have made interesting if rather
dangerous reading. We had to talk low and carefully a lot of
the time, as the situation in this country is not all it might be.
Nadine believes in de Gaulle as in God, and says Churchill is
making the biggest mistake ever in trusting Spears, of whom
she cannot say enough bad. By the way, Beirut was really in the
Lebanon – a state of its own with a rather farcical government.
We crossed the border into Syria proper coming here. That
Sunday evening was one I shall remember vividly – how lovely
is a keen and animated conversation amongst people who really
have something to say!

I must confess to you, before we go further, about Saturday's
shopping expedition. We wandered quite by accident into a
most first-class shop. It is owned by one Michel Terzis, and he
is a robber, but everything in his shop is good and genuine and
I had rather be robbed in a place like that than in the bazaars
where the things are often trash. Oscar Grasso was in there, and
he, being an Italian and a wealthy man, has a great appreciation
of beautiful things. He also knows how to handle the Oriental
salesman, and I was duly introduced to Terzis and his minions as
'the lady who sings with our orchestra', and Turkish coffee was
brought along. Then began a dazzling display of silks, brocades,
jewellery, furniture, leatherware and so on, all really lovely stuff.
I had worked out a careful budget beforehand, and am now
a good haggler with no finer feelings left when it comes to
bargaining. However, I had intended to buy nothing that day. I
came out having spent £17. Don't be alarmed, my darlings, I've
been saving ever since we came abroad in order to buy here.
And every single thing I got in there was a bargain, as Terzis
wanted my custom for an advertisement. I told Nadine, who has
lived here for over two years, exactly what I paid for everything,
and she was overcome at 'the old robber' as she calls him, having
let me have such gifts. I fell heavily for a pair of aquamarine
earrings that struck me as a perfect match for my pendant.
Two very lovely stones not at all well set in native silver, which
he reduced after some time from £5 to £3.[8] You would have
been tickled to see us in Terzis's – we were a couple of hours
wandering round and looking (luckily you can look at wares

to your heart's content and no need to buy in this part of the world). Monsieur would come creeping up and whisper in my ear, 'Mademoiselle – for you – just for you – I have decided I will make a leetle reduction – already it is a gift, but I will make you another price – promise me you will tell no one – for you and for you only, because I wish you to have them – I will make you this offer – the earrings for £4.' Whereupon, despite many compliments on my beauty, I would steel my heart and say, 'No thank you, Mr Terzis, I am really not buying earrings today.' He would go away, and ten minutes later he'd be back again! It's all such fun and really quite an art, gauging how far they will go. It is very muddling though, changing in one's mind from the £ sterling to the £ Syrian, as they will cunningly quote a price in sterling that is really more than what they ask in Syrian, but the exchange is so complicated that one can't work it out. Also they alternate between yards, metres and the Turkish 'pic' of 27 inches. I have notes in a little book of what I can afford and how much of each measure to ask for.

On Monday I woke up with a fearful hangover, having slept very badly owing to the rocking-horse tendencies that my bed had suddenly acquired! This Palestinian sherry is poison, and I shan't touch it again. Luckily we didn't leave for Damascus until 1.30 p.m. so I had pretty well recovered by then. (Note – not altogether – I can still remember how the mountains rose and fell alarmingly during the bus drive.)

What money I hadn't spent in Terzis's went on leaving the hotel. They have an amazing system whereby each of the umpteen bellhops carries part of the luggage part of the way! However, eventually we were embarked, and set off for what must be one of the loveliest runs in the world. Syria is a country of immense diversity of colouring and landscape. The Beirut side of the mountains is dark, with grey craggy boulders, loamy soil and heavy cedar trees. Over here the earth varies from pure dazzling white chalk to light red, and the main tree colour is the golden-green of young poplars and willows. Yesterday was a day of clouds too – heavy rainstorms sweeping over, with rifts of hot blue sky in between. As we came up over the first and highest barrier, we plunged into damp woolly mist. The place where they'd been skiing a fortnight ago was bare sopping earth, water everywhere, and no flowers as yet. Then we came down out of the cloud, and had an incredible vision of the second barrier across that wide fertile plain I told you about – cloud-shadow everywhere, with here a shaft of sunlight, there a silver rainstorm, ahead the mountains frowning and purple beneath a storm, and far below the plain smiling and sun-dappled. We came down through the last wisps of mist and into the light – our road curling to and fro in amazing bends, and the valley below like a flat sea of cultivation. It must once have been a lake, very beautiful in its ring of mountains; it is now a fertile haven between the two ranges that rise very steeply on either side. Streams bowl across it everywhere, and the orchards are in full bloom. I have two clear pictures of it – our road through an avenue of young poplars, golden-green in the sunlight, with the mountains beyond blue-black under the storm; and a little peninsula into one of the brooks, scarlet with anemones against the turquoise of the water. Then we started off on the climb over the second range – not so high and rocky as the first, with shrubs and broom and some sort of wild fruit tree covered in white blossom growing on the slopes, and upland valleys where goats and sheep graze on the new grass. Then down into Damascus, following a steep gorge. One follows a mountain river that is now in heavy spate of thick green water – chalk cliffs rising creamy-white and steep on either side, and a fringe of poplars, willow, aspen, alder and other unknown trees on each bank. The water is run off into countless canals and channels, and often it is on both sides of the road at once, flowing at different levels, the rushing together and meeting with a terrific surge of cross-current, and off again to turn a mill-wheel somewhere, its force broken by baffle-walls or tree trunks.

The town is fascinating and beautiful and I long for days in which to explore it. We only got here at about 4.30, and went straight out to the Transit Camp where the men are staying, and which was a rude shock after the loveliness of the run. It is a mud-village like the lowest native quarters, with dirty huts that have broken windows, no light or heating and not a stick of furniture – just bare floor. The Band have been to many camps and they are all rather bad, but generally better than this. People seem to expect troops in transit to live like pigs, and I suppose the fact that most of them only spend a night at a camp passing through explains why no one bothers to make the place comfortable. However our poor men have to live there, and keep instruments and stage kit clean and smart. They have no beds, only bed boards to sleep on, which is hard on the elderly ones and the people who are low-grade in health. Also they are not tough and fit like ordinary troops, which is a thing people forget. Johnny went straight off to see Welfare Officers and Area Commanders and I think things are being done. I do hope so; we have many reporting sick anyway, with tummy trouble and suchlike. Also several found the run up to Sannine too much for them, and are dreading our trip to The Cedars – the next mountain warfare place we go to, 6,000ft up. The height and steepness seemed to shatter them. Two of our brass players who have chest trouble have Doctor's Certificates forbidding them to play at heights of over 1,000 feet, which all tends to make life difficult. Cairo has refused them a higher rate living allowance, which would allow them to 'live out' in YMCAs or Church Army Hostels, so they have to go wherever they are sent. I feel awful being in such luxury here. I have what must be the bridal suite – huge bedroom with most comfy bed, and a balcony looking out South West to the snows, over a lovely little mosque with twin white minarets, and big bathroom and a sort of hall – all to myself.

It is quieter than Beirut here. My room there was high above the main street, sunny and interesting as one had a view of the fruit bazaar up a side-road, but very noisy, with trams clanging along and the Syrians performing their usual voluntaries on terrific klaxons. An interesting feature of driving here is the notices one sees up: a red board with 'Malaria. Camping forbidden for five miles'. Then five miles on a green board with 'Malaria. Camping allowed for ten miles. Use nets'. And so on. The only thing in favour of the malarial mosquito is that it does not fly more than 2 miles from its birthplace, so the danger areas can be plotted fairly accurately. Talking of flying – a little detail that is rather illuminating about Paiforce – so bare and hot and impossible is the country that the birds nest inside houses wherever they can. Whenever we did an afternoon show, there was always an obbligato of sparrows carrying on their nest-building quite unperturbed!

19TH APRIL 1944. DAMASCUS

Here we are in the middle of two shows at a camp some miles outside the town – rather lovely with some of the largest hills in this part of the Lebanon, rising to the South and still well snow-covered.

J and I had such an interesting time yesterday afternoon and again this morning. We set off to find the bazaars, and asked our way of a funny little man who firmly picked us up and insisted on showing us round. He was not at all the usual guide or tout, and turned out to be most extraordinarily helpful and interesting, though at first we did our level best to shake him off. He has literally taken us everywhere, and insisted upon our taking local trams, which are very cheap, instead of gharries, and walked miles himself, and was quite contented to wait ages while we photographed or bargained. We have seen so much in a morning and afternoon that I hardly know where to begin. Yesterday we were swept right through the main bazaars, as we were assured they were only for tourists, and generally rather expensive and not too good. We stopped to look through the archway of the main citadel, which is now taken over by the Syrian Gendarmerie, and we made friends with some of the gendarmes and ended up by being invited in and allowed to take photos (all strictly against orders) and of course consuming the usual Turkish coffee. It was all very comic; we were posed in a lovely group consisting of self, the Sous-Officier, and several others, when suddenly Monsieur le Commandant appeared and they all fled in terror. However he averted his eyes tactfully, and turned out quite friendly. We were shown the lovely police horses, kept in stables thousands of years old, hollowed out of the walls, and we climbed the battlements, and looked out over the roofs and four hundred and forty mosques of Damascus. We saw the Civil Prison, and were shown age-old loopholes, from which the Arabs threw bombs at the French in 1925. There was a bird's eye view of the famous Omayad Mosque with its great marble courtyard. Eventually we tore ourselves away after fond farewells and promises to send photographs to all and sundry. The Sous-Officier turned out to be also the Bandmaster of the Police Band so he and Johnny got on very well. Most of them spoke a bit of French, and our little guide, who speaks umpteen languages, interpreted in Arabic when things got involved. Well, we walked all through the Old City, where the things that are sold in the bazaars are made – mostly by poor Armenians or Greek Orthodox Christians, as the Muslims here tend to be well-to-do. We saw iron and steel work; brass and inlaying being done; brocade being worked in little side streets on an incredible contraption of pulleys that looked too Heath Robinson for words, on which the worker controls the different colours of silk on pedals, just like playing the organ (this was very beautiful – dusty old mud-walled rooms with sunlight playing on priceless silks and thread of pure gold and silver. But the workers are at it from dawn till dark – laborious and patient work that must be a fearful strain on the eyes); then we watched old men carving out wooden pegs, chessman and suchlike, squatting on the ground, right hand doing what looked like playing the double bass, but which rotated the wood, the left hand controlling a sharp knife, and the left toe applying the necessary pressure. An old boy this morning made two beautiful lemon-wood chessmen for us in a couple of minutes. The price was 25 piastres or about 6d, but I gave him 60 for his unique big toe.

Our next visit was the most amazing of the lot – glass-blowing; a crowd of men and quite small boys squatting round a furnace, pulling out molten glass on the end of a four-foot iron tube, swinging it airily around to get it to the necessary shape (missing each other by inches) then blowing it out, the whole process of turning out a jug, vase, or whatnot, taking just a few minutes. We saw the place where Paul was let down from the window in a basket, and the famous East Gate, and the Street called Straight, and many lovely mosques. And lastly we went into a very well-known shop called Nassan. Asfar and Sarkis is *the* one, but it is very expensive and catches the rich tourists. All those who are in the know go to Nassan, who has a marvellous shop – room after room of silks, furniture, carpets, etc. mostly their own work. We had very little time left so we promised to come back next morning, and dashed home for a quick high tea and pack. Then our show at the Garrison Theatre – it started very sticky, but we really 'got them' and ended up by having a most enthusiastic audience.

19TH APRIL 1944. DAMASCUS

Am rushing to try and get this finished during Show No 2 here, but keep having to dash in and sing.

20TH APRIL 1944

Couldn't get any more done last night, and have forgotten my ink tonight, so here goes in pencil. I'd just finished telling you about our Tuesday afternoon's exploring in Damascus. Well, yesterday morning J and I set off to go back to Nassan's shop, and we did our best to avoid the little guide, but he found us trying to board a tram, and again refused to be shaken off – and again we were ultimately very glad he was with us. However, I spent two hours in Nassan's, and ended up by coming away with another dress-length of brocade! It was a slow business; I had completely fallen for this particular one the night before, but it was too expensive. There was a marvellous character of a salesman – one Monsieur Gabriel, with whom I thought I could bargain, 'tho really it is not a haggling sort of shop. However this morning young Mr Nassan was behind the counter in person, and wouldn't hear of any reduction beyond the 10% that I'd already been offered. I was just about to walk out when Mons Gabriel, who is the Sales Manager, came rushing out. There followed the usual beating about the bush and coffee-drinking, and eventually I was persuaded to go back into the brocade room. Well, of course the outcome of it all was that I got my length – 6¼yds roughly, 40ins wide, for £10, which was the price I'd fixed on as my maximum possible. It is a glorious one, darlings – it is their Grade 1 Artificial Silk brocade, which washes (in fact every length is washed and dry cleaned before selling) and it is 'Sun and Shadow on Snow' – a pale ice-blue ground, with the pattern of warm apricot – the whole effect glowing and warm, yet with all the folds mysteriously blue. After we concluded the deal, which I did with Monsieur Gabriel, Nassan having retired in disapproval, I saw all over the huge shop, and took a photograph in the big room full of lovely furniture. Then we went and saw the garden, the rabbits and chickens, and the Nassans' house – a nice Oriental one with a cool courtyard full of orange and lemon trees, roses, lilacs and vines – and met Mr Nassan again and managed to thaw him. The firm has been going for 90 years, and before the war used to supply most of Liberty's silks – I longed to spend pounds there – they had some exquisite things, including a mosaic table ordered by Lawrence on King Faisal's behalf and never delivered as Faisal abdicated and left the country. The pure silk brocades and the gold and silver ones are unbelievably mouth-watering – and ruinous! After we had eventually said our goodbyes, we set off again – we saw the Gate of St Thomas and Ananias' House, all in the fascinating Christian Quarter. The old walls are still v well preserved, with houses built into them. The colour everywhere is most vivid – Armenian women with lace veils, Bedouins with children strapped on their backs and dressed in magenta, yellow, scarlet and blue, Circassian Cavalry with curly lambskin hats, skull-capped Jews, donkeys, mules and ponies, but here gaily be-tasselled and hung with bells. Coolies jog past with long poles on which are slung full shopping baskets that they are delivering for housewives (an idea for war-time shopping!); and there are men with marvellous brass contraptions slung on their backs clashing a pair of brass cymbals and carrying baskets of oranges, which they squeeze into a glass for a few piastres.

20TH APRIL 1944. BAALBEC, SYRIA

We continued on our way, past the myriad little shops where
whole families work, from the youngest boy to the oldest
grandpapa. I suppose that is how they develop such uncanny
skill at their handicrafts – the precision work I've seen done
with the most primitive of tools is amazing. Our last visit was
to the gold and silver bazaar – a huge roofed-in area where
countless small tradesmen ply, each with a little sort of cubicle
and a stall displaying his wares. Our little man took us straight
to the two which he said were best, and we watched small boys
doing the delicate filigree work. I bought three silver bracelets,
and two brooches – for Pam, Liz, and an adorable baby one
for Jane, and the brooches for Mrs K and Mrs M. Then home
(stopping to look at some lovely ruined Roman Gates and to
peep into the great Court of Omayad Mosque) – through the
bazaars – long alleyways with arched tin roofs still full of bullet
holes from the Arab troubles – where there are quarters selling
nothing but shoes; shop after shop with great strings of leather
sandals of every colour, some gleaming with beads or brass studs;
then masses of baskets; then flowers and pot plants; then harness-
shops, the steel bazaar, the brass bazaar, all in the cool shade of
the cobbled alleys. In the centre of it all, our guide showed us
a very beautiful mosque, which was where the camel-caravans
used to stay when they came in to market in the old days – the
animals in the courtyard, and their owners in little rooms all
round the gallery. By that time it was past two, and we'd had no
lunch and had to be off for our two shows at Qatana at 3.30,
so we said goodbye to our guide – a little Greek Orthodox
Christian, who had really been extraordinarily interesting and
nice – we gave him £5 Syrian, or about 11/- each time, so he
did well out of us. But we had so enjoyed it all, and would never
have found our way to the glass-blowing or brocade-making or
other things that took place in the little houses tucked away up
the side streets, without his help. A hasty lunch, and pack, then
off for our two shows, which were extremely successful.

Chapter Seven

Baalbec to Cairo

Here I am putting pen to paper again – 'tho there won't be time
for v much tonight. Every day is so interesting here, and I now
know the show so well that I can write up till about half a bar
before having to make an entry! If only the playing conditions,
audiences and organisations were up to the beauty of the
country, one could be perfectly happy. I couldn't say anything
before, as while we were at Beirut my letters were being
censored at the DNSE office, but things here are rather sticky.
The OC of DNSE, one Maj Cowles, is, I think, completely dead
and useless and incompetent. The attitude when we arrived was:
'Well I can't think why you have come here. I have nowhere
big enough to play you, only small audiences, and no transport,'
which was very encouraging! Cowles is being relieved, and
his successor arrives any moment, so we have also suffered in
the changeover. We keep arriving at places and finding no one
expects us or knows anything about us – such a waste of time,
as we have only a very short time left abroad, in which to tour
Palestine and play in Jerusalem and Cairo, where they want us
badly for straight concerts and broadcasting.

23RD APRIL 1944

My darlings. This letter has lapsed for 2 days, and in the
meanwhile I have had such a lovely lot of mail from you – many,
many thanks. The garden sounds really lovely, but I am worried
that you are all doing too much in it – please be lazy and don't
worry about dandelions, or weeds on the terrace, or planting
masses of potatoes. We are so enjoying our stay here – the hotel,
a 'Wog' one, is very pleasant – moderately clean, good food
(though only native bread and a tendency to have goat cheese
in everything), hot water at night and a lovely mosaic terrace
flanked by two lilac trees in full bloom, where one can sit
drinking coffee or beer in the shade, and looking across the little
main street to the ruins. Several good shops, and an amusing
crowd of British, French, Polish and Lebanese, all on leave or
holidays – the former tend to be interesting people, as this is a
quiet place with no sophistication. But the ruins – they are the
most beautiful and enormous and fascinating that I have seen
anywhere, and they put the Pyramids and Babylon completely
in the shade. Baalbec, or City of Baal, is believed to be the
home of sun worship. It was the old Heliopolis (there is of
course one near Cairo too), and the most famous and holy city
of this part of the East for thousands of years. The Phoenicians
built a great temple to Baal, of which only enormous 440-ton
blocks of marble remain; then came the Romans under Julius
Caesar; they identified Baal with Jupiter, and erected the most
marvellous temple on the Phoenician foundations. It is one
of the archaeological wonders of the world, and despite Arab
attempts to destroy it when they re-conquered the country,
Christian efforts to convert it into a church, and Constantine
the Great pinching many of the pillars to build into St Sofia,
it remains the most beautiful and impressive sight. It consists
of a great entrance; a hexagonal courtyard, a huge Inner Court
with double porticos of pillars all round, two baths 72 feet long
where people purified themselves, and a sacrificial altar 66ft
by 60. Then surmounting all this is the Temple of Jupiter, built
on an artificial mound – originally an immense place with 54
pillars 70ft high round it; now only 6 pillars remain standing,

but all the bases are there. Beside and below this is the Temple of Bacchus, also huge, with the most exquisite remains of carved stone ceilings and Corinthian capitals that I have ever seen. Then there is a small Temple of Venus. The three gods were a Trilogy, Bacchus being the son of Jupiter and Venus, and the rites and ceremonials connected with the worship of the two latter were very sensual and orgiastic — hence bitter attempts by Christians and Arabs alike to destroy the temples. Most harm has been done by earthquakes, though, and I've seen no air-raid debris to compare with the ruins of those enormous pillars.

23RD APRIL 1944. PALMYRA HOTEL, BAALBEC, SYRIA

I was trying to convey to you some sense of the impressive sight that is Baalbec — we are all photographing madly, and this morning Johnny, Hurwitz, all of the Band who have good heads for heights, and self had a marvellous time scrambling all over the ramparts and roof of the Temple of Bacchus, getting some striking pictures by lying on our tummies and photographing straight down fluted pillars onto the heads of tiny figures, or posing on the edge of cornices with terrific drops below, and standing beside the six remaining huge pillars of the Temple of Jupiter with a big drop to the courtyard in front of us, being photographed from underneath. The Germans began excavating at the end of the last century, and had to remove successive layers of Byzantine and Christian and Arab superstructures, churches, forts, etc. Then the French got down to it in 1937, and the place is now very much as it originally was. But the reconstruction was interrupted by the war, and the great central court (which has niches for 330 statues and held 3,000 people) is littered with bits of capital, fragments of ceiling, plaques, busts, gargoyles, sections of pillar and every sort of debris, some of it partly pieced together, the rest just numbered and left. Lizards dart in and out of the crevices, kestrels nest everywhere high up in holes in the stonework, and mimulus waves from walls and pillars and between the paving of the courts. The sun beats down incredibly hot, though we are over 3,000ft up, and it is easy to see how this place, in its fertile, secluded valley with snows all round, became sacred to the Sun, God of Life and Prosperity and Voluptuousness. Beneath the great temple and the courtyards is a maze of underground vaults and passages, icy-cold even at midday, where pilgrims lived and where the sacrificial animals were kept. There is an interesting theory that originally a temple was built here by Solomon as a present to Balkis, Queen of Sheba. Look up 1 Kings IX 17–19, Gran darling. 'And Solomon built…and Baalath and Tadmor…' (Baalbec and Palmyra, which is near here), and etc., mentioning the Lebanon later on. There are very many other interesting buildings and remains near here – this part of the world was the home of sun-worship with its terrific rites and ceremonial, and the Greco-Roman influence which succeeded the Phoenicians, incorporated Baal into its own Pantheistic worship, and carried the religion to even greater heights (and depths) of pomp and luxury. The proprietor of our hotel, M Alouf, has written a book on the ruins, which is now out of print, but he has lent us his own copy of it. It is the official work on Baalbec, and has been translated into many languages and he is an acknowledged authority – the book is extremely interesting and I have read it all in an afternoon.

Yesterday I went to Damascus as the Band were playing for sports – 6 hours' travelling to play for an hour and a quarter in the grilling sun with no one listening – typical of the arrangements here! However, I wandered round Damascus and photographed. Met Capt Taylor (Welfare Officer at Qatana, where we did 2 shows) and he joined us for lunch at the Orient Palace, came for a walk through the bazaars after and then took J and me to eat delicious strawberries and cream before we left to return here. He also bought me some lovely sweets, and took photographs of me in a very good shop, goggling at an immense box of candied fruit, then clad in a lovely brocade dressing gown! (The latter will be funny as I had drill slacks and shirt and heavy shoes on underneath and they would keep showing!) Capt T as you will have gathered is a keen amateur photographer and is having an exhibition soon. You can imagine what he, J and I were like all on the go together with our cameras. When bitten by the photographic bug, one thinks nothing of lying on one's

back in the middle of a busy street to get a striking angle, or
scaling dizzy heights and lying on the tummy on the edge of
abysses to achieve dramatic effect!

23RD APRIL 1944. PALMYRA HOTEL, BAALBEC, SYRIA

How lovely it is to think that ere very long I may be showing
you all my pictures and treasures – what a time we will have!
I will really have masses of photos – some very interesting
ones amongst them, what with my own, Manny Hurwitz's and
Johnny's. There is a chance that I may get the ones that were
confiscated by Censorship back. They have gone to Cairo, but
Capt Taylor has contacted an Intelligence friend who is going to
ask what is the matter with them, and put the point that they are
important for RAMC Records. The funny part is that the ones
taken are all snaps of bridges – the Faisal Bridge, Baghdad, and
the bridge at Ahwaz, which was built by the Germans, and both
of which one can buy PCs of in any shop! This business of being
taken over by ENSA has been a terrific success and we have
had innumerable comments in our Completion Book (which is
signed by a Senior Officer after every show) such as – 'We hope
ENSA will do more in this line' and 'Such a joy to hear a clean
show' etc. I have all our Completion Books, and our write-
ups really are very good. What pleased all the ENSA people
immensely was that after a show we did for the Americans in
Persia, they gave us a write-up in their troops' paper, saying
'Thank you ENSA. Our USO shows can produce nothing like
this and have much to learn from you' – or words to that effect
– I am v afraid that as Beric Holt's letter and parcel of papers to
you went down, the ones he sent home to the Press in England
must have gone down too – just my luck!

24TH APRIL 1944

Again I am writing during the show, and will try and finish this
off tonight – tomorrow we leave at 9 a.m. for our 200-mile run

to Aleppo, where we are spending some five days. I believe it is a fascinating old place, again with a marvellous bazaar, but am now quite broke, having borrowed from J and spent all my Cairo money on ahead, including your £10 present, Mum darling, which I hadn't intended to touch! Brocade could easily be my downfall! Am sorry to leave this fascinating place. It is alive with Roman ruins – our hotel is built above the old theatre, and there is the complete old town buried beneath the present-day houses. Alas, I went and woke up with a silly sort of bilious attack today – I think the result of rather hot sun, probably – and I didn't feel fit enough to go out and snoop about – however it is wearing off. Have replenished my brandy here, and got my small bottle filled with excellent three star stuff for 4/-, not bad. Johnny offered me the night off tonight, but I should hate to break my record of not having missed a show.

25TH APRIL 1944. CLARIDGES PALACE HOTEL, ALEPPO, SYRIA

Here we are in a new abode again, and masses of news and experience, both pleasant and unpleasant, to recount. No more mail. I hope that it is a lovely, warm, still Spring evening, and that you are all gardening amidst the daffodils and primroses and violets. I am sitting behind a couple of screens offstage during our first of two shows here. Not a bad hall, 'tho a trifle small for us; but only half full. Organisation here is appalling (I mean in all Syria). We keep doing two nights at the same place, to half-empty houses, when one show would have been heaps. And oh for some classical concerts! I long to get down to work again, because I know that technically I've improved – we are all sick of the old Variety shows and much in need of rehearsal, but it's almost impossible to get any. However, here there is a very nice room with good piano at the DNSE Office, and I can go there any afternoon.

Before I go further, let me warn you not to be misled by the name of this hotel. We were shown on arrival into two small and dirty rooms, each opposite a lavatory of quite unbelievable smelliness, with very little ventilation, no fly-netting over the windows, and no mosquito nets provided. We felt pretty gloomy about the whole thing, especially as the service seemed to consist of one willing but greasy-looking lad who did everything from carry the cases up to serve meals. However, we went to a cinema, to cheer ourselves up, and saw the marvellous film 'All This and Heaven Too', at which I wept non-stop for an hour. We then came back and had dinner outside in a very pleasant courtyard with roses in bloom and a fountain. However when I went up to bed I saw something suspicious-looking crawling on the wall. Immediately Johnny, who is my adviser on all insect matters, was summoned, and he said it was a bug. We looked around and found several more large ones, which we slew forthwith. It seemed a bit late at night to change rooms, so I decided to try and stick it, and we moved my bed into the centre of the room and had a good search everywhere, killing everything we could see. I eventually got into bed and dozed fitfully, being dead tired after our long run here, but at about 1 a.m. I could bear it no longer! I made a dash for the light switch and revealed a bed that was literally crawling! Well, for about a quarter of an hour I went berserk armed with a Penguin book, and the bed was splattered with red stains of squashed bugs, but as fast as I bumped them off, so others appeared. So I girded the old blue and white dressing gown round me, and sallied forth. First I woke poor Johnny, then I went downstairs and had a very trying interview with two porters who spoke little English or French and thought I was being fussy anyway – apparently every other room was full, so we climbed back to my little hole armed with a flit-gun, and one of the porters turned back my mattress, stripped the bed and soaked everything with flit. Not a bug to be seen. But J, who knows bugs, tried to persuade me to sleep the night in his room on a lower floor as he said flit had no effect whatsoever on them. He was right…so it ended up with my sleeping on his bed, and him sleeping most uncomfortably on the floor, poor dear! And even then my rug and two small pillows we brought down from my room were both inhabited. We were too sleepy to be amused, but in retrospect it is very funny, especially the thought of me dashing around the room battering away with a copy of Henry Williamson's 'The Old

Stag' while the porter flitted phlegmatically and the bugs
chuckled in their crevices.

26TH APRIL 1944. CLARIDGES PALACE HOTEL, ALEPPO

I changed rooms the next day, and have a very nice and quite
clean place now, much cooler and better ventilated than the first
and plus mosquito netting. It is on the first floor, opening onto
the courtyard where one has meals. This is a real native hotel
– very few guests and those Syrian or Arab, with an occasional
officer passing through. It is not the best hotel in town, and
today a very nice Captain, the DAPM I think, called in, having
heard via the 'bush radio' that I had been badly bitten, and
offered to take us straight to the best hotel and fix us up there.
However we have only two more nights, and anyway we both
have very nice rooms here now, so it isn't worth it. (Bush radio,
as you probably know, is the mysterious means whereby news
gets around out here.)

Now, I want to revert to Baalbec and our lovely run here on
Monday. It was really very reminiscent of Kurdistan – a high,
fertile plain rolling on for miles, flanked by mountains, with the
same villages perched on hillocks and heavily fortified. We had
a glimpse of the high mountains above Tripoli, well snow-clad
still, then gradually they dwindled to queer-shaped chalk hills,
and we came down from the rather more than 3,000ft altitude
of Baalbec. Our first stop was at Homs – the town out of
bounds because of typhoid, and very sad and shuttered-looking,
but a big NAAFI on the outskirts still open. I was recovered
from the previous day's bilious attack, luckily, and thoroughly
enjoying the run, and I managed to put away my third and
fourth fried eggs for the day very happily (having had two for
breakfast not long before!) though Johnny was convinced I'd be
sick in the bus! We stopped for a while at El Hama to see some
amazing and enormous waterwheels that are very famous. They
are made of cedar wood and last 1,000 years without needing
renewing as cedar, on account of its thick resin and fine grain,
is water- and worm-proof. They turn slowly and massively,

pushed by the current, and emitting weird squeaks and shrieks, and they feed water on the system of dredger buckets, to several stone aqueducts that supply the town. The two biggest wheels are some 70ft in diameter. And now, Mum darling, I would like to give you a brief impression of her mother's daughter hanging out of the side of the bus nearly going mad trying to identify the strange and lovely flowers that flashed by – it was tantalising in the extreme – and of course the only halt we had in the country was on a high and rocky path where nothing but the tall spiky pink thing that I described in the letters about Sannine grew (incidentally, it is an asphodel). But oh! The flowers amongst the crops and in the grass! Wild gladiolus; irises; scarlet poppies, anemones and tulips; yellow daisies in big, brilliant cushions; a bright purple flower that is, I think, a monkshood; something pink like a big flax that I couldn't identify; flowering thistles with flat, spiky tops; anchusa; big, pink convolvulus; a small blue fellow like our dwarf Michaelmas daisies; clouds of mustard and (I think) gypsophilia; several curious green flowers, and a sort of extra-big sorrel; and a thousand more fascinating things that whirled past under my nose. Then the birds – do you know, I think that all the kingfishers in the world must come to North Syria to mate. The telegraph wires on the 189-mile run from Baalbec to Aleppo are beaded with big blue ones and little black and white fellows, some paired up, some still single. They must be kingfishers – heavy heads and dark bills, brilliant blue and mushroom pink and black, but it seems incredible to see so many on that somewhat arid plain. Books of reference do not exist in the East – a flower is just a flower to the Oriental mind, and one bird the same as another. We came into Aleppo at teatime, having left at nine. As David Hassan (who has driven us from Cairo, and knows our ways) put it when asked as to the length of the run: 'Four hours' drive; four hours' cups of tea.' Still, one sees the countryside!

26TH APRIL 1944. CLARIDGES PALACE HOTEL, ALEPPO

Aleppo – a grey and rather monotonous-looking city, without
the 440 mosques and the canals of Damascus or the sea and
mountains of Beirut. A really Oriental place, very dirty and
dusty, with the most marvellous bazaars – all in cool stone
passages, with fan-vaulted roofs and skylights every twenty
feet or so letting in shafts of sunlight. They stretch for literally
miles, leading off in all directions up steps and down steps – a
rabbit warren of a place, with donkeys and mules clopping over
the cobbles and scrambling on the stairs, and no room for two
beasts to pass, laden as they are here. Johnny and I, going out to
explore, were rather luckily picked up by an agent of one of the
best shops here – Marco Polo House. By way of advertisement,
these agents will show one all over the town free – we have had
two mornings with a very nice Syrian boy who speaks beautiful
French. But of course we also spent hours in the shop itself!
And it is the devil of a place to get out of with any money left
in one's purse at all. However the things are lovely, and cheaper
than elsewhere, as they get Turkish silks easily and also are off
the beaten track. Yesterday there were three Air Force officers
who had flown up from Cairo to buy £2,000-worth of stuff
for the RAF shops in Egypt, and they said this was the most
inexpensive place in the Middle East. It certainly has more
pure silks than anywhere else, but I am still very happy about
the lengths of brocade I have, as they are unique colourings
and patterns such as I've seen in none of the ordinary shops.
However, I have fallen for a jacket-length of the real pure silk
and gold thread brocade – stuff that is pretty well everlasting. It
is a very delicate pattern of Chinese red and gold on cream and
will wear over almost anything. Oh the silks and silk mixtures
they have there – mouth watering! We have seen the very
impressive Citadel – crumbling old Arab fortifications and palace
remains on a hill dominating the town, with very interesting
Roman water storage tanks underneath. And a nice mosque; and
of course miles of bazaar with the usual fascinating handicrafts
in progress. Also have visited the branch of the v good
photographer we go to in Beirut, where I had all my Baalbec

photos developed – J and I between us had well over 100 prints made, many of them really publishable. We made ourselves quite unpopular in Baalbec by doing so much photographing on our own and never employing the quantities of local men who pursue one with antiquated box and tripod cameras. As one said to Manny Hurwitz – 'Nice photo? Very clean, very hygiene, very sentimentary.' By the way, Johnny and I are hardening our hearts about tipping – you should see the subterfuge we employ, both being awful cowards about it, to leave unnoticed! Really it was ruining us before, as there are so many servants in the hotels here. We left the Palmyra, Baalbec, in good favour though, as I said very genuinely that I intended to go there after the war, the manager pressed two lovely branches of lilac into my hand as we left. The poor things died though in the heat of the bus, despite an 'elevens' when we stopped at the NAAFI at Homs. Another remarkable thing I noticed during the run here was the ploughing – vast areas all so symmetrically done, in the age-old manner of donkey, camel or bullock yoked to the wooden plough. We also passed innumerable herds of goats and sheep, and I blessed them as they were my only hope of seeing flowers – passing them involved slowing down and much shouting and yelling as the herdsmen tried to clear the road!

28TH APRIL 1944. ALEPPO, SYRIA

Here we are again doing our show – it is so hot today that they have been spraying the roof of our little theatre with fire-hoses to try and cool it down. It has made no difference though, and my make-up is beaded with sweat. Funnily enough it is not a very tiring heat as it is very dry – Beirut is much more exhausting, as it is always damp there. And also I bathed this afternoon, in a very nice pool in which the Band have lived ever since we arrived. I have no costume or cap, mine being in the bottom of my trunk in Cairo thanks to the misleading information we had from HQ there. However, I managed to hire one today – rather too wide and big, but with a bootlace borrowed from one of Johnny's shoes I managed to keep body and soul together. However, a cap was another matter. Women do not really bathe much here, and I think my costume was a man's one as the top was rather scanty! So I pinned my hair up in Edwardian style and, entering the water in a dignified manner, I progressed about the bath in a stately breaststroke – I was the only female there, and today being the Moslem Sunday, there were crowds of Syrian boys from about ten upwards who were most intrigued to see an English girl bathing. The Band are all beautifully tanned; they ran races and dived, and Johnny, despite his years and too much smoking, and having swum once since the war, still managed to beat them all, which delighted him. One of the drivers we collected at Beirut has been Lebanon Diving Champion three years running, so I'm hoping to get a few hints from him when I have achieved a bathing cap. Have sent to Cairo for my things, so as to have them for Tel Aviv at any rate.

We are more comfortable in our hotel now – the new rooms are quite comfortable, but it is an awful dump re food and service and hot water. The chef wanders about in a lounge suit and trilby hat, and I used to mistake him for a guest at first – but if one approaches him firmly and demands lunch, he proves very amiable and goes off still plus trilby, to produce it.

I'm still overcome by the size and beauty of Baalbec, and we all talk much of it. Beneath the big Temple of Jupiter, 50ft high on its artificial mound, there is a space where the biggest block of stone in the world was to be placed, to form a level terrace beside the temple. The block is hewn and squared and lying in a quarry some miles away – it must be 25ft high by 15 deep by 100 long, and calculations have proved that the incredible number of 40,000 men would have been required to shift it. Perhaps that's why it lies unmoved still. There is a very famous ruin, St Simeon Stilites (can't spell) near here, which we have had no time to see, and between Tripoli and Homs is the most beautiful Crusader Castle, the Krak des Chevaliers – I'd like to see the latter. We are due in Beirut on Thurs next, play every night there, and leave for Palestine on the Sunday. We are doing one orchestral concert, thank goodness.

1ST MAY 1944. HAKIM PALACE HOTEL, TRIPOLI, SYRIA

Here I am, 8.30 a.m. of a hot morning in Tripoli, sitting down to write this to you before breakfast, as we intend to spend all day bathing. First of all, a lovely bundle of mail from you on arrival here – up till Sunday, April 17th, and I am so delighted that all my letters and the parcels eventually turned up. Our plans after being much changed now seem fairly fixed. Our tour to Palestine is cut rather to our disappointment, owing to lack of time. We leave Beirut next Saturday after 2 shows only there (they have an outbreak of meningitis, so do not welcome crowds), and we go straight to the Canal Zone, for how long I do not know. It will be very hot there, and the Khamsin will be blowing. But its one advantage is that it is, I believe, all work in big places with big audiences. And do not worry about the heat; I find that it is suiting me very well – I am a Child of the Sun, like you, Mum! Do you remember our last day at Aleppo when they were spraying the theatre roof with fire-hoses to try and cool it? The RAF people kept coming up and saying 'How do you find the heat is affecting you?' and I told them we had spent the afternoon swimming and sunbathing, whereupon they were very surprised and said that it was 98° in the shade that day. Since I began bathing I feel a different person and have a huge appetite again. The sea and baths are all beautifully warm. During the RAF show I arranged for a letter to be rushed to Cairo, asking for my bathing kit to be sent to Jerusalem, and of course got here next day to find we weren't going there at all!! However, I was determined I would swim yesterday, as it was sweltering, and you would have laughed to see what I did. Johnny had a very old and rather dated costume, which I persuaded him to relinquish in favour of trunks. I then pinched his costume, and in an hour's hard work took a foot out of it and converted it into a very smart halter-necked suit for me! I was so bucked with myself when I'd finished. It is not quite Paris Plage, but looks nice on not too close inspection! We set out yesterday afternoon to find a place the Band had discovered near the Transit Camp they are living in, and we had an awful hunt. Eventually we hiked back some way, and found that true to style the boys had got into a private place, and were swimming from a splendid spot marked 'For Naval Personnel Only'. However, though a couple of officers in immaculate ducks came down to go sailing and gave us a funny look, they said nothing! The background of the place is not exciting – a railway yard in the Dock area – but there is a changing hut, and one goes straight into 12 or 15ft of water with raft, spring board and 12ft diving board. Also it is just us there – and that in this country of rather unpleasantly curious native youths is a great attraction. I am still capless, and swim in stately fashion, but the new swimsuit is admirable! This town is a typical seaport – romantically evil-looking dock areas, not very good shops or cinemas or hotels, all very dirty and disease-ridden but redeemed by exquisite snow mountains rising behind it, and the lovely blue of the sea washing it clean and a fragrance of orange blossom and flowering trees even in the meanest street.

1st May 1944. Hakim Palace Hotel, Tripoli

Don't be misled by the name of this hotel – it is rather the same brand as the Claridge Palace at Aleppo! But the rooms are slightly cleaner, and there is a sort of lounge, with Arabic woodwork, stained glass, purple cushions, gilt pineapple mouldings in the corners, sham scarlet hibiscus, and a piano, where I can practise peacefully every morning. The food is awful and flies swarm on filthy tablecloths, and there is no hot water at all, but there are pleasant balconies with lovely sweet-smelling pot-flowers and shrubs, and some English people, and it's about the best hotel in Tripoli, so one can't grumble. Anyway it is one up on Aleppo – we were quite glad to leave there, as it somehow seemed dirtier and hotter and dustier than other places, and had no fine views or attractive streets. Even here, to my surprise, there are no decent cafés or shops. Beirut is full of lovely patisseries and has excellent shops of all sorts. We are looking forward to getting back to the Regent Hotel there.

We left Aleppo at 9.00 a.m. on Saturday morning, and had a marvellous run here. It is very curious how the building styles change as one goes north and inland; I saw a type of house I've seen nowhere else between Homs and Aleppo – mud beehives[9] with just a door and no windows – quite the most primitive things we've come across. The villages looked like apiaries clustering on their hillocks. However the people wear very bright clothes and decorate their donkeys and mules with coloured tassels, so the monotony of the mud-grey is relieved. The ploughing season is in full swing – everywhere amazingly straight furrows being ploughed, with never a tree in sight for a marker, and funny uneven-looking pairs such as a camel and a mule, or a donkey and a bullock yoked together. We passed through El Hama, and the biggest waterwheel had stopped – probably having its 1,000-yearly overhaul and repair! Then we got to Homs in time for late lunch at the NAAFI. That unfortunate town is now out of bounds for typhoid, typhus and meningitis, and the NAAFI seems to be suffering from the general despondency – it is a horrid place, and we ate our sandwiches and drank nasty tea and got out as quickly as possible. I had arranged to have the mid-morning halt by a field full of flowers, so that I was able to dash out and collect a few of the ones I'd been wondering about – but I was none the wiser, as I didn't know them. However, I am listing all flowers known and unknown, and doing rough sketches with short descriptions of the latter. The run from Homs to Tripoli was perfect. It was over low hills, with the big snows on our left and most beautiful upland streams and valleys opening out on either side – the turf was blue with some prickly-leaved flower I can't identify, which grew like a carpet with a fine tall thistle, dark purple and striking, standing up amongst the blue. The villages are stone, with red-tiled roofs and that peculiar feeling of freshness and purity that one has in the mountains, which was a welcome relief after filthy Homs. The 'blue birds' were about (am now doubtful if they are kingfishers after all), and also a bird like the common kite-hawk, but snowy white with black wingtips. We came over a low watershed, and ran down towards the sea, which was like sheet-gold in the evening sun. Then we turned and ran south along the coast into Tripoli – again the tall canes, and funny prickly[10] cactus that grows hereabouts. We had a glimpse of the Krak des Chevaliers castle, but it is too far from here for us to be able to go to see it, I fear. Tonight we play at a Mountain Warfare place, but quite low down. Our show at the Cedars, the big one 6,000ft up, has been cancelled I am disappointed to say.

4TH MAY 1944. REGENT HOTEL, BEIRUT

Here we are back again, and such a lovely lot of letters awaiting us. I have not the remotest idea when we return, except that our contract expires during the first two weeks in June. I shall not know when we leave until after we get on the boat, I feel sure. And I can assure you that even the ship's officers during the actual voyage do not know what port they are going to. I shall not be allowed to ring you from the port, so the first you will hear will probably be a call from London saying 'Arriving next train'!! At the moment we know no more than that we get on a train for Ismailia on Sunday.

We had very nice audiences for our last two shows in the Perroquet Theatre, Tripoli, despite its being a most dreary old place with bugs and an appalling smell of drains. Alas, no more bathing as the weather turned wet and grey. However, on our last day J took me deep into the most fascinating bazaar area, which he had discovered on a solo photographing exhibition. Funny crumbling old arches, remains of beautiful houses, walls dating back to Roman days, roofless churches, all converted into a thousand tiny shops where the usual patient craftsmen sit doing incredibly laborious and slow work, with minute boys wielding hammers or polishing by hand. The most fascinating thing about the ME is the use to which that commonplace article the petrol tin is put. The social and economic fabric of this part of the world would collapse, I feel sure, were tins in general to cease to exist suddenly. Whole areas of the bazaar were employed in making things from them – oil lamps, cooking utensils, coffee pots, shoe-shine outfits and gazouses (or contraptions in which soft drinks are sold by itinerant vendors), boxes and containers of all sorts and bridal chests which will have 'Pork Soya Links' (or the name of a peculiarly revolting American sausage meat supplied in large quantities to their and our troops) stamped all over them. Besides this, the petrol tin is used for roofing houses, as a lavatory, to carry water, as a chair with a wooden bar fixed across the top, as a reflector for stage lights, to make oil-drip stoves, and a million other things – as we were wending our way back, enraptured, through the clatter of hammers, with the usual crowd of small urchins tailing us, and pointing out my trousers and battle-blouse to all newcomers with great glee, we happened to glance up a little cul-de-sac, and there was a nice old stone house with two lovely great trails of scarlet geranium drooping from a balcony. We stopped to admire it, and an old lady caught sight of us out of the window and started signalling frantically. It was some time before I gathered what she wanted while she picked geraniums for all she was worth, and eventually I decided she wanted me to go into the house. So I climbed the steep stairs, and the dear old thing came dashing down from upstairs, threw her arms around me and kissed me, and pressed the flowers into my hand. Conversation was limited as she had nothing but Arabic, however we parted on the warmest terms, after meeting her daughter and baby, and being offered coffee, which we unfortunately hadn't time to accept.

5TH MAY 1944. BEIRUT

We left Tripoli after breakfast yesterday, and had a very lovely run here all along the seashore, with the water lapping rough grey rocks and a mass of flowers growing amongst them – including a very attractive short, close, bush-like privet, and lots of pale green things that might be a hellebore, though in leaves and growth they are like aconite. (Damn – am writing this during rehearsal, and a huge flea has just hopped onto me and lost himself in my battle-blouse – am in a perpetual state of being bitten by something or other!) It is a joy to be back in a clean hotel eating really good food again – we are here until Sunday when we leave by train for the 24hr journey via Haifa to Ismailia. A lorry is going by road with a few men and part of the baggage. The rest goes by van, and an NCO and three men have to live with it on its three-day journey. Last night we did a variety show in this nice hall of the Transit Camp, and tonight is orchestral – am singing 'Caro Nome', 'L'été', and a group with the piano. There have been some excitements in this town during our absence. As our waiter put it while we awaited our food last night, 'We have had here since four days a Revolution!' He made a histrionic gesture towards the window and a peaceful-looking street. Seeing we were unimpressed, he hastily added, 'Today is of course very calm,' and proceeded to tell us gory stories of how quite ten people had actually been killed in the street fighting. As a matter of fact the curfew has only just been lifted, and there were posses of sheepish-looking Lebanese soldiers wandering about the streets yesterday, but today even these have departed. The trouble was, I gather, that the Lebanon Govt was meeting, and the two parties, one pro-French control, the other pro-Lebanese independence, clashed, the former rather curiously being the revolutionary body. However, I doubt if anyone really knows or cares what happened. As the waiter proudly added, 'It is here only our second revolution' (the other having been quite a high-class affair in November last). And who would deny these people the fun they get out of these little fracas? Personally, if I ruled an Eastern country, I'd stage-manage a quiet little bust-up every year as a sort of safety valve, and to give them something to talk about for the next twelve months.

The Band are playing extraordinarily well – Fingal's Cave for one, and I have been sitting back and loving it after days of variety. The enjoyment of this tour has been purely topographical, to quote J, and the difference after our happy time in Paiforce most marked. There has been the awful feeling of being continually up against people and conditions – difficulty after difficulty, and the show not at its best as a result. In Paiforce everyone at any rate tried to help. We are all rather short-tempered and generally browned-off now! And to make matters worse, it has decided to pour with rain at a time when rain should not be falling here. The Band are in tents in the Holiday Camp, which is lovely in summer, and right on the beach for bathing, but not so good in this weather. Also the travelling arrangements are for them to do the awful journey to Ismailia 3rd class, which is all wrong, and J has to go and wage yet another battle about that, poor dear.

Harry Roy's remarks were most interesting, and should bear good fruit, though of course he has left a fearful name out here. His Band had the best of available accommodation in hotels and for travel, whereas we being a military party get the worst. Also it is a fact that he was offered a plane here to fly him to Cairo, and he refused to take the (negligible) risk as he said his insurance did not cover air travel. But he is right in that the vehicles and drivers supplied to DNSE are awful on the whole. If the Army would turn over just a very few British drivers to ENSA it would make a world of difference, and the vehicles would be decently serviced and maintained, so breakdowns would be halved. However, I adore this town and shops, and shall be sorry to leave it.

7TH MAY 1944. THE TRAIN BETWEEN LYDDA AND GAZA, PALESTINE

Here we are bowling along in the train – a setting sun on the left, and on the right a huge moon rising over low hills covered with grove upon grove of oranges, lemons, grapefruits and limes. The windows all wide open, though it is 7.15 p.m., and, further down the train, the Band and other troops hanging out of the windows of their 2nd and 3rd class carriages, and sitting on the steps with their legs dangling out over Palestine. Johnny has just dived out during a short halt at Lydda, to grab a cup of tea and two bits of NAAFI slab, and he ran into a Major who had seen and loved the show at Shaibah – a nice coincidence. However, as we have now played to some 60,000 troops out here, I suppose it is not so strange. We have not the remotest idea of our plans, or of where we are staying yet – we just arrive at 5.30 a.m. hoping for the best! Our final classical concert in Beirut was very successful – a nice audience, and J was delighted as, though he had been dreading the evening, the Band played beautifully. I got through 'Caro Nome' and 'L'été' and some

solos with piano fairly well, all considered. Next morning all
my heavy baggage went off early by lorry, leaving me gloriously
free for a day of enjoyment – not one of laziness though! J
and I were up betimes, and fought our way through crowds
celebrating the anniversary of the overthrow of the Turks, to the
Remount Depot, where we were taking a chance on getting
a ride – our friend Corporal Bosher was out, but a very nice
Sergeant Gulliver produced two horses for us, and what is more
came with us himself. I was v relieved, as I had ridden the horse
J was to have and knew it pulled. Eventually he went on the
leading rein, and I was thankful the Sgt was there. I had a very
nice chestnut with a decent mouth this time that would have
been an excellent ride if it had been able to walk. We had a most
beautiful ride – a real long one of nearly 2 hours, right through
the tall forests of fir or pine trees with their curious flat tops
of foliage and bare trunks like slim columns, and out on the
sea-shore, with amazing blue water lapping red sand, and the
Sannine massif gleaming in the morning sunshine. On the way
back I discovered that Sgt Gulliver had been in the Household
Cavalry, and had also been stud groom to Jack Speed before
that. He knew Douglas and Nicola and Ronnie and Maria, and
was shocked to hear of Ronnie's death. Wasn't that strange? We
talked so much about them all, and about Knowlton. He told
me that the big house had 365 windows, one for each day of the
year, which I hadn't known. He also remembered 'Mrs Speed,
who sang a lot'. We parted great friends, after I'd taken several
photographs. We had a quiet afternoon – nice Tony Vickers,
the BBC Sgt, came to lunch and we had a farewell tea at the
Patisserie Suisse, and a stroll along the seafront, which was very
lovely with people canoeing and swimming and sailing. Then
a cinema and back to dinner to find Capt Taylor, the Welfare
Officer from Qatana near Damascus (who rather fell for me I'm
afraid!) having arrived for the night. We joined up for dinner,
and he gave me some nice photos he'd taken of me at Damascus.
I firmly went to bed v early – luckily the nice 'By the Way' party
we knew in Baghdad had just arrived, and I introduced him to
them and fled upstairs!

7TH MAY 1944. IN THE TRAIN

Do hope you can read this – whenever the train achieves more than about 20 mph it rocks wildly. Night has fallen too, and we have a rather anaemic light, however there are halts every fifteen minutes or so, which helps. Our next stop is Gaza, for dinner, or rather some sort of NAAFI meal. J and I are very lucky in having only one other young Anglo-Indian RE officer in with us, so we'll be able to sleep fairly well – not that it is really worth sleeping, as we have to stop for a 'tea and haversack breakfast' at Kantara at 3.00 a.m., which sounds particularly revolting. However, I have much to say, and no thrilling literature to distract me as I've just unravelled the mystery of 'The Silk Stocking Murders' at a single session. Have also devoured some v interesting French guidebooks on Syria and the Lebanon, and am learning much I didn't know. Heard a little more about the troubles in Beirut in an undertone from Tony Vickers. Apparently it all did centre round a spot just outside the window at which our hotel waiter made his histrionic gesture! Somebody appeared riding on a white horse, wearing his grandfather's suit, and surrounded by followers who threw a bomb at the Petite Sérail, which I gather is the seat of the Govt. He wore his grandfather's suit because the old boy had been a leader of the country, and it had been foretold that one of his descendants would come and save the Lebanon wearing aforesaid suit and riding a white horse. After which fine début, the gentleman seems to have fizzled out. There were quite a few shots during our concert on Friday night – I heard them plainly from my dressing-room. However, everyone is extremely friendly to us, unlike Palestine where things are once more quite tense. We lunched in Haifa today, and had time to notice that many shop windows have iron grilles over them, and despite that much of the glass is smashed.

Later. Gaza now – am alone while J gets his food – have had mine in the Officers' Mess with the nice young Anglo-Indian while J guarded the luggage – funny – in that crowded, noisy place the wireless was giving forth Ravel's 'Pavane pour une Infante Défunte', and that sad remote music was extraordinarily appropriate to the wartime throng of travellers somehow – I've always felt most alone and drawn into myself in railway stations – you know, the strong feeling of ships that pass in the night – strangers entering one's orbit and then vanishing into the darkness like comets, and the imagination giving one a sense of journeying far beyond the limits of earthly travel. We left Beirut at about 8.30 this morning, and ran between the exquisite flowery Syrian hills and the sea. Those funny prickly cactuses I described turn out to be 'prickly pear' and are producing orange and pink flowers between their spikes. (By the way, when throwing myself from my pony I had to be careful to avoid them!) Then we came to the frontier, and a fascinating stretch of creamy chalk cliffs and gorges where we went in and out of tunnels, with dazzling glimpses of that whiteness falling sheer into blue water. The country flattened out and became much more dull and European-looking, though the sand beaches were very lovely. Now we are inland, the hill alas left far behind!

This is where we leave my diary. Our last months in the Middle East were so packed with happenings that they would take a book in themselves. So I have tried to summarise the most interesting and significant of them, including the journey home.

We stayed first in the pleasant garden city of Ismailia, where the streets glowed with flamboyants, their scarlet streaked with gold towards the centre, the masses of blossom so thick and solid that the branches were bowed down and the normally upright trees looked like weeping willows. The Band were at last happy in a holiday camp on the shore of Lake Timsah where they could bathe at will. I was at a good YWCA, and Johnny and I hired ancient bikes so that we could get to the beach in our spare time. It was already very hot in early June, and that enervating wind the Khamsin blew constantly. Our shows were all outdoors to huge audiences sitting round on the sand, and we were harassed by every sort of flying insect, all intent on suicide; they got themselves twangled in violin strings, down the tubes of wind instruments, and even into my mouth as I sang, though Johnny did his best to wave one arm across my face while conducting. A few days in Suez were unpleasant, with a basic and unfriendly hospital and a constant sickening smell of oil from the refinery. But we had a great day at Sakkhara visiting the step pyramids, and were delighted to see the *Orion* passing down the Suez Canal, disproving the rumour that she had been sunk. We also got word via ENSA that our dotty Egyptian driver Miserahi, known as Misery, had surpassed himself when driving one of their parties around in his old bus by going one night to see if he had enough petrol with a lighted match. ENSA was now minus a bus, and a load of costumes and props. Misery, needless to say, survived! We played at a huge hospital on the canal where I re-met Miss Hill, now Matron there, having been transferred from Shaibah in Iraq. Her greeting was typical – she looked at my dry untidy hair and said, 'My dear, I'll send my hairdresser to you straight away!' I discovered she had a Harvey Nicholls hairdresser who she had managed to keep as her batman! I remember too going to an after-show party at a mess in Port Said where I almost leant on an enormous furry spider, which was sitting on the bar. She was kept as a pet, largely to scare the wits out of visitors; and she loved her drink!

Back in Cairo we were warmly welcomed back at Helmieh where I stayed at the same mess with my South African ambulance driver friends. It was a tremendous excitement to hear that the D-Day landings had at last taken place, but we were all worried about the Germans' latest weapon, the V-1 rockets known as doodlebugs because of the pulsating drone they made, which were raining down in and round London (one of the first landed in the copse next to our garden. My mother went out to have a look next day, and found a huge crater).

We began a hectic round of shows and broadcasts, sometimes two a day, and ENSA asked if we could stay for another three months, but the War Office refused. Some of our jazz musicians played in a popular Cairo nightclub where King Faisal went twice to hear them. Johnny and I were busy developing and printing our masses of photos with our War Graves friends, and to my joy some precious photographs, which had been confiscated in Teheran for some obscure reason, were returned to me unharmed, thanks to a friend in Intelligence. Somehow final shopping had to be fitted in too, and one day my South African friends and I found a famous perfumery shop in the heart of Cairo. After a happy if expensive hour we took a garry back to Helmieh and everyone passing thought we were mad, all sniffing each other to a chorus of 'I say, try my Lotus Flower!' 'Secret of the Desert lasts well!' and 'Can you remember if Harem Nights was on my left sleeve or my right hand?' We giggled so much we nearly fell out of the garry.

We had a most unpleasant engagement to perform for a special tea party in the garden of the British Embassy. The temperature was 110°F in the shade, so we set up under a tree while our audience sat on a terrace in the distance and couldn't hear anything as the mike didn't work. No one greeted us or looked after us though we saw the Lady Ambassadress, who shall be nameless, among her guests, and we had to come and go by the tradesmen's entrance, 'just like servants' fumed Johnny. We had made a special effort to be there as we had to rush off to a big troop show out in the desert that evening. There was one occasion when we had an audience of about 10,000, all sitting round in the moonlight as far as the eye could see. Another time we were driving back very late in brilliant moonlight and we had to halt at a level crossing behind a shifting mass of grey, which turned out to be herd of fifty to sixty donkeys. The herd boys, all riding bareback, were singing wild songs and yelling at the animals, and eventually the gates opened and we poured across – a whirl of silvery dust clouds and twinkling legs and ears, all the donkeys going flat out ahead of us, their little hooves muffled in the sand so that they were like a phantom herd. The unpleasant side of life in our barracks was the constant war we waged against ants and cockroaches. My plate of late supper, left in the fridge for me, would be ringed with cockroaches every night. I got used to brushing them off and eating what was left. Far worse was the havoc wrought by tiny black ants, which were able to get into the most hermetically sealed of tins. They loved eating clothes, and favoured what my headmistress coyly called one's 'intimate garments'. We were all in the same plight – there wasn't a decent knicker left in the whole unit!

The culminating somewhat stressful excitement was the arrival from the USA of international soprano Lily Pons, with her conductor husband André Kostelanetz. He took over our band, with which he was delighted, for three big broadcast concerts, and I had the thrill of singing in one of them in place of Lily Pons. I had been asked back to give a recital at Music for All – a lovely occasion shared with pianist Gerald Gover, who I was to meet again at Glyndebourne. Johnny made a most beautiful orchestral arrangement with violin obbligato of Richard Strauss's song 'Morgen!' for me, which I sang whenever we had a classical audience. We gave a farewell Variety show at the Ewart Memorial Hall, and finally on 29th July we found ourselves at Port Said, homeward bound and all together this time on board the SS *Banfora*. She was a dirty old Free French boat with a Chinese crew who spoke no English, full of assorted families with children going back to England, lots of smells, and bugs in the cabins. Johnny found himself with the boys in a hammock on the troop deck. We were two in my cabin, joined by a mother with small baby who was not potty trained as he had had dysentery, and whose nappies she would wash in our one small basin.

Despite screaming children and 700 more people getting on at Gibraltar the journey turned out to be fun. We auditioned for a show, but talent was lacking and anyway there was no room. So we started up a radio station and I learned to be a DJ. This was tricky as our 'studio' was six foot square, the door tended to fly open when it was rough, knocking us into the piles of mixed records, needles had to be changed often, and I used to perform what became known as a Harry Parry, catching the old gramophone sleeve in the speed control so that 'Melancholy Wood' came over as a quick foxtrot with Bing Crosby singing alto.

We berthed on the Clyde – I think at Gourock – and sat there for two days struggling with officialdom and the dreaded Customs. Eventually a large bearded man came to our cabin and assessed my list of dutiable articles as follows: 'Brocade £4.10.0 – for your own use, I suppose? Hmm, better say it's made up. Tobacco – you chew that I expect? All right. Sweets 2lb. OK. A small remnant of silk – also made up, I suppose?' He found my five filigree brooches and bracelets, marked 'For presents'. 'Hmm. Value £2 – I can't mark that off. You may have to pay a little. An officer will be along later.' He never came, and I got through scot free as did most of us.

Landing was a nightmare for some; one family had thirty-nine cases and nowhere to go. My tiresome neighbour with a baby that cried unceasingly threw a crying fit herself when told she must make her own arrangements for her baggage. However she achieved a complete squad of fatigue men to help with her two trolleys of bags all labelled 'Baby Blake. Wanted on Voyage'.

Johnny, the band and I found ourselves on a slow all-night train to London. The NAAFI provided newspapers, cigarettes, pork pies, rock buns, chocolate, and successions of cups of tea as we chugged slowly south. It was over – and Johnny pulled out his photographs and we looked at Syria.

Chapter Eight

The War Years, 1944–45

SS *Banfora* docked in Greenock at 5.00 p.m. on 10th August 1944. My marching orders were to proceed to Aldershot on Saturday 12th, a journey that took all day and night and culminated in the sight of a flying bomb (the new V-1 rocket) crashing nearby as we crossed London, a grim reminder of the world we were coming home to.

The rest of 1944 is rather a blur in my memory. The first euphoria of being at home with my beloved parents was followed by bouts of depression as the war dragged on. The Germans were throwing everything at us and our bombers roared overhead nightly, heading for their industrial cities. The doodlebug I saw crash to the ground nearby as we were passing through London on our way home from the Middle East was a terrifying thing with an evil pulsating drone as it came nearer and nearer. The air was full of prayers from many people who had never prayed before. 'Oh God, please let it pass over me and fall further on!' A shameful prayer, but we all confessed to it.

My mother had arranged a special treat for me, three nights at the Mayfair Hotel in London, to go to performances of *Madam Butterfly* and *La Bohème* at the Haymarket Theatre, given by the Sadler's Wells Opera, later to become the English National. We arrived at our hotel to find we had been given a magnificent suite on I think the fifth floor. We soon found out why. The few other guests had all booked rooms as low down and near to the air raid shelters as possible. We didn't even try to get down during the frequent alarms. I remember leaning out of the window to watch the doodlebugs go flaming by almost at rooftop level. My constant prayer while I was abroad had

215

always been 'Please God, let me live long enough to sing Mimi!' so those two wartime performances were magic for me. Bells would ring loudly in the auditorium every time a doodlebug came in our direction. Anyone was at liberty to get up and go, but no one moved and the singers and orchestra carried on as if nothing was happening, even when a doodle engine cut out overhead to be followed by a bang that shook the theatre.

My voice and I were equally overstressed and tired after the weeks of travel and incessant performances, sometimes two a day, in the Middle East. Colds and laryngitis succeeded each other, and Dino Borgioli told me that the enforced rest would be the saving of my voice. The band was touring up and down the country and I sang with them whenever possible, but it was into the New Year before my voice was fully recovered.

Very soon after I got home a firm of London solicitors rang up to inform me that my father had just died. They had traced me through a full-page photo and article in the *Sunday Pictorial* the previous weekend, and I did so hope he had lived long enough to see it. As he had been found dead in his flat in Marylebone there had to be an identification and inquest. My mother refused to let me go to identify him, as I had not seen him since I was a little girl. It turned out that he had died as a direct result of his First World War wound. After a night of very heavy bombing in North London some of the shrapnel that they had not been able to remove from his brain had shifted and killed him. We got a sad and moving letter from a close woman friend of his – and I was so happy to know that he had had such a friend – saying that he had been very strong and brave, completely overcoming his drink problem and holding down a job although he had been ill with meningitis for many years. He never ceased to adore my mother and was so proud of me. He had actually come to hear me sing somewhere but had not made himself known. Why? My mother and I were deeply saddened by his death, and I have always felt guilty that I did not track him down and visit him in time. He can have been only in his early fifties when he died, an unrecognised victim of the First World War.

In September came more sad news. I was always in close touch with my childhood friends of the Folkestone days. Elizabeth had married young and had a daughter, my godchild. Now news came that her husband had been killed on the Italian front aged twenty-three. Soon after she came to stay with us. She was pregnant with their second child at the time but like so many young war widows was brave and uncomplaining, and some months later produced a healthy son.

On 17th September the disastrous Battle of Arnhem began. The British 1st Airborne Division and the Polish 1st Independent Parachute Brigade were parachuted and glider-landed to secure the bridge over the Rhine at Arnhem, in an attempt to break the German front line and hasten the end of the war. They were dropped too far back from their objective and although a small group of British paras made it to the bridgehead they never managed to secure the whole bridge. Pinned down by heavy German fire, they were almost wiped out, and surrendered on 21st September. Arnhem was in fact not liberated until April 1945. We at home knew nothing of this at the time, but later I heard that a very special man, the only one of all my young friends whom I really felt I wanted to marry, was missing. He was the only son of friends of my parents, and we had met just before the war at a house party. We talked about many things, music, mountains, and the spiritual background to all life, which we both believed in. I was a very unsophisticated teenager, too young for him at our first meeting, but he visited us and brought me a pile of books with different approaches to the spiritual, from Ouspensky to Krishna Murti and Madame Blavatsky, and Kugy on the Dalmatian mountains where he had done a lot of solo climbing. I saw him last when he was on leave from the Parachute Regiment, and I felt I let him down badly. He had to leave very early in the morning, and I – always bad at getting up – overslept. When I woke and shot out of bed I found he had gone. An extraordinary sense of desolation swept over me, as if I knew I was not going to see him again. Some time later I got a letter from him telling me that he had found someone who was, as he put it, 'my wife in the sight of God'. Then came the news that he was missing at Arnhem. And just as the youngest of my Three Musketeers, Ronnie, was lost without trace at Dunkirk, so Nigel disappeared at the bridgehead. We hoped for years and years that somehow, somewhere, he might one day turn up, perhaps having lost his memory, all the wild ideas one has when a much-loved person vanishes. Maybe one day a farmer ploughing near the bridge may come upon an identification bracelet where a shining young life was cut short.

Meanwhile I was keeping very busy in London, studying Russian because I wanted to add some Russian songs to my recital repertoire, and working on my Italian with a dear Italian lady Signora Foa, whose son Giorgio was head of the BBC Italian department at Bush House. My accent improved rapidly and I was thrilled to be asked to do several broadcasts in Italian, reading the news and taking part in plays. I also started doing concerts for another splendid character thrown up by the war, Sylvia Bruce-Lockhart, who organised music in unlikely places such as air raid shelters and gun emplacements. I had met her husband in Beirut where he was serving in the army, when I went in to HQ to ask if there were any horses I might ride during my stay in the Lebanon, and came out having been given a part to play in a Shakespeare reading. Sylvia drove a small van in which I travelled together with a tiny upright piano and a white-haired elderly lady accompanist. I remember a concert on Blackheath Common where there was a Z-battery emplacement. We were in full flow to about twenty men in an army hut when the air raid warning went off. In seconds the place was empty except for us three, me with my mouth still open singing the Hebridean love song as the deafening roar of the Z-batteries going off rocked the little hut. I don't think we scored that night; the bombers went on their way, soon after came the all clear, and the concert was resumed.

At some time I did a week on Southend Pier with Mantovani and his band. I have no record of how this went except for a cryptic note in my diary, 'Horrid little man!' I assume it can't have been my best week.

One day I went along to rehearsal with the band and found our compère Michael Lyndon was not there. Mike, my friend and companion who had taught me so much when I was the rawest of novices to the stage, who was kind and thoughtful and fun to work with, was gone. When I asked why I was met with embarrassed excuses. I was probably the only person in the band who hadn't known. Mike had committed the unforgivable sin for those days, not just of being gay but of being caught. I could not find out where he went or what happened to him. I hope he drifted back into the professional theatre because he was multi-talented, a singer, dancer and actor. But I grieve to this day that I never said 'Goodbye, and thank you.'

In the autumn of 1944 I was renting a room from a friend in

Marylebone. She was on night duty, doing secret work in connection with the French Resistance at the Special Operations Executive headquarters in Baker Street. I was often the only person left in the big block of flats at night and it was eerie and frightening during raids, but I hated the thought of being trapped in the claustrophobic underground shelters. I was nearly blown up by a rocket while in Kodak's in Holborn, trying desperately to get hold of photographic paper to print my Middle East photos, and had another near miss soon after. It was the V-2 rockets now, and at least you could not hear them coming like the awful doodlebugs. It was a sad, dark time, with uncertain overcrowded train journeys to London and bitter cold weather. The one bright spot was when I heard that a BBC audition I had done in September, very badly as I thought at the time, had been successful.

I remember a happy and peaceful home at Christmas (no bombs), followed by splendid skating when the local ponds and lakes were frozen hard for six weeks. We even played hilarious and painful shinty with up-ended walking sticks and a rubber ball on our big garden pond.

By New Year 1945 the war news had begun improving at last. I find in my diary an entry 'Cold again. Snows. News marvellous – everyone has been so depressed but the cloud seems to be lifting.' The literary agents A P Watts wrote that they had had an excellent reader's report on my edited Middle East letters and were looking for a publisher, but sadly the severe paper shortage intervened, though John Murray would have published could I have found 500 reams of paper for him.

On 8th May VE Day came at long last. The dark backdrop that had been with us ever since September 1939 was lifted and an extraordinary sense of tranquillity came with the thought that all over Europe the killing and dying had stopped. We hastily scraped together what food we could and had a small party, followed by a bonfire at which a fine effigy of Hitler was burnt. The next night I did two celebratory shows with the band. But the rejoicing for many of us was muted because we had friends and relations still involved in the horrible war in the Far East.

My life of the last five years was beginning to disintegrate. Johnnie left the army to conduct a touring company of *The Merry Widow* for

Jack Hylton. He eventually re-married, having divorced his first wife, but sadly died in his forties of a heart attack. Our relationship had deepened from close friendship to something more intimate while in the Middle East, but we both accepted that it must cease when we got home. As he had said from the beginning, there were to be no regrets. It was an interlude typical of wartime, which left me with only happy memories.

The band seemed to melt away. Our final concert scheduled for 2nd August 1945 was cancelled, so it turned out that my last concert with them had been a small affair on 12th July. The professional jazz and classical musicians rushed off home to try to rebuild their interrupted careers, the regular army musicians returned to what must have seemed a very humdrum life of barracks and parades. It was strange after so many years of close companionship and hard work, much fun, much good music and a smattering of danger. 'Thirty Men and a Girl' had disappeared without trace like a pricked bubble.

Looking back, I see myself at that time as a very fragmented person, whirling around like a Catherine wheel, not knowing who I was or where I was going, singing a great deal in recitals, oratorio and concerts, but also leading a hectic social life. My diaries tell of a constant round of parties, of going to concerts and opera and plays whenever I wasn't singing (tickets were amazingly cheap) and of meeting many interesting people. There is a cryptic note in my diary for 25th January 1945: 'Lunch at the Ritz with Habib, Baroness de Rutzen, Field Marshal Lord Berwick and Princess ?? (*sic!*)' – I can remember absolutely nothing about this star-spangled occasion except that the Habib mentioned was a charming, cultured, extremely wealthy middle-aged Lebanese, also a prince, who had recently befriended me. Whether he saw himself in the position of a sugar daddy I don't know, but he was quite sensitive enough to realise quickly that I was not sugar baby material. I was never any good at networking, and these grand friends soon faded from my life.

Then on 7th August 1945 came the news of the horrendous bombing of Hiroshima, followed by VJ Day on 15th August. Once again Trafalgar Square was full of people rejoicing. The world was at last supposedly at peace.

The Post War Years, 1946–47

I see the post-war years as a period of confusion when we were all looking for a new direction to our lives, and failing – at first – to find one. Somehow we were not as happy as we had expected to be. Looking back, I see it was inevitable that, after the high tension of the war years, the whole nation somehow fell flat. Winston Churchill went, seemingly abandoned by those he had so recently inspired, the socialist government came in, rationing went on as relentlessly as ever, our wounded and our starved prisoners of war, many fresh from the horrors of the Japanese camps, came back to us different, and many families went through emotional and psychological trauma brought on by the return of loved ones who had become strangers. The war years had broken down age-old barriers of class and rank. Our empire began to melt away as one by one our colonies took their freedom. It felt as if our old country was young and vulnerable again.

At the same time there was a new awakening of interest in the arts. Music clubs sprang up all over the country, the orchestras and opera companies re-invented themselves and people flocked to listen to music and look at pictures as if starved after the bleak war years. All this interest may have been fuelled by the recitals CEMA had been sending round the country to the most unlikely venues and audiences, and the splendid National Gallery lunch-hour concerts started by Dame Myra Hess, to which I went whenever possible. I remember one marvellous wartime recital with Benjamin Britten and Peter Pears, and another with Michael Tippett, all of whom had spent the first part of the war in New York as conscientious objectors. They came home, bravely I thought, and here they were making music to a packed audience of young men and women all in uniform who gave them a warm reception. I felt proud to belong to a country that could be so kind and tolerant.

The summer of 1946 brought a magical holiday when my parents and I were once more able to go to Switzerland together with my closest friend Pam, who had just been demobbed after six hard years in the WRNS. The Alps have always been very special for my family. It all began when my mother was a desperately homesick little girl sent home from Ceylon, where my grandfather was a tea planter, to boarding school in England, together with her two brothers. She was put in charge of an elderly cousin for her holidays, and 'Cousie', as she was affectionately christened, was an intrepid traveller. She used to take my mother to somewhere near Annecy in France, and they would go for long walks into the mountains, with Cousie mounted on a mule and my mother hanging onto its tail when the going got too steep. She adored these holidays and developed a love of mountains and alpine flowers that never left her.

In 1946 we all went out by train, travelling as cheaply as possible because the travel allowance was something ridiculous, like £25 per person. My mother had heard of a small mountain hotel halfway between Wengen and Scheidegg, at Wengernalp. For the last part of the journey on the mountain railway from Lauterbrunnen Pam and I stood on the footplate between carriages in a daze of happiness, breathing in the keen sweet mountain air and enraptured by the flower-covered slopes and the perfect silver cone of the Silberhorn towering above us. We were the only people to get off at the little halt for Wengernalp, but there waiting for us on the platform were our host and hostess Herr and Frau Consett who owned the little Hotel Jungfrau. They hugged us warmly, telling us we were their first English guests since the war, and describing how they had been used to stand outside night after night counting our bombers as they roared overhead on their way to bomb enemy targets, and how distressed they were if they counted fewer returning. The mountain flowers were memorable that summer, and Pam and I used to take our shoes off and run downhill through the thick carpet of colour. There was a fierce and unexpected storm when nearly two feet of snow fell overnight, and the Consetts, knowing we were all keen skiers, dug out pairs of old skis for us. We went up on the train to above Scheidegg and absolutely disgraced ourselves on the way down, laughing so much that we couldn't stay upright. Sadly now the slopes are all scarred by great bare swathes cut by the winter pistes: we were lucky to see them when they were undamaged.

When I got home I went to the Caledonian ball in London, which seemed to be from another age. Otherwise everyday life continued grey and difficult, though artistically things were fizzing. On 5th November I moved into my first very own flat, christened by my mother 'The Gusset', rent £2.10.00 a week. It was a top-floor back room in Hans

Crescent, which just held my small bed, an armchair, a little upright piano, a corner cupboard, a chest of drawers and a Baby Belling cooker. There was a half-sized bath and a separate loo. In this tiny space I gave singing lessons, had coaching, and gave parties – with a maximum of four guests.

By Christmas 1946 I was on track again, engaged in a project I found tremendously rewarding, the setting up and running of the Wigmore Hall lunch-hour concerts. At that time it was the custom for serious young classical musicians to give one or more recitals in a London venue to which the national press and top agents could be invited. The most prestigious venue was the Wigmore Hall, but the cost of hire and publicity was way beyond the reach of artists just returning from the war. With the help of two friends, Cecilia Keating, violinist, and Hubert Dawkes, pianist and organist, with whom I had been doing recitals for CEMA, I drew up a budget for lunch-hour concerts that would cost £100 per concert inclusive, which could be shared by say three artists at a cost of £33 each. I approached the Arts Council, who owned the Hall, and the top London agents Ibbs and Tillett, and asked them for their co-operation. The latter were rather astonished at first, but we were able to negotiate a very reasonable hire fee and Ibbs became enthusiastic supporters and agreed to manage the concerts for us. All depended on getting the approval of the Hall manager, Mr Brickell, a rather choleric red-faced gentleman with a black moustache who obviously thought the whole scheme was way beneath the dignity of the Wigmore Hall, and who nearly exploded when I put it to him gently that it would be so nice if our lunch-hour audiences could get a cup of tea or coffee with their music. Impossible! Such a thing was unheard of. There would be crumbs on the carpet! His cleaners would all give notice. Beneath his irate exterior, however, Mr Brickell concealed a heart of gold, and before long I was hunting for a suitably modest firm of caterers.

We booked our first series of six Wednesday lunch hours to be launched on 12th March 1947. Word got around quickly and applications to take part poured in. Cecilia, Hubert and I gave the first concert to a very good audience and most of the national press, and we had to book a second series immediately. I am proud to read the names of the musicians who took part, many of whom later became famous. Dennis Brain, that incomparable horn player, appeared twice.

The Robert Masters Quartet took a whole concert, and Martin Lovett, Norbert Brainin, Peter Schidlof and Sigmund Nissel, who later formed themselves into the Amadeus Quartet, all played as soloists. There was a great drama about either Sigmund or Norbert (I can't remember which), as it turned out he had no papers and at the last moment the Home Office refused to allow him to appear. He was in the dreadful position of being a stateless refugee, a non-person, and I had a battle with officials, who relented in the end and allowed him to play.

The day after the great occasion of the first lunch hour I was back at the Wigmore Hall to audition for the English Opera Group (or EOG), Benjamin Britten's company, which he had launched at Glyndebourne the year before with his new opera *The Rape of Lucretia*. I remember I was feeling very depressed as I felt I had not sung well at the concert the day before, and after the audition I wrote in my diary that I sang rather badly, the big aria from *La Traviata* first, then the high soprano role of Lucia in *The Rape of Lucretia*, which I had been studying specially. Three of the directors of the EOG, Anne Wood, Joan Cross and Eric Crozier, all of whom had come to the concert the day before, were there, and all said nice things about it. But Benjamin Britten was ill, so nothing could be decided, though Eric Crozier, the producer of *Lucretia*, had a long talk with me explaining that they wanted to take several young singers to Glyndebourne for the coming season to understudy and be trained, and he would like me to understudy Lucia. It was a breathtaking thought, but of course Ben's approval was required.

On 29th March I sang again for the EOG with Ben present, at 10.15 a.m. on a 'pouring, filthy day'. This time I sang part of Rosina's aria from *The Barber of Seville*, followed by my warhorse the *Traviata* aria, and after that almost all the role of Lucia. That wonderful coach and dear man Hans Oppenheim, who had prepared me meticulously for Lucia, struggled along through the awful weather, though he was a sick man, to accompany me, as the piano score of *The Rape of Lucretia* is very difficult to play. In my diary I wrote 'Sing so badly – am sure I have failed.'

There ensued a wait, which seemed to me forever. At last on 12th April came wonderful news. I was offered the Glyndebourne season, followed by the option of tours on the Continent and at home, as understudy for the role of Lucia!

I was delirious with excitement, but was brought down to earth because the programmes for the next series of lunch hours were overdue and I found myself having to address a great pile of envelopes. I was busy with the odd small concert and some oratorio, also had to begin work on a programme for my second Wigmore Hall lunch-hour concert, which was fast approaching. Soon after we began London rehearsals for Benjamin Britten's new opera *Albert Herring*, a setting of a Guy de Maupassant short story 'Le Rosier de Madame Huisson'. It was an amusing story transposed from its original French setting to a village in rural England, where the mayor and local worthies headed by the formidable Lady Billows fail to find a girl of suitably pure reputation to be elected as their May Queen for the forthcoming May Day festival, so they elect Albert Herring, a blameless and timid youth whose mother runs the village greengrocer's shop. The story of how the villagers conspire to fill his glass of lemonade with neat gin at the May Day feast is a simple one, but Ben and librettist Eric Crozier produced a cast of superb characters written with many of Ben's favourite singer friends in mind, and dancer and choreographer Frederick Ashton produced with so much wit that we were often helpless with laughter at rehearsal.

We all went down to Glyndebourne on 18th May, I having let The Gusset for the summer, and I found myself in very nice digs in Lewes with another new girl to the company, Anne Sharp. We had breakfast and dinner at the White Hart Hotel nearby with all the rest of the company, and a fleet of cars ferried us to and from Glyndebourne daily.

Those first weeks were magical, and as I had no responsibility beyond attending understudy coaching and rehearsal I had time to enjoy the lovely gardens and lake and the whole beautiful setting. In fact I spent almost every minute in the theatre watching rehearsals of *The Rape of Lucretia*, *Albert Herring*, and Gluck's *Orfeo*, which was being put on by Glyndebourne. The whole running of the theatre fascinated me and seemed to me the height of professionalism and efficiency. In our lunch break we would all queue for an excellent 2/- meal at the big canteen where an oak tree grew up through the centre of the hall. Often one would see Mr Christie himself standing way back in the queue chatting with the stagehands as he waited his turn. The casts I was watching were star-spangled. Kathleen Ferrier, who was singing both *Orfeo* in the new production and sharing the role of Lucretia with Nancy Evans, was a tall and beautiful figure often dressed in white shorts and shirt having been playing tennis with Ben and Peter. Otakar Kraus was again singing Tarquin, the lustful and arrogant Roman prince who eventually rapes Lucretia. It was a shock to be introduced to a middle-aged balding gentleman of middling height and indeterminate features, but before long I was lost in admiration of Otakar's extraordinary power as an actor, the ease with which he moved from the evil Tarquin one night to the unctuous Vicar Mr Gedge in *Albert Herring* the next, and also his skill in making himself up. Singers do not usually get help with their make-up, and he took about an hour before each performance to create a haughty and aristocratic Roman nose for himself. He was a mine of information and advice for us youngsters and took a genuine interest in our development, sexual, I must add, as well as artistic. For him the two things went hand in hand. He was the first man I knew of that continental type which later became familiar – a married man who would sleep with as many pretty girls as possible while being a devoted husband and father. He did not consider it in any way unfaithful because his wife was special and forever.

I had a day's leave on 28th May to meet my parents in London and be presented at Buckingham Palace. It was a huge post-war garden party as there had been no presentations since before the war, so we did not get to meet the Queen individually. I remember very little about it except that I wore a short red and grey silk dress and a red hat, it was very hot, and I had hay fever. I got much teased by the company and Peter Pears christened me 'our deb'.

Peter and Ben, Anne Wood (who was Company Manager), Nancy Evans and her husband Eric Crozier, and Frederick Ashton were known to us as the Royal Family. I still addressed them as Mr Britten and Mr Pears, being very old-fashioned, and certainly we juniors were very much in awe of them. I was in the theatre every moment *The Rape of Lucretia* was being rehearsed, and it seemed incredible that only a year ago I had come down to a performance of it at Glyndebourne and had been so deeply disturbed by the power of the piece that I had been unable to sleep for two nights. It seemed tremendously new and modern and though I never loved it as I grew to love other operas it certainly held me in thrall.

Peter was my idol. I admired his artistry and his singing more with every day I listened to him. He was sharing the roles of male chorus in *Lucretia* and the title role in *Albert Herring* with Richard Lewis, also a fine artist. Off-stage Peter was tall and good-looking in a very English way. When he offered to help me with my singing I was overwhelmed, and found him a helpful teacher. I had the impression that we talked the same language, and I rapidly fell deeply in love with him, though I knew perfectly well that there was no future in it. Just once when we were walking together in the garden he put his arm round me and gave me a hug, and I knew perfectly well that there was what in modern terms we call a chemistry between us. I was still very naïve and unsophisticated in many ways, and it upset me deeply and filled me with revulsion when, at his request, I rang him first thing in the morning to fix the time for my singing lessons and he was obviously in bed with Ben. Peter won several female hearts but never so far as I know swerved from his partnership with Ben. Lennox Berkeley, on the other hand, who had been very much one of their inner circle, was at Glyndebourne with his newly-wed wife. Their son Michael was to become one of our top composers and broadcasters. I met many most interesting people at Glyndebourne, including John and Myfanwy Piper, E M Forster, and Ronald Duncan, librettist of *The Rape of Lucretia*, of whom more anon.

I got another day off to go down and do a broadcast for BBC Wales in Cardiff, and on one occasion my parents came to Glyndebourne and spent a happy day going round the garden, and watching Frederick Ashton, who was a friend, rehearsing *Albert Herring*.

We had met Fred when we were guests of mutual friends in the West Highlands. My mother and stepfather were about to get married so he fondly christened my mother Bridie. The children of the house party were commanded to produce an entertainment for the grown-ups one rainy day. This was during my ballet period, and I had the nerve to choreograph a short dance for myself and perform it before the great man! If I remember rightly he remained discreetly silent.

Albert Herring had its first performance on 20th June 1947. We all thought it was a brilliant production, with a cast including Joan Cross as Lady Billows, Gladys Parr as Florence, Peter as Albert, Betsy de la Porte as his mum, Frederick Sharpe as Sid, Margaret Ritchie as Miss Wordsworth and Nancy Evans as Nancy, all giving deliciously witty characterisations. However the press reaction was on the whole cool and all those concerned were deeply disappointed after the long rehearsal period and all the thought and work that had gone into the production.

I was beginning to feel a little frustrated with so much looking and listening, and felt I wasn't earning even my modest salary of £8 a week. Then on 1st July I went in to attend a rehearsal of *Lucretia* with orchestra conducted by Norman del Mar. Lucia was being sung by a Viennese soprano Irene Eisinger, as Margaret Ritchie, for whom the role had been written, was busy with her new part in *Albert*. The morning seemed to go smoothly, but after lunch I was suddenly called to go on to the stage. No Miss Eisinger. It transpired that she had thrown a terrific temperament and departed for Vienna in floods of tears with some sort of a nervous breakdown. The reason given was that she was furious because she had not been asked to sing Lucia in a recording and broadcast of the opera later in the year. This was no part of the Glyndebourne season and Ben naturally wanted Margaret to record the role she had created. So I was rushed onto the stage for the afternoon rehearsal of Act 2, sick with fright and finding the orchestra 'very disconcerting' as I had only ever worked on the role with piano. I was also handed a new short aria Ben had composed for Lucia (perhaps in an attempt to placate Miss Eisinger!), which I had to sight-read from manuscript. Ben listened in the auditorium. After the rehearsal there was a performance of *Albert*, and in the interval Eric Crozier told me that Irene Eisinger was probably not coming back, and asked if I could be ready to sing the first night, which was also a Third Programme broadcast, by the following Monday. I was stunned, but feeling sick with fright said I would try to do it. I was deeply grateful to Hans Oppenheim who had prepared the role so thoroughly with me in London. I couldn't sleep from a mixture of fear and excitement and I wrote in my diary:

> Am I right to say I will try to do a big first night
> and Third Programme broadcast? Mr Britten is away
> conducting his violin concerto in Cheltenham. Eric
> Crozier tells me that he has spoken to Irene Eisinger's
> Doctor husband on the telephone, and they have agreed
> she had better withdraw from her contract. It's incredible
> – the sort of thing that doesn't happen to me! Feel sick.

The Company is told at lunchtime and all are so sweet…
yesterday was told I can sing at the Zürich concert too –
am thrilled!

My diary for Thursday 3rd July went on:

Cannot believe this is happening to me. A Glyndebourne
First Night! Awful day today – orchestral rehearsal with
Mr Goodall, who is very wrought-up, owing I think to his
'Trovatore' going very badly at Covent Garden, and who
gets very impatient and conducts very unhelpfully, and
thoroughly upsets the already very strung-up cast, so much
so that they are nearly going on strike. Things v tense
and unhappy. Benjamin Britten gets back after travelling
most of Tuesday and Wednesday nights, and a great success
yesterday (with his violin concerto at Cheltenham). He so
sweet and encouraging and furious with Reggie Goodall,
though so tired he can hardly stand. I start rehearsing at
10.30 and do an hour on stage with piano, then till 1.30
with orchestra and movement, Act 2 only. Then 3 hours of
Act 1 with piano and movement in the Organ Room.

Poor Reggie was conducting from manuscript and having very
short sight needed to bury his head in the music and do a sort of
breaststroke with his arms. It was impossible to detect a down beat.
There was a refreshing moment of levity when several of the senior
members of the cast, such as Norman Lumsden and Dennis Dowling,
shouted down to him 'For God's sake stop swimming, Reggie!' He
was not amused, but we all had a relaxing giggle.

FRIDAY 4TH JULY:

Am in a sick panic today – probably the result of
yesterday's rehearsal. However Benjamin Britten has
spoken to Mr Goodall who is much nicer and more
helpful. We do my big dread, Act 1 Scene 2, which I have
to do for the first time with orchestra and movement.

Go on with piano after lunch. Back to Lewes and study my score feverishly. Was fitted for my dress today. Mabel Ritchie's is all right with a little alteration. [Note – clothing rationing was still on.]

The first time I heard the opening music of Act 1 Scene 2 played by the orchestra, when Lucia runs on stage singing 'Oh what a lovely day!' I stood with my mouth open unable to find the right note to start on. I was greatly comforted to know Margaret Ritchie always found it difficult too. She advised me to stand in the wings humming the note during the whole musical interlude when the curtain comes down on Scene 1 and large heavy scenery has to be changed in the very short time dictated by the music. So I planted myself firmly in the wings humming away and refused to budge as large beams rose and fell around me, and Jock, Glyndebourne's first-class but irate stage manager, swore at me under his breath for being in the way.

SATURDAY 5TH JULY:

Still v panicky. Today we are on the stage with orchestra until teatime – have part of our scenery, and get into my dress and sandals after lunch. It is beginning to take shape, but the cast so tired – Flora Nielsen, Norman Lumsden, even Nancy Evans who is so wonderfully calm, seem nearly at breaking point, as strung-up as I am. It must be a shock for them and for Mr Goodall suddenly getting me landed on them.

SUNDAY 6TH JULY:

Rehearse all morning, with Kathleen Ferrier for the first time. She dead tired after the big first night of 'Orfeo' last night, but so funny, has us all in fits – a marvellous sweet personality. Woke feeling calm after the awful panic of the last few days – and not sick any more. Public Dress Rehearsal at 6.00 to a large and enthusiastic audience goes well. The two quick scene changes before the Women's

scenes are a nightmare, never having been rehearsed –
various minor props get mislaid, but nothing vital. In
some amazing way rather enjoy it. Stanford Robinson and
Lorelei Dyer here preparing for tomorrow's broadcast.
Have my hair dressed up by Paul Schneider – it actually
stays up and looks quite effective.

MONDAY 7TH JULY:

Still feel incredibly calm – cannot believe this is happening
– my operatic debut at Glyndebourne – with Third
Programme broadcast thrown in. Rehearse all morning.
Rest after lunch in the Green Room. Performance begins
at 5.35. Very nervous but in an unreal sort of way – am
too tired to feel much, I think. Very long interval (1½
hours for the audience to dine) which is trying. Many
famous people in the audience including Karl Rankl. We
are all terribly nervous but the opera goes without a hitch
except that I am late on for one cue due to a black-out
[I think I must have meant mental, not lights!] but it is
not noticeable. Have masses of flowers and presents from
almost every member of the company. Do my own make-
up and hair in different style with very effective plastic
curls on forehead.

I also noted that although very relieved it was over I was rather
disappointed by the reaction of the audience afterwards. *The Rape of
Lucretia* was not a popular piece with British audiences. The next day
The Times had a very mixed notice, but I got a nice mention, and noted
that the opera as a whole was far more favourably viewed than last
year. The cast was Emily Hook (female chorus), Richard Lewis (male
chorus), Kathleen Ferrier (Lucretia), Flora Nielsen (Bianca), myself
(Lucia), Otakar Kraus (Tarquin), Norman Lumsden (Collatinus), and
Dennis Dowling (Junius). Sadly my parents were in Switzerland and
could not get back for their daughter's big day. I got good notices in
The Times and *News Chronicle*, and a favourable report for the broadcast,
which I found out about only some time later.

Our next performance was two days later and my diary entry starts once again:

> Ghastly day. Awful rehearsal in the morning. Mr Britten conducts (piano only) and I can't do anything right. It's cold and damp – voice awful – everyone very depressed. Get very upset and have a good cry. Performance at 5.30 with Lord Harwood and the Princess Royal (he came Monday too). Opera starts during a thunderstorm and suddenly lightning strikes the Glyndebourne power house and all the lights fail. This lasts 20–30 minutes, then the lights come on and we start off again with the tent scene, but the lights go again. Mr Britten and Peter Pears rush round and comfort us as we are by now a little jittery. However the second time the lights come on and stay on. But Mr Christie's wonderful emergency lighting, which failed to come on when wanted, blazes out in the middle of Collatinus's aria (a dark scene!).

I wasn't happy about my performance, but next day I was sent for from the office and told they wanted me to go on singing Lucia, except for the odd special performance that Margaret Ritchie would do. My salary was raised from £8 to £15 a week so they must have been quite pleased with me.

I got many letters saying that the broadcast on Monday had been excellent, and Mrs Christie (singer Audrey Mildmay) sent flowers and a sweet letter. But the last show at Glyndebourne was again very fraught. I was given intensive production rehearsal as had been criticised for stiffness on the stage. Apparently I had a bad habit of standing in fourth position (shades of my ballet training!) and Eric Crozier used to shout 'Don't dance, Elisabeth!' from the stalls. I find in my diary:

> Today again awful rehearsal in the morning. I wish everybody wouldn't contradict each other as to what one should do. And Reginald Goodall and Mr Britten contradict each other over the music too. Practise after lunch as voice seems bad, and Mr Britten of course wants the Linen Trio quieter and quieter (a difficult soft high

piece for the soprano). Good audience for our last show and feel I do Act 2 a bit better but Reggie Goodall upsets me terribly by raving at me for dragging. I didn't know I did as can't hear the orchestra, or see him well owing to the brilliant lights.

I was 'bitterly upset' by Reggie's outburst just as I was getting a little less nervous. However a few days later there was a studio broadcast of *Lucretia* sung by the original cast, which Ben asked me to attend – so that I could hear how it should be done – and after it was over Reggie apologised to me for having been so cross and told me I had done very well, because Margaret Ritchie had just dragged in exactly the same place during the broadcast! It was like being a yo-yo. I never knew if I was up or down.

The last night of *Albert Herring* however was riotous. The unfortunate cast had to make a short film of the opera after rehearsal in the morning, so had very little rest before the 5.30 performance. Everyone was in high spirits, and there was a lot of mischief. In Act 2 Sid, the errand boy, played by Dennis Dowling, had to bicycle onto the stage with a crate of lemonade bottles for the May Day feast. He was supposed to stop stage centre and call out 'Sorry, Miss Pike! Punctured me bike!' but the brakes had been removed so he swept on and straight off the far side, singing as he went and disappearing with a crash into the wings. Ben was conducting, and he was not amused. Worse was to come. The cast had been vying with each other to break down the senior singers – i.e. make them laugh onstage – and everyone, even Joan Cross, had been caught and reduced to fits of giggles, except for Peter Pears who had iron self-control. On this last night a tumbler full of neat gin was substituted for the lemonade Albert has to drink publicly at the party. He downed it – every drop – without batting an eyelid. And nothing was said in the interval before Act 3, which starts with a long solo scene of very tricky music for Albert, who is supposed to come home drunk after having been on a bender. He had to climb on a chair and light a gas lamp, which goes off with a bang at precisely the right instant in the music. The cast gathered in the wings listening expectantly. Surely a whole tumbler of gin must have some effect? But no – not a quaver in the music was misplaced, the gas went *bang!* at exactly the right moment, and the iron man had won!

As ever with *Albert* the audience was enthusiastic. It was a very happy piece. The singers were a real crowd of jokers, and rehearsals were full of laughter. When Albert disappears on a spree after the May Day feast dressed in his white suit, the entire village turns out to hunt for him. There is a dramatic moment when the little boy David rushes in shouting 'There's a big white *something* in Mrs Williams's well!' It was a hot summer, and Mr Christie, whom I remember as a large kindly person, used to wear a white linen suit, so inevitably he became known as the 'big white something', and if we were up to some mischief the warning 'Look out! Here comes the BWS!' would ring out.

I had had to do several rehearsals in the children's roles of Emmie and Cis, which I was covering, and in our opening scene Anne Sharp and I had to bounce a rubber ball against a half-door while singing 'Bounce me high! Bounce me low! Bounce me up to Jericho!' Ben was a wizard with balls and he could do this bouncing the ball off the ground so that it ricocheted off the door and he caught it in exact time to the music. Annie and I never succeeded; I remember crouching down behind the half-door with her, dressed in our shabby gymslips and black wool stockings, waiting for our cue. She rolled large blue eyes at me and in a tone of disgust exclaimed, 'Grand Opera indeed!'

The atmosphere of *Lucretia* was quite other, and those who had been in it for the first season agreed it was not a happy piece. The young would have said of it nowadays 'bad vibes'. Ronald Duncan, who had written the libretto, was a strange and to me rather sinister presence in the background. I can't remember ever speaking a word to him; he was always there watching and listening, and he became part of the bad dreams I was beginning to have. Any merriment there was in the *Lucretia* performances usually stemmed from Kathleen Ferrier. At the end, when she has killed herself, and is on the ground with her nurse Bianca and her maid Lucia lying across her body weeping, there is a very strange incongruous piece of music that we didn't like played by the orchestra. Unseen by the audience, Kathleen would begin to make strange squeaking and grunting sounds in irreverent imitation, and we would all three become convulsed with laughter, which the top two of the pile hoped would appear to the audience as spasms of grief. One day Bianca (Flora Nielsen) and I were summoned to the office by Anne Wood, who was not amused, and told us in no uncertain terms that what she called 'this lamentable pile' must cease forthwith.

25 *Above: Dennis Arundel taking a rehearsal of Cimarosa's* The Secret Marriage. *Phyllis Thorold at the piano.*

26 *Right: EP taking a rehearsal.*

27 *Peter Gellhorn, Music Director of London Opera Players from 1950 until his death in 2004.*

28 *Left: Charles Farncombe, d.2005, Guest Conductor with the company for many years.*

29 *Above: Our early "house" production of Puccini's* Tosca *with Henry Howell as Cavaradossi.*

30 La Belle Hélène *by Offenbach, Director Tom Hawkes. Robina Vallance as Hélène and Adrian Martin as Paris, the costumes designed by Malcolm Pride and made by students at the Wimbledon College of Art.*

31 Left: Dr Joseph Parry.

32 Below: Barbara Parry-Smith and EP at the museum at 4, Chapel Row, Dr Parry's birthplace in Merthyr Tydfil.

33 Bottom of page: 4, Chapel Row with Doreen Widgery and Barbara Parry-Smith, remaining grand-daughters of Dr Parry. L: Mansel Richards, Head of History at Cyfarthfa Castle School, whose pupils won the Prince of Wales Committee Jubilee Award for work done on the cottage, and the plaque designed and made by Dewi Bowen, sculptor and Head of Art (C. Left).

● Barbara Parry Smith, Dr. Joseph Parry's grand-daughter, and Elizabeth Parry, Dr. Parry's great-grand-daughter, examine the model of the row of cottages where the great composer was born. ABOVE: The team who produced he new exhibition.

34 Left: Offenbach's chamber opera A Husband On the Mat *with Marian Hughes and EP.*

35 Below: Three's Company *by Antony Hopkins, with Graham Godfrey (L.) and Robert Bateman as Mr Love and Mr Three.*

36 Left: Margaret Brownbridge, pianist, coach, repetiteur and keyboard player with the company.

37 Top left: Cosi fan Tutte *by Mozart, directed by John Ramster, with Valerie Reid as Dorabella and Naomi Harvey as Fiordiligi.*

38 Top right: Tosca *by Puccini, with Khosrow Mahsoori as Cavaradossi and Margaret Pearman as Tosca. Director Tom Hawkes.*

39 Below: Falstaff *by Verdi, director John Ramster. The cast at dress rehearsal on stage at the Yvonne Arnaud Theatre, Guildford, January 2000. C. Alan Fairs as Falstaff.*

40 *Learning to climb at the Quintin School, St John's Wood.*

41 *EP on a Mountaineering Association course in the Lake District.*

42 *Early morning camping by Loch Duich. Dorothea Gravina listening to a flock of male Eider Duck calling.*

43 Above left: Guide Willi Truffer on the Leiterspitzen, Zermatt.

44 Above right: Guide Celso Degasper with a client on Torre Wundt, Dolomites.

45 Right: Guide Gilles Josserand with Nigella Blandy on the descent from the Grépon, Chamonix.

46 Below: Sidney and Hilary Nowill on a col above Bay Göl, Hakkâri, SE Turkey.

47 Above left: The Innominata Ridge, Mont Blanc, Nigella Blandy and John Varnay climbing.

48 Above right: Bivouac Cravéri on the Peuterey route, Mont Blanc. The party having second breakfast.

49 Below: The "ferry" crossing the river into Zanskar.

Unfortunately Ben had a row with the Christies, a difference over casting, I believe. Glyndebourne cast internationally, but Ben composed his operas very much with his singer friends in mind. When the EOG season at Glyndebourne ended it was for good, and the next year Peter and Ben set up the Aldeburgh Festival. Before we left Mr and Mrs Christie asked me to return to Glyndebourne in 1948, but although very flattered I refused, as I felt my loyalty was to the EOG, which had after all given me my first chance. In retrospect I think I made a very big mistake.

Our spirits all revived as we set out on our continental tour. For the first week we stayed in The Hague and performed both *Albert* and *Lucretia* at the Kurhaus at Scheveningen before moving on to Amsterdam. I got to sing the Lucias because Margaret Ritchie was busy in *Albert*. We loved The Hague but hated hot, crowded tourist-filled Scheveningen, where the Kurhaus was quite unsuited to opera and the unskilled stage staff struggled with our heavy and complicated scenery. By now I had good friends among the young members of the company, especially Enid Vandyk who had joined as our secretary at the same time as I had, Alice Lidderdale our touring stage manager, and of course Anne with whom I worked in *Albert*. In Amsterdam we managed to fit in a motor-launch tour through the canals, under old bridges and past the fascinating gabled houses. I also got to the Rijksmuseum but was in a state of nerves as I had to sing Lucia the next day. Enid and I were sharing a tiny stiflingly hot top-floor room, there was a big thunderstorm, I didn't sleep at all and got up with a relaxed throat. According to my diary I cried at rehearsal (I hope not noticeably) and wrote that I was muddled by so much contradictory advice and dreading the performance. We rehearsed music all morning then went on the stage at the Stadtschoburg in the afternoon, but got nothing done as the Dutch stage staff were in a state of mutiny. Everybody lost their tempers and Reggie was awful. Feel I can't get through, but after a bad start the Linen Trio doesn't go too badly. BB was very upset as it was a bad performance.

We managed to visit several art galleries before packing up to move on to Switzerland, where I was meeting my parents for a week's holiday before rejoining the company in Lucerne.

This was still real wartime-style travel. A group of us caught an overnight train to Basle, sitting up all night second class. Trains went painfully slowly and made strange detours, as there was so much unrepaired bomb damage. We went via Belgium, Luxembourg and France, stopping for over an hour at Maastricht for security and customs checks. Luckily we had been issued with special food coupons to buy food for the journey! Tickets were checked about six times, eventually the old engine broke down, and we arrived very late in Basle. I shot onto the first train to Lucerne, where I found my parents waiting for me with our car. Despite the very small amount of money we were allowed to take abroad – still something like £25 each – they had managed to stretch their allowance so that I could join them for a week at our little mountain hotel at Wengernalp, where we had had such a blissful holiday the year before. It was the perfect break, mountain walking, eating and sleeping, before I rejoined the EOG on 10th August in Lucerne.

My accommodation there had been arranged in a little hotel, which was in a bad way after the war. My small dirty room produced several bed bugs and I felt I was back in the Middle East. When I complained mildly to the landlady she flew into a rage, told me to find another hotel and swore she had no idea what a bed bug looked like! It transpired that many of Lucerne's lovely old painted buildings were badly infested and would take a long time to clean up as they were all subject to preservation orders. The town was packed, but luckily Enid Vandyk offered me a small room in an apartment her family had taken at the Wilden Mann Hotel. I had great fun with them, and no responsibility, as I was not required to sing at all in Lucerne. This was as well, as I was sick for a couple of days, probably the result of the amazing rich non-rationed food in Switzerland, which took all our stomachs by surprise after the frugal fare in the rest of post-war Europe.

I sat in on the performances, two of each opera, which were enthusiastically received. Ben conducted *Albert Herring*, which the cast said made all the difference. He was indeed a very clear and decisive conductor, with great big hands like a policeman, which were easy to see. We bathed a lot, and wandered in the lovely old town with its painted gables and wooden-roofed bridge, the green waters of the rushing river, cool deep arcades looking out onto the lake, and the luscious fruit stalls and market on the cobbles. One could wander forever. But alas, there was nowhere to practise. We were all short of money and struggling to get more because the shops were mouth-watering. We girls helped the men to buy presents for their families, and I managed to get hold of an extra £20, my diary does not relate how! This enabled me to go and hear Menuhin playing the Bartók concerto with Ansermet conducting. The Berkeleys arrived to join our party, and Enid and I dined with them. We managed to afford several trips on the lake, and one night a group of us, including Otakar Kraus, Dennis Dowling and Anne Sharpe, hired a couple of rowing boats. I noted that it was 'lovely if slightly dangerous – much singing!' – this despite the fact that Otto was always ticking us young ones off for singing in the streets, which was, he said, very unprofessional.

On the day of our final performance I took the Berkeleys round the shops, which amazed them, then decided with difficulty how to spend my remaining few francs. At 6.00 p.m. there was a company meeting. *Crisis!* There was no money left to pay our salaries or the hotel bills, and the British Council was refusing to send the 13,000 Swiss francs we needed.

The performance of *Albert* at 8.15 began inauspiciously with the curtain failing to go up, then Betsy de la Porte (playing Albert's mum) once again missed a tricky but vital entry cue, there were many other small slips, so that although the audience was enthusiastic Ben was furious and unapproachable.

It was arranged that the British Council would meet all the hotel bills and, I assume, the travel home, as the company had completely run out of cash and we were to all intents stranded. Anne Wood, Gladys Parr, and one or two others including myself, were the last to leave, and we had a special wagon-lit carriage from Lucerne to Calais direct. We left Switzerland at 9.25 p.m. and reached Calais at 2.30 p.m. the following day. I can't remember what happened about the salaries, but am sure they must have turned up in due course. Our double-bass player was caught at the Swiss customs with the case of his instrument packed solid with nylon stockings, ladies' silk underwear and black cherry jam! We were equally loaded but luckily got away with it.

On 2nd September I was summoned to the EOG office for a 'little talk' with Eric Crozier, which I had been dreading. To quote:

It is far worse than I'd anticipated. LD is to do Lucia
again (all performances in the provinces as well as Covent

Garden), but the worst is that they do not ask me to do
Emmie but want Anne Sharp to do it and are offering me
the smallest part of Cis. Leave feeling quite stunned and
can't stop crying.

I was strongly advised by Dino Borgioli and many of my friends
and colleagues not to accept this offer, but a few days later, afraid that
I would be out of the EOG altogether if I refused, I accepted it. I had
kept most of the autumn free for their tour and could not afford to
lose it.

I was so deeply depressed that I felt a sudden urge to go home to
the comforting arms of my mother and stepfather for my twenty-sixth
birthday on 3rd September. It was not a happy one although Mum
and I spent a lovely afternoon brambling, which restored my values
somewhat. The following day I went back to London, had a lesson
with Dino Borgioli, then went to the Cambridge Theatre where a
tenor pupil of his was singing the Duke in *Rigoletto*. The opera seasons
at the Cambridge Theatre were run by one Jay Pomeroy, who was
reputed to make all his money in black-market whisky. We wished
all black marketers would use their ill-gotten gains so well; Pomeroy
brought many first-class international singers over and the performances
were a boon to opera-starved London. Dino was Vocal Director to
the company and Pomeroy's lady friend, Daria Bayan, was one of the
leading sopranos. She was a pretty girl with much charm, but her Gilda
in *Rigoletto* was inadequate, though the production by Carl Ebert was
brilliant. The conductor, Alberto Erede, was also excellent but he had
a long lugubrious face and a temperament to match. He regularly
reduced the singers to tears, and Dino would admonish him saying
'Alberto, you must give the singers hope! Without hope a singer can do
nothing!' Erede was insanely jealous of his mistress whom he had left
behind in Rome. From time to time he would rush off to Heathrow
clutching a revolver and swearing he was going to shoot her mythical
lover. It was Dino's job to go after him and bring him back in time
for the performance.

The day after *Rigoletto* I was back at the Cambridge Theatre to
hear my friend Maureen Springer sing Rosina in *The Barber of Seville*.
Maureen and I were Dino's 'babies' and he used to teach us together
first thing in the morning for what was I'm sure a very reduced rate.

She had an amazingly high coloratura voice with a lovely velvety quality; she also had great style and charm on stage. Her father had been a barrow man in the Covent Garden market, and she said there was absolutely no musical talent in her family. She electrified audiences in Dublin by singing a G in alt during a performance of the title role in *Lucia di Lammermoor* when she was only seventeen years old. Had her voice been a little bigger she would have been phenomenal; as it was she married tenor Murray Dickie, and they went off to Vienna and had a good career in opera there.

The EOG autumn tour began with a week at Newcastle-on-Tyne. I had a big Sunday night concert at the Pier Pavilion in Southend, then got a train to Fenchurch Street and a car to King's Cross to catch the overnight train north together with Ben, Peter and other members of the company who had been working late. I was sharing digs with Enid and we found ourselves in a huge comfy double room for three guineas a week each, including a good north-country full breakfast.

I did my first performance of Cis in *Albert Herring* that evening, to an enthusiastic audience. From my diary: '*Ben conducts and is so clear and helpful. What a change after Reggie Goodall!*' The following evening Ivan Clayton conducted *Albert* and I noted after that the children's scenes were still not satisfactory – probably the wretched ball-bouncing went wrong. The first *Lucretia* followed, conducted by Stanford Robinson. Joan Cross had been asked to help with the production of the women's scenes, which were now far more fluid and less static. I wrote in my diary after:

> It is a fearful performance. Poor little ★★★ (my replacement) is frankly bad.

Next day I wrote:

> People are rather upset about last night. One by one most of the company have come up to me privately to say that they think I should be doing Lucia. Am torn between longing to sing it again and being so happy in 'Albert' which is not nerve-wracking but great fun.

My morale was boosted by auditioning for the distinguished choral conductor Dr Hutchinson, who was complimentary and promised me an engagement.

The next week was our very important one at Covent Garden. I can remember meeting Fred Ashton on the Underground and hearing that he was very depressed because he thought *Albert* would be a dismal failure in the vast spaces of the Royal Opera House. The dress rehearsal the next day was very tense and there were various hitches over the scene changes. The following morning I had a TV audition, which I wrote was 'awful – appalling accompanist', then I rushed back to Covent Garden for a short rehearsal and the first night of *Albert*, which went well despite Fred's forebodings, with a warm reception from a good-sized audience. However I noted:

> The Press has been mixed as usual – on the whole I think better than Glyndebourne, usually favourable for the music but not so good for the libretto and plot.

On Friday came the first *Lucretia*, with the second cast singing.

> Emilie Hook (Female Chorus) has a fearful cold and cracks twice but sings well otherwise. Richard Lewis (Male Chorus) has a bad blackout otherwise very good. Nancy (Lucretia) magnificent despite bronchitis, all the others good except ★★★ whose Act 1 is fair, but her Act 2 in spots pathetic.

I noted:

> Lucretia has had indifferent press with mention of bad singing and some criticism of ★★★. 'Albert' is great fun – goes well – am so enjoying Cis and Covent Garden now.

The next week we gave *Albert* with a partial broadcast on Monday, and again on Wednesday, Thursday and Saturday. *Lucretia* was performed once, and the lovely little song for Lucia that Ben had put in at the last moment had to be cut because ★★★ couldn't sing it. So ended my first year with a professional opera company. It had been a series of ups and downs – like the curate's egg, 'good in parts'.

Chapter Nine

The Post War Years, 1948

The EOG's new production for 1948 was an adaptation by Ben of that English classic *The Beggar's Opera*. It was to be produced by Tyrone Guthrie, which was an exciting prospect, with costumes and sets by Tanya Moiseiwitch. All of us junior members were going to have to re-audition for the 1948 season. Joan Cross, who was going to sing Mrs Peachum in the new production, as well as carrying on with her roles of Lady Billows in *Albert*, and the female chorus in *Lucretia*, helped me to prepare two of the songs of Polly Peachum, the soprano heroine of *The Beggar's Opera*, which Anne Sharp was also studying. We auditioned at the end of January, and Ben stopped me halfway through the first of Polly's songs and said it was not at all how he visualised it. I sang it again trying to do as he wanted, but saw I wasn't making any impression, and Joan Cross later apologised for having misled me about how to sing it. In the end all us younger members of the company were offered parts as the men and women of the town. Actually we turned out to be a scene-shifting chorus, but Ben placated us by promising that each one of us should have a single solo line! Not a very exciting prospect, but we all wanted to work with Guthrie and stay with the company. The result was an amazing chorus, with Gladys Parr and Jennifer Vivian among the women and Dennis Dowling and Norman Lumsden among the men. Anne Sharpe was thrilled to be offered the role of Polly, but on one condition, that she leave her present singing teacher, whom she loved and whom she had studied with for years, to go to the newly discovered Viennese teacher Mme de Reusz. This lady, who was now teaching in London, was flavour of the month with the top people of the EOG. They all went to her, Peter Pears, Joan Cross, Anne Wood, Nancy Evans, even Kathleen Ferrier, who did not however stay long. Pressure was also being brought to bear on me, but I did not want to

change teachers, involved as I now was with the organisation of the
Wigmore Hall lunch-hour concerts, preparations for my own second
recital there, quite a nice variety of other engagements, and attending
classes at the newly formed Opera School.

This much-needed venture was the brainchild of Joan Cross and
Anne Wood. To date there had been nowhere for singers to go to
learn stagecraft. Now at last we were to have classes in acting and
interpretation, mime, dance, body language and elocution. Kurt Jooss
took the movement classes, and was a revelation to many of us. I shall
never forget one of his basic lessons in body language: how to get up
off the ground in ways that portrayed (a) happiness, (b) sorrow, (c)
extreme illness (very useful for operatic heroines who are always dying
or getting thrown to the ground), simply by the use of different muscles.
He told us he had developed his muscle control when doing forced
labour in a German camp (he was Jewish), when he would have died
if he had not taught himself how to keep on working by varying the
muscles he used. The head of music, who coached us in all our roles,
was Peter Gellhorn, probably the most brilliant opera coach in the
country.

I was at last rather unwillingly persuaded to go and listen to my
various friends' lessons with Mme de Reusz, and was impressed by
the way she worked with them. My voice had a natural vibrato, which
was I feared getting a little wobbly, and although the high notes and
coloratura were brilliant under Dino's tuition, I felt that the middle
range of the voice did not match up. I was devoted to him and had
been with him since 1943, but I plucked up my courage to talk to
him at last. I remember I dissolved into tears, but he was kind and
understanding, and told me I could always come back to him at any
time. So it came about that together with almost all the members of
the EOG I began to have lessons with Mme de Reusz. It was I think
the second big mistake of my career, the first having been to refuse the
offer of the Christies to go back to Glyndebourne. Had I gone back
there I certainly would never have studied with Mme. Her system was
totally opposed to Dino's, and I had to go right back to the beginning,
singing very softly on an 'oo' vowel with no high notes allowed. At
the same time I had somehow to fulfil my engagements for concert
and oratorio and continue with my career. Life was to become a
series of ups and downs – mostly the latter – as I strove to change my

method. Not all teachers suit all singers, but I had yet to learn this and I struggled on with Mme for several expensive and unhelpful years. It was not until long after that I learned that one of the BBC listening panel, who had heard the Third Programme broadcast of *The Rape of Lucretia* in 1947, listened to a broadcast recital of mine in 1948 and gave an unfavourable report, which started: 'Can this be the same voice I heard a year ago?' Singers are a real bore on the subject of their voices, so maybe I will write a special chapter later on, which can easily be skipped by readers.

To get back to *The Beggar's Opera*, we started work on the music and the pages of dialogue, and we had much hilarity over the latter, for which patient Basil Coleman was coaching us. Dialogue is every singer's nightmare, even when it is quite ordinary, but we were supposed to be a very low-life crowd, women who were mostly whores and men who were brigands or pimps. Our first efforts at eighteenth-century bawds and bandits reduced us to tears of laughter. We got better, but I didn't feel most of us were ever wholly convincing.

Ben was always a law unto himself about casting, and insisted that Peter Pears should play Macheath, a macho, charismatic and womanising ruffian usually sung by a baritone. As Peter himself put it: 'I shall just have to be the pale and interesting sort!' I don't think this interpretation entirely accorded with Tyrone Guthrie's view of the character, but Peter was such a superb artist that in fact he made a great success of it. Ben had disappointed poor Anne Sharpe terribly by not giving her the role of Polly after all, though she had dutifully changed singing teachers and gone to Mme de Reusz. Instead he gave it to mezzo Nancy Evans, who provided Peter with a much more mature and sophisticated – and extremely beautiful – Polly. And Annie joined us in the chorus.

The rehearsals were brilliant, and the production turned out very strong and realistically squalid and ugly, with its movable sets of great clothes horses hung with ragged laundry, which we repositioned ourselves for the various scenes. Our clothes were suitably drab and dirty, with the odd touch of tawdry finery. We girls wore low-cut hessian blouses, and Otto Kraus, who was playing a deliciously villainous Lockit, was anxious to ascertain that we were not wearing anything as bourgeois and incorrect as bras under them. He looked. I wasn't. For once I think I surprised him! Joan Cross was amazing as

Mrs Peachum; no problems for her over a fruity cockney accent. She gave us a splendid piece of advice: 'Be as vulgar as you like, girls, but never be common!' Gladys Parr, a distinguished Wagnerian singer, was a priceless old bag as Mrs Trapes, and Rose Hill a sharp and witty Lucy. There was so much to be learned from them all, and Tyrone Guthrie, after offering the chorus a few pointers, told us to get on and develop our own characters. I was Mrs Slammekin, clumsy and awkward, and I made my first entry by coming on, tripping and falling flat on my face. It raised a laugh – I can't think why. I had just learnt how to do stage falls and was rather pleased with myself! Norman Lumsden and Dennis Dowling amused themselves by coming on with a revolting assortment of bulbous noses, boils, ulcers and carbuncles. They would stick their heads out through the laundry and shock us with something more disgusting every night. We all had special make-up classes taken by Joan to help us achieve a genuinely Hogarthian effect.

Preparation periods for a new production were luxuriously long in those days. We had a full cast sing-through of *The Beggar's Opera* on 6th March, followed by scattered music and dialogue rehearsals. Tyrone Guthrie came for the first time on 16th April, and had his first full rehearsal with the company followed by more London rehearsals, then we all travelled to Cambridge where we went into digs for intensive rehearsal followed by the opening night at the Arts Theatre there on 24th May. According to my diary the audience was distinguished but flat, and the next day's press was bad. We played there for a week then went down to Aldeburgh. To my great surprise Ben himself asked me to cover the part of Miss Wordsworth in *Albert Herring*, and I was called on to rehearse it frequently as Margaret Ritchie was often unavailable. Oh how I longed to play that part! Margaret unfortunately was an ardent Christian Scientist and was never ill (though a wicked rumour circulated that she had once gone mysteriously absent for a fortnight to have her appendix out!). One day when we were all having coffee together during a rehearsal break in Aldeburgh and discussing a nasty cold that was circulating, I happened to say: 'Oh dear, I've got a nasty sore throat starting.' She leant across the table, patted my hand, and said: 'It's not the throat, dear, it's the mind behind it.' She continued to call on me to sing the high off-stage passage she found a strain in *Lucretia*, which meant I had to be in the theatre for all *Lucretia* performances just for those few off-stage bars. Peter said: 'Spit in her eye, dear!' but I didn't and I never did get to perform Miss Wordsworth.

During that prolonged rehearsal period I was also busy with other things. My own second Wigmore Hall lunch-hour recital had been on 11th February, followed by a rush to Glasgow for a broadcast on the 12th, and a concert up at Kelty on the 13th. Lessons with Mme de Reusz were unhappy. She began insisting that I must open my mouth far wider when singing, wide enough to accommodate the width of three fingers. 'Wie ein wallfisch, darleeng!' ('Like a whale!') she would repeat. But my jaw was not hinged like a whale's, and the resulting efforts were disastrous. I was having a lesson a day, and was not supposed to sing out, so I became deeply depressed.

I was sustained by some great music, including Bach's B minor Mass and *St John Passion*, the latter memorable with Kathleen Ferrier and Peter Pears, who was still my idol. I heard Flagstad in *Tristan and Isolde* and Furtwängler conducting Beethoven's Ninth Symphony and a remarkable recital by Ben Britten and Peter. Plays included *The Lady's not for Burning* and *Coriolanus* with John Clements, Alec Guinness and Rosamund Atkinson, of which I wrote 'The most terrific and exciting play I have ever seen.' Fascinating that we have now almost sixty years on been reading *Coriolanus* in my U3A class, and agreed that it was rather dull and political and not one of the Bard's best! The Clements production must have been very strong and our U3A reading of the play very poor! I saw it twice, and also the same company's *The Taming of the Shrew* (I think with John Clements and his wife, that delicious actress Kay Hammond) and became a Shakespeare addict.

I kept on meeting up with old friends from the RAMC band and our Middle East days. Oscar Grasso seemed to have resumed his position as virtuoso violinist at the Hungaria, and we had a great party one evening in the Chelsea flat of my friend guitarist and singer Eric Lukis, to which Oscar was invited. He turned up in a huge car with the head chef and his wife and the head porter. Eric, who played and sang folk songs in thirteen languages, was getting some cabaret work in London and was suffering greatly from stage fright. He tried a new remedy for it, which was being widely advertised, but warned me off trying it too because of the disastrous result. He said he went on to do his songs so slaphappy that he started off in the wrong key, couldn't get through the song, had to stop and start again giggling happily the while, and made a complete fool of himself. He was very funny about it, but never got another engagement from that particular venue!

After a long cold winter, the spring and the New Look came in, and clothes rationing must have been eased, because I have rapturous notes about ballet-length skirts and two new uncrushable (a new development) summer dresses from Debenhams for £2 and £3.

We had to re-rehearse *Albert Herring* for a broadcast with a new little boy, the last one's voice having inconveniently broken. I think I did some of the rehearsing of Miss Wordsworth, but again found myself singing the child's role of Cis for the broadcast. I was also studying Haydn's lovely work *The Seasons* as I was booked to sing the soprano solos in the 'spring' and 'summer' sections with Dr Eric Thiman and his choral and orchestral society at Dartford. I have a note that I was for once pleased with how I had sung, but the very next day, after a full day of rehearsing *The Beggar's Opera*, I had a very bad evening lesson with Mme, followed by black depression.

The 1948 Aldeburgh season was great fun. Anne and I stayed at Sandhill, the lovely home of Mrs Galsworthy, where we had stayed in 1947. There were visits to art galleries, lectures on Gainsborough and Constable, a concert in the parish church with the Zorian Quartet joined by Ben and Steve Wright for the Mozart Clarinet Quintet, and a superlative recital by Ben and Peter. It all ended with a big party at Crag House for Lord Harewood and his guests, to which we were all invited. I wrote that I had fallen in love with Aldeburgh and hated having to leave.

On 24th June, after some re-rehearsal, we all met at the KLM Centre in London en route for Amsterdam. Ben, Peter and several others arrived late having attended the memorial service for John Tillett of Ibbs and Tillett, so long the foremost British concert agents. There was a big press send-off at Heathrow where we were much photographed boarding 'an enormous 4-engined Skymaster specially chartered. Feel terrified as it seems impossible for it to take off'. Take off it eventually did, alarmingly near the end of the runway, not surprising as it carried not only the full company and orchestra but all the scenery, costumes and props for *The Beggar's Opera!* The press was out in force to meet us at Schipol, and it was good to be back in Amsterdam. There followed a hectic week of performances launched by a lecture recital the day we arrived, followed by two performances in Amsterdam, two in

Scheveningen and one in Rotterdam, all interlaced by amazing parties at which vast quantities of smorgasbord and far too many glasses of schnapps were consumed. We found time to revisit the Rijksmuseum and the Van Goghs in the Municipal Museum, and to do a boat trip round the canals. We had a party at the British Council of which I wrote: 'Lovely house in the Herrengracht. Walk home alone and enjoy seeing the city by night.' I wonder if one could do that safely now, sixty years on.

When we got home we went straight off to Cheltenham for a week of *Beggar's Opera* and *Albert Herring*, with a matinee thrown in, and for once there is no mention of depression in my diary. The shows seem to have gone well and been successful. I remember a visit to Tewkesbury where we visited the beautiful and impressive abbey, and tenor friend Max Worthley took me for a boat trip on the Severn, which as we were in a skiff and there was half a gale blowing and he was no oarsman, was exciting! On the Thursday, after singing in *Albert* at 2.30 and *The Beggar's Opera* in the evening I wrote in my diary: 'I feel so exhilarated. I do love this life and the stage!'

A week later we were off again to Knokke in Belgium where we stayed in a hotel overlooking the beach and had icy swims in the North Sea. Sadly our performances of *The Beggar's Opera* in the very unsuitable Casino fell flat. We each had £5 in Belgian money to spend and on the last day I bought all the food and drink I could for the family, and we arrived very late for our boat at Ostend, with no money for porters, so had a struggle to make it on board plus a mountain of luggage that included eggs, a big ham, many bottles and a huge kite! Two days later we were back in Cambridge where we spent a week in a heatwave doing performances of *Albert* and concerts. We went on the river most days and did the classic thing of breaking our punt pole and getting back shamingly late for rehearsal. We used to swim from our punt, and I fell in love with the cool brown river water with green weeds streaming in the current. It was deliciously soothing after the cold sea at Knokke.

It was a rich and happy time, the small roles I was singing were no problem for me, and Mme de Reusz was at last allowing me to study songs with her instead of endless exercises. It couldn't last. Quite suddenly I find in my diary: 'So desperately depressed just now as seem to be making no headway with all these expensive lessons.' Mme had quite suddenly forbidden me to practise on my own. Looking back it seems to me that I did much better when I was away from her for a while, but when I got back she always brought me sharply to heel and destroyed what confidence I had managed to build up.

The beginning of September saw the EOG rehearsing for an important week at Sadler's Wells, with Gladys Parr, who had had a bad fall and nearly broken her ankle, struggling gallantly onstage as she was in both operas and had no understudy. Audiences were enthusiastic and most nights were sold out. After a particularly riotous performance of *Albert Herring*, which included several small mistakes and a late final curtain (said to be Eric Crozier's fault) Ben gave us all a severe telling-off about making mistakes, whereupon Eric stood up and told him that some of us were getting a fear complex about mistakes, and the atmosphere became very tense. Ben was a perfectionist, and Peter was always word- and note-perfect, but we lesser mortals sometimes fell short of these standards. By the end of the week I wrote: 'All very tired. Peter, Otto and Gladys have played every night, principal parts. I don't know how they do it. I'm tired enough with my little bits.' That week I also wrote: 'It has dawned suddenly on me in the last few days that I am, or could be, terribly in love with PP. I have been through agonies as I must not and think I can still kill it.' By now this was serious, and no longer a Glyndebourne infatuation.

We were at Sadler's Wells for a second week with alternative casts going on, and we were also starting to rehearse a re-organised version of *The Beggar's Opera* that Tyrone Guthrie was working on for a live broadcast for the BBC. It was chaotic at first, but once the last performance at Sadler's Wells was out of the way we could all concentrate on the broadcast version. It was very different and used a narrator, but it became the most marvellously vital and alive presentation. The BBC were amazed at how quickly we had prepared it. It was not their habit to let outside producers direct the operas they presented, but Guthrie was brilliant and they were thrilled by the results he got. We had to act as much as if we were giving a stage performance. My diary tells me: 'Tyrone Guthrie sits at my table for lunch. He is so interesting, the sort of person who draws one out and listens to one, in preference to talking himself.' It was typical of Guthrie to have gone round sitting at different tables to talk to us lesser mortals.

We did four performances of his special broadcast version on the

Home and Third Programmes. Unfortunately halfway through this very pleasant week I had a bad lesson with Mme. She used to make us share lessons as she thought we could learn from each other. I can't remember who my sharer was but know I was deeply ashamed because I cried in front of her. It was so galling to share with singers like Annie Sharpe who had a lovely natural very high soprano voice, which never seemed to give her any problem. In our digs we used to tease her because she could get out of bed in the morning and lie in the bath singing up to E in alt. It didn't really help me to listen to her because my voice was a different sort of animal. I just got more depressed. But eventually I wrote: 'During the morning my nightmare depression lifts and am back to normal.'

There followed a week in Birmingham. Our dingy old-fashioned dressing room under the stage was icy, which did not help the many people with colds and 'flu, but the shows went well and we got good press from among others that doyen of critics Eric Blom. And a group of us were in excellent digs where our wonderful landlady gave us a hot meal at 10.45 p.m. each night when we got in from the theatre, all for £3 a week!

On the final Saturday we gave a matinee of *Albert* and *The Beggar's Opera* in the evening. Ben made a speech and thanked us for the great success of the season. He was very sweet to me personally and said encouraging things, but I knew that although I had worked hard, as we all had, in fact I had sung nothing that showed off or developed my voice and I seemed to have lost my nerve about singing.

I was having some back pain so I went to an osteopath who found that my spine was all awry and started me on a course of treatment. We were by now embarked on a week of performances at the People's Palace, and the crashing fall I did every night on my first entrance probably did not help. I told the osteopath about my depression and he said it could well be caused partly by the displaced vertebrae in my neck and at the base of the spine. Towards the end of the People's Palace week we were all summoned to a tea party before the show. Peter and Ben both spoke, and we were told that Anne Wood had resigned (she and Joan Cross became directors of the newly formed Opera Studio) and Elizabeth Sweeting was taking over the management of the EOG from an office in Aldeburgh. Poor Enid was now out of a job.

The Post War Years, 1949–50

At this time I was seeing a lot of Ruth Railton, a friend from long ago whose parents used to have a house on the shores of Loch Linnhe. Ruth was an outstanding person, a fine musician and conductor, with the long auburn hair and wide grey eyes of a Pre-Raphaelite angel. She later formed the National Youth Orchestra, and stabilised its finances by somehow getting into the office of the great Cecil Harmsworth King of *Daily Mirror* fame. She cast her spell over him, got the financial support of his newspaper group, and eventually married him. She came to many of our EOG performances and greatly admired Ben's music. Another delight during a rather depressed autumn was a visit by the Comédie-Française, which came to the Cambridge Theatre for a long season (Jay Pomeroy's opera having vanished, probably due to a final bankruptcy). My friends singer Jean Warrand and composer Christopher Shaw and I were all Francophiles, and we went time and again to their brilliant productions.

It was a long, cold winter, and many of us battled with colds, coughs and laryngitis, wishing that we played the violin or the piano or any instrument that could be restrung and repaired, unlike the voice. There were several artistic goodies such as the ballet *Cinderella* at the Royal Opera House, with Moira Shearer exquisite in the title role, and Frederick Ashton and Robert Helpman the funniest-ever ugly sisters. I was with EOG friends and we all went round to congratulate Fred afterwards. We also went to *The Marriage of Figaro* with Elisabeth Schwarzkopf as Susanna, Sylvia Fisher as the Countess and Geraint Evans in the title role. We started off in the 2/6 seats and by Act 4 had reached the stalls circle!

In March came exciting news. We had heard rumours that Ben was writing a children's opera, and Elizabeth Sweeting got in touch to tell me it was definitely happening, and Ben had a special part for me in it. Incredible and flattering, and I could hardly believe it. I was filled with a mixture of excitement and fear. At the same time Nicholas Choveaux put me on the small list of artists he promoted, and Ivor Newton, for whom I had a great admiration, asked me to do a concert with him. It was too good to last. Mme de Reusz suddenly refused to allow me to sing the Countess's aria from *The Marriage of*

Figaro, which I had been performing for years, because she said the high As at the end were too much for me – I who had always had an easy and thrilling high C. I knew from what people told me that the middle range of my voice was now rounder and fuller in quality. But was the voice better or worse as a whole? One of the agonising things about being a singer in those years was that you could never hear yourself as others heard you. The only way was to pay a large sum of money to make a record, and unless you went to a first-class – and very expensive – firm like HMV the results were often of a poor quality. I felt vocally very lost.

Mme de Reusz and I went to the Albert Hall to hear Peter Pears in the *St Matthew Passion*. His singing of the Evangelist was perfect and deeply moving. In the dressing room afterwards we met Ben, who told me he had written an aria for me and given me a lot to do in the children's opera. He had written the whole piece in ten days and it was to be called *Let's Make an Opera!* The cast was to be Gladys Parr, Anne Sharpe, Max Worthley, Norman Lumsden and myself, joined in the second half by six local children. In May we got our copies and found that the first part was a play about writing and preparing an opera called *The Little Sweep*, which we performed in the second half with children, and with audience participation when everyone joined to sing four lovely birdsongs.

We had a run-through at the house of Erwin Stein, a director of Ben's publishers Boosey and Hawkes. His beautiful daughter Marian (later to become Lady Harwood) was playing the four-handed piano part together with a colleague, and they, a string quartet and Bert Wilson, the virtuoso EOG percussion player, constituted our orchestra. It turned out, we all thought, to be over-percussive, and I wrote: 'Bert alone makes as much noise as a full orchestra.' I was called Miss Parrish in the play section and Rowan in *Let's Make an Opera!* To the delight of all the cast Basil Coleman was to produce, with Norman del Mar conducting. When my contract came it also included the understudies of Lucia in *Lucretia* and Miss Wordsworth in *Albert Herring*. This time £18 a week!

On a frivolous note, I was enraptured by two lengths of shot taffeta I bought for concert dresses. The material was a novelty and was lovely, one length gold shot with grey, the other blue shot with green. The taffeta was stiff, standing out all round and rustling as one moved. Styles were flatteringly feminine, with full-skirted ball gowns and tight waists, and pretty dirndl skirts in fashion for daywear. At last we began to forget about khaki and woollen bloomers. And that April 1949, sweets finally came off the ration.

All in all I was in a happy frame of mind, but it wasn't to last because just before the EOG gathered in Aldburgh for rehearsals and the launch of the festival, Mme pulled my singing of my new role to pieces.

The Aldburgh experience was frenetic that year as we tried to rehearse *Albert* and *Lucretia* as well as prepare *Let's Make an Opera!*, travelling for an hour by bus to Ipswich daily to rehearse with our six school children there. The small boy who played the Little Sweep in the opera, Sam, was splendid, but the others didn't know their parts at all and needed hours of work. Conductor Norman del Mar was wonderful with the children, and later on with the audiences when they had to sing the enchantingly atmospheric birdsongs.

There were not enough rehearsal spaces at Aldburgh, and I remember all our dialogue rehearsals had to take place in the ladies' lavatory at the Jubilee Hall! We had orchestral rehearsals at a boys' club with a tin roof under which we cooked, while Bert and his large selection of percussion deafened us. I was in everything, singing the little off-stage bit in *Lucretia*, and Cis in *Albert*, understudying and occasionally singing at rehearsals for both operas and preparing the new *Let's Make an Opera!* I also had a small solo part in a Holst psalm at two church concerts. These were lovely events held in the big parish church. Ben conducted the Jacques Orchestra for the first, his *St Nicholas* cantata, then the Holst piece in which Peter sang the principal part and I had my little solo. For the second concert Leslie Woodgate conducted Handel's 'Ode to St Cecelia's Day' and we repeated the Holst psalm. I remember too another poetry and music concert in the church with Robert Speight reading most beautifully.

Preparations for the first night of *Let's Make an Opera!* were increasingly hectic. I was struggling with a bad back. As Nanny in Part Two, 'The Little Sweep', I was supposed to carry my friend Anne Sharpe off stage. Anne, although small, was very solidly built, and at the final rehearsal we had to repeat the scene for the sake of our six children, and that was too much – my back gave out. There was no time to worry about it, the producer cut the carrying bit out, and we pressed on. Vital props and costumes came too late for us to rehearse with them, the first play section was too long and difficult for singers to put across (it was later cut altogether), and it all came to a head very appropriately on 13th June, the day before the first night. To quote:

> Black Monday! We start on a rehearsal of 'Let's Make an Opera' on the stage at 10.00 a.m. My costume is here at last, and is nice. We all wear what we have of our costumes. The play part is chaotic – no Robert Keyes to accompany, so Marian Stein and Kate Shanks who are playing the four-handed piano part in performance have to take over. They are very bad. Norman del Mar is furious, stops the rehearsal during Scene 1 and says he won't go on.

So there was no rehearsal that day. On the 14th I wrote:

> Yesterday was awful. Gladys Parr said that in all her years she'd never known such a state of affairs the day before a premiere. Eric Crozier came round to all the cast and gave us a pep talk, which only made bad worse. Norman Lumsden was the most worried as he has such a lot of dialogue. Rehearse with Norman del Mar in the morning. Public Dress Rehearsal at 2.00, 1st Night at 7.00. Feel utterly calm, and both go miraculously well and are a terrific success, largely thanks to Norman del Mar who is wonderful with the audience – they sing like anything!

My parents were there, also Mme de Reusz down from London to listen to her many pupils. It was a miracle that we got through with all the children considering that we had never had all our props before.

Next day there were good notices in the *News Chronicle*, the *Birmingham Post* and *The Times*, in which I had a favourable mention, though the local paper said my words were difficult to hear. Peter and Ben gave a final recital, which was quite wonderful, as Annie put it 'almost inhuman'. The festival ended with a ball to which Anne, Dennis Dowling and I went. Annie and I found it rather dull – not enough men!

My parents had gone on ahead to the Alps and found a small hotel 6,500 feet above Chamonix near the top of a telepherique. My childhood friend Pam and her elder brother joined us, and we walked and explored and tried to get into training for the great family project my mother had dreamed up, a guided excursion up the Glacier des Bossons to the Grands Mulets hut, at which climbers spent the night before climbing Mont Blanc. The Guides' Bureau in Chamonix was dismissive and not a bit helpful, describing our tour as a '*promenade de grandmères*', but we realised it must be a bit more than that when we were told we must take an aspirant guide, or trainee, as well as the full guide, and hire ice axes, and crampons for Pam who had not got proper mountain boots. The old guide we were given was one Albert Tournier, son of a famous guiding family, who had himself been a well-known guide in his young days, but was now reduced by age and too much cognac to taking out parties of trippers like ourselves. We must have looked a most unskilled and unlikely bunch as we got off the *téléphérique* at the Station des Glaciers and set off to cross the great stretch of the Glacier des Bossons. At first we followed a horizontal track under a great menacing wall of seracs. As we paused for a breather my mother looked up apprehensively at the wall of ice towering above us and asked old Tournier, '*Est-ce que ça tombe souvent?*' (Do they fall often?) to which he shrugged his shoulders and replied '*Parfois.*' We hurried on. At the far side of the glacier we roped up, my parents with old Tournier and John, Pam and myself on another rope with the aspirant. The climb up to the hut was on steep, deep slippery snow and our young guide went far too fast, so that Pam and I arrived at the hut exhausted. The parents with Tournier followed at a gentler pace, and we all had lunch, during which the old boy drank far too much *crépi* (wine) and our young aspirant deserted us for the much more remunerative and interesting job of taking a Swiss climber up Mont Blanc the following day. We would have been in a real mess if it had not been for the guardian of the hut, himself a guide, who had to go down to Chamonix for provisions and who volunteered to take John, Pam and me. In retrospect it was a hilarious descent, and frightened as we were we still managed to laugh a lot. Old Tournier got lost among the many small crevasses on our descent route and eventually fell into one, cutting his nose. My stepfather held him and pulled him out, and he was so ashamed that he begged my mother to clean up his nose so that the other guides wouldn't see. I still have a clear vision of looking back up at them and seeing my mother setting off firmly in what she thought was the right direction while my stepfather set off equally firmly the opposite way. As both were roped to the old boy, who was standing still quite befuddled, they didn't get far and from below it was very funny. We careered off again behind our young guide, racing down and leaping over small crevasses in his wake until quite suddenly the rope went taut round my waist and I was pulled back into one I had just jumped. The guide was quick as lightning to hold me and pull me out, and Pam, who was behind me, was almost in tears with emotion, gasping 'What happened? What happened?'

'Pam, you're standing on the rope!' came a cold voice from her brother at the rear. She was. In fact it was firmly impaled on one of her crampons. The arch crime of mountaineering is to stand on the rope that must be kept taut between you and the next climber at all times. We got down more or less unscathed, feeling as if we had climbed Everest, and we called our tour after a comic family series then very popular in *Punch*, 'The Bristlewoods in the Alps'. We were stiff for days, but we had made it to the Grands Mulets – and it was a lovely change from opera!

I soon found myself back at Aldburgh with my kind hostess at Sandhills. Annie should have been there too, but she was suffering from nervous prostration – some sort of a mini-nervous breakdown. We were rehearsing *Let's Make an Opera!*, and a young soprano called Pamela Woolmore was called in to take Anne's place. She seemed to know the music suspiciously well, and it was then that I found out that while I was away there had been a recorded broadcast of which I knew nothing in which she had taken my part. I realised that she must have been groomed to take my place, which explained why she knew the piece so well. Annie arrived, but had to go straight to bed, so Pamela played her part at the first performance. I wrote: 'She did wonders, but is very sophisticated and mature and looks all wrong.' She was of course much more suited for my part, for which she was intended. Annie was persuaded to get up, and got through the second performance. The doctor said her condition was due to worry and nerves – not uncommon in the EOG. There was one show of *Albert Herring*, in which she and I played our usual children's parts of

Emmie and Cis, a useful reminder for our forthcoming Scandinavian tour.

Soon after I got home I got a letter in Ben's handwriting:

> After two nights of dreaming of Ben and Peter, today
> get a letter from Ben which I hardly dare open. It is as
> I thought, that they have decided to replace me for the
> broadcasts – it contains much criticism and is rather
> hurtfully worded – though I suppose he meant to be kind.
> Am desperately upset. Start a long letter in reply.

That afternoon 2nd September I made my birthday cake and iced it ready for next day, writing: 'Continue on my long letter to Ben. I don't think he need have done this – it will do me so much harm professionally. I am really angry about it.' I had a nice twenty-eighth birthday on 3rd September, and after writing about it I noted that I had sent off a carefully revised and thought-out letter to Ben that morning, in which I had been frank, and wondered how he would react. He was surrounded by a crowd of adoring admirers at Aldburgh and was unused to any sort of criticism. Mine was of the way young artists were dealt with in the group, and I reminded him of Dino's words, that without hope an artist can do nothing. Young singers are tender flowers, far more vulnerable and unsure of themselves than they often appear. Mostly they crave for encouragement and appreciation, and if given a chance will blossom.

There was a day of rehearsal in London at which Ben did not appear. I showed his letter to various friends, who were horrified, and to Mme de Reusz, who said I should say 'Mr Britten, I have not deserved this' and refuse to go on the Scandinavian tour. I could see now that the company had Pamela Woolmore ready in case I should do just that! But it was too late, I had my contract, and I had turned down a lot of other work so could not afford not to go. I think I was useful to the company too, because I was singing small parts in both the operas we were taking, and understudying major roles in both. I was a good musician and would not have let them down had I suddenly had to take on either of my understudy roles.

We went by overnight boat from Harwich to Esbjerg, and during the journey Margaret Ritchie buttonholed me and we had a long talk all about Ben's whims and how one must suffer them in silence, which of course I had not done. When we arrived in Copenhagen we were whirled straight in to a press reception before going to our hotel rooms, and the usual large quantities of smorgasbord and schnapps were consumed. It was Sunday evening, 11th September, and a party of us was taken to the closing night of the famous Tivoli Gardens. Annie and I went on the scenic railway of which I wrote 'Terrific fun – terrified!' then on the great wheel. I shall never forget Annie, who was a strictly brought-up Church of Scotland lass, looking at me with great round eyes as we were poised at the fearsome top of the great wheel and exclaiming 'And on a Sunday too!'

We gave two performances and a broadcast of *Lucretia* and two of *Albert Herring* in Copenhagen. The press was ecstatic about the shows, and we could understand why when we went to *Rigoletto* at the Opera House. It was so poor that we came out after one act. We were reminded that conditions in those countries that had suffered defeat and occupation so recently were still very hard. However, there was a sumptuous party given for us by our sponsors, an ambassador's reception, and finally a farewell press party at which Ben was presented with two enormous laurel wreaths. Next day we sailed for Norway, and paused when passing Elsinore, for him to drop them overboard in tribute to the Bard.

The second week of our tour in Norway was even more hectic and fun-packed than the Copenhagen week. After a night on board we were all up at 6.00 a.m. to see the fjord and beautiful approach to Oslo:

> The Press swarm on board and interview and photograph
> for two hours before we can land. We are all going to
> private hosts. Roy (Ashton), Annie and I to Mr and
> Mrs Hurum; he is Music Critic to Aftenposten which is
> sponsoring us. Arrive there to find they are giving a party
> for us all at 1.00, and my bedroom is in use as a dining
> room. A wonderful party with much food and drink – it
> goes on and on – people rest on sofas and divans – then
> we go to a Press tea at the Press Club and tea consists of
> red wine and open sandwiches – then all on to a banquet
> in our honour. For this we go up into the hills by special

train to a restaurant high above Oslo. Meet many charming Norwegians. Wonderful food and drink.

The day already seemed endless, but at the insistence of Mr Hurum a large party of us including Ben, Peter, our Norwegian impresario and Annie walked all the way back down the mountain.

The next day there was a rehearsal and performance of *Albert*, with the first act broadcast, in the presence of King Haakon and the Crown Prince and Princess. Afterwards we all went to the Press Club for schnapps and a meal, the latter very slow but delicious. I spent the next day in bed with a heavy cold, missing the ambassador's party, but did a performance of *Albert* in the evening. The press here was rapturous – even better than Copenhagen. I wrote:

> This household is amazing and so Bohemian. They have
> taken all the doors down so that we can circulate for the
> lunch party. Very little convenience – one bathroom and
> small washbasin, and one lav. outside. Privacy is nil, but
> food and drink overflows and people are always wandering
> in and out through the bedroom I share with Annie.

There was a well-organised day of sightseeing, which was enjoyed except for the *Lucretia* cast who came straight back to rehearsal at 5.00 and performance at 8.00. The day was also rather spoilt for me because Annie got a letter booking her for *Let's Make an Opera!* in November and December, but I heard nothing and wrote that I couldn't help feeling hurt and angry.

After the last *Lucretia* there was a farewell party given for us by *Aftenposten*. It was a riot – toasts, speeches, and cabaret acts by all the high-ups, even Peter and Ben and Joan Cross – and we got to bed after 5.00 a.m. The next day, our last, there was a performance of *Albert*, which was a huge success. Mr Hurum had decided to throw yet another farewell party in his house for us. I don't think they bothered to go to bed, and poor Mrs Hurum was hectic all day preparing food, during which she managed to burst a tin of tomato ketchup all over my new taffeta frock. We had to turn out of our bedroom, which was in use for the party again, the drawing room was transformed into Act 1, the shop scene, from *Albert*, while the next room held Lucretia's bed!

It was a crazy time; how the principals managed to turn in splendid performances night after night I just don't know. At the final party we sang – among other things – most of *The Beggar's Opera* and lots of the children's opera, Peter and Ben did folk songs and their special blues, and Peter and Joan danced the cancan. We had three hours' sleep, then boarded an all-day train to Göteborg in Sweden. I remember sleeping and waking over and over again, and always we were passing through great forests of pine and larch and fir. At Göteborg we got on a Swedish boat. The men were all in third class, the women in second, which caused some unrest, Ben being particularly fed up, but we all collapsed onto our bunks and slept like logs. We spent all the next day on board, and I wrote: 'It's been a wonderful trip – very bittersweet for me as I feel it will be my last with the Group. No word from Ben, and the others are all booked for the winter season of the Children's Opera.'

In fact the final *Albert* in Oslo had been my last with Ben and Peter and Joan and all the rich talent of the EOG. Annie and I ended up still singing the children's parts of Emmie and Cis in *Albert*, and I can't say the EOG had done anything to further our careers or develop our voices. It had been rich experience, which I wouldn't have missed for the world, but I feel it was lost time vocally. All the joy in singing, which I had felt at the beginning of my career, and the self-confidence as a performer I'd built up during the war years with the band, had vanished. I could think only of Ben who used to be there in the wings watching me during the children's opera. He had golden-yellow eyes and he rarely looked straight at one. I used to feel that night after night he was there confirming his belief that there was no talent to be found in me.

The human psyche is so strange. I can remember nothing of what he said or wrote to me, or of what I wrote back to him. But certainly some sort of strange personality entanglement had happened because I dreamt of him and of singing in his operas night after night, and the dreams recurred for many years. Now at the age of eighty-six, writing down these disturbing memories has caused me to have a 'Ben dream' again, though he did not appear in it himself. A few nights ago I dreamt that I was booked to be in a new opera of his. I can see a pretty blue dress, which I was shown and told I was to wear. Some music arrived, but no calls for coaching or rehearsal. Then it was the first night, and the music had started, and I was in the wings desperately trying to find out when I had to go on and what I had to do. No one seemed to see me. And suddenly I realised that the part I had been offered was so unimportant that it didn't matter if it wasn't there at all. Another dream that kept coming back was of me singing in an opera of his that I knew well and had done many times. I recognised it and remembered the phrases I had to sing well, but there was always something wrong – I had mislaid my score, I couldn't remember an entry, I was late on because I couldn't find my way to the stage in a strange theatre, or I could not find my costume on the dressing-room rack – all dreams harassed performers will be familiar with. But when I woke up the music I knew well in my dream world was forgotten and Ben in fact never wrote any such opera.

By November I was working on so many things that I had no time to miss the EOG. There was a performance of *Elijah* coming up, and a BBC recital of English song, and two operatic concerts in schools with baritone Dennis Dowling for the Arts Council, also Violetta in *La Traviata*, which I was working on with Joan Cross at the Opera School. The schools concerts brought me together with pianist Phyllis Thorold, who became a great friend and later my partner in the formation of the Opera Players. Mona Tatham and Ian Macphail, assistant music directors at the Arts Council, came to the second concert, and Mona, herself a singer, came to our lunch-hour auditions the next day and was enthusiastic about my voice. Apparently she had been worried about it when I was with Dino, but now saw an enormous improvement and said it was fine, so even and controlled.

A few weeks later she rang to ask if I could take over a fortnight's tour with a special chamber music group whose soprano had fallen ill. This was a very fortunate introduction, as I seemed to fit well into the group Music in Miniature. It was organised by cellist Vivian Joseph, and consisted of rising young clarinettist Gervase de Peyer, Yvry Gitlis, violin, pianist Margaret Chamberlain and Vivian himself, who also introduced the music with charm and wit. We did ten concerts all over South Wales on that first tour.

Although I seemed now to be an outcast from the EOG, 1950 brought me quite a healthy crop of solo engagements – on one happy day in March a *Messiah*, a *St John Passion*, and a *Merrie England* came in, the latter through Ibbs and Tillett who were taking an interest in me at the time. Henry Foy was now running the EOG and seemed genuinely anxious about my relationship with the company. He rang to offer me two seats for Ben's 'Spring Symphony' at the Albert Hall and told me I was to be sure to go and greet Ben and Peter in the artists' room after it. I did so very nervously, and both were extremely kind. It must have been post-performance euphoria! About a month later Henry rang to offer me Mrs Slammekin in *The Beggar's Opera*, Cis in *Albert Herring* and the understudy of Rowan in *Let's Make an Opera!* for a very small salary. I accepted with reservations, but later rang and turned the offer down. The link was at last firmly broken.

Seen retrospectively, June was a time of new beginnings. I had my first-ever brochure printed, and circulated it to some 1,000 music clubs and schools. To my great surprise Mme de Reusz passed on a number of her pupils to me, and I also acquired two or three of my own, so they all had to be fitted in to the schedule for regular lessons. And Phyllis Thorold, who had played for our Arts Council school opera concerts, invited me round for coffee to discuss finding some way of making opera more attractive and intelligible to the children. We agreed that it would be better to present one opera at a time instead of a jumble of excerpts, to use a narrator and to show the children how powerfully words and music together can tell a story. We chose *La Bohème* for seniors and *Hänsel and Gretel* for juniors, and agreed to get to work cutting these two to the fifty-minute time limit set by the London County Council (LCC). We were both tremendously excited by this project, especially when the Arts Council agreed to see a run-through in September.

I promptly rang Anne Sharpe to ask her to sing the part of Gretel, for which she was perfect, being petite with fair hair and blue eyes and a very young face. But when I tracked her down to her home in Scotland she told me she had done nothing for two months as Mme had made her so nervy that she felt she could not sing at all and had gone back home. I was very shocked that this should have happened to Annie, who had one of the most easy and natural voices I have ever heard. We talked for ages, and it was then I decided that I too would leave Mme as soon as a suitable moment arose, because she had such a negative effect on me. It would have to be after the summer though, as I had arranged to go to Salzburg with her, where her son-in-law Josef Kripps was conducting at the festival.

I was not looking forward to Salzburg, but it turned out to be a fascinating interlude. We stayed at a charming typically Austrian mountain hostelry, Distelalpe-am-Gaisberg, 3,000 feet above Salzburg. Mme was there with her daughter and son-in-law, also Irmgard Seefried with her husband, distinguished violinist Schneiderhahn, and their baby, and Erich Kunz and his wife. Later we were joined by Lord Harewood and Erwin Stein of Boosey and Hawkes. I also re-met Walter Legge whom I knew from the RAMC band classical concerts, when he used to bring his latest protégée, a young and beautiful auburn-haired violinist down to play concertos with the orchestra. I was to have daily lessons with Mme, and the first two were very depressing. I wrote: 'I feel so rebellious and inclined to give up, but will not.' We went to *The Magic Flute* in the Felsenritterschule – an amazing outdoor venue created in the old riding school. The cast included Seefried, a lovely Pamina, Kunz, a marvellous Papageno, and Lipp as Queen of the Night. Two days later it was *Don Giovanni* with another fabulous cast. I noted: 'Seefried adorable as Zerlina, Kunz a memorable Leporello, Gobbi as the Don looked and acted well but sang badly, Schwarzkopf was a good Elvira. Lluba Welitsch as Anna had trouble with her big aria (Non mi Dir) owing I think to the tempi.'

Due to a lot of intrigue, the Mozart operas, which had been conducted the previous season by Kripps, were conducted this year by Furtwängler. The great man was no opera conductor – the tempi were deadly slow, and his *Magic Flute* ran fifty-five minutes longer than the Kripps version. The singers came up to our hotel and cried on Kripps's shoulder. I shall never forget *Don Giovanni*. We were very close to the stage, and for her beautiful aria Welitch sang supported by her lover Don Ottavio. I saw her nails digging deep into his arm as she ran out of breath and was forced to break one of those sublime phrases. If eyes could have killed, hers would have incinerated Furtwängler.

There was deep intrigue going on. Kripps, who had suffered during the war years because he was Jewish, was now being accused of being a communist. Both Furtwängler and more especially Schwarzkopf had worked for the Nazi regime. Austria was currently quadripartite, and the political intrigue was cutthroat and bitter. The Kripps camp, including Mme, were all distraught, and Kripps, having been ousted from the mainstream repertoire, was conducting only Britten's *Rape of Lucretia* and I think the odd concert. In my diary I wrote: 'All so unhappy about terrible intrigues to brand him a Communist.' He and his wife wanted to follow Mme and come to London, but denunciation as a communist would bar him from getting an entry visa. The communist witch hunt was already well underway.

Mme had been doing her usual tactic of knocking me down then building me up again, as I wrote: 'Suddenly have a lesson which goes marvellously. Feel I have made a stride and discovered a new muscle-control to get openness inside my mouth and palate, and fullness of tone.' Oh dear, I cannot think what I meant, but it cheered me just as my parents, who had driven out from home, arrived to join us.

Unfortunately the Kripps *Rape of Lucretia* was only a moderate success. I noted that '…not all the singers were good enough – especially Patzac, who has no voice left but speaks well, as Male Chorus (the Peter Pears role), and Analies Kupper the Female Chorus.' The three other men were good, but the Lucretia, whose name I cannot read in my diary, was not at all good-looking, and was badly dressed and made-up. I had been spoiled with Kathleen Ferrier and Nancy Evans!

Back in England soon after, Phyllis Thorold and I immediately set to work rehearsing our potted versions of *Hänsel and Gretel* and *La Bohème*. Phyllis had originally visualised a purely concert performance with the necessary cuts linked by narration. But I found it impossible to give any idea of live opera without action, so in came movement. And who would present a witch without a broomstick? Or a Mimi in her first touching love duet with Rudolph, minus her candle, which blows out at such an opportune moment? In no time we had full production with costumes and props, and I was in my element. We always sang in English and put great stress on diction, because it was essential that the children, and later our adult audiences, who were many of them unfamiliar with opera, should know what was going on. One of the characters used a simple narration between acts to cover the cuts and set the scene, and at first in the schools we reckoned to use available chairs and tables. We spent about £5 each on these first two presentations, and we ran them at the Wigmore Hall for Mona Tatham and Ian Macphail, assistant music directors at the Arts Council, on 6th September, and again in a more polished state for Sir Steuart Wilson, the director of music, on 16th October. He and his wife were already friends of Phyllis Thorold, and coincidentally he had known my father in the First World War, when they were wounded almost simultaneously. He was a big man in all senses of the word, and had gallantly made himself into a very distinguished tenor, though he had lost one lung and part of the other as a result of his wound. When we first talked about potted opera to him he said: 'It won't work – I know because I tried it.' However he agreed to see what we had done, and was generous enough after to say that it was good and worked well. The Arts Council was at that time running the music in London schools, and, to our joy we were offered four performances each of *Hänsel and Gretel* and *La Bohème* for schools and a full-blown tour of music clubs with *Don Pasquale* in the New Year. The Opera Players were on their way! Little did we know what lay ahead.

Nothing is more desperately boring in a musician's biography than annual lists of engagements and works performed. I have ventured to write the post-war years in some detail because they were both formative for me and to some extent, in the case of the EOG, part of musical history. The fight to establish the Opera Players will also be dealt with thoroughly, then we shall move into the broad sweep of the middle years, and through the new doors that were about to open for me, bringing much joy and a second career as a lecturer.

Chapter Ten

The Story of a Small Opera Company

In 1980, at the request of my board of directors, I wrote the following account of the early days of the Opera Players.

The Opera Players, like Topsy in 'Uncle Tom's Cabin', just growed from a very small seed sown in the spring of 1950, when singers Elisabeth Parry and Denis Dowling and pianist Phyllis Thorold were asked to give a series of operatic concerts in London schools. Before singing each aria or duet they had to explain the story of the relevant opera to the children. After struggling through ten plots of varying complexity the artists were as bewildered as the children. Over a cup of tea Phyllis Thorold suggested that we should stick to one opera per concert, singing as much as possible of the music and linking the excerpts with narration so that the children could see the story as a dramatic whole and hear the well-known tunes in their proper context.

We got together a group of six young artists and began work on concert versions of Hänsel and Gretel for juniors and La Bohème for seniors, but soon realised that we could not give a true idea of opera without using movement. This led to the need for a Witch's broomstick, a candle for Mimi, and eventually to simple costumes which we improvised, begged or borrowed. When the two 'potted' operas were ready we approached the Arts Council. The then Director of Music, Sir Steuart

Wilson, said 'It won't work – I know because I've tried it.'
However he asked us to present what we had prepared to
his Music Staff at the Wigmore Hall, and afterwards was
generous enough to say that what they had seen and heard
was good. We were offered eight school performances –
four of each opera – in the autumn. I shall never forget
the first 'Bohème' to a school of physically handicapped
children in a very poor area of Islington, using the coke
stove in the narrow hall as the attic stove, with a lad in
a wheel chair in the front row crying all through the
last act and saying after that it was smashing. Nor shall I
forget the stink bombs thrown at us a few days later as we
knelt singing the prayer to the fourteen angels in Hänsel
and Gretel. Despite this episode the success of the school
shows resulted in an Arts Council tour of music clubs in
the New Year, and rapid growth from 27 performances
of two operas in our first season to 124 of eight operas
in 1955–56. We had extended to two-hour performances
for the public, and already had a number of very talented
young singers working with us, Thomas Hemsley, Norman
Platt and Eric Shilling amongst them.

We realised early on that small must be good, and asked
Peter Gellhorn to become our Music Director, a post he
held until his death. An opera score played on the piano
by Peter was memorable. I well remember him standing
behind the unfortunate Phyllis at an early 'Bohème'
rehearsal and admonishing her, 'I do not hear the fourth
horn.'

Geoffrey Dunn produced all our early operas, and his
previous experience with the Intimate Opera Company
singing in and producing small-scale opera was invaluable.
As an actor he was able to help us all enormously in those
days before the existence of opera schools, when singers
learnt stage skills by trial and error.

My partner Phyllis Thorold and I ran the company
between us, she providing the administrative experience
and a growing expertise with costumes, which eventually
led to her becoming an expert in period embroidery

(she did all the embroidery work on the splendid Queen Elizabeth costumes for Glenda Jackson on BBC TV). I was the Heath Robinson thinker-up of portable scenery, and because of my previous stage experience in charge of presentation and productions, writing the narrations, programme notes and general publicity.

We made all that we needed (clothing coupons were in force when we started) and we travelled by train, often trundling barrows up and down the platforms ourselves when porters shied away from our mountain of peculiar poles and bundles. Gas piping supported curtains (or sometimes didn't – we gave the shortest-ever second act of *Bohème* when the whole lot fell forward enveloping the cast just as the curtain opened at Street in Somerset). Garden trellis was a cheap and portable standby for garden scenes, and a keen amateur operatic cabinetmaker improvised a collapsible couch-cum-bed, which appeared glorious in gilt and red satin for *Don Pasquale* and shrouded in old army blankets for Mimi's deathbed in *La Bohème*. One night when Rudolph lowered Mimi – me – onto it for the dying scene there was an ominous crack. He knelt, back to the audience, supporting it and me with shaking arms. 'Bloody leg's broken,' he gasped while I sang those exquisite and tragic phrases. Tom Hemsley, our Schaunard, grabbed an enormous saucepan, which was one of our stage props, and shoved it under the bed, where it looked like a mammoth chamber pot, and Act 4 continued. Rudolph unfortunately got the giggles and I had to sing out to the audience over his heaving shoulders as he buried his head in my lap. By the end most of the audience was in tears and we were congratulated on a marvellous last act – 'So moving,' said one dear soul, 'with the tenor sobbing on the bed.'

Another time, perhaps during the repair to the couch, we asked the society that engaged us to supply a bed. On arrival by train, we found the station yard empty except for a horse and cart. On the cart was a magnificent brass bedstead. 'You the opera?' said the carter. 'Jump up, I've been sent to fetch you.' We got onto the cart and clopped through the little town to our hall, feeling that all we needed was a bell and drum to announce our arrival in true *commedia dell'arte* style. Another early memory is of losing our one and only quill pen, and chasing a flock of geese through a muddy farmyard in Lincolnshire.

We played in everything from Nissen huts to disused churches in those days, for a fee of four guineas each (three for school matinees), and I remember a barn in the Midlands so bitterly cold that our audience all came with rugs and hot water bottles, and our breath hung in clouds as we sang. The men rushed off down the village street to the pub in full costume and make-up at the end of Act 1, and came back with a bottle of rum. After that Act 2 went with a swing.

In 1954 I discovered a score of *La Cambiale di Matrimonio* by Rossini on the Rive Gauche in Paris. It was a short comic opera set in London, with only six characters and no chorus. I translated it during five days in hospital, and we gave it what we think were its first performances in Britain. Soon after Phyllis made a copy of Donizetti's *Rita* from the British Museum – a very amusing work for just three singers – and translated it from the French. We doubled it with *Pepito* by Offenbach, which was produced for us by a then unknown young director called John Copley. Tenor Kenneth Macdonald and baritone Eric Shilling were with us for four happy years at this time.

Season 1955–56 must have been a marathon – 124 performances including a new *Escape From the Harem* for the Mozart bicentenary produced by Clive Carey specially for a tour of Northern Ireland. We must be the only company ever to have given twenty-eight performances of the *Seraglio* in four weeks – one-night stands with only one cast! (Another record might have been much later in 1984 when our singers sang *Tosca* four times in forty-eight hours, two orchestral rehearsals and two performances.)

This is how I wrote in 1980 about the birth and early growth of the Opera Players. Not a word about the background situation, our painful and nerve-racking struggle for survival with the Arts Council, because in 1980 the Arts Council was still very much of a presence for us. Although they had failed to get rid of us, and had come to accept us as an irritating fact of life, they were still in a position to discredit us nationally, and even more important to veto our appeals for financial assistance to, for example, at a later date, the National Lottery.

Back in 1950 the whole situation was complicated by the fact that some of the principal Arts Council officials were old friends. There was Sir Steuart Wilson, who was a keen critic but also a firm supporter of ours, and who had been a friend of my father in the First World War, and the two assistant music directors of the day, Mona Tatham and Ian Macphail, who much later became the chairman of our company.

The music department had its own company called the Grand Opera Group, which it financed and toured extensively. This was a concert group of four singers introduced and compèred brilliantly by ex-Glyndebourne baritone and producer Douglas Craig. This group was the pride and joy of the music department. Then we came on the scene offering our shortened and simplified versions of a complete opera, fully produced in costume with props, furniture, basic scenery and all the available stage lighting. We sang in English so that our audiences could follow the plot, and used a narrator to set the scene and fill in any gaps left by the lack of a chorus. We were the first company to offer potted opera in this more dramatic and colourful way, and at first the Arts Council was keen to sponsor our school work and music club performances. We were greeted with great enthusiasm by our audiences and often booked back immediately, hence the rapid rise in our performances from 27 in our first season to 124 in our sixth. Our season, or operatic year, ran from 1st September to 31st August, which fitted in with the school year and the programming of most opera houses and music societies.

We left for our first Arts Council tour of music clubs in April 1951, and opened at Radcliffe-on-Trent in a disused cinema that was being energetically swept by a nice young curate as we arrived. My dressing room was up a ladder in a loft – my rough army touring experience stood me in good stead! The organiser was delighted and immediately booked us for a return visit. Two nights later Phyllis and Tom Hemsley, who were driving, were woken by the police at 3.00 a.m. and told to move her car and our hired van from the place where the hotel night porter had told them to park. It was snowing, and Tom found he had no driving licence, so I had to drive the van for the rest of the tour. The Arts Council's regional music director chose to come to our Friday-night show, which was in a borstal – a vast hall and an extremely unwilling tough audience.

Back in London I was off at once for a short tour with Music in Miniature, and got back to the gloomy news from Phyllis that there had been much criticism from the Arts Council regional director, who had seen only our borstal show. An added knock was that the Arts Council had had one of its annual artists' concerts, or hiring fairs, for the regional organisers and music club secretaries. The Grand Opera Group had taken part, but we had not been invited.

In April I had a memorable fortnight's break to sing the soprano lead, Iphis, in a staged version of Handel's oratorio *Jeptha* in South Wales. As if the piece were not long enough in itself, the organisers added a half-hour's variety programme on at the end, so that the evening lasted for over three and a half hours. They are gluttons for musical punishment in the Valleys! There was a mammoth chorus of some 150, who crowded the wings to watch every minute of the goings on, so that it was a free fight getting on or off the stage. At the end the heroine is about to be sacrificed by her father when God miraculously intervenes, and this involved my lying on a slab while tenor Gabriel Todd waved a large knife over me. Blackout had to come at the exact moment when the knife was descending and the voice of God is heard. Night after night the local electrician failed to get the lights off at the right moment, which left Gabriel and myself on the spot, he swearing under his breath while I tended to get the giggles. Despite the chaos, and having to work out most of our own production, they were such lovely enthusiastic people that I wrote afterwards of 'happy happy weeks!'. The role of my mother in *Jeptha* was sung by Norma Morgan, a local girl who was a lovely singer and actress. We became good friends, and I was able to arrange for her to come to London, where she got a scholarship for the Opera School. Later she became one of our soloists and sang a moving Mimi in *La Bohème*.

In April Phyllis and I were stunned to hear that we were one of the Arts Council's sponsored groups for the coming season, and they were offering us two tours of *Don Pasquale* – but only on condition that we got rid of two of our singers (one of them was Norman Platt, a fine musician who later founded and ran Kent Opera, which was to have a distinguished career of first-class performances, until the Arts Council withdrew its financial support and the company was eventually forced to close). This was a terrible dilemma for us, and we refused to make an immediate decision.

But a dream of mine was about to be realised; I was going to study in Italy! Singer friends told me of the Accademia Chigiana, held at the home of that great music lover and patron, Count Chigi, in his beautiful Palazzo Chigi in Siena. *Corsi di perfezionamente*, or master classes, were held during July and August for young professional musicians. I applied for the class of Maestro Giorgio Favaretto, and after a short mountain holiday with my parents at Macugnaga under the great south face of Monte Rosa, I travelled down to Siena and arrived to find that all my papers had been mislaid, so that I was not expected. I found myself unaccountably having tea with Count Chigi and the Accademia's secretary Olga Rudge, a charming and interesting American lady who had been the mistress of the great American poet, Ezra Pound. I found a nasty room for the night, and auditioned for Giorgio Favaretto the next day. Luckily I was one of the two singers to be accepted, and I was awarded an Italian government scholarship. This was in answer to prayer, as I had only my return ticket and about £20 in my pocket. The scholarship covered all tuition, and provided money to rent a room with an Italian family for two months and pay for the hire of an upright piano, which had to come all the way from Florence and be carted up many flights of stone stairs. We lived with the shopkeepers and poor townsfolk in tall elegant thirteenth- and fourteenth-century houses, which soared above narrow paved alleys, and which were now divided into an apartment on each floor. I remember feeling I could reach out and shake hands with the people in the room across the street. The rooms were stone-floored, bare, cool and clean. Siena had been bombed in the war, and the Roman acqueduct, the town's only water supply, had been cut. When the people were asked what they would like their reparations money to be spent on, aqueduct or theatre, they unanimously chose a new theatre as theirs had been destroyed. The aqueduct was patched up somehow, and by 1951 we got running water from seven to nine a.m. and again from seven to nine in the evening. Every vessel and bath and basin was filled each morning, and enough had always to be left to water the wonderful geraniums on the balconies.

Every house was full of music students, and the streets rang with the sounds of practising. We soon discovered the public baths, where a fierce female attendant dispensed towels for a small sum, and where one could have a cheap hot soak. We also swam in the small town swimming pool, where the water, which was rarely changed, must have been very insanitary by the end of the long hot summer. We had a very modest sum of money left over for food when rent and piano hire had been paid. Breakfast consisted of a doughnut and coffee en route for morning class. For lunch and dinner we mostly went to a wonderful family restaurant called Grottino's, right on the main Piazza del Campo. Like all Italians they adored music and had a soft spot for music students, and they produced enormous piles of plain boiled rice with a generous knob of butter on top and as much grated parmesan as you wanted, all for a very modest sum that could be negotiable if you were broke. We drank local red wine. We were in Chianti country, and the water from the aqueduct was not recommended, but the wines were superb. We worked all morning, then had a siesta and started work again at five o'clock. After supper we would sit out half the night in the welcome cool of evening, putting the world to rights, and reading Dante and Italian poetry in the moonlight with a group of student doctors. They teased us and pulled our legs unmercifully, a favourite joke being the Italian word for fig, a fruit that was cheap and abundant in Siena. Was the noun masculine or feminine? If you got it wrong you found you had asked for a male penis, which could be embarrassing. The doctors were studying at the local hospital, which they said was beautiful, with thirteenth- and fourteenth-century frescos all over the walls but absolutely no modern equipment.

There was only one other 'English' in Siena that summer, and she was 'doing' Dante at the university. We were duly brought together and became lifelong friends. She and I went about with a quartet of four young doctors, one who was a communist, one who had been a fascist under Mussolini, one who had fought in the hills as a partisan, and the fourth whose political alignment I cannot remember except that it was different from the others. They were the best of friends, and our discussions about the war were fascinating. Sometimes they would take us to a particularly beautiful ruined castle or cloister and read poetry to us by moonlight.

Soon after I arrived in Siena I was invited to Sunday tea at Palazzo Brucchi by an amazing English woman who gave tea parties for English-speaking students. She had come to Italy years ago as a very young girl doing the Grand Tour, had fallen in love with and married a wealthy Sienese aristocrat and had never gone back to England. During the war the front line rolled back and forth around Siena, and their big country house was taken over by the Germans as an officers' mess. Although Mrs Brucchi never lost her English accent the Germans accepted the explanation that she came from northern Italy, and not one of the locals betrayed her. The German officers would sit chatting to her in her great dining hall not knowing that just under their feet there were escaped Allied soldiers and airmen hiding in the big wine cellars on their way north.

My class with Giorgio Favaretto was multi-national. He spoke only French and Italian so my Italian improved rapidly. The whole class sat and listened to each other, and I found this very nerve-racking at first, as I was unused to being taught publicly. It was a salutary and toughening experience in front of an adult and sophisticated crowd of young artists, and I soon went out and bought a fan and learned to flirt with it and throw temperaments and weep on Maestro's shoulder with the best of them. Maestro did not teach singing; we were supposed to have sound techniques by the time we joined his class. What he taught was interpretation and style, body language and how to present ourselves and our music to the public. You had to put 100 per cent of yourself into every song you sang and you had to project 'gioia' to your audience even if what you sang was tragedy. After all, why do we stand up and sing to people at all, if not to bring them joy in the beauty of the music? There were concerts going on all the time, and one could catch occasional glimpses of the greats such as Segovia, or the members of the Thibaut-Cortot-Casals trio on their way to give a master class.

We studied in Palazzo Chigi, a huge and echoing place of marble floors and wood-panelled aule (big rooms) hung three deep with paintings by the Italian masters. There was a private chapel dedicated to St Cecilia, an ornate marble and gold small concert hall where the students' concerts took place, and a walled courtyard lit by flares at night where chamber concerts were held. Count Chigi was a splendid, six-foot-six, white-haired patriarch whose noble family had been closely connected with several popes over the ages. He married an English girl, but sadly they had no children, and although they separated he as a devout Catholic could never remarry. History has it that he was once persuaded to travel abroad, but got only as far as the frontier where he was smitten with homesickness and turned round and came home again. Although Siena in 1950 was a communist city, he was much loved, led all the church festivals and marched at the head of all the processions. This could happen only in that delightful mixed-up country Italy! The Queen of the Belgians was an old friend of Count Chigi and often stayed with him. She was particularly fond of coming to Maestro's classes to hear the young singers, and I sang for her several times.

No cars were allowed inside the city walls (nor are they to this day) but the Vespa was the latest thing, and the Italian girls were just plucking up their courage to try them, riding side-saddle behind their boyfriends with knees demurely clamped together.

Beloved Siena, I fell deeply in love with it, and with a handsome Dutch tenor in my class. When I got to know Wim, I fear that I abandoned my jolly quartet of young doctors to go off with him. We used to wander outside the city walls through the vineyards and olive groves in the moonlight. He was most appropriately studying Schumann's wonderfully romantic *Dichterliebe* with Maestro, and that music is still very special to me.

Siena was a unique experience, and I was to return there several times, but none of them equalled the aching romance of that first summer with the multi-national crowd of young musicians so recently liberated from the horrors of occupation and war. I put on dark glasses and cried all the way back to England by slow train, while trying to read Pirandello.

At home I tried hard not to let my parents see how depressed I was on my birthday, and how horrified at being thirty! Mentally I was away in Siena with Wim, who still had his big concert singing the *Dichterliebe* ahead of him.

But life had to go on, and we had to face up to telling our two singers that they had to go. This we both felt was a dastardly thing to do, but unless we did it there would be no more work and no more Opera Players. However we delayed telling them for as long as possible. I also had to decide whether or not to go back to Mme de Reusz for lessons. When Maestro had heard me sing on arrival in Siena, he had said to me: 'Where do you visualise your voice as coming from?' Without a second's hesitation I pointed to my forehead where Mme had always told us we must have an imaginary cross from which our voices issued. Maestro was horrified. 'No! No! No!' he cried. 'You sing from your stomach, from the soles of your feet, from your whole body!' Added to this, a well-respected London singing teacher told me my voice was placed much too high, and should really have been a strong lyric. So the decision was easy. I left Mme feeling disillusioned with singing teachers in general!

Sir Steuart Wilson introduced us to a very young bass baritone, Tom Hemsley, who was just down from Cambridge. Tom was a natural comedy actor with a fine voice so he became an excellent Don Pasquale, though too young for the part. Tom was given the great honour of singing the role of Aeneas in Purcell's *Dido and Aeneas* opposite the great Kirsten Flagstadt. She had agreed to come to London to sing Dido in performances to be given in the garden of her friend Bernard Miles. Her fee was a glass of Guinness per night! This was music for music's sake alone, and the performances with small orchestra were lovely. Tom got into trouble early on in rehearsal when the producer asked him to embrace Mme Flagstadt at a certain point. She was a large and well-built lady, and Tom, totally in awe of her, didn't know how to start. He said he tried this way and that way but never managed to enfold her in his arms to the producer's liking. 'I'm so sorry, Mme Flagstadt!' he eventually blurted out. 'I'm accustomed to something a little smaller.'

Eric Shilling also sang with us a lot but was already becoming very busy at the Sadler's Wells, soon-to-be English National Opera. Both these singers had great futures. Stanley Pine, who came in to double with Norman Platt, was a stylish and aristocratic-looking baritone, who made a good Dr Malatesta, but he had had a very tough war and his health was not good. He had been a POW in, I think, the salt mines up near Poland. In the last days of the war when the Russians were advancing from the East and the Germans retreating from the West the prisoner of war camp was hastily closed down and guards and prisoners fled together, determined at all costs to avoid the horror of being captured by the Russians. They struck southwest and had a terrible long march of some 500 miles during which many died of starvation and illness before they at last ran into the advancing Americans. Stan's digestive system had unfortunately suffered bad damage. Through him I learned a valuable lesson. I still had Glyndebourne standards in mind and wanted – impossibly – our small company to achieve excellence. As a result I must have nagged everyone intolerably, because one day when we were all in the train together Stanley said: 'Elisabeth, I dreamt last night that I was throttling you!' This was a big joke, but I took it to heart, and realised I must be careful with these men, many of whom were older than I was and had been through so much.

With Music in Miniature I did a concert at the Leas Cliff Hall, Folkestone, and who should be replacing Yvry Gitlis as solo violinist for this concert but Emmanuel Hurwitz – Manny of the RAMC band days, now on his way to a distinguished solo career. It was a great reunion, and it was also a concert for which I got a really good press criticism. To this day I get a warm glow when I remember it. I remember too the black depression that could descend all too quickly after just one bad notice, even though it was in a provincial newspaper out in the sticks.

In October Phyllis was summoned to the Arts Council to see Mona and there followed a mysterious conversation. Mona suggested that we should do a 'command performance' for John Denison, who had succeeded Steuart Wilson as Music Director. They were considering taking us over and financing us!! Phyllis and I did not like this very much. Either they were just looking for a final opportunity for the new man to turn us down, or, if they were genuinely thinking of taking us over, we would lose all our identity, our ability to choose our repertoire and cast the artists we liked. This would have given them the monopoly they probably wanted.

On 13th December a letter came with a complete volte-face. There was to be no financial help at all for us, and Norman and Leslie must go at once or the Arts Council would not use or recommend us anymore. They were graciously prepared to hear alternative singers as soon as we liked and would give us an early decision.

I was having hospital visits at the time to track down a missing kidney, and who should I meet at St Thomas's but Miss Hill from the Shaibah General Hospital in Iraq, now a matron here. It was a great reunion, and incidentally I have managed very well on one kidney all my life.

Shortly afterwards we had a tour of *Don Pasquale* coming up, and a crisis because Stanley Pine, our newly approved Dr Malatesta, was unable to sing one of the performances. I hunted in vain for another baritone who knew the role in English and in our translation. No question of course of getting Norman Platt back, not that he would probably have agreed to help us out after the shabby way we had just treated him. There was no alternative but to ask Douglas Craig, manager of our rivals the Grand Opera Group, who I knew sang the role. Douglas agreed, and he did a brilliant job, mastering our production and cuts, and doing the compèring that fell to Dr Malatesta in our version, perfectly on very little rehearsal. It had all, I hoped, gone off smoothly, but the result was a series of thoroughly unpleasant meetings with the Arts Council. Mona, speaking in her office to Phyllis, actually said: 'Of course, you realise we shall have to kill you?' Douglas, reporting back to Mona after his performance with us, had said: 'Why is it that ladies of gentle birth can never give a good performance?' (aimed at me) and then reported Phyllis for indecency, because in our unisex dressing room she had been walking around in a pair of voluminous and all-concealing black wartime bloomers, which she wore under her evening dress in cold weather! Phyllis promptly let it be known that the sight of Douglas getting into his corset to underpin his eighteenth-century coat and breeches had been at least equally distasteful! Shortly after Douglas sang with us we heard in a roundabout way that he planned to send out the Grand Opera Group with a fully produced and costumed version of *The Barber of Seville* after Christmas. I suppose we should have felt proud that he had pinched our idea, but we were depressed, angry and very worried as the Arts Council had all the resources to do a first-class job whereas Phyllis and I had to find what money we could spare for production costs.

There was a meeting that Phyllis and I went to at the much-dreaded Arts Council office at which we were so scathingly criticised and our poor little company so torn to shreds that Mona rang later that evening to ask if we were all right. No, we weren't, but we were more determined than ever to survive. A little bunch of primroses arrived next morning just as we were setting off on tour with a card, 'To two Plucky Players' in Mona's writing.

In December of 1952 poor Phyllis was once more summoned to the Arts Council to be told by Mona that we were much worse than two years ago, and she could no longer recommend us even for schools. This was devastating, and did not make for a happy Christmas. Fortunately our many bookings and excellent press reports did something to reassure us, but Phyllis found out that certain people were deeply jealous of our success.

After many auditions, runs and reruns, we found a cast that satisfied the Arts Council for *Don Pasquale*. Eric Shilling and Tom Hemsley were both excellent in the role of the Don, but sadly for us, Tom went off to do very well at a theatre in Germany before long. A new Irish tenor, John Carolan, who had a fine natural voice, was accepted for the role of Ernesto, and I seemed to be tolerated as Norina. We had problems with John, a strange character who tormented Phyllis and me by deliberately arriving for our schools shows about two minutes before the start, so that we were on the verge of cancelling by the time he strolled in. I probably nagged him unmercifully despite the fact that on stage we were always playing love scenes, as I was Mimi to his Rudolph, Norina to his Ernesto, and so on. One day he got his revenge. He was standing behind my chair in the first act of *Bohème* and just as I was about to sing the aria 'I'm always called Mimi' he put his hands on my shoulders and pinched me really hard. I never let on, nor did I tell him that he had in fact broken some small blood vessel so that I developed a large purple tumour on the front of my left shoulder. That was why I spent five days in hospital translating *La Cambiale di Matrimonio* while it was removed!

In July I went to Genoa to give a concert together with Giorgio Lippi, cellist and father of Simonetta, a friend from Siena. It was a great thrill for me, and I put together a programme of all my favourite English songs from Elizabethan up to the present day. The concert was for the Britannic Society in Palazzo Durazzo, a small select crowd in a typical marble hall with helpfully resonant acoustics. We were taken out to lunch by Italian friends to a famous eating house called the Bucci di San Matteo, where a delicious lunch went on until four o'clock. The concert began at 9.30 p.m. and three of Italy's top critics turned up, one of whom read out my translations before each song. It was nerve-racking because he insisted on sitting at the piano following every note, but he genuinely loved the programme – one of the favourite moments being two very contrasted Armstrong Gibbs songs, 'Silver' and 'Five Eyes'. The write-ups were effusive and generous, but I fear they cut no ice at home!

The following spring I returned to Genoa for another concert with Giorgio Lippi, then joined Phyllis in Rome for lessons with Giorgio Favaretto. I also coached with David Ricci for opera, and was encouraged by his praise for my voice and technique. The great Previtali had been told about me and wished to hear me, so I auditioned with him feeling extremely nervous. Although his comments were favourable, nothing came of the meeting. I think this was the time when Phyllis and I, looking for digs in Rome together, nervously told the landlady that we were musicians, and please might we practise in her flat? Her face lit up and she said: 'On one condition, that I may bring my chair and sit in the corridor outside to listen to you!' On another occasion Maestro had given one of his very late-night parties at which all his pupils had to sing. Next day he went to apologise to the people upstairs for the noise, to be met with a reproachful, 'Maestro, why did you close the windows? We could not hear properly!' Shades of London, where any mention of music usually got one thrown out forthwith. The English song programmes in Genoa and the repertoire I studied with Maestro came in very useful as I had several broadcasts from Paris, Brussels and Basle at this time. Perhaps because of the fame of Benjamin Britten, English song was very popular on the Continent and I usually included some of Ben's folksong settings and pieces from his song cycle *On This Island*.

In summer I joined my parents for a short time in Zermatt, then went back to Siena, delighted because Phyllis was there, engaged to play as assistant accompanist to Favaretto. Siena was as magical as ever despite the lack of Wim. All the doctors were there, and many friends from my first year. I persuaded Maestro to let me sing one of my show pieces at the final concert, then on the journey home I had a forty-eight-hour romance with a very beautiful young Roman. We met in a second-class compartment and got talking; his mother was Irish and he was on his way to her home for a fishing holiday. The chemistry between us was perfect, and I am ashamed to say we flirted outrageously, being sorely tempted to get off the train in Switzerland and stay there in the mountains!

Back in London there was much to do as we had a busy season ahead despite the Arts Council. I was finding out about preparing interleaved prompt scores, and planning our own Opera Players' writing paper. And a friend from EOG days who was a clever props and scenery maker had turned up, and made us a handsome collapsible spinet, and even a practicable raised balcony on which the heroine could stand and be serenaded in the moonlight, for our new *Barber of Seville*.

We were to be lent eighteenth-century costumes for *Don Pasquale* by the Royal Opera House, and up to the eleventh hour nothing was forthcoming. When we did finally get them they were excellent, but Phyllis vowed it was not worth the uncertainty, and from then on she supervised the making of our own costumes in her dining room, which used to be converted into a temporary workshop.

A friend of mine who was training to be a photographer let us invade her small flat to have our first photographs taken. How we managed I don't know, but Mimi's bed and the dying scene were squeezed in, followed by Don Pasquale with us in all our Royal Opera House glory! People were so good to us. I went to Nathanwigs to hire and was taken under the wing of Miss Dolly, who fitted us up with various men's tie wigs for a minimal cost. We had the same wigs for years, and eventually she wrote to say that they were so old she did not want them back, so they were ours! Another bonus was that Phyllis had inherited from her mother one Miss Willoughby, ex-milliner to Her Majesty Queen Mary, later personal maid to Lady Ampthill. Willoughby turned all her skills to the stage and produced, among other memorable headgear, the long black shovel hats worn in *The Barber of Seville*. These were so well made that I have only recently disposed of them fifty years on.

As time went by the presence of the Opera Players on the musical scene came to be accepted and the dreaded meetings at the Arts Council office ceased. We auditioned and booked our own singers, producers and designers, and our main contact was to discuss which new operas we should put on so that there should be no overlap. However, we still had hidden problems to contend with, as a friendly music club secretary told us when she tried to re-book us. When the renewal of her club's annual Arts Council grant was being discussed, she was told they would get it on the condition that she engaged the Grand Opera Group for the following season.

It is interesting to note that we need not have been afraid of the Arts Council's *The Barber of Seville*, which took the road just after ours. Despite the competition we sold nineteen *Barbers* in the first season, forty-eight in the second, and sixty-four in the third.

We asked Peter Gellhorn to produce our *Barber* for us, though he had never produced before, and he made an excellent straightforward job of it, basing the movement entirely on the mood and tempo of the music. We also created a record, I think, by asking him to sing a major role, that of Dr Bartolo, in it. We thought it would be very good for a conductor to see just exactly what it is like to be up there on stage singing. He said he found the experience both of producing and performing very interesting and was sure he was the only conductor in captivity to have sung in his own production!

Phyllis, who was particularly interested in the educational side of our work, became friendly with Dr Russell, then Director of Music for the LCC. He was enthusiastic about our shows, which were 'directly provided', i.e. fully paid for by the Council in those happy days when we came under the heading of Class Tuition. He gave Phyllis a list of all the London schools and allowed her to choose which ones we should visit. She chose the poorest and most deprived, and arranged them geographically so that we could visit two junior schools a day with our fifty-minute *Hänsel and Gretel* performance, travelling our poles, curtains, witch's oven, costumes etc. in her car and reaching our second school in time to eat a hearty pre-Jamie Oliver school dinner before the afternoon show. Once in dockland we found a little boy crying in the front row. On being asked what the matter was he said, 'My father says opera is cissy and he'll wallop me if I go!' We used to ask the children if anyone knew what an opera was before starting. The answers were illuminating. 'It's when you all sing together very loud' and 'It's singing and dancing and my mum goes every Saturday night' were just two.

When we did our shortened *La Bohème* or *Don Pasquale* or *The Barber of Seville* for the senior children we could of course fit in only one a day. Their comments were extremely apt. One school was told we could do only a shortened version because the opera was too long, and the retort was: 'Well, if they hadn't repeated themselves so much we would have had time to hear the lot!' Librettists take note! Another child wrote after *Don Pasquale*, 'We were told the lady was rich, but she wore the same dress all the time.' I rushed home and made myself a grand second-act costume, and somehow found time to change into it. You cannot get away with anything with children. Our generous budget from the LCC allowed us to give fifty-plus performances a year, and this was our bread and butter during our early days.

In 1960 we took an important step forwards; we decided we would perform with children as well as for them. *Hänsel and Gretel* was the obvious first choice, with local schools singing and acting the gingerbread children, providing a Dew Fairy and a Sandman if good enough voices could be found, and dancing the 'Angels' Pantomime'. I devised simple production and choreography, details of which were sent to teachers in advance together with costume sketches and suggestions as to the easiest way of making or improvising them. The teachers prepared the children, I went to them for one preliminary rehearsal, and we had a dress rehearsal on the day of the performance. *Cavalleria Rusticana* and *Pagliacci* were offered in the same way for senior schools and adult choral societies. The success of these early experiments matured into a policy that made possible the incorporation of local choral and operatic societies, schools and even occasionally orchestras, into every full-length opera we offered.

When we went to Northern Ireland the troubles were already underway, and our three successive tours there brought various problems. Larne was very shocked by *The Escape from the Harem*; they substituted another title and sat in stony silence during the more racy bits of dialogue. The following year we were advised that it would give great offence if the sleazy priest Don Basilio in *The Barber of Seville* was presented as such, so the Reverend Father of the English translation became a layman, which gave the singers a memory problem. The real heroine was pianist Phyllis Thorold, who was under orders to play 'God Save the Queen' before each performance – whereupon half the audience would sometimes walk out.

In 1960 we still had no staff, stage or secretarial. Phyllis's first small second-hand Austin burst into flames as we arrived for a show at Tettenhall College, Wolverhampton, but after this event we each acquired an estate car. We would pack costumes, props and scenery, load it into the two cars, drive to the performance, unload with the help of local people and our own singers, set up, perform, repack and reload, and often drive home late to change operas and set off again the next day.

Later on as I ceased to sing major roles in the operas, I learned the basics of stage management and lighting, which could be hazardous, as when we started there were many archaic and dangerous dimmer boards still in use. I well remember dimming down for the final moonlit garden scene of *Don Pasquale* at a well-known boys' public school, praying it would end before the board became red hot, while a boy stood poised behind me with a fire extinguisher at the ready.

One of the more fearsome things during my stage-managing career was setting up and detonating the stage maroon when the Witch's oven blows up in *Hänsel and Gretel*. The first time I did this, at Yeovil, the local electrician, a huge fat fellow, was laid on to help. We wired things up for a trial run, he clutching the maroon and two naked wires perilously close together against his stomach. We then lowered everything into a dustbin and put the lid back on (a mistake!). I retreated, but he refused to budge and made contact, whereupon there was a massive explosion, the bin split and the lid flew up into the wings breaking a window en route. I peered anxiously through the dust and saw him shaking with the happy laughter of the very fat. 'Aaaar!' he said. 'They aaavn't 'eered nothin' like that in Yeovil before!'

Dennis Arundel produced *Fra Diavolo* by Auber and Cimarosa's *The Secret Marriage* for us during the 1960s. Rehearsal space was always a major problem and expense for us. And at the time of *The Secret Marriage* production we were using a church hall near Chelsea Barracks, where we had a free show every morning as the guards marched past, band, mascot and all, on their way to Buckingham Palace. One day as the sound of the band was fading away a couple of very red-faced military policemen rushed into the hall. 'Whose is the green Morris Traveller double-parked outside?' Mine, of course, hastily parked, unloaded, locked and then forgotten. 'Madam, are you aware you have obstructed Her Majesty's Forces in the execution of their duty?' I was – it was all too clear. There was just room for the guards to march four abreast between the two rows of parked cars. Mine – double-parked – must have caused chaos. What did they do? Break ranks? Form twos? The mind boggles and I had visions of the Tower. I still regret not having seen what actually happened!

As a follow-up to *Hänsel and Gretel* we put on Benjamin Britten's *The Little Sweep* in 1967, and the then director of music to the LCC selected three of the toughest schools in London, where we were to perform it together with the children as an experiment. It was a great success, with even the most difficult and uncooperative kids vying to take part or help in some way.

In 1963 the Opera Players had been formed into a limited company and registered under the Charities Act, with a board of directors headed by Anne Wood. We were now able to begin much-needed fundraising, and were soon in receipt of an Arts Council grant, which grew steadily until it was abruptly terminated in 1979.

To celebrate the newly formed company and our first grants we put on *Die Fledermaus*, and for the first time afforded ourselves a proper team of Michael Alfreds, producer, music director Peter Gellhorn, and a young designer Dacre Punt, who later became well known to television viewers through his work on BBC series such as *To the Manor Born*. Emile Belcourt, our first Eisenstein, went on to sing the role for the English National Opera, and was only one of many who have been through our ranks and gone on into the national companies. By now we had a long list of singers waiting for auditions, a large mailing list, and produced a new brochure annually. We needed good photographs of our productions, and among many people who helped us on our way was photographer Zoë Dominic, who for a very nominal fee took as much trouble over our small sessions as over her work at the Royal Opera House.

The question of finding patrons arose after we became a limited company, and again I met with so much kindness when I wrote to people. Sir Robert and Lady Mayer (he of the Saturday morning children's concerts fame) were our first two. Soon after I wrote to J B Priestley to tell him of our work, and said it was largely due to my having become stage-struck as a result of reading and re-reading his book *The Good Companions* that I had thought to put together a similar group of touring opera singers. We never asked our patrons for money directly, but out of the blue came a cheque from him for £100 with the message that he had just sold a picture and thought the money might come in useful. Benjamin Britten too kindly agreed to be on our patron's list, and his name was of great value. One year I was invited to the Woman of the Year Luncheon (more because of a small mountaineering expedition I had been on and written about than because of music) and one of the speakers was Lord Redcliffe-Maude. I was enormously impressed by what he said, and wrote to him asking for his patronage, which he kindly granted us. Sir Isaiah Berlin and Geraint Evans also joined the list, and I am very grateful to them and many others for the support they gave to our small organisation.

About this time some happy impulse made me pick up my pen and write to Mary Glasgow – whom I had never met – to invite her to join our board. She responded with typical warmth, and soon became our chairman, in which position her enthusiasm and positive approach were invaluable for many years. As a result of her interest in the educational aspect of our work we commissioned Antony Hopkins to write us a children's opera for our twenty-first season. Richard Church was approached to write a libretto, but somehow the partnership did not work. After a wait of some months, we got a happy postcard from Tony, on holiday in Austria, to say the idea for *Dr Musikus* had suddenly come to him and he had written the whole piece, words and music, in a week, mostly on the pages of a book about motor-racing that he was reading. We ran it for a short session at the Arts Theatre in London, and it went very well with its blend of wit, humour and cleverly disguised educational content, as well as the various kinds of audience participation and the children's orchestra of percussion, bells and recorders. Eric Shilling produced, and sang the title role, and Antony Hopkins rehearsed the children beforehand, introduced it and played the virtuoso piano part. A week in a proper London theatre was a treat for us in those days.

Our two long-suffering small cars trundled a growing collection of props, costumes and collapsible scenery around the country. We toured all over the place, and I have photographs of my old Morris Traveller in Scotland and the New Forest within a few days of each other. Phyllis – whose car was better – carried the costumes; I had the rest in and on my Morris. Occasionally things would fly off the roof, as on the awful day when heavy gas piping narrowly missed a following lorry. The driver, having let fly a real mouthful, helped me to reload.

When *Bohème* mark four went on in 1968 with excellent sets by Gerald Kitching, a van became essential. At first we hired, and the hell of driving a large vehicle, often with peculiarities due to old age and hard use, straight out from a well-known hire firm into the traffic round King's Cross, is something I shall never forget. One vehicle refused to go into anything but first gear. I ground round the block and back into the garage where a mechanic with a scornful 'women drivers!' expression said 'Come with me!' and leapt into the driving seat. Triumph – he too could get it only into first gear. The next vehicle that was produced would not lock, but that was a minor evil. Thankfully we were later able to buy a Bedford Workobus – a dear vehicle that travelled far and wide driven by Phyllis and myself.

By the end of the 1970–71 season we had given 2,010 performances of twenty-four different operas. *The Barber of Seville* was in the lead with 583, closely followed by *Hänsel and Gretel* with 512. By our twenty-first birthday singers who had worked with us included Thomas Hemsley, Norman Platt, Eric Shilling, Laura Sarti, John Kentish Kenneth Macdonald, Edward Byles, David Johnstone, Emile Belcourt, John Dobson, John Winfield, Bernard Dickerson, Philip Langridge, Ramon Remedios, Bryan Drake and Michael Rippon. Our twenty-first birthday party was held in a blizzard at – suitably – the Alpine Club in South Audley Street. Baritone Donald Francke showed the Laurel and Hardy film of *Fra Diavolo* and we had a great party – Phyllis and I unable to believe how the years had passed.

During the 1970s the life of the Opera Players flowed fairly steadily, if any operatic journey can be described as steady. We put on a new production each year, raising money through an endless series of appeals to the smaller charitable trusts. Many, such as the Chase Charity and the Leche Foundation, supported us regularly and generously, but we were always short of money. Opera is a musical black hole. We ran each production until no one asked for it anymore. Some of our singers stayed with us for years and became the backbone of our company, maturing into heavier and more dramatic roles as time went by. Others came and went like meteors, doing perhaps a couple of seasons with us before passing on to greater (and better paid) things, or returning to their home countries, Australia, Canada, New Zealand and many others. The tide of bookings ebbed and flowed, averaging about 100 per annum. Each year I put together a new brochure and sent it out to all the listed music clubs and education authorities, and to the bigger public and private schools.

In 1971 Chelham Opera, a company doing similar work to ours and with whom we shared various singers, merged with us, bringing with it some useful additions to our costumes, music and props, and two new productions, *The Magic Flute* and *La Traviata*, which we ran in 1972 and 1973.

In the summer of 1973 my partner Phyllis Thorold resigned from the company. I had unfortunately been unable to tour for a time because of my mother's illness, and sang only very occasionally, so our original happy collaboration had been interrupted. Her resignation was a great blow as her work for the company in so many spheres seemed irreplaceable. She was an amazing person of many talents. In the war she had risen to the equivalent rank of colonel in the Red Cross, had served in Russia, flown in the bomb racks of a plane sent to bring British POWs home from Europe, and received an OBE for her services. She became a brilliant costume-maker and embroideress to help the Opera Players. And she was of course a fine pianist, having studied cello, piano and singing at the Royal College of Music. Christopher Shaw, who had been Music Director for Chelham Opera, took over playing for performances together with Alexa Maxwell, while Peter Gellhorn also played whenever his busy life allowed.

To date our performances had almost always been piano accompanied and given without a conductor. This was very good training for our young singers, who had to know their music thoroughly and learn to listen to each other and not rely on a conductor. As we slowly gained confidence and started to approach the small theatres, another of my great ambitions, to present our performances with orchestra, became possible. And I ventured into the mysterious world of the Musicians' Union – only to retreat hastily vowing to leave all future negotiations to a professional fixer, those vital people, usually musicians themselves, who arrange orchestras of all sorts and sizes, dealing with such complications as porterage (for large instruments), overtime, accommodation, VAT and suchlike. I dealt happily with the same fixer for several years, and he paid me one of the greatest compliments I have ever had. 'Elisabeth,' he said to a mutual friend, 'is the last gentleman in the business.'

When I first tiptoed nervously into the world of the commercial theatre manager I got the impression that I was looked on as a big joke. Few women ran touring companies in those days – apart from the formidable Mrs Phillips of the Carl Rosa. I got used to being greeted with a patronising 'My dear little lady' attitude. My endeavours to explain the aims of our company and its young artists usually fell on deaf ears. 'What I want, dear lady,' managers would say, thumping their desks, 'is NAMES. Bring me NAMES and then we can talk business.' Difficult to explain that the names they wanted cost far more than they were prepared to pay, and that we were bringing them the names of the future, young, fresh and enthusiastic, often giving performances that would have graced far bigger and more distinguished stages. And how smelly and dirty many of those little old theatres were backstage in the post-war days. They were soon to be swept away and replaced by clean modern but somehow soulless civic theatres. Gone were the bow-tied managers of old, replaced by young men with BAs, but little experience of the realities of theatre life.

In our very early school days we had limited our singers to four or five per opera, each quite probably wearing several hats during the course of the show. As we began playing for music clubs and theatres this number increased and we no longer needed a narrator to fill the gaps. Our fees were a simple question of economics; what we charged had to cover everything including travel costs. Accommodation, when essential, used to be arranged by the committee members of the clubs or societies we visited, or in staff quarters or sanatoriums of schools. Room-sharing was unavoidable, and even bed-sharing not unknown. I found our two baritones on the station platform one morning in fits of laughter. 'It's been a crime all the time we were in the army but now we are being asked to do it!' I apologised and said I would try to ensure that the same thing did not happen again! The usual way the accommodation was sorted out was that after the show we would come on stage with our bags as soon as we had changed and line up feeling rather sheepish. Prospective hosts would look us over and more or less say, 'I'll take that one.' Unfortunately many hostesses were single or widowed women who would not dream of taking a man home – women didn't eat so much breakfast and sometimes even stripped their beds! Unfortunately most opera casts contain many more men than women.

We ended up in some weird places. In one stately home, rather sadly run down and shabby, to which we were taken after our show, our soprano confessed to being hungry – which we all were – after we had been given just a pot of tea and a few biscuits. There was a long pause, and eventually the only remaining servant came in with a silver salver with large dome, which looked really hopeful, and placed it on the table. When the dome was removed it revealed one tiny sandwich. I can't remember if it was at the same place where we were riveted by the sight of a mouse running up and down along the sofa back just behind our hostess's head. We could see it, but she couldn't. Enormous self-control had to be exercised until it finally disappeared. Young artists now require hotel accommodation, and in single rooms at that. Luckily in the 1960s anything was still better than the war!

We never, even in our later days, travelled a big chorus. In most of the eighteenth- and nineteenth-century operas we presented, the soloists sang the same line as the chorus in the ensembles. Any opera that relied heavily on its chorus we put on only if we could get a local choral society or a school choir to join forces with us. We took to doing this with operas such as *Cavalleria Rusticana* and *I Pagliacci*, and we eventually offered the possibility of local participation in most of our repertoire, particularly *Die Fledermaus* and *Tosca*, where we could include choirboys and some male voices in the great Act 1 finale. All this meant that we had to acquire a large wardrobe of spare costumes.

We also offered coaching for local choirs and orchestras with Peter Gellhorn, and preparatory production sessions with our producers. There were some happy results, with Dennis Arundel going several times to Cheltenham College to train senior boys and girls for *Pagliacci*, while Peter went to the Strode Theatre at Street in Somerset to coach orchestra and chorus for *Cavalleria Rusticana*. He was extremely critical and never pulled his punches. The lady cellist dissolved in tears and had to be comforted and persuaded back to her instrument. Worse was to come. We had a gifted young Irish-Italian director who went down to Street to produce the chorus scenes. He walked in to the first rehearsal to find all the chorus ladies proudly attired in brand-new brilliantly coloured sateen dirndl skirts they had paid for and made themselves. He exploded – he was young and had not yet learned tact – and, in a tirade of Irish-Italian English, he tried to describe to them what a crowd of poor Sicilian peasants should look like. All the pretty new skirts were scrapped, to be replaced by sombre blacks and dark browns and greys over heavy shoes. The chorus was not happy. But together with the lady cellist and the rest of the orchestra, they learnt something. And the end performance was real and powerful and they loved it.

It was my job as manager to sort out all these sometimes dramatic problems. Once when we were putting on Mozart's *Cosi fan Tutte* Dennis Arundel and Peter Gellhorn almost came to blows over the question of tempi. Peter with his Glyndebourne background favoured slow tempi. He liked to spin out the glorious music into silken threads and weave it into a noble tapestry, and he coached the singers to do this. Dennis, a theatre man, said it was quite impossible that two young girls awaiting their lovers should sing their opening duet in such a way, and his idea of the tempo was almost double Peter's. He walked out, and I rushed after him to the nearest bus stop and pleaded with him to come back, to the great interest of the queue. It was essential that he should return as production was too far advanced for there to be a change. It seemed impossible, but he came back, and eventually a compromise was reached.

My own first-ever experience of producing a chorus came very early in the life of the company when I went down to Colchester to prepare 150 teenagers to take part in *Cavalleria Rusticana* with us. It was a nightmare, as they were self-conscious, awkward and unwilling at first, and I was suffering from laryngitis so could barely make myself heard. There was room for only about fifty on stage, so I had to divide them into a large group who sang in the orchestra pit, and a smaller lot, hopefully the most able, who would sing and act. I picked a young couple to walk across the stage during the famous interlude, only to find that those tough kids, who probably knew far more about sex than I did, were frozen with embarrassment when asked to put their arms round each other in public!

In 1974 we put on *The Marriage of Figaro*, directed by Douglas Craig, after several days of auditions, which brought in a lot of talent, including a leggy young mezzo called Eirean James, who made a delicious Cherubino and eventually made her way to the Royal Opera House. We had what experience had taught us was the ideal blend for this production – fifty per cent experienced singers who had already performed their roles, and fifty per cent new young artists making their debuts in this important opera.

Phyllis Thorold had always been in charge of our accounts and had refused to register for VAT as she felt strongly that charities should not have to do so. In the winter of 1975 Customs and Excise caught up with us and ordered us to pay arrears of tax since April 1973. We had no money to meet this crisis, but the Arts Council kindly came to our rescue and paid the bill. I dreaded having to cope with the VAT returns, but a charming young man from Customs and Excise came to see me and told me he had just spent two years in the Highlands of Scotland teaching local postmistresses what to do. 'If they can do it, you can,' he said. 'Just ring me if you have a problem.'

In 1976 Christopher and Jean Shaw made a brilliant translation of Offenbach's *La Belle Hélène* for us. Costs of scenery, props and costumes had by now escalated alarmingly, and we knew this particular piece needed a first-class production and setting – but how to afford it? We asked Tom Hawkes, whose productions I had always admired, to direct, and to my delight he agreed. I then plucked up my courage and arranged to go and see Malcolm Pride, the then head of the theatre department at the Wimbledon School of Arts. I remembered the marvellously witty *Orpheus in the Underworld* designed by Malcolm, which ran for ten years at Sadler's Wells in the 1950s. I explained our painful lack of funds, and he agreed that the senior students of the costume and design course could make our scenery, furniture, costumes and props as a project for cost price. I asked him if he could suggest a student designer too, whereupon he said that he loved *La Belle Hélène* and would like to design it himself. This was a fantastic offer from a top designer and my heart sank as I blurted out that unfortunately we were totally unable to pay the sort of fee he commanded. He replied that there was no question of a fee; he wanted his students to have the experience of working for a real live show on fully professional designs such as they would meet later in their careers.

We held auditions and chose two young mezzos, one a beautiful and gifted girl straight from the Royal College of Music, who was to become a memorable Hélène, the other quite different but also gifted who sadly left us almost immediately to take up a resident position at the Berne Opera House, and two young tenors, Adrian Martin and Keith Jones, peering hopefully at their trousers as we tried to ensure that they were neither knock-kneed nor bandy legged – unfortunate features for a kilted hero. We were lucky as both were upstanding types with sturdy legs and figures that looked good in extremely scanty costumes.

Because of our collaboration with the Wimbledon School of Art we had the unprecedented luxury of a week's rehearsal in their theatre with scenery and costumes, followed by two public dress rehearsals, one for each of the two casts. It was a stunning show. As more enchanting costumes and sets kept appearing (five changes each for Helen and Paris and two each for all the others) my mouth became drier and drier as I tried to calculate the cost – gorgeous headdresses, sequins, beads, boots, helmets, swords, even a boat for the finale – Malcolm must have seen my face because he came over to where I was standing at the back and whispered in my ear, 'Don't worry, we are only £30 over budget.' I could hardly believe it because our total budget for costumes, scenery and props was a mere £600!

The party after the final rehearsal was wrecked for me by the sight of our stage staff aged eighteen and nineteen struggling to get everything loaded into our modest van – a nightmare as there was far too much – to leave that night for a tour in Wales. The show opened next evening in a tiny hall in Bettws y Coed, with a few light bulbs as sole illumination and an acting area so small that Hélène's Act 2 bed, a huge circular affair, entirely filled it and had to be climbed over by anyone needing to cross the stage. The cast was billeted in the village with slightly shocked members of the local community, and Paris's landlady, obviously overcome by his Act 2 slave's costume, which consisted of a few strategically placed lengths of chain, kept repeating as she gazed at him, 'There's beautiful legs you have!' but not a word about his voice, which upset him a lot.

After the big event of *La Belle Hélène* we reproduced *Tosca* for the following season, and this was a 'house' affair, translated by Doreen Murray (Tosca), directed by Frederick Westcott (Scarpia) and designed and largely made by John Ford (Spoletta). We lacked a heavier voiced tenor to sing the role of Cavaradossi, so I went to the English National

Opera, with whom we had a cordial relationship by now, to ask if they had a young tenor they would like to try out in this role. They suggested a fine Australian singer who had recently auditioned for them and been taken on, though they could not employ him immediately. His name was Henry Howell, and we had him with us in *Tosca* for two seasons before he went off to South America and an international career. My heart warmed to him from the start. When I somewhat shyly tried to explain to him the rugged conditions of some of our work he said, 'Don't worry, love – I've been running a company just like this all over the outback and I wouldn't hire anyone who wouldn't carry the cases.' He was as good as his word; on arrival Henry – a massive fellow – always picked up the heaviest case in sight.

The autumn of 1978 saw us back, cap in hand, at the Wimbledon School of Art, for help with a new production of Mozart's *The Seraglio* by the successful team of Tom Hawkes, Director, and Christopher Shaw, Music Director. This time Malcolm Pride selected a senior student, Martin Grant, to design scenery and costumes as his degree project, and at the public dress rehearsal adjudicators including Peter Rice came to assess his work. It was a charming Turkish-Victorian affair and Martin got a good degree as a result.

The *Seraglio* production was overcast by the shattering news, received via a press release, that our Arts Council Grant had been withdrawn in common with that of several other companies. It was little consolation that we were not alone. Our first reaction was that we would have to lie down and die. An emergency meeting of directors was called, however, and we resolved to launch an immediate appeal for financial aid and try to carry on. Robert (now Lord) Skidelsky who was then on our board wrote a fine article in *The Times Educational Supplement* about the importance of our work, and the John Lewis partnership came to our rescue with an on-going grant for running costs. This was a huge relief because getting money for running costs is extremely difficult. Trusts are happy to support an exciting (and newsworthy) project, but no one wants to contribute towards the nitty-gritty of the daily expenses.

When the blow about our Arts Council grant fell we were in the process of commissioning another children's opera for the Year of the Child, and I had suggested a young English composer, Richard Blackford. The Arts Council had agreed to pay the commission fee, and this arrangement held good, so we went ahead heartened by the knowledge that Ted Hughes (later to become Poet Laureate) had agreed to write the libretto. The Royal Opera House had become interested in both project and composer, and we had a meeting at which they generously proposed to meet seventy-five per cent of the cost, estimated at £20,000, of putting the opera on and running it for two weeks at the Round House in the New Year of 1980. Richard Blackford and his collaborator the young American director Michael Hackett were determined to produce the opera in the round; in fact it was all very much of a young people's creation, with David Syrus, then a *répétiteur* at the Royal Opera House, making his debut as an opera conductor. There was an orchestra of eight drawn from a brilliant young instrumental group called the Fires of London, each of whom had a virtuoso part to play (the percussion part was even scored for a water gong, which had to be immersed in a bath of water). The players were seated all round the circular central platform on which the action took place, which proved awkward when the conductor found a large singer blocking his view. The opera was called *The Pig Organ* and was based on the fairy tale of *The Princess and the Swineherd*. We had a double cast of five professional singers, and three teams of six children playing the musical piglets. There was no scenery, but Malcolm Pride again provided fantastic costumes, and very effective lighting was devised by the Royal Opera House crew. A fearful struggle with Equity to get a work permit for American director Michael Hackett, without whom Richard refused to allow the opera to go on, was resolved only at the eleventh hour, then everything became so easy with the Royal Opera House behind us – adequate rehearsal on their premises, tiptop stage and wardrobe staff, and Malcolm to design the costumes and some incredible props. The main problem was orientation, as performing on a circular stage with gangways radiating out like spokes of a wheel led to singers and children frequently losing their bearings and taking a wrong exit. The only constant factor was the conductor, and he had his own problems when he found the singers standing with their backs to him much of the time. It was an exciting and stimulating experience, though the Royal Opera House and the Opera Players lost a lot of money over it. We grew very fond of the Round House and were sad to hear of its demise. (Note – fortunately it was soon up and running again.) British conservatism about music is such that *The*

Pig Organ had only one provincial booking – a sad state of affairs for young composers. Admittedly the water gong was a menace to tour and caused a flood at our first and only touring date!

Fearing that *The Pig Organ* might not book we had put on Rossini's popular *Cenerentola* at the same time, using excellent costumes that came to us from Chelham Opera, having started their life in a production at Sadler's Wells. It sold well, and brought us our one and only groupie! We were playing at the Church Stretton Festival, and before the show the secretary came up and asked me to meet an admirer of our company, who had come a long way to see the performance. That was how I met Ena Wordsworth, opera buff and particular lover of the nineteenth-century works of Bellini, Donizetti and Rossini. Ena became a good friend who followed us round and soon ran our Friends' Association. That first evening she was talking about how she had never seen a *Cenerentola* production with the ideal heroine she imagined. 'Now there,' she said pointing to where one of our singers was standing, 'is my dream Cinderella. Young, slim, and beautiful, with waist-length golden hair.'

'That,' we told her, 'is your Cinderella for tonight. And she has an amazing voice too.'

In the 1979–80 season we had given 119 performances. In the following year the number fell dramatically to twenty-five, largely because of a second severe blow, the ending of our twenty-five-year relationship with the LCC, for whom we had been giving between fifty and sixty directly provided schools performances a year. Cuts in educational expenditure were the cause, and our work for schools in the provinces came to an end at the same time. In future schools would have to pay for concerts or operas, and this most of them could not possibly do.

During the lean season I concentrated on fundraising, got in £17,000, and we had a major stroke of much-needed luck. The Intimate Opera Company, which had been in existence for fifty years, presenting a unique repertoire of one-act operas for three singers, ranging from Arne and Mozart to Horowitz and Antony Hopkins, closed down, and we took over all its music, costumes and productions. With the ever-deepening recession this was just what we needed to enable us to offer low-priced and entertaining performances suitable for all types of audience and venue. In the spring of 1981 Charles Farncombe asked us to perform two of these chamber operas, Handel's *Apollo and Daphne* and Mozart's *Bastien and Bastiennne*, for his festival at Llantilio Crossenny in Wales. The operas were put on in the beautiful old church of St Teilo, with a small orchestra, and were so successful that we went back for many years. We formed London Chamber Opera, which worked with its own small orchestra of ten to twelve players, as the outcome of the Llantilio performances.

At the other end of the scale, and as an extension of our work with children, in autumn 1981 we launched a major production of *Carmen* in which both senior- and junior-school choirs could join us as soldiers, smugglers, cigarette girls and gypsies. They loved it (though one headmistress objected to her girls smoking on stage even though we assured her the cigarettes were only props ones). A generous grant from a small trust enabled us to have practical touring scenery built and attractive costumes made, and *Carmen*, directed by Frederick Westcott, proved a great attraction with its rousing music and dramatic story. Children and teachers from all over the country took part in it with us and found the experience exciting and stimulating.

A further development to enlarge the work of the company in the community was our new production of *Die Fledermaus*, directed by Eric Shilling, which we took to the opera house in Jersey. Eric went over in advance to produce the local choral society, then sang with us for a week in his much-acclaimed (at the English National Opera) role of Colonel Frank.

Another example of work we consider to have been of real value was the joint productions we gave for two February festivals in Milton Keynes, when Peter Gellhorn rehearsed and conducted the local chorus and orchestra, and our producers worked with the chorus, to put together with our soloists high-quality full-scale performances of *Die Fledermaus* in 1983 and *Tosca* in 1984.

In 1985 I wrote for my directors:

> We continue to be fraught with problems. Storage
> is expensive and uncertain, and we have had many
> traumatic moves. Rehearsal space is becoming more and
> more difficult to find and is very costly: we have used a
> rich mix of Quaker Meeting Houses and church halls,
> competing with Yoga, Alcoholics Anonymous, Floral Art

and numerous other homeless organisations for free time. Props and costumes have to be shuttled from place to place by car, and we have never had anywhere we can rehearse with our scenery or put it up to repair or repaint it. Our transport is once more limited to hired lorries and my ancient Austin Maxi, now on its second time round the clock. Our Organising Secretary, contemplating our second-hand typewriter bought in 1963, remarked sadly after her first six months with us 'I see now that the Opera Players is not a job, it's a way of life.' Our future is more seriously threatened financially than ever although we flourish artistically. Our needs are modest and cannot possibly be pruned further, but some form of stable funding is urgently required. We hope to win through as we have done in the past, but the next few months will prove critical.

In 1992 I added:

I wrote the above account in 1985. Seven years on we are miraculously still here, probably more securely established now, with our own stores and a well-equipped office, but with the same financial problems which seem to afflict opera at every level. The past seven years have been as full of drama and disappointment and satisfaction as the first thirty-five. The Arts Council did us a favour when they took our grant away. They made us into tough survivors.

Elisabeth Parry. 1992.

Chapter Eleven

The Parry Family and London Opera Players

Much of the later history of the London Opera Players, as we now called ourselves, depended upon the Parry Trust and is tied up with my rediscovery of my Parry heritage, which came about through a network of musical cousins. I had completely lost touch with my father's family until I got to know my Bramhall cousin – she who ran the music club there and asked me up to give a recital. She put me in touch with my great-grandfather Dr Joseph Parry's only surviving granddaughter, Barbara, who lived in Bristol, a remarkable and lovely person, and it was Barbara who told me that I was his last surviving great-grandchild. Through her I at last began to find out how much he still means to the people of Wales and what a very remarkable man he must have been.

Joseph was born in Merthyr Tydfyl, the son of an ironworker whose wife, another Elizabeth Parry, apparently had a lovely contralto voice and sang in the local chapel choir. The little boy joined his father at the age of nine, to work first in a coalmine and later at the Cyfarthfa iron works. He worked barefoot with the other boys, and sometimes their feet got so painfully burned by the hot cinders that his father would have to carry him home in the evening. He would have earned something like twelve and a half (old) pence for a fifty-six-hour week. He had a very good voice, and also sang in the chapel choir where he probably learned to read music by the tonic sol-fa system, but he was seventeen before he learned to read and write. He showed astonishing musical ability from the first. His father was one of many who emigrated to the USA to escape the grinding poverty in the Valleys and seek a better life. He left in 1853, and found work in Danville, Pennsylvania, where, amazingly, in a year he was able to save enough money to buy a house and send for his wife and family to join him. They travelled over in one of the special ships laid on to carry the families of emigrating miners to the New World, £5 a head for passage in the hold. It must have been hard for Elizabeth with four small children, but they were provided with mattresses and food, and there was a special doctor to look after them.

In the USA the family flourished, and Joseph's talent was soon recognised. He sent compositions home to Wales for the principal Eisteddfodau for several years, always winning first or joint first prizes, whereupon the Welsh mining community formed a group and collected enough money to send him back to London to study at the Royal Academy of Music. He studied piano and voice and composition with the distinguished English composer Sterndale Bennett, and now for the first time he was able to become musically literate, to hear great orchestras and go to an opera, which for him was a mind-blowing revelation.

He got a scholarship to go on to study music for Cambridge, where he was one of the first Welsh miner students, and he got his BA in 1871 followed by his doctorate the next year, an extraordinary achievement for one who had only so recently learned to read and write. For his thesis he presented a work for male voice choir for which he imported one of the finest choirs from South Wales. His early strength must have been choral music, which of course was all he knew in his youth – that and hymns. Hymn tunes poured from him, and his rolling and noble melody for 'Jesu Lover of my Soul' is still loved to this day. Although his teacher was anxious for him to stay on in London, Joseph felt he owed so much to his people that he returned to work in Wales where he became the first Professor of Music at Aberystwyth University. There he insisted that the university choir, which until then had been male voices only, should become mixed so that he could present his first opera, *Blodwen*. The authorities and the Church rather frowned on this development, but it went ahead, and after a first presentation with piano he orchestrated the opera and it received many performances all over Wales. It had a Welsh libretto – the first opera ever to be written in Welsh – for Joseph's loyalty to his homeland was such that he wrote many of his vocal compositions to Welsh words, though the family spoke English in the home.

He married a Welsh girl in America and brought her home to settle in Wales, though he continued to revisit the USA. A fine organist, he had to boost his income for most of his life by taking positions as church organist. He was also a good pianist with a pleasant baritone voice, he taught and lectured, and compositions poured from his pen, operas, oratorios, songs, cantatas and hymns. He was asked to take up the newly created position of Professor of Music at the University of Cardiff, and he became a figure who was almost idolised in Wales – their first ever son to become a doctor and a distinguished musician at home and in the USA, where there is a Parry Society in Danville to this day. He had a large family, and it became a big joke that he named all his sons after musicians he admired. The eldest, my grandfather, was Haydn, and there was Mendelssohn, always known as Mendy, and Sterndale, after Joseph's composition teacher – but history does not relate what he was called in the family! Rumour has it that there was also a baby Beethoven who died at birth, but I have not been able to authenticate this.

My grandfather Haydn was also a composer, apparently very brilliant and expected to surpass his father, but sadly he died of pneumonia at the early age of twenty-nine while living in London and teaching music at Harrow. He is buried at Highgate Cemetery, and I have recently learned that my father was buried beside him. I have a faded and delightfully Victorian obituary notice of Haydn's death in 1894, which reads:

> The talented young Welshman had been offered an opportunity of showing once for all the breadth and scope of his genius. He had the distinction of being offered a place on the programme of the Cardiff Music Festival. New works were to be got from the most eminent men – amongst those asked being Dr Dvořák, Dr Grieg. Sir Arthur Sullivan, Sir Joseph Barnaby, Dr Stanford and Dr Hubert Parry, and into this brilliant galaxy Mr Haydn Parry was admitted with cordial unanimity.

Haydn was already well on with the composition for this occasion when he died. I am so sorry never to have met my grandfather.

He left two children, my father, and a daughter who had a

daughter who actually produced a son, David, a film producer living in Hollywood. David was recently associated with the notorious production *Jerry Springer the Opera* – it's a good thing he does not bear the Parry name, or the ancestors would be turning in their graves! Unfortunately he is unmarried, so very soon Joseph Parry's line will be extinct. If only I had been the John my mother so wanted!

The place where Joseph was born in Merthyr Tydfyl, number 4 Chapel Row, is one of a row of six cottages which have been done up and are still all lived in apart from number 6, which is the Parry Museum, full of memorabilia, press notices, photographs, and music covering his life in Wales and in the USA. The cottage is tiny, just two up and two down, with the original spiral stone staircase, so narrow that someone even approaching obese would get stuck, and how his mother managed while pregnant I shall never know. A tiny kitchen was built on at the back, but there was no lavatory or bathroom. In this small space, in addition to her husband and four little children Elizabeth had to take in a lodger to help out their meagre income.

I was delighted and honoured when invited down to various concerts and festivities to unveil a plaque at Dr Joseph's birthplace, in 1978, to celebrate his 150th anniversary, and to cut the ribbon when the Parry Museum was formally reopened. Invariably his music would be played or sung on these occasions and every programme included his great favourite, the love song 'Myfanwy'. His music is totally out of fashion now, except for in Wales, being very Victorian in style. It was what my mother, a lover of the French school of music of Debussy and Ravel, scathingly dismissed as 'ancient and modern', after the traditional hymn-tune harmonies he favoured. As a composer his work has been dismissed as lacking in taste and unoriginal. As an all-round musician he was much loved and known in Wales as 'the great Doctor'. I was very touched to hear from Danville that a concert of his music has been organised and a plaque installed at his house there to honour his 150th anniversary. Sadly, he died quite young, aged sixty-one, and left little in the way of diaries or letters. After his death his wife Jane sold all the rights of his music to Snells of Swansea, where everything was destroyed by Second World War bombs. All that remains of his large output has come from private people, or been found in libraries and at the universities where he taught. But much has been lost forever.

I am so very proud of him, and wish I had got to know about him earlier in my life. It has been a revelation to me how much he is still loved and esteemed in Wales, where he liked to be known as 'always the little boy from Merthyr'.

I remember my Welsh Granny Parry dimly, and greatly regret not having met my grandfather Haydn who had died before I was born. In the 1970s I met up with some cousins from her side of the family. There was one couple, Eileen and Peter, who lived quite near me in London and whom I got to know quite well. They had no children, and after Peter's death I found to my amazement that he had left me all that they had, which was the contents of their flat. He had never spoken of having any relatives, so I went ahead with arrangements for the cremation to take place at Putney Crematorium. There were just two or three London friends of his and myself standing in the waiting room about to go in to the service when an usher rushed in saying 'Wait! Wait! There's a group of gentlemen coming up the drive!' It's a long drive from the crematorium main gate, and there in the distance were indeed four tall figures all in black looking like something from a Lowry picture. 'We are Peter's cousins from Cornwall,' they announced. I was covered with embarrassment and horrified to find that he had these relations whom he had never mentioned to me. What would they think when they heard he had left everything he had to me, a person they had never heard of? They turned out to be charming, and I invited them all to come up to the flat and choose what they liked of Peter and Eileen's things. The sale of all the remaining items brought in about £15,000, and as my parents had died not long before and I was feeling very rich (quite mistakenly, as I found out later) I decided I would turn this windfall into a small family trust in memory of my musical forebears. The income from the trust was dedicated to the opera company and would provide us with a regular small income.

I had always dreamed of establishing the Opera Players as a permanent feature, both to provide affordable opera to the smaller venues that had neither the cash nor the space to engage the nationals, and to offer young singers the experience of singing major roles without the strain of being catapulted straight from college onto the big stages of the national companies. Alas, in all our fifty-six years on the road we never managed to save a penny. Although our stockbrokers did wonders with our small capital, which grew magically, our costs always seemed to grow faster than our income.

I had moved from the Gusset to a studio flat over the Plague Steps in Knightsbridge, the wide pavement with plane trees leading along to the Brompton Oratory, where hundreds of victims of the Great Plague were buried in pits well outside the walls of London in those days. I shared the double bedroom with a close friend who was a florist. I would creep in in the dark in the early hours after performances, and soon after she would creep out to get to Covent Garden Market by 4.00 or 5.00 a.m. There was an aged geyser with long chimney pipe going up through the ceiling in the bathroom, a delightful big studio living room with a wood-burning stove and platform for a model, and a tiny kitchen leading to – joy of joys – a little roof garden. I put a trellis round it and grew a Russian vine, which rapidly enclosed the whole area, and planted window boxes and tubs, leaving just room for two deck chairs. After my friend left I let the flat for a couple of months each summer via the Universal Aunts. And who should be one of my first guests but Franco Zeffirelli, my ideal of the perfect opera producer, in London to put on Shakespeare's *Romeo and Juliet* at the Old Vic. He had with him his current boyfriend, and I was a little anxious as to how my dear white-haired weekly cleaner would react to the situation. I needn't have worried. She took 'the boys' as she called them to her heart, and went in every morning with fresh croissants for their breakfast.

Zeffirelli's *Romeo and Juliet* was perfection. The curtain went up on a medieval Italian street scene with a golden light in which he had somehow created the illusion of dust motes shimmering in the hot air. I could smell Siena and feel its August heat. The cast, with the seventeen-year-old John Stride as Romeo and a young Judi Dench as Juliet, was as perfect as the set.

I got back from my summer holiday to find Franco and his friend still firmly ensconced in my flat. I had to get back into it as the Opera Players' season was about to begin. I must be the only soprano on the planet who has thrown out the great Franco Zeffirelli! I stood over him and helped him pack all his overflowing possessions into brown paper parcels, then put him and them firmly into a taxi.

The final flat, in which I spent twenty years, was a ground floor and basement plus garden in Sumner Place. I had tenants to help pay the rent, but there was still room for my bedroom, an office with my faithful upright piano from the Gusset days, and a lovely drawing room with French windows that housed a big old concert grand I had been given, and yet had enough room for occasional small-scale rehearsals. Here, as if in answer to prayer, there came along the perfect solution to my secretarial problem in the shape of Margarita, just retired from the Civil Service, who had in her early days been on the stage, and who became a staunch friend. As she said rather wistfully after her first few weeks with us: 'I see now that the Opera Players is not a job, it's a way of life.' She certainly made it hers.

For the first time I could now accommodate our board meetings adequately, and when years later I left London we were lucky to be able to meet at the house of our then chairman Ian Macphail. Ian and his wife Michal Hamburg, daughter of the great pianist Mark Hamburg, whom I remembered from my childhood days in London, had a beautiful house and garden in St John's Wood where we had many delightful meetings, graciously entertained by Michal. At the age of eighty she still played brilliantly and was busy recording all her father's favourite repertoire for an American company.

I eventually went to live at my family home in Surrey, as a London address, which had been de rigueur in our early days, was now no longer considered necessary in the growing age of computers. And as soon as they came on the market, I was persuaded to purchase – reluctantly – Sir Alan Sugar's first ever PC, because I was told that everybody was now computerised. I was hooked from the moment I switched on, but to this day I am not computer literate. I struggled with that first 600-page manual until I reached a chapter that began 'You will by now be in despair,' which I found rather endearing. I then enlisted the help of a lady in the village and we struggled together, until she eventually confessed to me that her thirteen-year-old son was teaching her! The early PC had one superb feature called Limbo from which you could retrieve everything you lost. I miss it dreadfully on my clever Microsoft Word programme, and am still capable of losing my work irretrievably. Sir Alan would despair of me, as my business has been a loser all my life. My toe would not even get over the threshold of his office before 'You're fired!' would ring out. Nevertheless I am very grateful to him for many happy hours wasted with that little early computer. And I am pretty certain that not even he could make opera pay!

Board meetings gradually moved down to my home in Surrey, and we had many company parties and celebrations in the garden. We were fundraising hard, and Peter, one of our directors, spent most of a year struggling with the paperwork of a lottery appeal, which had to go via the Arts Council. The forms were so incomprehensible and difficult to answer that the organisers sent round advisers who came for free and literally told one what to say. Our sweet lady filled in one reply for us that was not strictly true, and when I pointed this out to her she replied, 'Never mind, dear, that's what they want to hear.' We succeeded in getting a grant towards the purchase of a much-needed van, but delivery was delayed because the grants people insisted that we must have disabled access to the vehicle. We explained that we were never going to carry people in the back, only costumes, props and furniture for our operas, but they insisted that we must install a ramp and fixtures to secure a wheelchair, all of which cost an extra £1,000. We had a sponsors' party and ceremonial handing-over of the vehicle at Losely Park, and our chairman was photographed in a wheelchair halfway up the ramp, which was then dismantled, never to be used again.

We have been blessed all along with amazing devoted and hard-working stage staff. After our early days of coping on our own with limited scenery, our first proper team were Nev and Bill, Nev as company manager-cum-driver-of-lorries, his friend Bill as designer and maker of scenery and props, lighting designer and stage electrician. Several times when we were very skint for money Bill would build sets in my garage and courtyard (my garage has always housed everything except a car). I would look out of the window to see him struggling to paint flats in a brisk breeze that blew them all over, then rushing to squeeze them into the garage as the rain began to fall. He was a skilful painter, and I loved to watch him. Once when we were very behind with a production of *Madam Butterfly* he painted a really exquisite Japanese screen freehand in about twenty minutes.

Nev and Bill were succeeded by Derrick and Jenny, a pint-sized couple of many skills who did everything required to get our shows on. Doing one-night stands, which was our usual lot, is the most exhausting and nerve-racking business for all concerned. Our stage staff did a three-day job involving travelling to the venue the day before the show in order to get in to the hall or theatre as early as possible on the day.

They had to get the stage ready for a 2.30–5.30 p.m. rehearsal with singers and orchestra. If this overran, the orchestra would have to be paid overtime, and it was often a nailbiting time for the manager counting the cost as the minutes ticked by. Performances usually started at 7.30 to allow for the obligatory break of two hours between rehearsal and show. During this break the stage staff were usually trying to finish the lighting that they had not previously had time for. The curtain would come down at about 10.15 and then the stage staff – usually with some local help, which also had to be paid for – had to take down and reload the set, the furniture and props, and the costumes. Many theatres charge overtime if companies are not out by 11.00 p.m. I made a habit of getting to venues about lunchtime so that I could unpack and hang the costumes and sort the wigs, shoes, personal props etc. to give the staff a bit more time. As manager there was no way I could relax until everyone and everything had arrived safely at a venue, the inevitable local difficulties had been ironed out, and the afternoon rehearsal had gone smoothly. From then on, the sheer professionalism of the company took over. They were great troopers, good at their jobs, and I knew that however tired they may have been after a full day of travelling and rehearsing, they could be relied upon when the curtain went up to give a good performance.

The Busy 'Nineties

I have been browsing through *Top Notes*, our biennial newsletter, which I started in 1991 for our newly formed Friends' Association. In retrospect I think the 'nineties must have been one of the company's happiest decades. The new music staff at the Arts Council did not know us and seemed totally uninterested in our existence, so we were now absolutely our own man. It was certainly a very busy decade, as I was reminded as I read of some of the immensely varied venues in which we performed.

One was Hever Castle in Kent, where we were first engaged to give an operatic concert during their summer season. The theatre by the lake is a perfect setting, the platform backed by a stone pavilion whose pillars open onto a big lake, which makes a romantic background. There, on a still fine evening, soprano Helen Kucharek sang the Water Nymph's 'Song to the Moon' from Dvořák's *Russalka* while a great heron flapped slowly overhead. We visited Hever with our full operas often after that, and not all evenings were so auspicious. We soon learned why one is presented with a large bowl of clothes pegs on arrival. The wind. Our penultimate performance of *The Marriage of Figaro* went as follows:

> It poured and blew, the rain swept in under the awning wetting singers and musicians alike, Susanna, used to the heat of Australia, sang the whole show wearing a borrowed pashmina, Don Basilio's shovel hat took wing, props blew off tables, and the music, despite being clothes-pegged to the music stands, kept blowing away and being nimbly retrieved by our quartet. The capacity audience arrived with rugs and macs, the artists were all heroic, and by the end of the evening, when wind and rain had ceased, that magical finale cast its usual spell.

We had a last performance at Hever, *Don Giovanni* in 2006. It was a dry night and everything was going well until the finale, when Don Giovanni was going down to hell via the steps down to the lake. Our fire effect and two smoke machines were functioning perfectly, and the whole scene was very dramatic, until a sudden impish gust of wind from the lake blew all the smoke back obliterating the singers and musicians. It was as if Hever was cocking a last snook at us.

Our travels took us north to two delightful and historic theatres, the tiny Royal Georgian Theatre at Richmond, Yorkshire, and the slightly bigger Georgian Theatre in Dumfries. Our first visit to the latter with *La Belle Hélène* resulted in our beautiful boat, our pride and joy, being demasted as it glided on to pick up Helen and Paris and carry them off to Troy. This made for a more than usually hilarious finale. Incidentally, due to a sudden train cancellation, our Hélène had missed her train north. She got into her car in East Suffolk at 10.00 a.m. and drove up, arriving just in time to get her breath for ten minutes, change and get on stage — to give a splendid performance.

At Pyrford Court, near Woking, we used to perform in a beautiful painted music room with just a bare parquet floor. Our conductor and musicians were behind us with the audience on three sides; I remember it being difficult to arrange for Tosca to throw herself realistically off the non-existent battlements. At Alresford we gave several operas on the terrace at the lovely home of Mrs Virginia Constable-Maxwell; and at Christie's we played in the auction room in aid of her favourite charity, the Paul O'Gorman Foundation for Children with Leukaemia; we performed in the Goldsmiths' and Fishmongers' Halls, and for several years in the big conservatory at Syon House, where I remember the gardeners fussing around terrified that we were going to damage the orchids; then there were the barns, a small one at Great Dunmow, and the huge and beautiful one at Cressing Temple, which had its particular problems because the cottage where the artists changed was several hundred yards away and there was a perilous climb up a wooden ladder to gain access to the backstage area – not funny in a thunderstorm wearing period costumes and high-heeled shoes. I always had to reassure our artists that our employers' liability was in order here! There was one terrible occasion when our unfortunate stage manager, reversing the lorry up to the barn entrance to reload after the show, in pitch darkness, took a small chip out of the twelfth-century wood of the great doorway. What a drama! For some reason Europe had to be informed, I imagine because the place is a world heritage site.

We played at Goodwood House many times as part of the Chichester Festivities, and there we performed on a small platform about twelve by fifteen feet in size, which was erected in the ballroom right in front of a large family portrait, I think a van Dyck. Every time the two young officers in *Cosi fan Tutte* flourished their swords the managing director nearly had a heart attack. How that invaluable picture survived our various visitations I shall never know. A complete change was Gray's Inn where we gave several performances in a marquee in the gardens. On one occasion we even had a distinguished QC singing the role of Scarpia in *Tosca* with us. We had had special small-scale scenery made for the occasion, only to find when we arrived that the marquee was several inches lower than we had been told and we had a race against time to take the tops off all the flats. The Grays Inn shows were very happy occasions, only marred by the appalling acoustics in the marquees, which seemed to eat up all the sound.

Not only did our stage staff have to cope with all these varied situations, but we also had some really horrendous journeys to undertake – to be found usually under 'Nailbiters' in *Top Notes*. To quote, there was:

> …a short but hectic tour beginning with 'The Magic Flute' in the Royal Georgian Theatre at Richmond, followed by 'La Cenerentola' at the Arts Theatre in Stamford, Lincs, then the Flute again for the Stroud Festival in Gloucestershire, on three successive nights. All three performances were sold out, but we did experience some logistic problems which gave us a few extra grey hairs. At Richmond not all the scenery would fit onto the tiny stage so it had to be left outside in the lorry. Costumes for the Flute were transported by Elisabeth in her car, a second lorry carrying the lighting technician and Cenerentola scenery came up to Stamford, and Company Manager Neville Ware had to drive the large lorry to Stamford and stay there to put on Cenerentola. Meanwhile the second driver took the Magic Flute scenery and lighting technician on to Stroud because the Flute took a day to set up and light before the show. Finally Neville drove the second lorry over to Stroud so that he could run the Flute performance.

Another such occasion was when we were performing *Tosca* with piano accompaniment at the Dumfries and Galloway Festival on 2nd June and we were asked at very short notice to stand in for another company at the Malvern Festival with two performances of *Tosca* on 3rd and 4th June. It was too good an opportunity to get into a new festival to be missed. I wrote:

> The Managing Director offered her invaluable Company Manager a strong cup of coffee and said: 'We have got to do the impossible,' and the resourceful Neville worked out a plan which would succeed if everything went like clockwork. The scenery van left Dumfries at midnight with Neville, technician Bill Bradford and an extra driver who drove all night. They reached Malvern for breakfast,

set up the scenery and lit the opera (this can take a whole day in itself) in time for orchestral rehearsal at 2.00 p.m. Peter Gellhorn was conducting a special arrangement made to reduce the large orchestra to eleven instruments plus a synthesiser. Meanwhile another extra driver in a hired car brought the cast from Dumfries for the rehearsal, with the exception of the Tosca and Cavaradossi, who were replaced by our other pair of principals, because it is not advisable to sing such heavy roles on three successive nights. By a miracle there were no major motorway or rail hold-ups and everyone arrived on time.

I did not add that I felt ten years older by the time we were all safely there!

Eric Shilling, who had been such a strength to us and had sung in almost all our operas since 1951, was now not singing very often, and was on our board of directors. He agreed to sing the title role in *Don Pasquale* with us for an open-air event at Chiswick House on August Bank Holiday, and I wrote in a profile of him:

> It was always a great occasion when he sang with us. The young learn so much from his immaculate musicianship and timing. His professionalism is an example – never late for rehearsal and always word and note perfect. He is the ideal colleague, kind and considerate, and amazingly modest about his long and distinguished career.

Chiswick House turned out to be his last performance with us, and sadly it was not a very enjoyable one. We were performing at the lake amphitheatre. The electric piano provided for our accompaniment had no music rack, we were expected to change in a small stone pavilion with no table, no chairs, no electric light and no water, the nearest loo, about a quarter of a mile away, was overflowing and had been closed, so we used the laurel bushes behind the pavilion as soon as it grew dark, and a playful breeze kept blowing away props and music. We were miked, and Eric forgot to turn his off as he came offstage at one point so the audience may have heard what he was thinking about the whole sorry affair! We were not happy bunnies.

In 1992 I wrote the following obituary in *Top Notes*:

> Sir Geraint Evans was a patron of Opera Players for many
> years, and his death is a particular loss to us. He and his
> wife came to a company party in my London flat, and I
> have a mental picture of this great man on his hands and
> knees mopping up a glass of red wine he had inadvertently
> spilled, then joining in our party with great gusto and
> advising me: 'Never put on anything without a Charity
> working with you, dear!'

Good advice, which I fear I was not in a position to follow up!

In the winter of 1992–93 we went through a severe financial
depression. The previous autumn we had had five engagements
cancelled because of the withdrawal of sponsorship or funding to our
bookers. We survived an all-time low in January when we had just
£1.85 in our account for a couple of weeks. However we did not go
into the red as did some of our less fortunate competitors. Financially
things were made more difficult when the National Lottery was
introduced. All charities seem to have suffered as people chose to
have a gamble with their charitable giving, and an organisation that
had been particularly good to us, the Foundation for Sport and the
Arts, which had been funded by money from the football pools, saw
its income drastically reduced, so that one had to join a queue even
to send in an appeal.

It was at about this time that we also lost two very good friends
and colleagues, pianist Alexa Maxwell, who had become the Countess
of Munster, and pianist/composer Christopher Shaw. Both had
toured with us and played innumerable performances in our early
piano-accompanied days, and it was Christopher and his wife Jean
who translated and arranged our witty adaptation of *La Belle Hélène*,
which stayed in the repertoire for years. Both died far too young,
in their sixties. Another down in our roller-coaster life was when a
young agency, QPR International, in which we had put our trust,
went bankrupt with all our newly printed publicity locked in their
office.

These were some of the accumulated 'Low Notes' in our newsletter,
but there were many 'High Notes' to counteract them. Ena Wordsworth,

Secretary of our Friends' Association, was a tower of strength to me for *Top Notes*, writing short articles of musical interest, and also producing delightful comic verses about the company and its operatic adventures. With a new director, Peter Andrews, helping actively with promotion, and a smart new brochure designed by another board member, Margaret Brownbridge's graphic designer husband Brian Couser, we counter-attacked the depression. We set about developing our educational work with the help of a new friend, Jean Taylor, and tenor Robin Green became our education officer. We offered Antony Hopkins' *Dr Musikus* and the ever-popular *Hänsel and Gretel* for juniors, and for seniors a very clever updated *Carmen* by Robin Green, translating the story to a contemporary setting of drug-smugglers and street gangs and their girls and called *Extasy*.

The following letter was written to the county music adviser from the headmaster of a Surrey school we visited:

> I want to tell you just how appreciative we were of our visit by the London Opera Players. Regrettably, I was unable to see the morning's workshop session as I was teaching. However by break time, excited comments from staff who were present were being received and by lunchtime I was expecting much from the afternoon's performance. However, I had no concept of just how excellent an interactive performance was coming [of *Dr Musikus*].
>
> Everyone was most impressed with the quality not only of the company but of what they managed to bring out of our own pupils. I have seen many TIE (Theatre in Education) groups in schools over the last twenty-six years, and as you are aware, am exacting in the standards I expect. The London Opera Players was well up in the top two or three that I recall.

After our performance of *La Belle Hélène* at Alresford in aid of Lifeline for Children, a new charity working for children in Bosnia, Rwanda and other war-torn areas, our hostess Virginia Constable-Maxwell in her closing speech said it was the best evening they had had in her fifteen years of presenting opera in Alresford.

Following *Tosca* at the Gatehouse Theatre in Stafford we received two letters that gave us particular pleasure as our outreach activities were very important to us:

> A group of us, all regular opera buffs, attended your company's performance of Tosca in Stafford on Thursday March 23rd, and I would like to congratulate you on two scores. Firstly, we all enjoyed it enormously, the sets, the singing, everything. Secondly, in such a cultural backwater as Stafford, to have such a large audience is praise indeed, although you may not realise this! Anyway, all-round praises.

And from a member of the local choir:

> I feel impelled to write to you on several counts following your production of Tosca in Stafford yesterday, in which I was privileged to play a very small part.
>
> First, to express my appreciation at the first-class musical experience which I had, seeing and hearing the performance both from behind the scenes and from the auditorium, an experience I know was shared by all who attended. I may say it was a pretty good house by Stafford Gatehouse standards!
>
> Also to express my thanks for the warmth and kindness displayed by your cast and crew, who made us so welcome and gave their time to helping us to enjoy the experience of assisting in a professional opera. Also for the time and patience of your Musical Director Peter Gellhorn. I was impressed by the relaxed and friendly backstage atmosphere. Thanks again, and I hope we added something worthwhile to the performance.

Dr David Dougan, Arts Officer for Essex County Council, said:

> I write to thank you most warmly for your two contributions to our new opera festival, especially the 'Belle Hélène' which I thought brought the Festival to a most satisfactory conclusion. I thought that your production brought out all the fun of the piece and that it was beautifully sung and played. You had two very credible principal players – and I must confess

I was captivated by your Hélène [Robina Vallance]! Many thanks for two most enjoyable evenings.

A new boost to our bookings was the success of *Cosi fan Tutte*, for which we engaged a young director, John Ramster, straight from several years at Glyndebourne, and a young designer, Peter Mackintosh. I said in *Top Notes*:

> Both John and Peter are in their twenties and are highly gifted young men. As rehearsals progressed the management realised with great relief that their trust in this young talent had not been misplaced – we have a stylish and charming production with fresh and attractive Empire-style costumes and a simple classical décor.

Our double casts were christened respectively Blue and Orange, less invidious than One and Two, and both were equally good so bookings were divided between them. It was the most affordable piece in our repertoire, and what with its cast of only six singers and its relatively light set, it continued to book right on after the millennium.

Tosca was still running well, and we were asked to perform it at the Thorndike Theatre in Leatherhead as part of the reopening – after refurbishment – of the theatre. The local operatic society was taking part with us, and we asked Richard Balcombe to conduct our small orchestra. The arrival and preparation for rehearsal was chaotic. I was besieged with questions, decisions, and difficulties over the placing of the Act 2 off-stage chorus, who said they could not see the conductor or hear the orchestra and who became very stroppy on being told they were out of tune. The young theatre manager kept on hovering in the background and saying he needed urgently to talk to me, but I kept on sending messages saying, 'Not now! As soon as the rehearsal is underway!' Once everything was sorted and they were safely launched into Act 1 I said to him, 'Right. Now what is it?' It turned out he had been trying desperately to tell me that the company he worked for had gone bankrupt and the liquidators were expected at any moment. It was quite unexpected, and he was not supposed to tell me, but apparently the entrepreneur who had undertaken the refurbishment and reopening of the theatre had vanished leaving 80,000 pounds' worth of debts. We had two options – to pack up and go home at once – but it was now too late for that, or to do the show, and he promised us that every penny that came over the counter in the bar or into the box office would be ours. It was good of him to have told us and made us the offer, because he and his staff had not been paid for three weeks. Fortunately I had director Peter Andrews with me, and he was a tower of strength. We sat over supper and worked out that as eighty per cent of the seats were already sold we could just about break even. Alas, most of the advance bookings had been paid by cheque or credit card and the theatre's account had by now been frozen. We had a marvellous audience, and of course told no one what had happened. It was a sad end to a very pleasant small theatre, which the townsfolk, headed by Dame Sybil Thorndike, had raised money to build and which they were proud of. We were left with £4,000 owing to us, and I think that was one of the first times I had to take capital from the Parry Trust to pay the company.

For our next new production, our mark three of Mozart's *Die Entführung aus dem Sérail*, we drew on the Welsh College of Music and Drama, and two of their second-year students did us proud. James Humphreys with a striking set, and Greek Melina Economou with attractive and very authentic costumes. Tom Hawkes, by now a valued friend, came back to us to direct, and our auditions produced an amazing young tenor, Marwan Shamieh (whose true nationality I never fathomed though I think he was Arabian). He was completely inexperienced and had actually come to London to study law. I remember he was shaking with nerves at the audition, but he came on and sang Belmonte's extremely testing arias with complete control and style and a very pleasant voice. Marwan was a very good colleague, and he was with us for two years, then he took off for Austria, first as a soloist with the opera at Innsbruck, then on to Vienna where I hope he still flourishes.

At the same time we took on an Iranian tenor for Cavaradossi, and after one or two nervous performances he blossomed into a fine performer who really looked the part with his mass of dark hair and fine features. He disappeared back to Iran eventually – a sad waste of a lyric tenor with great potential.

During the autumn of 1999 I spent hours working out a budget for our ambitious two-year educational project with Chelmsford Borough

Council to produce *Carmen* involving children in every aspect of opera. And Robin paid his first visit to the five selected junior schools (we found it was impossible to work with senior children because their syllabus is so crowded). The preparatory work of introducing the children to opera, which was something quite new to most of them, consisted of performing *Hänsel and Gretel* in the Civic Theatre with children onstage singing the Gingerbread Children; then came workshops, followed by two showings of *Amahl and the Night Visitors* over Christmas.

The *Carmen* budget was for two years of work, with tutors visiting the chosen schools to prepare the music, work with the children on the story and the characters, get them designing scenery and costumes, as well as posters and fliers, even teach them a little Spanish dancing, the whole to culminate in a week's work in the theatre before the performances, during which the children would get used to singing onstage, and would get a chance to help with the scene painting, and learn a little about stage lighting, and box office management, every aspect of putting on an opera. In June 2001 there would be two public performances, with orchestra conducted by Richard Balcombe and our professional soloists. The budget was a nightmare, due to variations in travel costs, and took me many days, followed by the putting together of a timetable with the schools for the tutors to visit. Robin Green took over here, and after we had agreed how many visits could be afforded from each tutor he had to fit them into busy school timetables. I had negotiated a total sum of £25,000 plus VAT with Chelmsford Borough Council, and I opened a special account to cover the two years of the project. I am proud to say that we ended up overspent by only a very modest sum, for which Chelmsford reimbursed us!

There were 150 children involved, and we had 75 onstage each night, which was really more than the theatre had room for. It was organised chaos, very exciting and moving. The teachers were splendid, and the children, in their extraordinary mishmash of homemade costumes as smugglers, cigarette girls, soldiers, matadors and so on, backed by the scenery they had helped to paint using the 'by numbers' system (1 for yellow, 2 for red, 3 for blue and so on – the most popular bit of the whole experience!), the children were amazing. Even some special-needs children whom we had included did their bit enthusiastically if inaccurately. A great performance it was not, but it succeeded nevertheless in being very moving.

Another near disaster, which I garnered out of the *Top Notes* 'Nailbiters', concerned our first visit to the Charter Theatre at Preston, where we were engaged to perform *La Belle Hélène* (with four new principals) and *Hänsel and Gretel* with local school children. To quote from *Top Notes*:

> We worked really hard to get the new principals ready, also to prepare the very good local children who were singing the Gingerbread Children and dancing the Angels' Pantomime with us, and all seemed well when our lorry left for the North on Thursday. We then had three crises in twelve hours, and have never in all our fifty years been so near having to cancel a performance. The Managing Director was busy trying to work out cancellation costs while dealing with the crises! On the ill-fated Thursday evening when the van had already left for Preston the phone rang twice in quick succession. First it was our new Orestes in 'La Belle Hélène' who rang to say there was no way she could sing next day because her father in Scotland was in intensive care after a major heart attack and she was already on her way North to his bedside. Next our orchestral fixer rang to say that the music posted in advance to the orchestra had failed to arrive. Both operas we were performing used special arrangements made for us; one was not duplicated, the other had a duplicate down in Wales. Which crisis to see to first? The wires hummed. Orestes would not budge, although we were faced with cancellation without her because the role is an unusual one and our other Orestes was on maternity leave expecting her first child very shortly.
>
> The crisis over the music was resolved first, when it turned out that the missing parts had not in fact been posted after all, but were safely in the van which had just arrived in Preston. Then our mother-to-be Orestes gallantly volunteered to save the situation – despite strong protests from her husband – and went to Preston next day and gave a marvellous performance.

Very fortunately Orestes is a trouser role and she was able to wear the baggy jeans which are really the 2nd Act costume throughout. It's a very active role with some dancing and I had visions of the baby arriving in the dressing room.

I had retired to bed the previous night thanking St Cecilia for the solution of these first problems – as it turned out, too soon. The telephone rang at breakfast time next morning. It was our Gretel, and there was no need to ask what the matter was – she was speechless with laryngitis and a chest infection. Her double was also expecting a baby very soon and there was no way she could appear on stage as a little girl! But she could sing, so she too got on the train for Preston, and sang Gretel on a cushioned chair in the orchestra pit while the voiceless victim gave a spirited acting performance on the stage despite a high temperature.

By the end of the century I was approaching eighty years of age, and I was quite determined that with the millennium a new and young person needed to be found to keep the company going. My directors were one of many boards to whom I owe everything for their support, and for their patience in dealing with a totally unbusiness-like managing director over the years. They were all agreed that we must seek out the right person to carry the company on into the twenty-first century, and in October 1999 the following announcements appeared in *Top Notes*:

The First Fifty Years

London Opera Players is entering a stimulating and exciting period in its history. Firstly, the Millennium then our own 50th birthday, involving the opening of our new touring production of Verdi's 'Falstaff' at the Yvonne Arnaud Theatre, Guildford, in the second week of January 2000. With the Company's future in mind I am very happy to bring you all exciting news for:

The Next Fifty Years

In September 2000 Eleanor Farncombe, who is presently a Director of the company, will take over the administration. Eleanor sang with us while she was still studying at the Royal College of Music in London some ten years ago, and her father, conductor Charles Farncombe, is an old friend who will be conducting 'Falstaff' for us at the Yvonne Arnaud in January. We hope to present a full profile of Eleanor in our next Top Notes, meanwhile my Board and I are delighted that a young and vital administrator will bring fresh energy, ideas and enthusiasm to the company.

The board backed me whole-heartedly over my dream of putting on Verdi's *Falstaff* to celebrate the millennium and the fiftieth birthday of the company. Verdi and Shakespeare – what could be better?

I invited John Ramster, who had given us a delicious and witty *Cosi fan Tutte*, to direct again, and went back to our super friends Malcolm Pride and Michael Pope at the Wimbledon School of Art for costumes. As ever they did us proud. Would that we had been so lucky with the scenery! We went to a young Glyndebourne designer, who produced a very clever design of a uni-set on a revolve, where the singers would rotate themselves for the six scene changes. It was a two-storey openwork structure in heavy Elizabethan beams mounted on three movable trucks, which cleverly portrayed the interior and exterior scenes, then split into three and opened up for the final scene in Windsor Forest with Herne the Hunter's oak centre back. The whole was set in front of a groundrow portraying Windsor and the castle, beautifully painted by one of the Glyndebourne painters, and at the back was a transparent backdrop backlit with trees projected on it. The model was a dream. Unfortunately the drawings were not completed in time, and what with Christmas 1999 and the millennium coming up all the set-builders in the country seemed to be fully booked. Only one firm in Cardiff could be found to undertake the work and it was not made clear to me or to our stage manager that this firm worked only in steel. The result was a metal structure weighing four tons, every inch of which had to be clad (covered in a sort of papier mâché) to represent wood. This although we had from the first stressed to the designer that the set would have to travel in a Ford Luton lorry and be handled by a stage staff of two!

Luckily we knew nothing of these horrors to come during the rehearsals, which were a joy. We had a double cast from the outset, and for once there were no weak links. We had three weeks of rehearsal, often with three sessions a day – expensive, but for once I was determined that no expense should be spared, and we'd had quite a successful fundraising appeal for this special occasion. Charles Farncombe and Richard Balcombe coached the cast, and Charles was to conduct the first week of performances at the Yvonne Arnaud Theatre in Guildford. He had made a reduced orchestration for our chamber orchestra of twelve players. But sadly he was taken ill and Richard stepped in at the eleventh hour, and did a brilliant job for us.

The last few days were the usual pre-first-night nightmare, with costumes, scenery and props appearing only at the eleventh hour. Here the great difficulty of not having our own premises became apparent. There was nowhere where we could put up a four-ton steel structure for a dress rehearsal. So lightweight models of the scene trucks had to be made for the scene changes, which had to be perfectly timed to fit the music, as the curtain came down only once during the performance. Our dress rehearsal had to be in an upstairs hall in Guildford with inadequate changing space for voluminous Tudor costumes, and difficult stairs up which the model trucks had to be carted. The dress rehearsal also involved our first meeting with the nine elves and fairies being provided for us by the junior department of the excellent and highly professional Guildford Drama School. They had been coached musically for some time, and John Ramster paid them two visits to produce the hectic last act in which they had to appear with the Fairy Queen and torment the unfortunate Falstaff. We also had a little boy to play Falstaff's page, and a very good young comedy actor from the Guildford School of Music and Drama – just the sort of local involvement we liked to achieve, though they had to be costumed and produced in a very short time. The dress rehearsal was a Saturday I prefer not to remember as it was also when Charles was becoming ill.

On Sunday we were able to move our sets and costumes into the theatre. Monday morning was for lighting, and in the afternoon the cast had a movement rehearsal on stage to meet the four-ton set with its three movable trucks and revolve, and to practise the five scene changes. At the same time the orchestra, provided by my good friend Bob, had a seating rehearsal to work out how they could best squeeze into the very small pit at the Yvonne Arnaud, which is narrow even with two rows of stalls taken out. I had come home briefly to snatch some lunch when the phone rang. It was Bob. 'Elisabeth, please come at once. There's a large heavy structure on the stage, which is moving out of control towards the orchestra pit. I shall have to call the health and safety people.' For once he sounded really agitated. I flew back to the theatre with sinking heart, to discover that our singers, pushing the trucks of scenery for the first time, had simply pushed too hard on the raked stage of the Arnaud, and were not familiar with the brakes, which had to be pushed down as soon as the set was in position. Bob was understandably nervous, as one of his leading violinists had recently been injured by a piece of scenery falling onto him in the pit at another theatre. I soothed him as best I could, and the move was repeated several times with no more problems to his satisfaction. No health and safety!

On Tuesday we had an afternoon dress rehearsal followed by the first night in the evening. It was one of those very rare and precious occasions when everything goes perfectly – a rare thing in opera! The complicated scene changes went quietly and in time to the music, the lighting was spot on, the singers and orchestra were at their best, and the performance had that magical quality that happens only on a really special night. I was so proud of them all and would happily have presented them at the Scala, the Met or Glyndebourne. The second cast did equally well on the second night, and we had enthusiastic and appreciative audiences all the week. It was a happy culmination to fifty years on the road.

The trouble with *Falstaff* began when we started to tour it. After the first two or three shows, with overloaded lorries and the set that took six men to put together and dismantle, something had to be done. The heavy steel structure just had to go. Luckily our stage manager Derrick was a very all-round theatre man, and he built a smaller wooden set for us, which we could use with the original trucks and revolve so that the production did not have to be altered. It was not as impressive as the original, but it went on our Luton lorries and could be managed by three stagehands.

As anticipated in our *Top Notes* announcement, in the autumn of 2000 Eleanor Farncombe took over the management of London Opera Players (we had added 'London' to our name because bookers often did so of their own accord, thinking perhaps that we sounded too much like a local amateur group), and I stepped back into the non-executive role of artistic director. As I mentioned before, we had known Eleanor for years, and she had even taken part in several of our productions. She had a very pleasant mezzo voice and had been on contract to a German theatre for several years. She had also had experience of stage management and had assisted her father on his foreign tours, so she was thoroughly familiar with the operatic world. We must have seemed like the Crazy Gang after the discipline of the German theatre world! Unfortunately our lovely *Falstaff* was not booking well, to our great disappointment. This was partly due to its having a bigger cast than most of our productions, at a time when escalating travel and accommodation costs were hitting all our bookers hard.

Not for nothing did Eleanor have a lighting-designer husband. We were rapidly modernised so that the lighting plans and the sets for our productions were carried by magic in her laptop computer. Eleanor often supervised our lighting herself, and through her we acquired a good sound system, with which we could amplify our invaluable synthesiser and the string quartet we worked with more and more often, as money for the chamber orchestra became ever harder to find. We even had feedback, smoke machines and a couple of closed-circuit TV cameras!

We put on *Don Giovanni* in a charming production by our old friend Tom Hawkes, and *Cosi fan Tutte* was still on the road, so in 2005 I decided as a final fling to raise money from the Parry Trust and put on *The Marriage of Figaro*, so that we would have three good productions on offer for the Mozart bicentenary. We held two days of auditions, heard many good young voices, and booked a double cast to start rehearsing in spring.

As the company grew up, so our singers got married and had families. By the 1990s there were so many small children that some sort of crèche had to be set up wherever we were rehearsing. The young mums and dads organised themselves very well, with one parent or a sibling always in charge. Vast amounts of toys and games appeared out of dads' rucksacks and I used to spend some time soothing worried caretakers. Account would have to be taken of feeding times, because all our young mums, as is the way today, breastfed their young. I shall never forget in our last *Marriage of Figaro* rehearsals the sight of our Figaro, his newly-born daughter hanging in a papoose round his neck, spreadeagled like a little starfish against his broad chest, sound asleep as he sang. She never stirred, even when the full cast let fly in the big finales. His wife Robyn Savestos was at the piano and would be conducting all our performances. We are very proud that we had a gifted young woman conductor as our music director for our last years.

The position had become vacant when Peter Gellhorn died in his nineties, to be succeeded by Charles Farncombe, who sadly also died a few years later.

A particularly happy memory is of a performance of *The Magic Flute* we gave in Wells Cathedral with Peter conducting on his eightieth birthday. It was a charming production by Tom Hawkes with costumes and sets by the Wimbledon School of Art – one of the best in our by now considerable repertoire. And it was a magic occasion, with the beauty of the music and the wonderful setting perfectly matched. The main aisle sold out early on so closed circuit TV was installed and the nave seats were all sold as well. It was a day of non-stop rain, and the stone-floored and walled dressing space in the cathedral was dank and chilly, but nothing could damp the excitement of the show.

I was particularly sad when Margaret Brownbridge, our assistant music director, pianist and keyboard player, who had been a tower of strength to me for years, resigned from the company. I wrote in the *Top Notes* autumn 2003 edition:

> It is with great sadness that I have to tell our friends that Margaret Brownbridge is leaving the company in the New Year. She has been part of the fabric of our work for many years now, and her high standard of musicianship and sense of style have been a vital part of the standard we strive to maintain. Young singers have been influenced by her playing and disciplined by her music rehearsals, and our more mature

artists have always enjoyed working with her. It has been the constant background of her musical integrity which has given our performances a distinction which I venture to say is all our own.

We were lucky in that Charles Farncombe was also a first-class coach of young singers, and he gave unstintingly of his time when he took over most of the conducting in Peter's last years. After his death we were lucky to find Robyn Savestos, now married to baritone Peter Grevatt, who had joined us aged twenty-one, and graduated via chorus and small parts to singing the lead in many of our productions.

Much earlier on a heaven-sent person had appeared to fill another gap, actress Jennifer Thorne, or Jenny Croft as we knew her when wearing her other hat. Jenny was one of the non-singing members at the Royal Opera House, Covent Garden, where, I discovered, some eight actors and actresses were regularly employed to take on the heavy acting in violent or highly dramatic scenes, and to do the energetic dancing, which would be too much for the chorus to undertake while singing. Jenny was extremely musical and knew her operas backwards (she has recently been starring as the 'Madam' in the Act 2 café scene in *La Bohème*), and she is also an extremely competent dressmaker.

Apparently there had been a crisis in the Opera House wardrobe and they had called for helpers. Jenny came forward, and discovered a new talent in herself. She was in effect head of our wardrobe for years, and a vast help to me. She designed and made the costumes for our successful *Cosi fan Tutte* production (apart from the tailored soldiers' coats), and she was amazing at adapting garments for different sizes of singer. This was vital to us, as some of our costumes lasted for years and in their time were worn by large and small.

Our last *Marriage of Figaro* was a happy production, directed by Brenda Stanley, with costumes made by Jenny. Brenda had joined us to sing a delicious Blonda in Mozart's *Escape From the Harem* mark one. She went on to join our board and also directed operas for us. Thanks to the very hard work of director Peter Andrews, we had a tour of twelve performances for the new *Marriage of Figaro* in the summer and autumn of 2005. And we had a new 'groupie', New Zealand baritone Robert Williams, who was going later to make his debut in the role of Figaro with us. He came to every show, and when we were at the seaside he organised barbecues for the cast between rehearsal and performance.

Nevertheless, ever since 2000 the company had been struggling. There were only eighteen opera performances between the beginning of November 2003 and the end of November 2004, and seven booked for the first half of 2004. Since Eleanor joined us we were for the first time paying a modest managerial salary. We gambled quite a sum of money on some part-time professional help, which alas did not raise a single booking. We tried a last appeal, which Bryn Terfel kindly agreed to spearhead after talking with our president Philip Langridge. Unbelievably this too failed.

We realised we were no longer financially viable for the size of theatre and hall for which our performances were originally intended. With an audience capacity often in the region of 500–600 they inevitably lost money on us. We now often performed with a first-class string quartet led by Rolf Wilson with Robyn Savestos conducting from the keyboard, as even our ten- to twelve-piece chamber orchestra with the added fee for a conductor was too expensive for many venues. We also had to travel a special lighting man to deal with our computerised system. Council-backed theatres were strictly accountable and their councils would not tolerate losses as there was little or no spare cash for the arts. The really large venues, which would have been financially viable, required a larger scale of production with bigger scenery and larger forces. Many of our regular bookers could no longer pay more than £2,500, or at a stretch £3,500 plus VAT, for one show, and this did not cover the fees, travel costs and accommodation for most of our performances. Our competitors – and at one time there were about seventy of them, all struggling for bookings – seemed to get round this by paying very little, and cutting down on rehearsals and other costs. But we never compromised over standards and every performance was re-rehearsed.

Eventually the only solution was to subsidise each show, as we found some of the other companies were doing. For us this involved tapping the capital of the Parry Trust, which was already committed to backing our *Marriage of Figaro* production costs. We reached the point where there was enough capital left to run the company only frugally for two more years, with not a penny extra to meet the cost of a yearly new production, buy us a new van, or meet any of the unavoidable maintenance expenses.

My board and I agreed to call it a day and close down while the company's flag was still flying high with three good Mozart productions on the road for his bicentenary year. We decided our final performance would be on 24th November 2006, *Don Giovanni* at the lovely old Buxton Opera House, where *The Marriage of Figaro* had been so successful the previous year. The theatre was the ideal size for London Opera Players, and we had a very happy evening, which went off well to a good audience. Several of the board made the journey north, and directors, singers, musicians and staff all partied at the hotel afterwards. At least Buxton wept for us; it rained in torrents!

And that was it. Fifty-six years had passed, and the important post-war niche we had been created to fill was no longer empty. Our national companies, most of which did not exist when we started out, now divide the country between them and all have small-scale educational touring groups, so that it is possible for people to reach a fully professional opera performance from anywhere – except perhaps the Outer Hebrides! I have been privileged over the years to enjoy one of the most exciting and fulfilling experiences in the world, the coming together of an opera from auditions to the final performance stage. Listening to the development of music and drama, as singers and musicians grow into their roles and become a team, is a joyful and rewarding affair. Now at last the 'Good Companions' have disbanded – nevertheless thank you, J B Priestley, for having inspired the idea.

★★★

At the time of writing, the final affairs of the company have at last been wound up. Our costumes were sold by Bonhams. One lovely old blue brocade embroidered coat made by Phyllis Thorold many years ago, and worn by many tenors in *The Barber of Seville*, which I had reckoned would fetch £10 to £20, was priced at £300 by the experts!

The residue of the Parry Trust capital was placed in the capable hands of the Welsh National Opera Company. In February 2009 the WNO's new production of Mozart's *The Marriage of Figaro* was funded partially by money from the Trust and enabled a rising young baritone,

David Soar, to make his debut as a principal in the title role of Figaro. An annual bursary in the name of the Parry family is being set up to help gifted young singers, and should be in place by 2010.

Chapter Twelve

Mainly Mountains

During the troubled early 'Fifties, when the Opera Players were struggling to establish themselves, and life in London was becoming increasingly busy, a second strand in my life was shyly creeping ahead. The seed was sown when my parents, holidaying in Zermatt while I was studying in Siena, met up with someone my mother described enthusiastically in a letter to me as 'a charming tall young Englishman who took me on a glacier!'. This was a tremendous excitement for her as she was passionately interested in, and very knowledgeable about, mountaineering, though she never climbed herself. The young man was Sidney Nowill, writer, mountaineer, photographer, a person of so many and varied talents that I could not quote them all. He used to come regularly to Zermatt, which my parents grew to love so much that we went there twenty-one years in succession. We joined up each summer with a multinational group of habitués who always stayed at the historic Monte Rosa Hotel, from which so much early climbing history was made, including Whymper's ill-fated first ascent of the Matterhorn.

Those were wonderful days in the early 1950s. Zermatt was still a big village, and the spider's web of chair lifts and gondolas, which now crisscrosses the mountains, did not exist. There was of course the famous Gornergratbahn, its old red carriages creaking and groaning up the cogs of its steep track to high up where the summer snow still lay. There was also a delightful slow quiet chairlift up to Sunegga, now a mass of tourists who come very quickly up a horrendous sort of train in a tube, but then so solitary that we bathed without embarrassment – or costumes – in the Gründje See in our pants and bras. Otherwise one walked, and getting up to the Höhnli Hut, the starting point for climbers of the Matterhorn and a favourite destination of my mother's, was a long 5,000-foot climb from the village.

Those were the days when the huts were all supplied by mules, and they could be a serious hazard on paths that had a vertical drop on one side and a rock wall on the other. Passing places were not provided. The mules' loads were calculated so that they were wide enough just to fit onto the paths without bumping against the rock and pushing the mule over the edge. The animals learned to walk on the outside edge of the paths with their loads just clear on the uphill side, leaving no room for a body even of the slenderest proportions. So when you heard the bells of a caravan drawing near, you hunted for a niche into which to squeeze yourself while the caravan passed you with its crate-loads of bottles swaying and jingling cheerfully. The muleteer had quite often stopped off to have a chat with friends, but the mules knew exactly where to go and nothing would stop them until they reached their destination, so it was *sauve qui peut!* on the paths, and unsuspected climbing talents were discovered as people scrambled for safety. Now supplying is all done by helicopter, at great expense, and although that has its own excitement it has none of the romance of those patient and determined mules.

My mother's charming young Englishman became someone who opened up a whole new life for me by introducing me to climbing and mountain travel. As soon as we coincided at Zermatt he asked me to join a party of his friends to climb on the Riffelhorn, a small rocky peak above the village, which is to rock climbers what the nursery slopes are to skiers.

'I couldn't climb,' I said. 'I've got no head for heights.'

'Nonsense, everybody can climb,' came the reply. So climb I did. And found that I enjoyed it; it is rather like chess, where you have to work out several moves ahead. Sidney had American friends with him. The husband was an experienced climber; his wife, like me, was a novice. He roped her up and led her up one of the Riffelhorn's easy routes, and we watched poor Steffie, who was a small girl, struggling to follow her tall husband up the rockface. She eventually got herself so stretched out in her frantic hunt for holds that she looked like a little starfish, clamped onto the rock, too terrified to move hand or foot.

'Mind out, Bob!' called Sidney, in the sort of voice men use to describe their wife's shortcomings to other men. 'She's a bit extended.' Whereupon Steffie was hauled ignominiously to the top – and never tried again!

I was a doubtful starter, as it was true that one of the two recurring bad dreams I had when young was falling from heights. The other was appearing on the stage, and that ghost had by now been well and truly laid. The heights fear took a little longer to subdue, and never wholly left me, in that even when I was doing big climbs, I always hated sitting on a narrow ledge with my feet dangling over space, trying to eat a sandwich or have a drink. For two years I climbed just mild routes while trying to decide if I loved or hated the experience. Then I met a much-respected Zermatt guide, one Willi Truffer, the old-fashioned type who had a great respect for the mountains and their plants and animals and birds. He took a Nowill cousin and me up the Trifthorn, a proper small mountain, with an easy but exposed rock ridge leading to the summit. I can hear him still, exasperated by our timorous progress, calling out, 'Walk! Walk! Just like in Piccadilly!' Easier said than done when your legs are shaking with fright!

But there was the Matterhorn, rearing up proudly at the head of the valley, so beautiful and remote and impossible-looking, yet being climbed by all and sundry, it seemed, during the tourist season. The guides reckoned they could get anyone who was reasonably fit up the 'normal route' after one or two practice climbs. Indeed my companion on the Trifthorn got up it a few days later, and Sidney Nowill reached the summit by the Zmutt Ridge, one of the most difficult and dangerous routes on the mountain. That made my mind up for me!

The Zermatt guides treated their clients exactly like registered parcels, which had to be delivered safely at all costs, and beginners were hauled up on a tight rope and lowered back down again. The Matterhorn was too great for that. I decided that I wanted to climb it properly, not just up and down the 'tourist route', but traversing across and down into Italy. So I set about really learning to climb.

Back in London I joined a Mountaineering Association evening class held at the Quintin School in St John's Wood. I also rang a couple of London-based climbing clubs. The secretary of the first, a man, said: 'What's your grade?' When I confessed I had no idea he rang off.

50 Philippa Treadwell on the Hanuma La, Zanskar.

51 Contraband at our camp, Bay Göl. Tribesmen coming back from a foray into Iraq.

52 Dorothea Gravina near the summit of the Gran Paradiso, Italy.

53 Coming down Liathach in the Torridon hills in early Spring with members of the Ladies' Scottish Climbing Club.

54 Our buses below the Tururgart Pass in Kyrgyzstan on the Silk Road tour in 2005.

55 Hänsel and Gretel by Humperdinck, twenty-first century version, our most often-performed opera. It ran for fifty-six years. Penny Mathison as Gretel and Jessica Schlenther as Hänsel.

56 Above: Escape from the Harem *by Mozart, directed by Tom Hawkes, with costumes and scenery by students of the Royal Welsh College of Music and Drama. Cast from L.to R.: Russell Ablewhite (Pedrillo), Fiona Dobie (Blonde), Martin Nelson (Osmin), Marwhan Shamiyeh (Belmonte) and Nicola-Jane Kemp (Constanze).*

57 Above:Eleanor Farncombe, Manager of London Opera Players from 2000 – 2006.

58 Left: Fritillaries in the garden, Broadmeade Copse.

59 Top left: Mabel Moore and EP in the garden.

60 *Above:* The Marriage of Figaro by Mozart, directed by Brenda Stanley. Our 2005 production in rehearsal: Cast L.to R:Diane Charlesworth (Countess Almaviva), Justine Davies (Susanna), Philip Kay (Count Almaviva).

61 Left: EP in Chile, the Grey Glacier from Lake Grey.Patagonia, February 2007.

62 Below: The surprise eightieth birthday party given me by the company at the Marwick Hall, Puttenham. EP centre left of wheelchair.

The second secretary, also male, simply said: 'We don't want any more women.' How I had come to hear of the Mountaineering Association I can't remember, but it was far more welcoming – a professional body that ran courses all over the country and awarded certificates for varying degrees of competence. People roared with laughter when I said I was studying mountaineering in St John's Wood, but those classes were a joy, like a breath of fresh mountain air coming into our hectic city lives once a week. Our tutor, George Hall, was a maths teacher in a big London boys' school, and an enthusiastic mentor to young would-be mountaineers. His class came in all shapes, ages, sizes and backgrounds, and we all learned to tie knots, and belayed each other up the rib stalls, then abseiled off the top; we pitched tents in the gym, we learned basics such as 'Never pull on vegetable holds' (they tend to come away in your hand). We did map and compass work, learned the qualities or dangers of different rocks, and some elements of meteorology and geology, and one evening we arrived to find in large letters on the blackboard: 'About bivouacking. Don't.'– the principle being that you were incompetent if you got yourself into the position of having to, anyway at the stage we were at. But George did let fall a few words of wisdom about what to do if you were inevitably benighted.

Best of all, there were frequent weekends to Wales or the Lake District. We would meet under the arches at Charing Cross after work on a Friday evening, get into a hired coach and drive all night. There were no motorways at first, then the M1 and the M6 came along. We would stop in the middle of the night for tea and greasy eggs and bacon in a lorry drivers' café, arrive about 7.00 a.m. at one of the climbing huts that we had booked into, get a quick breakfast, put our boots on, and then off out, whatever the weather. We walked and climbed all Saturday and Sunday, boarded our coach again about 5.00 p.m. on Sunday, and arrived back in London just in time for the world's workers to reach their offices on Monday morning. There are huts for walkers and climbers dotted all over the Lake District and Wales, and in the 'Fifties and 'Sixties they were in a pretty basic state – dormitories with sagging two-tiered bunks and questionable dark ex-army blankets, a boiler that would have to be coaxed into life to supply the washbasins and kitchen with hot water, and a large communal living room with a wooden table and some battered old armchairs. George and various experienced types would patiently lead groups of novices up the rocks, and thus we learned the elements of climbing.

★★★

In Zermatt, guide Willi Truffer was to become a sort of mountain father to me. He had a large family, and they lived in a lovely old traditional chalet in the village of Randa, just down the valley. They were peasant farmers, with cows that lived in the bottom floor of the chalet all winter, then went off with the communal herds to the high Alps for the summer, when Willi was away guiding. The second of my three special mountain men I met on the enthusiastic recommendation of Sidney Nowill. My family and I went to stay at Cortina d'Ampezzo in the Dolomites and I started to climb with a fantastic rock climber, Italian guide Celso Degasper, for whom Sidney had a great admiration. Celso, a handsome and dashing man who spoke fluent German and pretty good English, was a delight to climb with. Here the amazing towers and pinnacles of golden rock were free from snow except in their deepest gullies, and soared almost vertically from flowery meadows. Celso would look up at a smooth shining rock wall, and say: 'Watch well how I do it.' Then he would glide effortlessly upwards with a series of smooth movements, ending up with a 'Tic! Tac! So it is done, and well' as he reached the belay stance. Following seemed impossible, and I accused him of taking the holds with him as he climbed. In fact the steep rock was full of holds, but they were far smaller than anything I had met before, often with just room for the tip of a boot or finger. One learned to trust them, to stand well away from the rock with heels down so that the toes of the boots were pressed into the holds. We grew to love Cortina, with its larch forests and rich variety of flowers and the smell of the juniper bushes in the hot Italian sun.

The Matterhorn, like all great mountains, makes you wait for it. Sometimes it cannot be climbed for days on end, even in the summer. When one has only two precious weeks at its foot, and one's guide may already be booked to other clients, it can be a frustrating and prolonged wait. The year Willi and I both felt I was ready was like that. At first the weather was good but he was not free, then the weather turned bad, and our fortnight's stay was drawing to a close. At last the weather improved, and there was one day left on which I could do the climb before we went home. But it would be Sunday, and Willi, a good Catholic, would not let a Sunday pass without attending mass. As we would have to spend the Saturday night at the Höhnli Hut and set off at 4.00 a.m. on the climb, mass seemed an impossibility. Switzerland is full of climbing clergy, and whenever one happens to be on his way up the Matterhorn, he will celebrate an early mass before leaving. Sadly there was to be no priest at the hut that Saturday evening. As a great concession Willi agreed to stretch a point and attend evening mass, but this meant that I would have to get back to Zermatt by 5.00 p.m. As I trudged up the Höhnli that Saturday afternoon I knew that it would be almost impossible for me to traverse the mountain and get back over to Zermatt in time. However, Willi arrived up at the hut beaming. He had heard that a climbing priest of his acquaintance was due in Zermatt that afternoon, so he went down to the station and pounced upon the poor man as he got off the train. 'Father,' he said, 'I have a crazy English woman who must climb the Matterhorn tomorrow. Will you come to the hut and celebrate morning mass for us?' His friend agreed, and everyone was happy. Willi had his mass at 3.30 a.m. and I knew I didn't have to kill myself to get back to Zermatt by five o'clock.

I don't have very happy memories of most alpine huts. Most of them are between 8,000 and 10,000 feet up, which is just the altitude band at which I used to get mountain sickness, went right off food, and couldn't sleep. So the early-morning departures, usually at 3.00 or 4.00 a.m., were always unpleasant, stumbling up steep moraines by the inadequate light of a candle lantern, which is all the guides carried in my early days. But slowly, as the magical mountain dawns crept up over the skyline and the snows began to glow with amazing red and gold lights, I would begin to feel better. By the time we reached 4,000 metres I could eat and drink and sleep! I've fallen asleep on many a summit, and was told it is just one of the effects of altitude, but it's an awful waste of prime time!

On that first climb up the Matterhorn Willi pushed me hard. On a Sunday in August there could be as many as 150 climbers on the 'normal route', and the main danger was being hit by stones kicked down by inexpert feet higher up. I was pushed on to pass group after group, and barely allowed time to step inside the historic Solvay hut perched halfway up the rocky ridge. As dawn came we were well ahead, and the view back down the slender line of the ridge dotted with climbing figures to where Zermatt nestled in the valley thousands of feet below was one of the unforgettable ones of my life. When we reached the summit, a long narrow ridge, with thousands of feet of space on either side, there were no congratulations from Willi. He looked at me somewhat doubtfully and said; 'Are you feeling shtrong?' I assured him that I was feeling very 'shtrong' whereupon he disappeared past the great wrought-iron summit cross and over the far end into Italy. The Italian side of the Matterhorn is very precipitous, and has been equipped with a number of fixed ropes to help the 'tourists', as the guides rather patronisingly call us, to get down the worst. There is one, a rope ladder called, I think, Jacob's Ladder, which dangles over a slight overhang. You are supposed to get onto it, manoeuvre yourself round and climb down on the inside next to the rock. I failed to do this and had an ungainly struggle to reach the bottom. Willi was waiting and watching. 'You did that very bad,' he said. It was his only remark the whole way down the south face.

We didn't get back to Zermatt until about 7.00 p.m., so it was as well that he had found the friendly priest off the train. I climbed many mountains with Willi after that, and a strong if silent bond developed between us. He was very strict with his own large family, and treated me like a sort of extra daughter. He was a great herbalist, and as we climbed up to the huts he would pick certain plants, which he then infused into a tisane, which he gave me to help my mountain sickness. In his voluminous rucksack, which weighed a ton, was a flask, which he produced as soon as the worst part of a descent was over, usually when we got back onto the first grass. Mixed with icy water from a stream it turned cloudy white and was known as 'Schneewasser', a potent and illicit brew that, however, many of the guides made in their homes, as it was a marvellous pick-me-up and settler of upset stomachs. As we got lower still we would stop at the first high cowshed and get milk from the herdsman. Alpine milk straight from the cow and drunk halfway down a mountain is ambrosia.

★★★

During the 1960s the Opera Players performed several times at Sherborne Girls' School. We were always most courteously looked after there, and Phyllis and I would dine with the headmistress, a distinguished and charming lady called Diana Reader-Harris (I have a feeling she later went into politics). The conversation turned to climbing, how I had gone to classes and courses and hoping to climb the Matterhorn that summer. 'You must come and tell the girls all about it,' said Miss Reader-Harris. She was not a lady to be gainsaid. I found myself agreeing to come and give a talk with slides to the girls the next year. I was already a keen photographer and had just started taking colour slides, so I already had quite a collection of pictures of our goings-on in the gym at the Quintin School, and various weekends in the Lake District and Snowdonia. I carted my heavy old Pentax camera on the Matterhorn traverse and managed to get a few pictures on the climb, so I put together a talk lasting just over an hour and went down to Sherborne feeling dreadfully nervous, to give my first lecture. At the end Miss Reader-Harris simply said to me, 'My dear, you must do this.' So I have lectured ever since! All the money I earned from my talks was saved towards guides' fees for the next season, which was a tremendous help, as I had to ration my climbs according to what I could afford. The modern generation of climbers think it rather wimpish to climb with a guide, but in my day, unless you were lucky enough to have a father or brother or boyfriend good enough to take you up mountains, the only way you were going to get up any of the big climbs was with a guide.

That Sherborne talk and Miss Reader-Harris's encouragement opened up a second career for me as a travel lecturer, which I carry on to this day.

Having decided that I really wanted to become a climber I went through several seasons in a sort of climbing frenzy. I knew that starting out at the age of forty, I would have to get a move on! The crux year was 1961, the Matterhorn year, and I had started to train during the winter with a Mountaineering Association winter climbing course in January in the Lake District. It was based somewhere called the Boat House outside Ambleside and I was given only a very vague description of how to find it, where two rivers meet, and with a map reference. I had no car, so I got a coach from Victoria Coach Station, which left at 10.00 a.m. and reached Ambleside at 10.15 at night. It was a pitch dark January night when I set out with a small torch and an enormous rucksack to hunt for the Boathouse. Nobody was around to ask, so eventually, seeing a faint light on my left, where I knew the lake should be, I got into a field and headed for it. A kind farmer put me right – I was in fact quite near – and I arrived at about eleven o'clock to a warm welcome and a hot meal at the home of guides Brian Marsh and Pete Deeley and their wives, who were running the course. It really was a boathouse, converted into a bunk house, where the rivers Rothay and Brathay meet, and from my bunk in the girls' room I could get straight out of my window into a boat.

I got away for one more weekend, followed by a week's rock-climbing course, when I completed my second grade and noted proudly in my diary that I had been promoted to leading several pitches at 'V Diff' standard. This is nothing by present-day standards and will make modern climbers laugh, but we had only basic pitons and karabiners, with hemp ropes, heavy boots, and none of today's complicated hardware. I never in my whole climbing career wore a hard hat!

There was no time for more, as we were very busy with the Opera Players, so it was 'Alps, here I come!' when the opera season ended in July. Before going to Zermatt, Sidney and I spent ten days with the third guide who was going to become important in my mountain life – Frenchman Gilles Josserand, a witty and delightful Parisian who had been a teacher (he spent a year teaching at the French school near South Kensington) and who had then qualified in the very severe Chamonix Guide School. Our first evening with Gilles was memorable. Sidney and I were invited to stay with him and his wife and three children in their small chalet at Rommes-sur-Cluses, to discuss the ten-day tour he had planned for us, moving from hut to hut, and starting from Chamonix. We were sleeping in the loft of his barn, where we laid our sleeping bags on sweet beds of hay and tried rather vainly to sleep, as a mighty thunderstorm circled the mountains around us, and lightning flickered and flashed through all the chinks in the woodwork. When we reached Chamonix next day the weather was terrible and climbing was out of the question, so Gilles suggested that to save hotel bills we should all stay in a tiny little converted hay barn, a *grenier*, which belonged to his mother. It was just two rooms, an upper one reached by an outside staircase, with a couple of bunks, and a downstairs one also with two bunks, a cooking area and a tiny loo and washbasin. As it turned out, we never got our tour as the weather remained awful and Sidney had a bad cold. Gilles did his best for us by taking us twice on the Glacier des Bossons – yes, the one I'd adventured on with family and friends all those years ago! – to practise cramponning, which was new for me. On other days he took us to awful wet cold practice rocks, where all the other guides in Chamonix had also brought their clients. And there we rather disgraced ourselves by failing miserably on many of the test routes. Poor Gilles, he must have been very shamed by us. He was a brilliant climber, and despite the disadvantage of being a Parisian and a schoolteacher while most of the other would-be guides were tough Chamoniards, he rose to being an instructor for three years at their top École Nationale in Chamonix, which led to his being pretty unpopular. To have his English clients disgracing themselves so publicly must have been awful for him. The few French women climbing were tough and competitive and I felt an utter wimp when I failed to get up a strenuous pitch and heard Gilles' disbelieving voice saying, 'Even my wife can do that.' Meanwhile the young guides frolicked around us, showing off on impossible overhangs while Sidney and I got more and more depressed.

At last the weather improved, and Gilles took me up to do a very easy route, the Midi-Plan ridge. It was so deep in new snow that at one point Gilles was uncertain whether it would be safer to retrace our steps or to carry on to the hut we were aiming for. In the end we carried on. And I disgraced myself yet again by getting stuck. Very deep snow is extremely tiring to walk through, and my legs had already reached the spaghetti stage when I suddenly floundered really deep into a snowdrift – and simply could not get one of my legs out. Gilles was very cross, as he had to come back and dig me out. Unless you withdraw your legs quickly and energetically the snow freezes and you find yourself in an icy plaster cast.

On the last of our ten days booked with Gilles it was fine, and he took me to do a quality rock climb on the Aiguille de l'M. At last I felt more at home because this closely resembled Dolomite climbing, but I was nervous because I knew there were some grade-five pitches, which were at the limit of my climbing capability. All was going well until fairly near the top, when we found ourselves on a belay stance behind a very slow party. They were young English climbers, good, but climbing guideless and spending ages studying their guidebook between pitches. Gilles, a rather impatient chap, decided to pass them by abandoning the normal route and taking a recognised variant, which involved traversing out to the left then up over a little overhang. It all seemed to happen in slow motion, and it exactly replicated an accident in a film we had watched in Chamonix during the bad weather. He reached up over the overhang, silhouetted against a very blue sky, and, as he pulled up, the handhold gave way and he fell backwards somersaulting as he went and dropping out of sight. I was not belayed, but the rope between him and me was running to the left up and over a large rough granite block. The block sloped outwards, but not too steeply, and I saw at once that if I put my full body weight on my end when he reached the bottom of his fall the friction might be sufficient to hold the rope in place just for a few seconds. When the shock came it lifted me off my feet, but the rope held, and in seconds the strain was off it as Gilles got back onto the rock. I heard his voice, sounding as buoyant and cheerful as ever, though he told me afterwards that he felt shattered, calling up, 'Oh well done! You are marvellous! This English technique!' though nothing could have been less technical than me hanging like a monkey on the rope! I wrote in my diary that at the moment of Gilles' fall I felt no fear, and something that was certainly not my usual slow self reacted for me. The English boys by now were on their way, except for their last man, who was sitting quite near me belaying them. He never uttered a single word during the whole performance. Gilles hardly said a word when he arrived up beside me, but carried straight on up, this time by the normal route. I slipped twice off the very first step up, because my legs had begun to shake so much. On the summit he thanked me for having saved his life and I told him I had to because it was my life I was saving too! As he fell he was sure we would both die and he thought, 'Poor Elisabeth – on her first alpine season!' He refused to accept his fee for the climb, saying, 'I behaved like an irresponsible boy, not a guide.' In fact all he did wrong was to fail to test the handhold before committing his weight to it.

The next summer, 1962, was to produce even more adventures. It started in the Dolomites where various friends had gathered to climb with Celso. Then Sidney Nowill and I went over by bus to Pontresina in Switzerland. He had a great plan that we should tour for a week with a guide, climbing the big peaks in the Bernina area, which was new to me. We did one or two small excursions, then went up to sleep at the Tschierva hut to climb Piz Roseg. The weather was a little too warm, always a bad sign, and avalanches had been rumbling down the mountains, which I saw were less rocky and more snow-covered than in the Zermatt area. We left the hut at 3.00 a.m., and set off on the long snow climb to the summit. By dawn we were traversing up a steep snow slope with a glacier high above us. I was plodding along, head down, in my usual early-morning state, when I heard a noise like a thunderclap from above. We all looked up and yelled 'Avalanche!' at the same instant. I was in the middle of the rope with Sidney bringing up the rear. He started to run back downhill while our guide shot off uphill shouting 'Oben! Links!' ('Up! To the left!') and for an awful moment I was left in the middle being pulled each way. Then Sidney realised his mistake and turned and started to race uphill as I did – our only chance of escaping the main body of the avalanche. Fear made us all sprint until the guide shouted 'Unter!' (down) as the avalanche was upon us, and we threw ourselves on our faces with arms over our heads. It was ice, and it pattered over us for what seemed ages. When it stopped we sat up and looked around for each other. Our last sprint had just taken us out of its main path, and Arthur was sitting up looking all right, Sidney had taken a knock on the head and was a bit stunned, and I was fine, or so I thought until I saw blood on the snow and realised it must be mine. I had two small cuts on my head, not serious, but bleeding copiously. By good fortune a whole class of young guides was training in the Bernina and happened to be following us up Piz Roseg. They had seen our three figures ahead, then the avalanche came down and they thought we were goners, but as the clouds of powdered snow settled they saw the three of us moving, and set off uphill as fast as they could to help. The young guides were all anxious to show off their first-aid skills to their instructors, and they pounced on me and enveloped me in yards and yards of bandage, which was no use at all. I've never laughed so much in my life as everything they did failed to stop the bleeding. Eventually they left us and went on up the mountain, but Arthur our guide wouldn't hear of my going on. In fact it took us two and a half hours to get down to the hut, and by then I was having dizzy spells from loss of blood. When we walked in at the door the hut was full of daytrippers, and there was nowhere to sit. I was by then fairly bloodstained, but no one got up to make room for me until Arthur shouted at them. I still had to walk down to the valley where an old horse-drawn bus took me back into Pontresina. The local doctor put seven stitches in my head and told me to rest for a couple of days. He said he spent his time patching up climbers in summer and skiers in winter. I did manage to do the beautiful traverse of Piz Palü before joining the parents in Zermatt, still wearing a headscarf because of my shaven head.

In August Sidney and I got our ten-day tour with Gilles, which had been aborted by bad weather the year before. This meant going up into the mountains carrying all we needed on our backs, which involved a ruthless weeding out of things Gilles considered unnecessary. He emptied my rucksack onto his kitchen table and I had great difficulty in persuading him that the sanitary towels I had packed really were essential. Nowadays when these matters are talked about quite openly I could have explained without any embarrassment that my periods came about every third week, that they were heavy and I lost a lot of blood and really needed that pile of STs (there being no internal protection available then). However, I remember being overcome with shyness.

We had an amazing tour full of excitements and new experiences for me. On a lovely morning we went along the spectacular Rochefort Ridge with France on our left and Italy on our right, then turned off and were confronted by an abseil down an ice cliff at the end of the Mont Mallet glacier, a sheer drop of over a hundred feet. Because we had so much to carry – cooking stove, fuel, pans, food, some bedding, spare shirts and pants, and so on – much of which went into Gilles' sack, he took only one 120-foot rope, so we had no safety rope to belay us. Sidney went down first, then came my turn. We did not use the modern metal *descendeurs* in those days, we abseiled 'classic', with the rope between our legs and up over our shoulders. This could be extremely painful on a long abseil, but Gilles insisted it was the safest way as there was nothing mechanical to go wrong. I went slowly down and realised as I neared the bottom that the rope was just too short to reach the ground. Beneath me yawned a *bergschrund* – the deep crack formed where the ice of a glacier meets the snow slope below. I was dangling over this not knowing what to do when Sidney shouted at me to kick hard against the ice wall and drop off as I swung out. The *schrund* was luckily quite a narrow one so I kicked and dropped just as the pain between my legs became so excruciating that I thought I would prefer death in the *bergschrund*! We were relieved when Gilles joined us and pulled the rope down from the rickety stake round which it had been fixed at the top. After that I think we were a little light-headed, and delighted by our night's lodging, a sort of triangular-shaped outsize dog kennel high on a rocky ridge with amazing views. It was the Periades bivouac, and there we sunbathed, then made our supper as rocks and snow turned pink and orange in the sunset. There was just room inside the bivouac for the three of us to lie side-by-side – it was very cosy. We had been up at 2.00 a.m. so we slept soundly until a storm broke during the night, the rain poured down, and the bivouac leaked like a sieve. I had the best of it at my end of the row. Gilles was at the other end at a slightly lower level so the water gathered round him. '*Je suis dans la piscine ici!*' he moaned. Nothing to be done except stick it out.

The next day we made a late start over the Col de Talèfre. It was extremely cold on the north side but we met the sun on top, and Sidney and I climbed on unroped up easy rocks to the summit of the Pointe des Papillons, urged on by shrieks of mock terror from Gilles. The hot Italian sun dried us out, and eventually overheated us as we did the nasty long descent on slushy melting snow and ice treacherously full of loose rocks. But once over the Triolet glacier we came to the tiny Rifugio Dalmazic, where the guardian plied us with far too much red wine and the men then roared ahead glissading down long *névées* while I came a bad third. At last we got down into the Val Ferret, where Gilles, despite having a heavy cold, insisted on getting into an icy stream and sitting there in his trunks washing. I was more interested in the gorgeous ripe peaches on sale at all the little farms, and we ate our way slowly along to Courmayeur. There the pension to which we had been recommended was full – in fact Courmayeur was overflowing with tourists, and it was only through guide friends of Gilles that we got three rooms at the very grand Hôtel des Anges. I shall never forget Sidney leading us into the bechandeliered dining room where dinner was in full swing. Smart Italian holidaymakers from the cities, the men all in evening dress, and grand dowagers all beautifully coiffed and bejewelled, gazed in horror as we strode in, after five days up the mountains sleeping in huts or bivouacs, still in our climbing boots because we had nothing else, and headed straight for a free table. Such is the presence of Sidney when drawn up to his full height and using his most imperious voice, that the grand head waiter scurried over to serve us in person, followed by the wine waiter, who found he had met his match as Sidney is a connoisseur! I can't remember what we ate or drank, but there was a great deal of it as we were ravenous despite the peaches.

From Courmayeur we climbed the Aiguille Noir de Peuterey, an awful stony seven hours up and seven and a half down, as we missed the normal route and kept deviating to avoid stone falls. It was worth it because of the tiny summit crowned by a lovely silver Madonna, where there was just room for us all to rest while enjoying the tremendous view over the south face of Mont Blanc. Sidney was more determined than ever to do the great classic route up the Peuterey ridge one day.

Our last climb of the trip was the Chardonnet by the Forbes ridge on a perfect morning. The views from the ridge are very fine, and Sidney and I took photo after photo. Suddenly I came over a hump to find Gilles' ice axe planted in the snow with the rope coiled neatly round it, so I picked up coils and axe and proudly led the final part of the ridge (very easy) to the summit where Gilles was sunbathing having got tired of waiting for all the photography! The French guides have quite a different attitude from the Swiss to their clients. You are not a parcel to be conveyed safely up and down the mountain, but a climbing companion learning to become an independent colleague. That at least was how Gilles saw it, and his approach led to stimulating climbs.

The day after the Chardonnet Sidney was unwell, but Gilles had a final treat in store for me, as he knew I loved Dolomite rock. It was a short but steep climb on the Pürtscheller ridge of the Aiguilles Dorées, which would allow us to get back to Chamonix for me to reach Zermatt that night. As we approached our climb the golden granite spires glowed red and orange in the sunrise. The crux pitch was a vertical wall with what Gilles described enthusiastically as an elegant crack running from top to bottom, the only possible way up.

He shot up like a monkey, disappearing round a corner far above, to what was presumably a belay stance out of sight. A voice floated faintly down to me: 'Climb!' I viewed the crack with growing depression.

After an interval I yelled back: 'How?'

'Jam!' came the reply. Not nice sweet jam, but wedge.

Another interval, then 'What?' from me.

'Anything that fits!' came the reply.

I tried wedging my fist in the crack. Much too small. A hip – much too big. At last I found my right foot would jam securely, leaving the left foot flailing desperately to find any sort of tiny niche that would help upward progress on the polished rockface, while my right hand and elbow in the crack somehow held me in place as I squirmed up. Progress was slow and painful, and exhausting. I knew that if I fell off I would swing on the rope to below where Gilles was belayed, and face a possibly far worse situation. At last I hauled myself over the top and round the corner where I could see him perched up on a ledge. He looked down at me and remarked somewhat distastefully: 'Every time I see you climbing towards me you are bleeding somewhere else.'

That night I rejoined my parents in Zermatt, and as I came into the dining room for dinner there was a round of applause led by the distinguished Swiss climber Alfred Zürcher, who in his youth had made the first-ever north-face ascent of the Eiger. Although he no longer climbed, he stayed at the Monte Rosa every summer, and his twin grandsons were with him, about to make their first ascent of the Matterhorn. He was full of encouragement for young mountaineers, and every time I came back from a hard climb there would be a pretty Swiss hanky and a note of congratulations from him on my plate at dinner. We all changed for dinner every night, even after I got back from the Matterhorn traverse at 7.00 p.m. I was in the dining room bathed and changed by eight. In those days we knew almost everyone in the hotel, a lovely collection of friends from Italy, Austria, France, Spain, all speaking in various languages, which became known as 'Franglais', as we would start in one language and probably end the sentence in another. It was splendidly epitomised by Virginia Graham's poem in *Punch*, which I cannot resist quoting in full as it became a family favourite:

Zut!

Donnes-moi mon mackintosh pelisse,
Es regnet beaucoup trop en Suisse,
Mais tout de même durch Sturm und Drang
Prenons un petit Spaziergang.
Oh Weh! Oh Weh! Der Matterhorn
Qu'il a l'air mouillé, triste et morne.
Wir konnen nicht at any Preis
Cueillir l'illusif edelweiss,
Nie monter par funicular
Pour sehen comme c'est wunderbar.
Alles in mist ist gar bedeckt,
Zut, c'est effroyablement schlecht!
Retournons vite, retournons schnell
To unser kleine, clean hotel.
Geh back, geh back und wieder let
Us legen down upon die Bett.
Lisons les livres we've lised before,
Schlafen ein bit mit Bernard Shaw,
Priestley et Maugham, une puissante cuvée,
Und blick der Schweiz from unter le duvet.

Virginia Graham,   Punch 1946

With warm thanks to Virginia Graham and *Punch* and apologies for any mistakes. It was a long time ago!

In June I went on my first-ever pukka expedition, thanks once more to Sidney. He and his family lived in Istanbul, and he had done much to pioneer mountaineering in Turkey. We went to the Taurus mountains in June to climb in the Ala Dağ amid the nomad tribes. Our small party consisted of his cousin Philippa, Nigella Blandy and myself, and we had all walked and climbed together before. Sidney said airily: 'We won't be taking tents. It never rains in the Taurus in June.' It did. There were several heavy thunderstorms. But we had splendid high-mountain bivouac sacks with hoods, into which you could disappear completely if need be. We had a horseman, Ibrahim, and four minute donkeys to carry our mountain of gear to various different base camps. It was all pure magic to me. The flora in the Taurus is amazing; great low bushes of sweet-scented daphne, pale clouds of night-scented stock, which we waded through in the dark on Sidney's favourite 2.00 a.m. departures, little golden fritillaries, still a few tulips and anemones out, and all the usual alpines when we got higher.

Dr Peter Davies from Edinburgh Botanical Gardens had heard of our trip and he wrote to me explaining that he was compiling the first-ever complete flora of Turkey. Apparently no British botanist had visited the area we were going to, so would I please collect for him? Despite my protestations that I didn't know how, instructions and enormous wooden presses arrived, the latter extremely unpopular when it came to loading the donkeys. I tried to make a routine of pressing the day's specimens as soon as I got back to camp each evening. There was usually a mountain breeze blowing, and soon blotting paper and specimens would be flying all over the Taurus. After watching me curiously for a couple of evenings, our old horseman quietly came and squatted by my side and provided the extra pair of hands I so badly needed. He loved helping, and we became good companions though he hadn't a word of English. One night when I was just too tired to get the presses out he went to Sidney in great concern to report that the Bayan had not done her 'presse' that evening and what was the matter? There are so many magical memories; a camp by a high lake where a solitary shepherd was staying with a flock of sheep and goats. With the traditional hospitality of the nomad people he brought us a gift – I think an onion. He offered it shyly to Sidney and looking round at all our bedding and gear said, 'You have so much, and I,' he broke off and shrugged. He had nothing, and that onion probably represented quite a hole in his meagre food supply. Another evening we were invited to supper with the head of a tribe camped near us. We sat in the open round a fire eating lamb stew from a big communal pot, using the right hand only, while the head man and Sidney carried on a deep religious discussion. Later one of the women led us three women discreetly to a little secluded gully, which we understood was the female loo area. What a sensible rule that the right hand is used only for clean things and eating, whereas the left only must be used for dirty jobs such as wiping oneself in the loo.

We climbed Demir Kasik, the highest peak in the Ala Dağ, by the Hodgkin-Peck *couloir*, the first ascent since two English climbers discovered the route twenty-one years to the day earlier. Sidney led Nigella on the first rope, and I led Philippa on the second. We were roped because the *couloir* held snow and ice deep enough to belay into, and also many falling stones; normally in the Taurus we climbed unroped as the summer snow was too shallow to hold an ice-axe belay. We were quite near the summit when we were halted by a steep slab covered in thin ice. Sidney did not think the ice would hold him, but I felt we had come so far that we could not let one short pitch stop us getting to the top, and for once in my life felt a surge of confidence that I could lead it. With Sidney's permission I did so; it went quite easily and I was able to bring up the others. We came down by another route, Sidney, abseiling down a steep slope, starting a small avalanche, and I sitting up at the top by the belay as all the others went down, watching ominous cracks spreading out from the piton we had driven into the rock to hold our rope. It held, but we had lost a lot of time and were benighted, sitting on a ledge with the sound of running water below us, getting more and more thirsty as we had emptied our water bottles long ago. Early in the morning we came back into camp through the sweet field of night-scented stock feeling very happy, to find poor old Ibrahim weeping with emotion as he had thought we were all dead!

Back in the village we were allowed to sleep overnight on the roof of the headman's house. They had even built a little loo up there for us, just three low mud walls and a hole right over the heads of the cows stabled below. We were invited in to a drink of fruit juice with the great man, and Sidney led the way, shaking hands warmly with our host. I followed, holding out my hand too, but he drew himself up, put his hand behind his back, and said, 'I do not shake hands with women.' Sidney let everyone think we were his three wives. I as much the oldest was the senior wife, Philippa as second wife gained much prestige because she could honestly say that she had three sons, and Nigella, the baby of our party, was the nubile young wife yet to bear children. We gave the headman, his wife and children a ride in our Jeep. They had never been in a motor vehicle before, and christened it the Devil Machine.

After four lovely weeks of climbing and flower-collecting we were all sad to leave the beautiful Ala Dag. Back in Ankara we were most kindly put up in great luxury by diplomatic friends of Sidney, but although it was nice to have a bath I got claustrophobic and couldn't sleep a wink after lying out night after night watching the stars.

Nigella and I had driven out to Istanbul in her car, a second-hand Morris Minor known as the Zoom. We forgot to bring a road map so picked one up at a BP petrol station, which marked every garage from London to Istanbul but no physical features. We found ourselves going over the Loibl pass into Yugo-Slavia, a notoriously steep affair, which now has a tunnel under it. The little car broke down early on and we had to reverse back for some way to a garage where a German mechanic sorted out the problem. When he heard where we were going he said, 'I think I had better accompany you girls to Istanbul.' The Yugo-Slav frontier guards on top of the pass were astonished by the arrival of two females in a little old car in the middle of the night, flying the small Union Jack we flew all through the Iron Curtain countries. When they opened the rear door to inspect our mountain of gear, a collection of cooking pots fell out, whereupon they hastily closed it and waved us through. Adventures included my nearly burning down a motel with our camp cooker when we were trying to make ourselves a cup of tea after a late-night arrival – we spent nearly all the night cleaning the soot off the walls with loo paper then made an early getaway! At the Bulgarian border we were pulled out of the queue by customs officers who had discovered our ice axes stowed away in the bottom of the car. They were convinced they were dangerous weapons, and we were held up until a young officer appeared who took one look at them and burst into a beaming smile: 'Ah! Sportiv!' he said. We beamed back and assured him we were very sportiv, whereupon we were waved through.

We drove into Turkey on a lovely moonlight night. It seemed very quiet as we turned off into the international airport to ring Sidney, who lived on the Asiatic side of the Bosphorus, to tell him we were nearly there, though a day late. The whole place seemed deserted until some officials woke up and became very excited. 'What were we doing there? Did we not know that there was a revolution going on and the country was under curfew?' If anyone had been awake we could well have been shot as we drove in! Having let off steam, they became very friendly, and let us sleep in the lounge until the curfew was lifted next morning. The revolution was a relatively mild and short-lived affair and we reached the Nowills' home safely the next day.

When we got back from the Taurus, Nigella and I got back into the little Zoom waiting for us in Istanbul, and set off to drive back to Chamonix, where we had a rendezvous with Gilles. The trip back was not without incident. At the Turkish-Bulgarian border there was a little man in a dirty white coat who appeared with a tray of syringes and insisted that we had to be inoculated for something or other. Gella and I refused, and an impasse had been reached when we were saved by a Russian woman who spoke French to me and Turkish to the whitecoat, and who appeared to be a person of some importance. I explained the problem to her and she convinced him that we had had all the necessary inoculations at home. It was a relief – we had not liked the look of those syringes. Arriving in Plovdiv after dark, we stumbled by sheer chance on the main hotel, the Palace, a huge crumbling old place with potted palms and a three-piece string orchestra in the dining room, which was full of comrades in rolled-up shirt sleeves and large tough women such as we kept seeing working in road gangs. Our vast double bedroom plus bathroom, loo and small entrance hall, cost about thirty shillings a night for the pair of us, and our dinner, with lashings of delicious local wine, was about the same price. My diary tells me that we liked Bulgaria, with its fertile fields golden with wheat, vineyards, flowers everywhere, the fine horses and sleek fat donkeys, and the cobbled E5 running between avenues of trees and many-coloured cystus bushes. It seemed friendly and welcoming after the arid reticence of rural Turkey.

We had problems with route-finding as we kept being deviated off the main E5 for roadworks and found ourselves after dark driving for miles on unmade roads, ending up in farmyards. And in Trieste we got into trouble twice with the police, once when I was driving (we did two-hour shifts at the wheel) and I went the wrong way round a roundabout, and once when Nigella drove up a pedestrians-only street. All the road signs were in Serbo-Croat and quite unintelligible to us. We could have been fined, but each time the police, who were fierce-looking armed types, let us off with a caution. Perhaps they liked the cheek of our by now tattered little Union Jack! In Rijeka hotel after hotel was full and we could not find a room, until a kind Italian who had booked two rooms for his chauffeur and himself heard us being turned away from the reception desk and immediately offered us his second room, sending the chauffeur out to find accommodation elsewhere.

In Italy we turned north and went to Cortina d'Ampezzo to rejoin my parents, who had been cruising in the Black Sea, snatched two days' climbing with Celso Desgasper, then drove across Italy, over the Petit St Bernard pass, and up to Gilles' chalet above Chamonix, as we had a precious week of touring booked with him.. He introduced us to a young Englishman, John Varnay, who was also staying in the chalet, and asked if John, who he said was a very good climber, could join us as a sort of unpaid porter to help carry all the gear we would need. Gella and I were delighted, especially when we heard John's sad story.

He and three friends had been climbing on the Chardonnet just a few days earlier, and had had a terrible accident on the Col O'Reilly, the very spot where Gilles had warned Sidney and me on our climb the year before. Tragically, two of the boys had been killed. Gilles came across John and the other survivor in Chamonix and took them under his wing. One wanted to go straight home to England, but John stayed on and Gilles said he needed to climb again immediately to regain his nerve after the shock. It worked out wonderfully, and John usually took Gella on a second rope while Gilles led with me.

For our first day he took us girls to climb the Grépon just to see how we were going. We started late, after a storm, up the usual route, then Gilles led us round to climb the south face, which drops sheer down to the Mer de Glace. The final pitch is up the Knubel crack, named after the great guide who made the first ascent. At the crux the crack appears to run out of holds, so Knubel got up it by reaching up with the long ice axe that the early climbers used, hooking it over a stone embedded in the crack, and pulling up on it. Unfortunately the stone has long since fallen out and anyway we couldn't have reached it with our shorter axes, so one has to do a horribly exposed and delicate move out to the left, then up, and back into the crack to reach the summit. Gella, a better rock climber than I was, managed this beautifully, but I slipped and needed a tight rope to get me up. Gilles later said he pulled most clients up that bit, and asked me, 'Elisabeth, did you see my legs shaking before I made the traverse?' I said no, I hadn't. He said he had not done the climb for some time and was very nervous at that crux move. I would never have guessed – he appeared to be moving with complete confidence. Perched on the summit of the Grépon we burst into song. We all three had the Burl Ives records of Irish folk songs that Gilles adored and knew by heart. When he was happy and all was going well on a climb it was: 'Come back, Paddy Reilly, to Bally James Duff!' If things got tricky it was a darker song, 'Brennan on the moor.' And at any time it could be 'Three Lovely Maidens From Bannion.' This Gella unkindly used to change to 'Bunion', teasing Gilles about his feet, which had not been improved by the very tough guide training when they had to demonstrate their ability to carry a full-grown man on their backs for a long way over rough ground.

How we laughed and sang on that tour! There was a marvellous moment on the summit of the Grépon just when we had been carolling away about 'Come back, Paddy Riley, to Bally James Duff!' Suddenly a very Irish voice sounded from the void beneath our feet, exclaiming 'Chroist! Me arms!' followed by a more distant voice, 'Are ye alroight, Paddy?' Two small Irishmen bowed under vast rucksacks appeared on top, having struggled up the Fissure en Z, the approach crack on the opposite side from ours. The summit of the Grépon with five people on it was a bit overcrowded! The Irish boys were trying to do what they called the 'traverse of the Eggles' – i.e. going up and down the whole group of the Aiguilles in a day. Good luck to them – they vanished over the top to descend to the attack of the next Eggle with a long, long way still to go.

There were stern moments however, as when the time came to abseil off the summit of the Grépon. This is awesome on the Mer de Glace side. Gella, an extremely good rock climber, lost her nerve and absolutely refused to go, sitting on the edge with her feet dangling out over space until Gilles physically shoved her off with his foot. I simply had to make up for my slip on the climb so I went off without a murmur and hoped I had regained a few brownie points! In fact I have always quite enjoyed abseiling – apart from the always awful moment of truth when you launch yourself – because I am lazy and it saves much time climbing down.

A couple of days later we crossed into Italy by the Col du Dolent, at the time only the thirteenth traverse of this col, which had been first climbed by Nigella's grandfather Edward Whymper. It is a steep north-facing ice climb. Gilles led with us all on one rope, John Varnay next, then Gella and finally myself on a short rope at the tail end. In the olden days on ice climbs the leader would have to cut each step, but we all had modern crampons, and Gilles led by front-pointing, i.e. digging the front two points of his crampons into the ice and climbing as far as the rope would allow while we stood still, then cutting out a stance and making a secure belay where he could bring us all up. This process is repeated over and over again, in our case for five hours, until one reaches the top. You stand, trying not to freeze, until called on to climb, and with only two people on the rope it is easy, with three more difficult, and with four, if you are last on a short rope as I was, you often don't reach a stance but have to stop with your weight all on your two front points. My legs were red hot, and even Gilles got tired leading and asked John to take over the last pitch or two, which involved negotiating a tricky corner. By the time the two men were safely on top, Gella and I, both climbing at the same time, each had a slip. She burst into tears on the summit and refused to go on, saying she was too bloody tired. The nerve strain had been terrific, but once on top, resting in the sun and eating a second breakfast, we soon recovered.

Once we had got down the steep part of the descent and were on easier ground we unroped and the two men rushed ahead. Gella and I caught up with them ensconced in a tiny four-berthed hut called the Bivouac Dolent, just ideal for us to spend the night. The lovely flowery Val Ferret where Sidney and I had eaten too many peaches the year before led us to Courmayeur, where we stayed, carrying on next day up the Val Veni and the steep path to the Gamba hut.

The highlight of the tour came after a certain amount of dithering as to whether we should or shouldn't do it. Finally in view of a good weather forecast and reassuring advice from the hut guardian about snow and ice conditions, we set off to traverse Mont Blanc by the Innominata ridge, one of the great classic south-face routes I had often read about. It was a marvellous and happy climb, with the most spectacular views as we little ants moved slowly up the massive face. We reached our overnight stop, the Bivouac Eccles, by afternoon, another small four-berth metal box perched dramatically on a projecting spur of granite and held in places by steel cables. Luckily it was empty. The logbook told us that three Polish climbers with an Italian guide had left that same morning. On the table was a large onion. It was a welcome gift; we had an excellent pasta supper much improved by that onion. Only two people could stand up at the same time in the hut; with the other two crouched in the bunks. When we wanted to go to the loo Gilles roped us up and lowered us to the edge of some slippery snow beneath the hut where we could hang onto the steel cables while facing inwards and perform like baby birds sticking their tails over the edge of their nest. We were pretty well acclimatised by now and we slept like babies – in fact we all overslept and were roused only by the rumble of an avalanche nearby. We climbed on a cloudless morning up the Brouillard ridge, which was ice-clad with cornices leaning now one side, now the other, with rock steps in between, and such spectacular views that death-defying photographs simply had to be taken. At the top we emerged onto a gleaming dome of snow up which we had to go to reach the summit. It looked to us quite innocuous, but Gilles warned us that it was probably the most dangerous part of the climb as the snow lay over ice and it would be difficult to hold anyone who slipped. We did not linger on the ample and featureless summit, but hurried on down to the big Gouter hut, only to find it was overflowing and they would not let us stay, though we did get some tea or soup. We carried on to a pleasant small hut lower down, the Tête Rousse, which was almost empty, and there we had a great evening of celebration. In my usual way when overtired, I couldn't sleep, but lay feeling supremely happy.

Home in Surrey there was the launch of the Opera Players' thirteenth season and my forty-second birthday. I wrote: 'Despite occasional qualms, and unbelief at being so old, I do truly feel that life begins at forty, as each year gets richer and more filled with interest.' Two weeks later I bought my first car, a second-hand Morris Traveller like the Zoom. The young today are incredulous. 'Aunt, do you mean to say you were forty-two before you had a car?'

During my parents' lifetime the years fell into a fairly regular pattern, singing and opera from September until June, and mountains, which involved annual visits to our much-loved Cortina d'Ampezzo and Zermatt, followed by the yearly 'fix' of Scotland in Skye, during July and August. Singing practice had, of course, to be kept up, and I had regular places such as school halls with pianos where I used to work in Cortina and Zermatt. Music was with me all the time I was climbing, usually some passage from an opera the company was performing or a verse from a favourite song, which would repeat itself endlessly and help me to keep up a rhythm as I plodded uphill. I shall never forget a particularly beautiful dawn and morning of radiant sunshine when climbing the Zinal Rothorn above Zermatt. The weather had been bad and it had snowed during the night, but now the sky was cloudless blue, and the untracked snow glistened and sparkled before us as we climbed to the elegant summit. The music that rang in my ears all the way was the exquisite passage in the second act of *Der Rosenkavalier* when the young page Octavian brings in the silver rose, token of purity, and presents it to Sofie.

There was an interruption to the usual pattern in 1966, when I was invited by Sidney Nowill to join another small expedition he was organising to climb in the Hakkâri Mountains in the extreme southeast of Turkey. This region, south of Lake Van and adjoining Iran and Iraq, had been closed to foreigners for forty years. It was the area known to us as Kurdistan, though the Turks refused to use that word and insisted it is Southern Turkey and its inhabitants the Southern Turks. The Turkish government reopened the area to foreigners in 1965, and Sidney immediately planned to go there the following summer. The party was to consist of himself and his wife Hilary, his cousin Philippa, who had been with us in the Taurus, Gretel Macquisten from the British Embassy in Ankara, English climber Peter Ledeboer, a Scottish climbing friend of mine, Esmé Speakman, a Swiss Guide Henri Salamin and myself.

I was very anxious to be able to communicate a little bit with the local people on this trip so I joined a Turkish language class at the Turkish Institute near Hyde Park Corner. Once a week a motley small group of us came together at 6.00 p.m. to do battle with the language. We ranged from high-up Shell officials and diplomats to mountaineers and travel writers, and we were taught by a ferocious little lady called Mrs Çandan (pronounced Jandan) who had been headmistress of a school in Istanbul, and who treated us all like naughty children. She had some cause for complaint because we were all busy people and we hardly ever managed to do any homework. We would arrive tired out after a long day, dying for a cup of tea, but nothing so cissy as a tea break was permitted, so towards the end of two hours' non-stop Turkish grammar we were all dropping off and having to nudge each other awake to answer Mrs Çandan's increasingly irritable questions. I am afraid I never managed to put a grammatical sentence together but I acquired quite a vocabulary of single words, which when strung together caused hilarity and mirth among peasants and tribes people.

The plan was that Sidney and Hilary, who spoke fluent Turkish, should go into the mountains first, with Gretel and Philippa, a horseman and his assistant and four packhorses carrying half of the mountain of gear and food, tents, etc., which we needed, and set up base camp. They would then send the chief horseman and horses back to collect the rearguard of Peter, Henri, Esmé and myself plus the other half of the supplies, which we were bringing from England with us. Peter was with Unilever, and they were experimenting with dried foods for expeditions at the time, so they generously gave us a large quantity of their products to try out. Esmé drove from Edinburgh to Van, passing through Switzerland to collect Henri. Peter and I, who had work commitments until the last moment, flew to Van, and managed to arrive at the same time as Esmé, who was there on the tarmac to greet us. Her car was left in Van and we hired transport to do the full day's drive south to the village of Yüksekova, which was the setting-off point. There the local *kaymakam* (governor) had made arrangements for us to sleep on the floor of a classroom at the school, as the children were on holiday.

I remember being woken in the night by a loud and persistent rustling sound. I found my torch and peered out of my sleeping bag to see not rats, as I'd expected, but a steady stream of large cockroaches processing in and out of one of our pile of kitbags, in which our supply of chocolate was packed. They had eaten through the wrappings and were having a feast. I left them to it and went back to sleep. The loo was some way off and it too had its wildlife interest. It was the usual hole in the ground, incredibly smelly, and for reasons that don't bear thinking about it had attracted a swarm of bees. Visits to it were hazardous and as infrequent as possible. We met up with our horseman, a rather dour elderly Kurd with no English, who was just back from taking the advance party to base camp. He had us up at the crack of dawn so that he could take ages loading his horses, which he did with great care that the weight should be evenly distributed. We understood why later, as the animals were expected to all but rock-climb at times. Eventually we set off to cross a wide plain, the Gevar Ova, which stretched to the foothills, beyond which we could see snowy peaks. There was a barrier before reaching the hills, and a vividly worded scribble from Sidney was sent back to warn us about what the advance party had christened the Snake Marsh. This consisted of a marshy area crisscrossed by a series of deep water-filled channels, which were reputed to be full of snakes. The first group had walked through there, which was all right for our leader who stood six foot two, but not so funny for his wife who was about ten inches shorter and who found herself up to the neck in snaky water. (Actually no one of us saw a snake, and they were probably the harmless water snakes anyhow, but the thought of them was off-putting.) On this his second trip, Fereç took pity on us and indicated that we could ride on the horses. Anyone who has ever tried to get onto the back of an overloaded pack pony will know that this is no joke, and one of us, on being heaved up, fell straight off on the far side. At last we were all in place, Fereç rolled up his trousers, and grasping the lead horse by the bridle he set off. The horses were joined nose-to-tail by a short rope. Result, when the lead horse after some persuasion slid down the muddy bank of the first water channel and struggled out on the far side, the horse following was pulled head first down into the water after it. It was chaos: my horse was submerged for so long at one moment that I thought it must be drowning, but suddenly, with a mighty snort and a big heave, up it came, with me luckily still on top. Henri fell off shortly after, and said that snakes or no snakes, he preferred to walk. At last we were all safely through, and we paused to regroup and rest the horses on the far side. They were feisty little Arab stallions, and they were soon grazing happily on the rich marsh grasses.

It was by now midday, and the sun blazed down. Esmé was having a migraine and had been remounted on the lead pony. I was bringing up the rear, panting along as usual and taking photographs. We were climbing steadily up a path between steep boulder-strewn slopes, when suddenly three figures carrying guns leapt out at us from behind a big rock. They threw Fereç to the ground and pulled Esmé roughly off her horse. As I drew level the only word of Turkish that came to me in this extremity was 'Meerhaba!' which is a friendly greeting rather like saying 'Hi!' to someone. The bandits, for that is what they obviously were, looked a bit surprised but said 'Meerhaba!' back. Our position was difficult. Fereç spoke only his own language, Kurdish, Henri spoke only French, the rest of us had a few words of Turkish between us. Resistance would have been foolish, as one of the young men was obviously very nervous and had a wild-eyed trigger-happy look about him. Henri was also very nervous and got angry, saying over and over again in French, 'We must do something!' Peter told him firmly to be quiet and do nothing. The leader was in army uniform and we thought they were probably some of Marshal Barzani's irregulars, who were currently fighting the Iraqis in the mountains not far away. They took us a little way up the hill to behind some rocks where they searched our pockets, took off our wristwatches, then sat us on the ground and proceeded to go through our rucksacks, demanding 'Para! Para!' ('Money! Money!') We just shrugged and said 'Para yok!' ('No money!'), which was true. There was no use for money where we were going, and all our wealth was in travellers' cheques. They took quite a lot of things, one passport, all our medicines, which they referred to as 'aspirin', and worst of all, all our cameras and film. This was awful, because Henri was making a film for a Swiss society, *The Times* in London was waiting for black and white pictures from Peter, and I was making an illustrated lecture. I managed to get my hands on the film with all the pictures I'd taken so far and got it back into my pocket when the men were looking away, which was some comfort. Meanwhile poor Esmé was really suffering with a blinding migraine headache. They had taken all our pills, but I asked the young leader if I could have some for my friend and managed to say that she had a very bad head. To my surprise he handed me back the big bottle he had taken from Esmé's sack, so I took out a couple of pills for her. 'That is going to be my revenge for my lovely new camera they've stolen,' hissed Esmé. 'That bottle is not aspirin. Its a very strong emetic I have for migraine.' I handed the bottle back to the bandit with effusive thanks, and we hoped they would all take them and be terribly sick!

We were getting a bit worried about what they were going to do with us, as they could have shot us in their hideout and been away over the border well before we were found. But they made it very plain to Fereç with plenty of threats that he was not to try to go back to his village, but take us on up into the mountains where there were no police or soldiers we could contact. He was terrified, and in tears because they had taken his one possession of any value, his watch. The horses meanwhile had been grazing peacefully by the track, so we set off up into the hills feeling very shattered while the bandits followed us from above until it got dark, guns at the ready, making sure we did not turn back. We made camp in a very pretty little glade beside a stream, and there a minor miracle took place. At the bottom of her kitbag Esmé, a keen photographer, found an old camera she had put in just in case anything went wrong with the brand-new beauty she had bought especially for the trip. It had a film in it, and later our friends supplied us with more film, so between us we were able to photograph all the time, though the old camera had no light meter, and many of the pictures were not of our usual high standard.

We slept peacefully by our stream, and next morning climbed on to a great welcome from the advance party. The base camp was in a lovely spot at the north end of an ice-studded lake, which stretched for some three quarters of a mile between spectacular rocky peaks to where a snow col led – we imagined – over into Iraq.

A friendly tribe of Kurdish nomads had their summer camp about half an hour away below us. Sidney's party had got to know them, and the morning after our arrival a delegation of the men, led by the young chief, and including the chief shepherd, who carried two shepherd's crooks as a status symbol, came up to welcome us. Later we went down to return their call, winding our way downhill through waist-high slopes of a feathery yellow flower like cow parsley. The advance party had not accompanied us, so conversation was a little stilted, but after a long wait we were honoured by being served proudly not with the usual tea, but with cocoa from a Cadbury's Bournville yellow tin! The tribe was young and handsome, both men and women in bright colours, the men in baggy long trousers and over-tunics with sashes and belts with knives stuck in them, the women in the same sort of thing, all with neat small turbans, and on their feet one and all wore black galoshes! These it turned out were homemade from old tyres, and provided stout waterproof footwear for snowy mountains. My few words of Turkish provoked the usual roars of laughter. Kurdish men are conscripted in Turkey and taught Turkish in the army, but their womenfolk mostly speak only Kurdish. I managed to chat to the women, mostly in mime, and got onto the subject of pierced ears with the little girls. I discovered that they had their ears pierced when they were five, and mine had been done at the same age. I tried to explain that I too had earrings and bangles and necklaces like theirs, at my home, but they were filled with pity for me because I had none on, and one of the older women bore down on me with a ring and a large needle and offered to pierce my nose and insert it then and there. I tried to explain that in my culture nose rings were just not done, and do hope I did not hurt her feelings too much by refusing her kindly meant offer.

We had a wonderfully happy time at that camp, climbing the highest mountain in the Hakkâri, Hendevade, and various other summits all about 13,000 feet in height. The rock was dangerously loose and fractured, much of it golden yellow and containing lots of yellow quartz crystals. Rockfalls crashed from the nearest peak down into our lake, but luckily the campsite was just out of range. One day we watched an amazing sight. We saw a brown mass of figures appear over the top of the col to our south, and realised it was a migrating tribe. They had a big flock of sheep and goats with them, and after one or two men had descended the steep icy snow of the col one wise old cow with a small bull calf at her heels made her way down, zigzagging carefully to the bottom to be followed by an avalanche of sheep and goats. They all halted at the bottom like a well disciplined army, watched over by big sheepdogs with spiked collars whose task was not to herd the flocks but to guard them against attack from wolves. Last to come down were the women and children, who glissaded happily on their bottoms from the top of the col, babies in their arms, great bundles of firewood on their backs, shouting and laughing in their favourite brilliant red and pink clothes. At the bottom a long procession formed up, led by the shepherds and their dogs with the lead rams and goats at their heels. They came right past our camp and stopped to talk to us. The shepherds wore strange stiff cloaks of animal hide, which stood out from their shoulders on wooden yokes. These became tents when the shepherds, who always stayed out with the flocks at night, curled up under the rocks to rest. I saw exactly what 'For he shall lead his flock' really meant.

Another day some tribesmen and their women passed our camp, and a little group of women stopped behind a big rock that hid them from our view. A short while after we heard what was unmistakeably the crying of a newborn baby. The little group emerged, one of the young women carrying a little bundle, which she showed us proudly, a healthy new baby, tight-swaddled as is their custom. She had crossed an 11,000-foot pass that morning carrying a very heavy bundle of firewood, and goodness knows how much further she still had to go before reaching her camp, so we thought the least we could do would be to offer her a cup of tea. She refused us courteously, then with a proud toss of the head as if to say 'What would I be wanting with a cup of tea?' strode off down the mountain carrying baby and bundle with no sign of fatigue.

Henri was horrified to discover that these people had absolutely no knowledge of the use of herbs. The mountain slopes were covered with lovely alpine flowers, gentians, primulas, and cushion plants, and many sorts of herbs found in the Alps, so like all good Swiss, Henri immediately set about gathering them. I shall never forget the sight of him crouched in the midst of a group of Kurdish women explaining to them in French how to make tisanes!

Groups of young men from the tribe used to disappear over the col for several days and come back loaded with great heavy sacks. When they heard we had been robbed, they said, 'You need cameras? We bring you cameras!' – and we had visions of all our stolen goods being sold back to us. One man came back carrying a portable radio blaring out Arabic pop, which seemed hideously incongruous. They opened the sacks to show us gorgeous silk brocades they were smuggling in, but below the fabrics were hard heavy metallic objects, which we were not shown – probably guns and ammunition for the Kurdish resistance.

Sidney wanted to go back to Yüksekova by a different route, but when he mentioned this to the young chief he was told that on no account should we go that way back. The tribe encamped in that valley were enemies of our tribe and would certainly shoot us.

It was not possible to give our friends anything directly, but we wanted to thank them because they had guaranteed our protection while we camped near them, and not a single thing was missing from our unguarded camp, though many of our possessions such as ropes and knives and compasses would have been invaluable to them. All we could do was to leave behind anything that could be of use to them.

When we started our march back we saw a shepherd on the top of the first ridge silhouetted like a biblical figure leaning on his crook. He called out a greeting, and we saw another man on the next top looking out for us, and so we were watched over while we passed through the place we had christened Bandit Land, until soldiers sent out from Yüksekova came to escort us the final part of the way. As soon as we were back in the village Fereç was arrested on suspicion of being an accomplice in the attack on us. Sidney defended him vigorously, and he and Hilary spent a miserable night in the Kaymakam's office while Fereç was interrogated and beaten up next door. Sidney had to give evidence at some sort of enquiry, but when we left Fereç was still in jail. We sent him a letter of thanks for his services and a new watch as soon as we got back to England, but never got a reply and have no idea what befell him.

My lecture about this expedition, 'Kurdish Kaleidoscope', was far my most popular to date. As my friends put it: 'If you must get yourself attacked by bandits, you can expect to dine out on them for a long time!' The lecture went on booking for years, as the Turkish government re-closed the area after our misadventure, and to the best of my knowledge it has not been reopened since. It is probably much unchanged to this day, full of unrest and sporadic fighting between militant Kurds and the Turkish army.

The next summer Sidney realised his great personal ambition, to climb Mont Blanc from the south by the great Peuterey route, and I was lucky enough to be in the party. We ended up as quite a caravan. There was Sidney, climbing with one of the great mountaineers of those days, Michel Vaucher, then there was Dorothea Gravina and a strong young English climber, Sylvia Yates, with an 'aspirant' guide from Chamonix, Dominique Blanchet, and me with Gilles Josserand and Gilles' friend Bernard Minet, an excellent alpinist. There had been considerable doubt as to whether we should get off at all. I was, as usual, very unfit, and on a training climb that aimed to traverse Mont Blanc de Tacul and Mont Blanc, I managed only the first summit, to the great dismay of young Bernard, particularly as he had taken me ice climbing the day before and I had fallen off twice! I had got so badly sunburned on the Mont Blanc de Tacul that I had to go to the doctor for special ointment for my eyes, lips and mouth. Then Sidney became unwell. Then I started my period at this most inopportune of moments. However, at the eleventh hour, the doctor pronounced Sidney fit to go, so finally we set off via the Mont Blanc tunnel. I noted in my diary that the guides' rucksacks weighed sixteen kilos, Sidney's was ten kilos, and mine was reduced to seven kilos, plus of course crampons, ice axe and camera. We all went up to the Monzino hut on the evening of 18th July, and after an early supper lay down and tried to sleep for an hour or so. I was filled with fear and foreboding, not of the climb technically, but about whether I would be able to keep going for two long hard days and a bivouac. Michel Vaucher did not arrive until after 10.00 p.m. Having spent the three previous nights bivouacking on the fearsome Bonatti route on the Dru with a client, he had rushed straight through the Mont Blanc tunnel and walked up to join us carrying a huge rucksack full of equipment, yet he seemed undaunted by the thought of having to get up again at 1.00 a.m. We left at 1.30 and spent hours crossing the Frênet glacier in the dark, a terrifying time of leaping over wide-open crevasses, climbing seracs, and crawling on our tummies along a narrow ice ridge. On the far side of the glacier we reached a point where there really was no way forward, until Michel cut an ice mushroom round which he fixed a rope so that we were able to lower ourselves down and climb out up the other side. The scenery in the cold dawn light was awesome, with the great black pillars known as the Dames Anglaises towering ahead up a steep *couloir*. At long last we reached a resting place, the tiny bivouac Craveri at the Brèche Nord des Dames Anglaises, where we stopped in welcome sunlight for drinks and a sleep. The guides were all in great doubt as to whether we should continue because ominous clouds were appearing and it was much too warm. It was Michel's decision, and in the end he said we would go on. This was the beginning of the Peuterey ridge proper, and there was some pleasant climbing that eventually brought us out overlooking the east face of Mont Blanc and the huge ocean of tumbled ice that was the Brenva glacier.

At five in the evening we reached the narrow ridge of snow and ice that leads in a series of steps to the summit of the Aiguille Blanche. Here we were halted by soft snow, which made further progress impossible, so we had to settle for bivouacking, in order to set off along the ridge in the early hours when it would have refrozen. The ridge was so narrow that we could lie only in single file along it, and Gilles cut me an ice platform facing out over the Brenva glacier, stuck in a couple of pitons and tied me on securely. Somehow the men boiled water and we had hot tea, but food was impossible. Dorothea was settled on a rocky patch just a little further back, and the others all found what places they could to stretch out. By turning gingerly onto my side I could lie looking straight down thousands of feet onto the Brenva glacier and chalet roofs and twinkling lights way below in another world. It was breathtakingly exciting and I didn't sleep a wink.

Next morning we started off at 4.00 a.m. and proceeded gingerly along the ridge, which was now a skating rink of ice with the cornices frozen solid. We continued over the summit of the Aiguille Blanche and eventually came to a sheer descent of 480 feet, down which we had to abseil in our crampons to the Col de Peuterey. It was a horrid descent, abseiling in crampons over ice and loose rock, and try as we might some of us relatively inexperienced climbers dislodged stones. I managed to hit Sidney, he hit Dorothea, and Gilles was also caught, but luckily none of the damage was too severe. It was a disgraceful display, and Michel and the guides must have been horror-struck as they saw us struggling down amidst the bombardment. I felt particularly ashamed, as the day before I had dropped my ice axe while rock climbing, and Michel, ever kind and patient, had soloed down the Brenva face to retrieve it for me. The snow down on the col was so soft that the only way to progress was to crawl on hands and knees. We stopped here for a cup of coffee and the making of final decisions, because this was the point of no return. If we went on forward our only option was to make the summit and reach the Vallot hut on the far side. If we turned back we would have somehow to descend to the Frênet glacier and hope to find a route through the crumbling ice. Clouds were now right down on the summits and a wind was getting up. It was decided our best bet was to go on, and there followed some mixed climbing up the Grand Pilier d'Angle until we reached the foot of a steep slope, which was often of snow, but because of the unusually warm weather it had melted and turned into hard ice. There was no time to cut steps in the ice, so Michel used what was then a modern technique of climbing a full rope's length using the front points of his crampons, then cutting out a platform and making a firm belay. He would then bring his companion up, belay him, and proceed up for another rope's length and repeat the process. We followed on using his platforms, and the last man on our three ropes had to retrieve all the pitons and ice screws, which were still in the ice, and send them up to Michel for reuse. It went on and on and on. At one moment Dorothea, for all her Himalayan experience, was heard to mutter, 'This mountain has no top – we are cramponning straight to heaven.'

It was sheltered on the ice wall. Mist was around us and light snow was falling, but I was hot and threw back the hood of my anorak. At last I could look up and see a big cornice above us, with a gap in it where Michel had cut a way through to climb out onto the summit plateau. I heard a great roaring above, which in my fatigue I did not identify, then I stepped through the gap and out into a gale-force wind. I desperately needed to stop for a moment to pull up the hood of my anorak, but Gilles for once became angry and refused to allow a moment's pause. 'C'est le Col Major,' he said. 'Le pire endroit des Alpes.' We did not know at the time that we were passing in the fog and snow close to two climbers who must have come up from the Brenva side, and who had sat down in the snow to rest and died where they sat.

Sidney, who had studied the Peuterey route most thoroughly, and who was a fine mountaineer, had been giving Michel route directions on the climb, and now as we battled on he knew something was wrong. The wind had dropped, and it should not have if we were going in the right direction. He called to Michel, and they consulted the compass, to find they were indeed right off course. With Gilles, who knew Mont Blanc like his back garden, our two ropes were still on course, but because of the whiteout the two others had not noticed us. They retraced their steps and luckily Sidney shouted and heard Gilles shout back. We were soon on the summit, but there was not a moment to lose, as it was getting dark. The route down was simple and in under an hour we were at the Vallot hut, which we reached at 7.30 p.m. It was hardly a welcoming place as there was even ice inside it, but to us it was paradise. Dorothea and I collapsed onto a bench and just sat for an hour before we could summon up energy to take off our crampons. Meanwhile the guides melted snow and brewed cup after cup of tea, and we at last had a bit to eat, I can't remember what. I do remember that I had diarrhoea and my period, and had to go out into the snow and gale. I must confess I did not go as far from the hut as decency really required!

Michel later told Sidney that the ice slope we had climbed was longer and more difficult than any of the three ice fields on the north face of the Eiger. It was a long way down next morning, and I was almost too tired to start, but kind Michel took my hand and ran me down the first steep snow slope below the hut, after which my legs got going again. What he accomplished with us, after he had already had three nights out hanging on the wall of the Dru, was incredible. For several of us that climb was the peak of our mountaineering experience, and I feel privileged and lucky to have done it, humble climber as I am. I put it down partly to my trio of mountaineering saints who were invoked almost continually on the Peuterey. They are St Bernard, St Christopher and St Antony of Padua. St Antony was thrown in for what the insurance agents like to call 'universal coverage' and because he always helps my family to find things. I was furious to find that St Bernard and St Christopher were de-sanctified by I think the last pope but one. My trio have stood by me through thick and thin and they certainly had their work cut out on the Peuterey, a climb described as follows in that mountaineer's bible the *Guide Vallot*:

> With the Innominata, it is the toughest, the most beautiful and the most difficult of the great routes on Mont Blanc... an expedition which must remain the exclusive preserve of alpinists of great experience.

It was amazing luck that in my short years of climbing starting in my forties, I was enabled to do both these wonderful routes.

The mountains were very kind to me that year, because a couple of weeks later with Willi Truffer and his son Bernard, now also a guide, Dorothea and I were at the Weisshorn hut hoping to do the traverse of this most beautiful of mountains next morning, weather permitting. Willi and I had gone up to the hut to climb it at least twice before, and always been thwarted by bad weather conditions. At last we were to be lucky. If you look at the Weisshorn from across the Zermatt valley you see a superb steep triangular mountain with crenellated ridges rising to a sharp summit. It is on a Himalayan scale, and to me more noble even than the Matterhorn. In my day the climb involved a four-and-a-half-hour climb in the dark up to the col on the south side of the mountain, where the Schalligrat or south ridge begins. My diary tells me that I felt very sick when we reached second breakfast place on the col, and Willi saved me by producing his precious flask of illegal absinthe from the bottom of his sack. His home brew did the trick, and I felt better and better as we got higher. We attacked the ridge at 6.30 a.m., and climbed up and up, over a never-ending series of gendarmes and crenellations of golden rock, which led straight up to the tiny summit.

We got there at a quarter to one, over six hours of climbing. By this time big clouds had gathered but it was still and ominously warm on top. We rested there until a rumble of thunder warned us off and we knew we had to get down quickly. Willi told us that the first part of the descent was the most dangerous bit of the whole route, and we must be extremely careful. It was steep snow over ice, the sort of condition in which it is impossible for the guide or leader, who is the anchorman at the rear, to drive an axe in and get a secure belay should someone slip. Our return route was via the north ridge or normal route, and by the time we had got back to the hut we had done a huge diamond-shaped climb. We still had a three-hour walk down to Randa, Willi's home village at the foot of the Weisshorn, and as we stumbled down in the dark enjoying the sweet resiny smell of the pine trees the candle in his lantern and the batteries in our torches gradually died. Then we spotted a welcome light flickering on the path way below…one of Willi's family on his way up to light us back down the last part of the steep path where gnarled roots stretched out to trip the unwary.

Dorothea and I caught a train back to Zermatt, where she still had to walk to the campsite up at Winkelmatten to reach her small tent. As we came level with my hotel, friends swooped out and took us to drink strong, heartening Irish coffee and tell them about our day. Now people climbing the Weisshorn are taken straight to the col by helicopter at dawn, which cuts out long hours of nasty climbing in the dark. I am glad that I did it in the old days when one actually had to climb the whole mountain.

The Peuterey, the Innominata and the Weisshorn traverse were undoubtedly the most memorable of all my climbs, and they stretched me far beyond what I had thought were my limits, which is proof of what I once read – that the average person in a lifetime never extends him or herself to more than about half their full potential.

Chapter Thirteen

My Family and Life Without Them

At home my dear Scottish grandmother, who had now lived with us for twenty years, was beginning to fail. She was a remarkable person. Born into a strict Scottish family in Aberdeenshire, she lost her mother when she was very young, and found herself as the oldest in a family of four having to run the household for her father when in her early teens. She had to submit the household accounts to him every month. Daily life included prayers morning and evening for family and servants, and she told me she cried herself to sleep many a night because she expected to go to hell, as she had a 'blemish' in the shape of a birthmark, and the Bible told her that only he (or she) who is without blemish shall go to heaven.

At that time Aberdeen was fortunate to have a brilliant German piano teacher, Herr Reiter, reputed to have been a pupil of Liszt – or was it a pupil of a pupil? Granny had lessons with him from a young age, and by the time she was seventeen she was so accomplished that he asked her to play a piano concerto with the professional Aberdeen Orchestra. Her father had of course to be consulted. Not only did he refuse to let her play, but he also stopped her piano lessons now that she was seventeen, because her teacher was a man. Poor Granny, no wonder she turned to everything from Buddhism to the British Israelites in later life!

She married a Forbes cousin, far enough removed for the strict consanguinity laws not to be involved, and quite soon departed for Ceylon with her young bridegroom. The choice of careers for poor collaterals in those days was limited: there was the Church, the army, the navy, or planting something or other in the colonies. Granddad opted for tea in Ceylon, where already several friends and relations were working. The estate he took on was quite high in the hills near Talawakele, and Granny often used to tell me how they went upcountry with all their worldly goods, including her trousseau and her beloved grand piano, on elephants. Her trousseau unfortunately fell off its elephant into a river en route, but her grand piano, with an elephant to itself, got through safely. She had her three children in the bungalow there, some forty miles from the nearest white person. The doctor got to them for only one of the births, but she produced three healthy babies, with no pre-natal or antenatal help, no mother to advise her, just the native women, who she said were marvellous, to help her while their men beat tomtoms outside. She was one of a generation of incredibly brave Victorian women. She learned to ride in order to be able to visit, and I have a photo of her riding sidesaddle on a pretty grey horse, dressed in long skirt, hat and veil, with a syce at the horse's head. She and Granddad named their estate Coreen after a moor in Aberdeenshire. They made a beautiful garden, grew first-class tea, and must have been desperately homesick as they could afford to get home – a six-weeks' journey – only very rarely. The estate passed to their eldest son, who wisely sold it when nationalism assumed dangerous proportions.

Granny and Granddad came to live in Folkestone, where she soon became quite well known on the bathing beach. She would take her collapsible bathing tent down onto the shingle, set it up, and walk calmly into the icy Channel waters when she was well over sixty. She never really learned to swim, but gave a good impression of it, doing breaststroke with her arms while keeping one toe firmly on the ground. This performance was called 'Heading for Dover' and we children teased her unmercifully about it. When she was living with us after the war she used to go to her beloved Scotland every summer to stay with her oldest son near Roy Bridge. As she got older it fell to my lot to take her up to King's Cross and put her into her sleeper. She knew all the sleeping compartment attendants, and they would welcome her aboard, see that she had her breakfast tray in the morning, and make sure she got off safely at Roy Bridge. Travel was easier and much more pleasant in those days.

By Christmas 1960 Granny was having serious falls and wandering out of the house, to be brought home often by kind neighbours. My poor mother was at her wits' end, and our family doctor recommended that Granny should go into a nursing home. We hated having to do this, but the doctor said 'It is her or you' to my mother, so a place was found and in January she went in. She was only twenty minutes away from us so could be visited often, but although the home was comfortable and kindly she hated it. I shall never forget her joyful little face, convinced that we had come to take her home, each time we went to see her, or her misery when we left. In May we had a happier visit, and had her reciting 'The Lady of the Lake' and singing with the remains of her sweet voice 'The Bonnie Banks of Loch Lomond', and that poignant song of the homesick Scots

> Oh it's hame, and it's hame, and it's hame I fain wad be,
> Where the broom is blowing bonny and the wind is on the lea.

She died peacefully not long after aged ninety-seven, and I miss her to this day. I can still hear her practising the piano. She played daily when she lived with us, and maintained a miraculous finger technique, which enabled her to play pieces like the Chopin Berceuse with a filigree delicacy that left the notes shimmering in the air.

It was in the 1960s that we noticed my mother was not quite her usual self. There were indefinable changes taking place in her character, which came out most obviously in her attitude to me. She needed me with her to help her to pack for going away, and change for dinner in the evenings, and so on, but sadly she began to resent my going off on walks with friends. She and my stepfather, who suffered from emphysema, became unable to do long or steep walks, and she, who had always been used to encourage me to go climbing or walking with friends, began to seem jealous, which was quite out of character with her usual generous self. The word Alzheimer's was unknown to us, and after several years, as she gradually lost her sense of time and place, she was diagnosed as senile. She covered it up gallantly, always looking elegant and beautifully turned out, and I think few of our friends realised how lost she really was. She never lost her intelligence, and in her later years would dumbfound her carers by bursting into fluent French. Once when we were on holiday I was stopped by a foreign lady who said to me: 'I must just tell you that your parents are the most beautiful couple I have ever seen.'

During the next few years things became progressively more difficult as my mother's condition deteriorated. A final great blow was the resignation of my friend and partner of twenty-three years, that truly exceptional person Phyllis Thorold, about whom I have written elsewhere. Because of my family problems I felt I must sleep at home as often as possible, and as I was by now singing only very occasionally, it was not necessary for me to go out with all the performances. We had recently amalgamated with the Chelham Opera Company, and had acquired some new artists who were not yet integrated into the company, and Phyllis, who was considerably older, understandably felt lonely and I think a little abandoned without me and decided she wanted out. The ex-music director of Chelham was Christopher Shaw, an old friend, and he took over playing for our piano-accompanied performances together with another old friend Alexa Maxwell, while Peter Gellhorn played whenever he could fit us in to his busy life.

Through friends I heard of someone who was to be of the greatest help to me in this difficult time. She was a small dynamic retired nurse who went and lived in people's homes for two or three weeks at a time where support was needed, looking after the sick, cooking, feeding dogs and cats, watering the garden and in fact doing everything that was needed so that carers could have a break. It was thanks to her that I was able to get away for a blissful ten days' camping and walking holiday in June of 1974.

A climbing friend of mine, Dorothea Gravina, and I took my little car and a couple of tents, and journeyed through Andorra, then westward along the Spanish foothills of the Pyrenees. In 1974 it was all still totally unspoilt and undeveloped. Our first campsite in Andorra was up a high valley just below the snowline surrounded by bushes of the big golden Mediterranean broom in full flower. The air was intoxicating with the sweet winy perfume. There were small wild daffodils everywhere too and gentians and soldanella peeping through the snow. On our first day we went up to the head of the valley, which was the French frontier, and climbed along a snow ridge over a succession of little rocky peaks. The only people we met all day were a pair of lonely French customs officials out looking for smugglers, who told us sadly that nobody smuggled on foot anymore. Everything important, they told us, crossed the border in lorries or cars.

From Andorra we drove south into northern Spain then turned west. We were amazed by the remoteness of the high villages lost up steep valleys, so cut off from the outer world that in earlier days they had had to become more or less self-governing. They were bleak and poor, with high gaunt churches, and each chimney pot wore a hat to keep the snow out. Now I hear that this part of the Pyrenees is being reborn, with an influx of foreigners buying up derelict farms for redevelopment at knockdown prices. The roads, rough and unmade when we were there, are now surfaced, and water and electricity are being laid on, all of which is doubtless putting much-needed pennies into local pockets. But the strange remote magic that we knew will be gone forever. We ended up near Los Encantados, the 'enchanted mountains', camped in a very wet field. I can remember as we were coming down from a high walk almost being swept off the path by an unattended mule returning to the village at a spanking trot with a full-grown tree-trunk flailing from side to side in his wake. I remember too the masses of delicate white paradise lilies in the meadows, and huge gentians higher up.

We spent the summer quietly at home, and my mother died in October, my stepfather, true to the end, managing to outlive her by just six weeks. She would have been lost without him, and he just managed to see her out, then slipped quietly away. They were eighty-four and eighty-six, and about to celebrate their fortieth wedding anniversary, not bad for a late second marriage, almost all of which was very happy. I had prayed that they would go together as they were truly devoted, so I was thankful that things had worked out as they did.

I realised that I had been mourning for the mother I used to know, as she had been before her illness, for several years before her death. Now was the time to be happy that she had moved on, and thankful for all that she had done to enrich my life, instilling into me her great love of English and French poetry, sharing the same two favourite bedside books, Victoria Sackville-West's *The Land*, and *The Anthology of Modern Verse*, the mother who was always encouraging me when I was a child to look, look properly, at the sky, the sea, paintings, flowers, all beautiful things, and who got impatient when I didn't respond. I remember one occasion when we were spending the night at the little inn at Corran Narrows on Loch Linnhe and there was a rare display of aurora borealis. I was fast asleep, aged four, when my mother seized me up from my bed and rushed me outside with her usual enthusiastic exhortation: 'Look! Look!' To her great disappointment I wouldn't look but was very cross and cried.

She revelled in naughty limericks – if they were really well turned and witty – and I was brought up on the verses of that brilliant and witty churchman Monsignor Ronald Knox:

Oh bother! Oh bother! Oh damn!
I've suddenly found that I am
But a being that moves
In predestinate grooves.
Not a bus, not a bus, but a tram!!

Or, heard muttered, as he was processing in to mass:

Oh God, for as much as without Thee
We are not enabled to doubt Thee,
Vouchsafe us thy Grace
In persuading the race
They know nothing whatever about Thee.

And what can you make of a mother who, while being of an extraordinary purity and fastidiousness in her own life, delightedly imparts the following to her teenage daughter:

A Lesbian girl of Khartoum
Took a pansy along to her room.
She got into bed,
Turned the light out and said
Who does what, and with which, and to whom?

She and I giggled happily over the rhymes while not being able to answer any of the questions! Writing limericks was one of Mum's favourite party games (it is not as easy as you might think – try it!)

and I realise more and more what rich and varied pleasures I owe to her.

★★★

Nous n'iront plus aux bois.
Les lauries sont coupes.

Theodore de Banville

Who but the French could imbue such few and simple words with such a deep sense of loss and nostalgia? After the deaths of my parents it was many years before I felt like returning to Zermatt. I found myself not only alone at the helm of the opera company, but in charge of the family home and a fair-sized garden. My friends all assumed I would sell it, but I loved it dearly and was determined to keep it going, so the first thing I did was to add onto a wing and do up the accommodation there to make two small flats that I could let. This proved a financial lifesaver. I never lacked tenants, first students from the Guildford College of Law and later more permanent residents who became good friends.

The old holiday pattern went by the board, which was timely as the opera season was also changing. Where July and August had been dead months for the London Opera Players, we now began to rely more and more for bookings on the summer festivals that were mushrooming all over the country. And then into the vacuum left in the house after the parents died came Mabel, the retired nurse who had helped me so marvellously during my parents' illnesses. She decided that the cat and I needed someone to look after us, and often came to help out if I was very busy in London or needed a short break. She was living in a small upstairs flat in Putney with very uncongenial neighbours, and it seemed only natural for her to move in with me permanently. She had come to love the house and garden, and particularly our cat Pussa, and she was heartbroken when he died aged fifteen. He had a happy last day, catching a mouse and still able to jump up onto the birdbath for a drink, but we knew he was failing and he was due to go to the vet the next morning. He died in the night, and Mabel, a true nurse who had been at the bedsides of many a terminally ill patient, never forgave herself that she had not sat up with him on his last night.

Mabel was a truly remarkable person, oldest child in a large farming family, born in a Sussex cottage, and used to walking four miles to and from school daily come rain or shine. The school she went to was what is known as a dame school, just one big room divided into two, with the boys one side and the girls the other. Her school had a most enlightened small library, including a biography of William Morris, which moved her to become a lifelong admirer of his work. She left school at fourteen to care for an elderly relative, and qualified as a nurse, though I think she would have liked, had there been any money, to study singing professionally. For such a tiny person she had an amazingly powerful rich contralto voice. She told me about her first meeting with Sir Sidney Cockerell when he became bedridden and needed a nurse. She stood at the end of the great man's bed feeling very nervous, and his first question was: 'What are your interests?'

She told him: 'Music and wildlife and reading.'

'Sing me something!' he commanded. So she sang that lovely traditional English song 'Have you seen but a white lily blow?' At his special request she stayed with him until his death some four and a half years later. He found out that she went into Kew Gardens, which was just up the road, every day during her lunch break, so he gave her a notebook and pencil and said she was to write down everything interesting that she saw for him as he could no longer get there himself. During her time with him she met many interesting people, including his son Christopher, inventor of the hovercraft, and Wilfred Blunt, the manuscript of whose book about Kew Gardens, *In For a Penny*, with pencilled corrections, I have here, together with a pretty chair from the workshops of William Morris.

Mabel and I already shared a great love of music and books, and of nature, birds, flowers, animals and all wildlife, then one day I discovered that she had fallen in love with Scotland years ago on a coach trip. From then on, Mabel's Scottish holiday became part of the annual calendar, and she turned out to be the ideal travelling companion, always ready to try out new B and Bs in strange places. We would go off, my small car piled high with gumboots, mackintoshes, maps, picnic things and bird books, and drive up the M6, getting more and more excited as we counted the painted bridges north of Manchester, then got first glimpses of the Pennines and the Fells, up over Shap, into Scotland, to reach Moffat, where we had found an excellent B and B with a kind landlady who became a friend. Next day came my very favourite bit of the route, via Crianlarich and over Rannoch Moor with its dozens of little lonely lochans, steeply down Glencoe to Ballachulish and over the once-hated new road bridge on past Onich, where I had spent magical times as a small child, to Fort William, where Ben Nevis would usually be wrapped in mist, and so to Kyle of Lochalsh and the ferry to Skye. We would stay there for several days while I took her to all the very special places my parents had loved, the one-track unmade road that wound its way high over the hills between Tarskavaig and Orde, where one might just glimpse an otter by the shore, the coppice near Isle Oronsay where the willow warblers sang, and the exciting road up and over to Glen Brittle with the Cuillins stretched out ahead growing ever nearer and more imminent as one descended steeply to the wide expanse of that wonderful sandy bay.

I had often gazed across the Minch to the Outer Hebrides from Duntulm with my parents, and longed to go there, but they were happy to stay with their friends on Skye. Now Mabel and I put the car on the ferry from Uig and set out to explore the Outer Isles from top to toe. Sometimes we would seek out the local tourist board for accommodation, but usually we would just see a little notice, B and B, in a lovely spot and stop there. We went up to the northernmost tip of the Butt of Lewis, and loved that wild spot with the dark cliffs and the dark sea foaming at their base, where waves that came straight from the Arctic ice broke endlessly against the rocks, and hundreds of seabirds nested on rocky ledges and wheeled in the unceasing wind, and parties of gannets crisscrossed each other, each group focussed earnestly on some preferred feeding ground. Nowadays there is a road, so access to the lighthouse is easier, but then you had to walk the last part of the way over short green turf full of tiny flowers, and it felt magically remote, knowing that there was nothing but the wild sea and the sea ice between you and the North Pole.

A favourite place to stay was at a croft on the west coast of Harris, near one of those bays of creamy coloured sand where the incoming tide conjures up a kaleidoscope of colours from palest sea-green to deep turquoise, and the water is so crystal clear that you can look down through it and see every detail of the shells lying on the sand and the kelp bending before the current. I once saw a mother shellduck with a big family of tiny ducklings leave the shelter of the long grass and rushes and lead her little procession anxiously across the great expanse of low-tide sand until at last they all reached the safety of the sea. In June, when there was hardly any night, the cuckoos calling ceaselessly from the trees in the glen kept us awake. And nearby Arctic terns nesting on the greensward where sheep grazed, screeched as the mother terns constantly attacked unwary sheep threatening to trample on their precious chicks. The shoreline was stained pink by carpets of sea thrift, and I remember a place where the plants were all under water at high tide and you could look down and see every detail of the flowers, which re-emerged quite unblemished as the waters receded. I once swam in a remote small bay where I found myself next to a pair of great northern divers, who were unafraid, as to them my head was just that of another curious seal bobbing up to look at them. Magical islands, with a great spiritual aura, where ruined chapels tell of the colonies of monks who once lived and taught there, and mysterious standing stones speak from a far more ancient past of man's endless quest for the meaning of life. Who placed those stones? What is their meaning? They are possessed of a life of their own, and if you hug them you will find that many are warm, reminding us that they are amazingly assembled from millions of whirling atoms, just as we are, but with a lifecycle that seems infinitely slow to our limited human vision.

From the uncounted lochans of North Lewis, where the landscape is not so much land interspersed with water as water interwoven with many-shaped threads of land, and the waters are dark as the peat bog from which they flow, on down past the high hills of Harris to the Uists with their causeways running across the sea to link the many islands, pausing to visit the RSPB reserve at Balranald, and on to the great sands where the army has a rocket range and to Loch Druidibeg where at certain times of the year the swans mass in their hundreds, past dark pools where the small native water lilies flower in the early summer, and to which the beautiful Bewick swans return from Iceland in the autumn – all is lovely here. And Mabel with her love of wildlife was a perfect companion.

More Delectable Travels

The years after the deaths of my parents were very busy ones and left me little time for thinking of things past. It was probably the time when I was most completely integrated with the Opera Players, as we still called ourselves, when we were such a small organisation that the manager was a sort of general factotum. Since my partner Phyllis left I had taken over the bookkeeping, and found to my surprise that I enjoyed it. It was restful to work with a medium that had an indisputably right answer, as opposed to musical and artistic problems that were subjective and open to so many interpretations. I had always enjoyed mental arithmetic and I loved our old broadsheet ledgers, which you could open up to see everything at a glance, without the dizzy scrolling up and down of computerised accounts. It was very satisfactory to add in my head the long columns of VAT, and then check them on my calculator only to find I had got it right! Since Phyllis's departure I had also had to take on the maintenance, packing and unpacking of the costumes, and convey them to the shows. Perhaps most important of all, although I stopped singing in the performances in 1976, I knew all the roles and the production of every opera we were running, so used to coach new singers, and also stand in for any character missing at rehearsals. We would have an ad hoc stage manager who drove a hired lorry and was responsible for the scenery at performances, but I had to stand in and do the lighting quite often. This was before the days of computerised systems, when one simply pushed levers up and down a lighting board. We really were Priestley's 'the good companions' in those days, and I felt I knew every inch of the company as a mother knows her child. All the travels I describe were oases in a hectic life, and rarely lasted more than ten days or a fortnight, fitted in when the company had no bookings. (The six weeks in the Himalayas was a once-only very special treat, undertaken with the agreement of my board!)

The big change from the regular family holidays started immediately when in 1976 Dorothea Gravina, who had been my companion on a trip to Andorra and the eastern Pyrenees two years before, joined me again to camp and climb in the west of the range. We set off as usual with the car groaning under a great load of gear, took the car ferry to

Bilbao, then drove along the Atlantic coast into the Basque country and up through the pretty whitewashed village of Burguete, where we were told Hemingway lived while writing *For Whom the Bell Tolls*, to the pass at Roncevalles. There we visited the lovely old monastery, a haven in medieval times for the pilgrims who were making their way to Santiago di Compostella. The nearest legitimate campsite was miles away at Pamplona, but we put our tents up behind a hedge in a field and everyone looked discreetly the other way. The next morning was Sunday, and we heard music and saw a procession approaching the monastery from the village below. It was First Communion Day for the children, the little girls all dressed in white, and the boys in the typical Basque men's dress of dark knee breeches with thick white woolly socks, white blouses with pale handkerchiefs knotted at the neck, and black berets. We were also lucky to see a wedding in the tiny modern church up at the pass. Outside three men were playing a sort of fife and drums and the local bagpipes. Inside the priest was addressing a young couple who must have been climbers, making many references to mountains during his address, and sure enough at the end of the ceremony an arch of ice axes was formed by their friends when they came out of church. Dorothea and I rushed to our car, got out our axes, and joined the line to the delight of the little congregation. We went on to the village pub to celebrate – a tiny ancient place where we sat in a circle on a bench that ran round the wall and enclosed a huge raised stone fireplace where complete chunks of tree trunks smouldered and smoked.

From there we drove down by a green river through great forests of young beech trees into the foothills of the Pyrenees, the sierras, where we saw extraordinary hidden churches where the early Christians took refuge from the Moors, old monasteries with creamy windows of sheet alabaster, wonderful carved stone doorways, and quiet old towns like Sos del Re Catolico, where I wrote in my diary:

> It is a dream of a place – preserved unspoilt, exquisitely
> patterned cobbled alleys between closely built houses,
> some brick, some plastered, many with overhanging carved
> wooden eaves and wrought-iron balconies from which
> flow torrents of petunias and pelargoniums with tubs of
> sweet-scented arum lilies at the doors.

One day we climbed 1,500 feet up to visit San Juan de la Peña. The monastery at the top of the hill was captured by Napoleon, who had heard of the great wealth of the monks, but they outwitted him and when he arrived he found nothing. He sacked the place, which has been rebuilt with, unfortunately, a corrugated tin roof and is not very interesting, though I wrote:

> The real wonder is lower down the hill, a steep cliff face. Here, tucked into the rock wall in a hidden gully where the monks must have felt safe from the Moors, the original monastery was started, they think around 922 AD. The oldest, lowest church, which later became the crypt, is in what is called Mozarabic style, a very rare 10th century construction with the apses hewn out of the living rock and all partially underground. One climbs up into a court, all overhung by a natural roof of loose-looking red conglomerate. Here the inner wall is lined with funerary stones of the Aragonese nobility (11th–14th century). On up into a later church, again roofed in the natural rock, where there is the pantheon of the kings of Aragon and Navarre, and cloisters, between precipice and cliff face, which have pillars with lovely variegated carved capitals (12th C).

Here, shrouded by trees and invisible from the front, the monks could safely teach the Bible to the illiterate faithful from the stories so vividly portrayed in stone. The flowers by the path were exciting, long-stemmed pink saxifrages curling out of the rocks, a mauve primula, African violets in rich blues and purples growing happily on the bare, stony soil, aquilegias, wild roses and honeysuckle, and great low clumps of the large-flowered golden Mediterranean broom.

Although it was mid-June there were hardly any tourists, and many campsites and huts were still 'cerrado' – or 'cerrao' as they pronounced it in this area. It means 'closed' and it was a word with which we were to become all too familiar. We wanted to climb the highest mountain in the Pyrenees, the Pic d'Aneto, so we paused to buy supplies at the village of Benasque at the foot of the valley, and here we were told the usual thing, that the Renclusa hut, which is the jumping-off point for the climb, was 'cerrao'. This meant trying to get our car with tents, food and climbing gear, as near as possible to the hut, and then carrying it all up. Our first campsite was one I shall never forget, in a meadow by a mountain river where gentle herds of dun cows with tiny calves and two placid bulls passed us going home in the evening and then woke us early in the morning, poking their soft noses into our tents but treading delicately to avoid our guy ropes A Scottish family camped nearby warned us that the track ahead was awful and the Spaniards, who were building a new road just over the river, were blasting without any warning, letting fly debris right across the river onto the track. We set off very gingerly next morning. I was fussed about my car, which had a low clearance with the petrol tank as the lowest point where it could easily be punctured by sharp rocks. In quite a few places I asked Dorothea to get out and walk ahead watching to ensure that I could pass safely. Things got worse and worse, until we stopped and I said I didn't feel like risking going on. As we were sitting in the car feeling depressed another car came round the corner towards us, and the man at the wheel stopped and assured us that if we could just make the next hundred yards or so, we would reach a good stretch of remade track, which would take us right to the foot of the path up to the Renclusa hut. It was a lucky meeting for us, as we reached a most lovely place where we camped by several cars whose owners were already up in the mountains. It was a good fifteen miles from our last night's camp and we could never have made it on foot. As the hut was still closed we had to carry up tents, bedding, cooking and feeding gear, all we would need for three or four nights, and next morning we struggled to load up. When I had finally hung everything onto my bursting pack I could barely lift it.

'I'll show you how,' said Dorothea. 'This is how the Sherpanis [Sherpa women porters] do it.' She laid her pack on the ground and lay down beside it putting her arms through the straps. She then rolled onto her knees and got it on her back. 'If they can stand up from kneeling with their load on their back, then they can walk with it.'

I struggled to my feet and we set off up the steep path, me with my small camping kettle and frying pan tied on outside dangling and clanking as I trudged. Somewhere near the top I gave up and threw out part of my load into a bush of alpine roses, to be fetched later.

Dorothea, aged seventy-one, a veteran Himalayan climber, never paused even though her load was heavier than mine.

The hut was indeed shut and barred, but there were a dozen or more tents already up, and we climbed on above them and found a perfect place by a stream to pitch ours. We had got there, and it was heaven – a dream place just below the snowline, with the richest profusion of mountain flowers I have ever known. There were sweet-scented bushes of a pink daphne, and the alpine roses with their dark rust-backed leaves, primulas of various sorts, farinosa, auricula, oppositifolia and minima (this is showing off, but in those days I really did know all their names!), and of course gentians aplenty, the trumpet and the star, in their blazing Oxford and Cambridge blues. And a thrilling moment on the trudge up, when my eyes, glued to the ground, suddenly became aware of unusual green and black leaves that I recognised from our garden, and I saw that I was walking through a field of erithronium, the dog-toothed violet, which I had never before seen in the wild. At that moment I longed to have my parents with me, as they would have so loved this very special place, and a great wave of homesickness for them swept over me.

The young men camped nearby turned out to be a Basque climbing club from Bilbao. They were warm and friendly, and egged on by them we set off next morning to tackle the Pic d'Aneto, despite rather dodgy weather. We had been assured down in the valley that it was quite a straightforward route. 'In summer grandmothers with walking sticks can go up it!' they had said. All very well when the snow has gone, but not so easy when there is still deep snow and no tracks to be seen! The mist came down, and we were plodding up a steep snow slope when we were halted by shouts from behind. We were going the wrong way, having overshot a col where we had to turn left to descend onto another glacier, and our good friends the Basques, who were on their way up another mountain, had seen us go wrong. They led us in thick mist to the crossing place, which we would never have found without them, and set us on our way. We reached the top, from which we had been told to expect the most spectacular view in the Pyrenees, in a whiteout, and could barely see the great silver cross and beyond it a little smiling silver figure of the Madonna. The last part of the climb is the only difficult passage, along an extraordinary sort of gangway of great granite blocks with – they say – spectacular drops on either side. Maybe it was as well we could not see these, as the blocks were unpleasantly slippery with melting snow. My only view was of Dorothea's backside as she progressed gingerly upwards.

The clouds cleared on the way down, and we saw our peak in sunshine. When at last we were able to glimpse our campsite way down below us, our two little tents looked very lonely. The Basques had packed up and gone. But as we got nearer we suddenly spotted two figures sitting on a rock and waving up at us. It was an example of true mountaineering solidarity – two of them had stayed behind to make sure that we females got down safely. There was a note pinned to my pillow in my tent, written in a sort of Greek calligraphy, which said that they had left and 'We wait your visit in our Pyrenees Basques. Goodbye Basios!' That was followed by a sentence we could not decipher, written in Basque using a script that looked rather like Greek.

Another vivid memory from that camp is of an all-time low I reached a few days later when we were caught in a thunderstorm and got back to our tents tired, soaked, and very cold. I crawled into my sleeping bag having taken off my boots and most of my wet clothes outside, and set to to make some hot soup on my little Bluet camping cooker, which I stood in the doorway of the tent. I must have dozed off because the next thing I knew I had knocked it over and a pint of boiling soup was careering down the groundsheet of my tent, which was tilted slightly uphill. It reached every corner. I could have wept – in fact I think I did – and I know I lay there surrounded by soup for some time before I could pull myself together enough to find a loo roll and start the laborious mopping-up process. Never camp without lots of loo rolls; they are invaluable in emergencies. Dorothea laughed when she heard what had happened the next morning. 'My dear,' she said, 'when you are cooking on a gradient, always stand your cooker inside one of your climbing boots!' It was a great tip, and the Thermos-shaped Bluet stood comfortably inside my boot from then on.

The one snag of camping in the Pyrenees is the mosquitoes, quite the most persistent and voracious I have ever known. They could bite through a thick woollen pullover, and they followed us up to over 10,000 feet, undeterred by lashings of repellents.

One day we climbed up to a pass opposite the hut on the French frontier, the Port de Venasque, a dramatic narrow gash in a black rock ridge, where we found the remains of a track used by the pilgrims to

Santiago di Compostella, so steep that it had been built up in a series of rock steps on the French side. And at the bottom of the pass on either side stood the ruins of small hospices where the monks used to succour the pilgrims and feed them up before their hard climb. The little blue mountain pansy grew high up here, with cushion plants and gentians, and great flat thistles like starfish, and by a small dark glassy lake we saw a chamois and choughs and ptarmigan. It was a rich day crowned by a descent through fields of asphodel.

Every day we would buy a bottle of the local red wine, which cost the equivalent of 2/6 a bottle, with the sixpence back if you returned the bottle! It was wonderful stuff, and we spent extremely happy evenings in our tents before falling into a drunken slumber. We took too many bottles of it home. But the customs official to whom we declared it on landing picked up one of our opened bottles, took a sniff, rolled his eyes ecstatically and returned it to us with a wink, waving us through.

Later the same summer Dorothea and I came together again to climb a mountain I had often seen from the summits of the Valais peaks, on clear days when gazing south into Italy. The Gran Paradiso loomed impressively above its smaller neighbours, and both Dorothea and I wanted to climb it. So after some days camping and walking with friends in Switzerland, we went over into Italy and drove up the lovely Val Savaranche, past picturesque old farmhouses, through pretty villages, beneath ruined castles perched on crags high above, to camp at Pont, where the road ended. The next morning we set off early up the path to the Vittorio Emanuele hut, which was the jumping-off point for our climb. It was crowded, I remember, and we shared a four-berth room with an English couple and two delightful children aged ten and eleven. We were in a national park, and to my joy a herd of the rarely seen steinbock was grazing nearby. I grabbed my camera and set out, making a big circle to come out the far side of them where I would be downwind, and managing to get there unnoticed. It was the rutting season, and the stags were far too busy fighting and chasing off their rivals to bother about me. They are big beasts, the size of our red deer, and it was a magnificent sight to see them rearing up on their hind legs and locking their great antlers with loud clashings, pushing fiercely at each other until sometimes one would be knocked off balance and tumble down the steep rocks, only to leap up and charge to the attack again. Meanwhile the hinds and calves grazed placidly, and barely looked up at the drama going on all around them.

Coffee was served in the hut from 4.00 a.m. next morning, and we set off by the light of our torches to grope our way along the rough path on a moraine to the foot of the glacier we had to go up. We had reconnoitered it the day before, but in the dark it was hard to stay on track amid the piles of grey boulders – and I was of course feeling miserably sick. It was bitterly cold, which didn't help, and as soon as we reached the glacier in the first grey glimmer of dawn, we roped up and put on our crampons. The ice was hard, our crampons gripped well, and we topped the glacier onto a snow slope, followed by another, and another, and another – endless sweeps of curve after curve of steep snow in the shade of the north side of the mountain, until finally at about 10.00 a.m. we came into sunshine and saw the final summit rocks above us. The narrow space was crowded as this is an easy and popular climb rewarded by tremendous views. Our English family had set out before us and had made it, plus the children, in splendid style, and various other hut acquaintances had shot past us on the way up full of encouragement and kindness. We found a sheltered ledge just beneath the summit Madonna, and relaxed in the sun. We were lucky to have a perfect day, and on the way down we took our time, savouring the fine views, and the excellent crampon conditions, which turn a tiring descent from a penance to a joy. Back in the hut, we all had soup and pasta, then Dorothea and I set off down to our tents in the valley. We were well satisfied, as we had done 5,000 feet of ascent and 8,000 of descent by the time we crawled into our sleeping bags. And gallant Dorothea was seventy-one years old, with acute arthritis in her knees, which kept her awake most nights. Although we didn't know it, that turned out to be the last 4,000-metre peak for both of us.

Another year I went on one of Sidney Nowill's memorable small expeditions along the Black Sea coast of Turkey, through Trebizond, now better known as a seaside resort than for its famous towers, up through the rain forests to the Kaçkar mountains where we hoped to climb the central peak. On the way up we passed the ruins of Sumela, a fantastic monastery built up the side of a vertical cliff. The guardian, who lived down below, handed us the biggest key I have ever seen and sent us off up hundreds of steps carved out of the cliff face to an old doorway where we could let ourselves in and wander in and out of the old chapels and chambers. Sadly most of the frescoes have either been defaced or fallen away, but the views are spectacular. We drove on up unmade tracks running with water from almost constant rain, through tall rainforest where strange dark objects that turned out to be beehives were attached at the tops of the trees. The honey gatherers must have climbed like monkeys and endured many stings to harvest their precious crop. Some of the honey made here is called 'deli bal', the mad honey, because if it has been harvested when the yellow azaleas are in bloom it is mildly poisonous, causing vomiting, diarrhoea and hallucinations. Legend has it that the locals decimated the army of Xerxes when he passed this way by showering his troops with gifts of milk and honey.

When we passed through, the forests were full of colour, with the native purple *Rhododendron ponticum*, which is now all too at home in Britain, and the bushes of wine-sweet-smelling yellow azalea, which we prize in our gardens, in full bloom. There were small dripping villages at intervals, and when we reached the one at the road head Sidney made himself known to the headman and asked if they could supply us with sixty fresh eggs to take to base camp. Pandemonium ensued, with villagers pursuing squawking hens in every direction. Result, six eggs only, rather a blow to our tightly planned food supply.

The people here are unlike those in any other part of Turkey. They are called the Laz, they have their own language, and they are far more like their near neighbours over the border in Georgia, being mostly fair with European features. We found them very friendly and helpful, and not yet accustomed to foreign mountaineers. They provided us with horses and several horsemen to transport our gear, and we set off on foot to the spot where Sidney had planned our base camp, on a high alp by a small lake. Here, above the treeline, with snow patches lingering around, purple rhododendron and yellow azalea gave way to a low bushy azalea with white flowers veined with green and many more familiar alpines. Not far above, to the south, was a moraine and small glacier leading up to a col, and from this col there rose to the east a steep ridge of mixed rock and snow rising to the summit, high, oh so high above, and usually swathed in mist, of Kaçkar Dağ itself.

We arrived at this camping place together with all the bulls, old and young, of the village herd, who had been separated from their cows and were being driven up to the high pastures for the summer. The herdsmen halted them just where we were pitching our tents and almost immediately pandemonium broke out, with all the dogs barking and all the bulls fighting each other, bellowing and milling around, as the big fellows took each other on while the younger ones all sought out others of the same age and size to fight.

At first we feared for ourselves and our tents, as they roared to and fro, and Sidney went over to a herdsman to ask what was going on. The bulls showed no interest in us, and the herdsman reassured us that it was normal procedure and would all soon be over. 'They are electing their president,' he explained. In view of the current political turmoil in Turkey we thought this was nicely phrased, and sure enough by the next day all was peace and harmony, the pecking order for the summer having been firmly established.

The weather was not kind to us in the Kaçkars. It rained incessantly, and from the glacier upwards the rain fell as snow. From the top of the col we could look south and see range upon range of mountains basking in hot sunshine. Our range was the barrier between the cool moist Black Sea air and the hot dry landscape that stretched away into central Turkey. We made several attempts at the summit, and on the last one Sidney and another of our party got within sight of it, but were turned back by the deep and unstable snow. That camp was the only place where I actually found mildew growing on my climbing boots!

I had always dreamed of one day getting to the Himalayas, but although I had been asked by friends to join their parties several times, the invitations had always been for September-October, just the vital beginning of the new opera season, when I could not possibly go. Then one spring day in 1983 the phone rang. It was Philippa Treadwell, an old mountain friend and a cousin of Sidney's, who had been to the Taurus and the Hakkâri and the Kaçkars with us. She asked me if I would like to join up with just herself and a Sikh woman friend of hers, Premalia, for a long trek to visit a little known kingdom called Zanskar in the western Himalayas. A couple of years before she and I had both read a fascinating book by French explorer and writer Michel Peissel, who had visited the country in 1976, and stayed there for months taking photographs and getting to know the people. There would be no problem about the dates for me as Philippa planned to go in mid-July and August during Zanskar's short summer. The country had rarely been visited and was unspoilt when Peissel was there; in fact he was reputed to be only the eighteenth foreigner ever to reach the capital Padum. The tiny kingdom, just 200 miles long, with 8,000 inhabitants living at an average altitude of more than 13,000 feet, lies in a Shangri La area protected all round by mountains and high passes. In 1983 it was in a sensitive zone, very near the Tibetan border where China had quite recently gobbled up a sizeable chunk of Indian territory, and where the two countries now had armies confronting each other. To get there before the tour guides discovered it was a chance too great to miss and I leapt at it.

Philippa, a seasoned Himalayan traveller, planned it all and discovered an amazingly cheap bucket-shop flight with Syrian-Arab Airways, which offered us return tickets to Delhi for just £190. Our overweight baggage, including tents, sleeping bags and bedding, was taken on board without a murmur and we reached Delhi safely and on time, to stay for a couple of nights with Premalia. We then took an overnight bus – the most uncomfortable vehicle I have ever ridden in – and drove from 5.00 p.m. to 8.00 a.m., starting off up the 'grand trunk road'. This was Kipling come to life, with its crowded scenes of donkey carts and camels and sacred cows, and people riding bicycles, pedalling rickshaws, driving battered old trucks and ancient buses like ours, all weaving our way steadily north. In the early hours we found ourselves climbing into the foothills of the Himalayas with a relay of young drivers each more reckless than the last, to be decanted in the mountain village of Manali.

Here Philippa had managed to make contact from England with an organisation grandly entitled International Trekkers. We hunted for it in narrow alleys and eventually ran it to earth on the first floor of a rickety chalet-style house. Then we had our first round with the manager, one Mr Chand. He was totally thrown by the arrival of three females of uncertain age (in fact all over fifty) asking for a team of porters and horses to trek north through Zanskar to the great monastery at Lamayuru. 'Impossible!' he kept repeating. 'Much too hard! Too long! Too dangerous!' There were nine passes between us and our goal, but Phil had allowed us plenty of time, two of us were mountaineers, and we were not worried about the route. We were worried as to whether we would ever get started though, because Mr Chand had a big German party to get on the road, and a couple of Italian climbers burst into his office while we were talking to him, and demanded a large number of porters and ponies to go and climb a major peak – all far more remunerative than we three women. For four days we went on clamouring at him, and eventually he found us three men, a pony man and five ponies, four to carry all our gear and food for seven people for twenty-eight days, the fifth because he said one of the ladies was bound to get tired and need to ride!

Manali was not geared for serious trekkers or climbers, and all the tinned food available was out of date, so someone had to do a long bus journey to get us the necessary supplies, but at last, for better or for worse, we were ready for the off. The first leg of the journey was to be by bus over the Rothang pass to a campsite at Darcha, where we were to liaise with our pony man. Mr Chand parted us with far more money than we had expected, knowing very well that he would never see us again, as we planned to go by bus from our last stop, Lamayuru, round to Kashmir and the lakes at Srinagar. We soon found that he had let us down in every possible way. It is the duty of a trek manager to equip the parties he sends out. We found that we had a Sirdar who spoke very little English and didn't know the way, a young 'cook' who had never cooked before (our proper cook having been given to the Italian mountaineers at the last moment), and a sixteen-year-old boy who had never been out of his village before. But our pony man, Tashi, who came to meet us at Darcha, was a treasure, and made the whole trip a success.

Philippa had a brand-new tunnel tent bought in Guildford, which the young man in the shop there had put up for her on the floor. Rule number one for camping is always stop and make camp before dark on your first night when you are not familiar with your equipment. We arrived at Darcha after dark to find the campsite half-flooded by heavy rain and a stiff breeze blowing. Poor Phil had a fearsome struggle with the new tent, which she was sharing with her friend Premalia. It was then we also discovered that we had no knives, five chipped mugs for seven people, no jugs for milk or water, a grotty cooking stove that had to be pumped all the time to get any pressure up, and worst of all, no rope. We had been told it was important to have a rope for use when fording rivers, and had asked Sirdar Norbu to be sure to have one, which he had failed to do. And our non-cook served just watery cabbage for supper, which occasioned a major row. So many other things went wrong at that first camp that Philippa was in two minds whether we should carry on. The final straw was when the ponies were being loaded, and four were piled high with all that Tashi would allow them to carry – about fifty kilos – and there was still a pile of stuff lying on the grass. After much argument, which was difficult as Tashi had no English, we got him to agree to take the riding saddle off the pony that had been intended for us, and load it with the remaining pile of gear. All round us were the most beautiful flowers, bushes of bright pink Himalayan rose, the fine unnamed mountains and snows we had come so far to see, and nothing was going to stop us now, so finally, at about midday, in cold monsoon rain, we actually set off.

The second night we reached a place where we had to cross a large and swollen river. We had been told we would find a 'ferry' for foot passengers, but the ponies could not use it so they would have to take another route round to a ford. After six hours of cold wet walking there was still nothing to be seen, until we spotted a steel cable crossing the water. This turned out to be our ferry and at last we understood why the ponies could not use it! It was a wooden crate suspended from the cable into which we climbed one at a time, to be pulled across by a man who had suddenly appeared on the far side! The ponies had arrived too, but they were on the far side of a deep wide torrent and it was far too dangerous for them to make the crossing before morning, when the snows above would have refrozen during the night and the water level dropped. They had all our food, sleeping gear and dry clothing on them, a depressing thought, as we were cold and wet. But all was not lost, because the friendly man who had pulled us over the river in the crate kept on repeating '*Oteli! Oteli!*' and pointing at a low round-walled pile of stones with a tarpaulin top, which turned out indeed to be shelter for weary travellers. This route seemed to be the main crossing into Zanskar during the short four months of summer. There was just room for Phil, Premalia and me to crawl into the *oteli* together with the friendly ferryman, who doubled as innkeeper. We sat leaning against the draughty drystone walls while he boiled a kettle on an amazing biscuit-tin stove and made us welcome hot tea and later cooked us rice flavoured with salt scraped from a block of rock salt. He let Phil and me share his small tent overnight, and Premalia had his son's, while he and a disconsolate Sirdar Norbu huddled in the *oteli* together with some Gaddi shepherds. These picturesque men in oatmeal-coloured homespun kilted skirts and tunics were members of a tribe whose job it was to come to the high places with their flocks during the summer. The rest of our boys were all across the water with the ponies and our precious bottle of medicinal whisky, which we could have done with! It was a freezing night, but next morning the ponies successfully made a very tricky crossing under their heavy loads to join up with us, the weather was fine, and we set off up the Shingu La pass.

We came upon one of the Gaddi shepherds, a handsome young man extraordinarily like Omar Sharif, reading a book by the track, and Premalia had a long talk with him about religion, as he told her he was studying the writings of his guru. She asked him, 'You are an intelligent young man, able to read and write. Are you satisfied with this lonely life up in the mountains?'

He gave us a lovely smile and replied, 'Yes. You see, God has given us just enough intelligence to enable us to care for our animals.'

We spent a night halfway up the pass, with a view of handsome nameless peaks, most of which were as yet unclimbed, then reached the summit at 16,500 feet the next day, in hot sunshine and deep soft snow, which was hard going for our courageous ponies. Mr Chand had sent our boys out without proper equipment and the poor cook had no dark glasses. Luckily I had a spare pair to give him before he was overtaken by the agony of snow blindness. Marmots whistled from the rocks, and gentians and primulas gave us the feeling that we were back in the Alps, but once over the top the scenery changed dramatically. We left the monsoon rains behind as they never cross the mountains into Zanskar, which has been described as 'the highest desert in the world'. It is all above the treeline, however it is no desert. The river we followed for several days was edged with flowers, edelweiss in profusion, many other alpines, pink cushion plants, great bushes of the pink wild roses, and joy of joys, beautiful Cambridge-blue Himalayan poppies.

After crossing the Shingu La the climate changed completely from monsoon rain to dry desert. Daytime temperatures reached eighty degrees Fahrenheit, but at night it could be freezing. We travelled down a long valley, branching off to go and sleep a night in a monastery called Phuktal, built in spectacular fashion on a sheer cliff overhanging a river. We shared the guestroom with some other travellers, including some scruffy pot-smoking hippies who were trading on the monks' hospitality. Premalia spent some time trying to convince our hosts that not all Westerners were drug addicts. After a meal of gritty rice and dahl, the monks put our group into a separate little side room and brought us bits of carpet to lie on. I was bitten all night, but Phil, lying beside me, never had a bite.

The Zanskari people are devout Buddhists devoted to the Dalai Lama, their language is a form of Tibetan, and they were governed from Tibet for some 800 years, until India decided to annex them in the nineteenth century. It was good having Premalia with us as she had long talks with the chief lamas, who showed us their library, and the old wooden roller printing presses on which they reprint their scriptures when necessary, and some lovely early wall paintings, all of which were not usually on view. Back at our camp, two large young Italian mountaineers with the tiniest donkey I have ever seen had arrived and pitched their tents next to us. The donkey, to which they were devoted, was in deep disgrace, because during the night he had slipped his hobbles and gone down to feast in the local headman's barley field, just not done in a country where people's tiny fields have to support them all the year round. The young men had paid the equivalent of £5 to get him back! They had bought him in Lamayuru, and were doing our route in reverse. We told them he could never get over the Shingo La pass, as he would sink without trace in the deep soft snow. 'Never mind,' they said cheerily, 'first we will carry him, and then we will carry the loads over!' As we were going in opposite directions we never found out how they got on.

We trekked for two days along the incredible gorges of the Zanskar River, traversing steep screes on the narrowest of tracks, where a false step would send pony or human being sliding inexorably down into the river to be swept away without trace. We were like ants in that huge landscape, and my admiration for our ponies grew and grew. The only time they were at all naughty was when a caravan came towards us and somehow they all had to squeeze past each other with their bulging loads on. Then the ponies would jostle and push, and our men had to hang onto their heads and tails to steady and steer them. It was terrifying on those huge near vertical sweeps of loose sand and stones, and my three mountaineering saints, St Bernard, St Christopher and St Antony of Padua, were bombarded with prayers for help! As ever they stood me in good stead, and our little caravan emerged safely onto easier ground as we neared our halfway mark, Padum, the small village capital of Zanskar.

We stayed for three nights at a delightful camping place there, with streams rushing down from the glaciers on Padma, the big mountain above us, and millers grinding their barley in a series of old stone waterwheels nearby, while their children played around us and looked after flocks of sheep and goats and their young.

The VIPs of Padum all came to greet us, and they turned out to be Indians sent in to fill positions such as chief of police (but there were no police), school teachers, a vet (though there was no doctor), and a bank manager, though we saw no bank and the Zanskaris rarely used currency. They were well-educated Kashmiris who were sent here for two-year stints of duty, and who loathed it: no electricity, no proper running water, no radio or TV, no postal service, no shops, just poor mud houses and eight months of harsh winter. It must have been awful for them, especially as the locals disliked them and had been known to throw policemen into the river! The Zanskaris never forget that India brought artillery into their unarmed country and bombarded their undefended little village capital. Their young king was away studying in India so we did not meet him, and later when Phil and I wanted to pay our respects to the old king at Zangla, our Sirdar absolutely refused to let us go, as the bridge to his palace across the Zanskar River, very long and of the swaying rope variety, was apparently too dangerous.

We were lucky enough to be visiting the great monastery of Karsha on the day of one of their big religious festivals, when they were playing the long Tibetan horns that take three people to handle, and which make a unique and unforgettable sound. After this Premalia decided to part from us, as she was more interested in Buddhist art than passes and had other monasteries she wanted to visit. We agreed to meet up again later on in Kashmir, and Phil and I went on our way with our four men and five ponies, who had now knit into quite a family.

The second half of the trek involved high camps amid wonderful mountain scenery, with mountains up to 22,000 feet in height. We crossed a series of easy high passes, while to our east were amazing views of untravelled gorges, through which mountain rivers thundered their way to swell the Indus and flow on into India. Our small party was swelled by three French travellers, two young Englishmen whom we had met at Darcha, and two groups of Zanskari traders, all with their caravans of ponies, donkeys and yaks. We also crossed paths with several Swiss and French parties, and the only British tour group that had reached Zanskar to date, the enterprising Exodus Company. By now we were all very short of food, and there was absolutely nothing to be bought in this poorest of countries, so our talk was often about food – gorgeous Parisian menus were dreamed up as we trudged. We also ran out of fuel for the Primus cooker, which I found good as we had to make sweet-smelling fires of dried shrubs and yak pats. (One large yak pat can cook a whole supper!) There was much gossip of accidents, all of people swept away crossing the rivers, which were exceptionally high after a hard winter. Some of it was untrue, but one very sad story turned out to be genuine. We heard it as we were crossing a river on a rickety wooden bridge, not strong enough for the ponies, who had to find a ford. Some weeks earlier a young Englishman trekking alone with his girlfriend reached this river in the evening, and not knowing that there was a bridge only a short distance further on tried to ford it and was swept away. With a heavy pack on he couldn't save himself and he drowned. His girlfriend was found sitting on the bank quite devastated, when by a miracle in that as yet mostly untravelled area an English party – I think it was an Exodus group – came by and was able to take her along with them.

This river was the beginning of our descent from the high mountains, and here the air was full of the scent of catmint, which grew in great clumps with pink bistorta. We never wanted to leave those lovely heights. Our companions all went their various ways, but Phil, who had masterminded our journey so brilliantly, had one more excitement in store. Instead of ending our journey to Lamayuru by the usual route, she had heard of a more rarely used track through some unmissable gorges, and although our horseman was not keen, for once she insisted and he agreed to go that way.

Almost as soon as we embarked upon the track through the Hannupatta gorges we realised why Tashi had not been keen to come that way. The gorges tower above the river in walls of yellow and grey and red rock, sometimes narrowing to strangulations, where there is room only for a narrow path built out on one side or the other, so that the ponies were continually having to ford the river as the path crisscrossed its way along. In one place there was no room for a path at all, and Tashi offered us the choice of swimming through the strangulation holding onto the ponies' tails or climbing steeply up over a rocky spur to rejoin the path lower down. Phil and I chose the latter, and came down to a place halfway through the gorges where someone had built a chorten, where you could thank the gods for safe passage so far and pray for their continued protection. In several places the ponies had to be unloaded as their loads stuck out too far and would have pushed them over the edge. Tashi had a very good way of gauging the width they needed. He would go ahead with arms akimbo, and if his elbow banged against the rock it meant we had to offload, and the men would carry the loads through until the path widened, then lead the ponies. There was a crisis when we met a trader with his caravan coming the opposite way. He was very nervous because he said the path a little further on had begun to fall away and he had been lucky not to lose a pony. Manoeuvring the two caravans past each other took good nerves. The heat meanwhile grew and grew towards noon, as the cliff walls reflected the sun's rays above us, and we began to feel claustrophobic and long for space and air. Eventually towards evening we were safely through, but Tashi had one more worry. The ponies were very thin as there had been no decent grazing for days. He went off to a little huddle of mud houses, and came back with some very poor straw for which he had had to pay an exorbitant sum. We at last found a cool and pleasant campsite beside a racing irrigation channel, and settled in for our last night of travel as we were due to reach Lamayuru the next day.

We owed much of the success of this trip to Tashi and the ponies. They were magnificent small tough creatures who walked along all day with no bridles or halters, had the whole of the Himalayas to roam in at night, but once Tashi had found them in the morning – and they did sometimes wander quite a way in search of anything edible – would walk straight back into camp with him and stand tranquilly to be loaded. The lead pony was black and very wise. I can still see him well ahead of the others topping the Sirsirla, our final 16,000-foot pass.

We spent three days in Lamayuru, and there our contract with our team ended. Tashi had to trek all the way back, and we left him with the ponies sitting by the roadside hoping for a client. The boys had enough money to hitchhike with us over into Kashmir (two days in lorries, much of the time battened down in the rear with assorted travellers, because it was illegal for lorry drivers to carry passengers, but there was no other way). After that I expect they went home by bus, but we had three blissful days at Srinagar in a houseboat on the Dahl Lake washing our clothes and eating too much. I shall never forget our arrival on board, filthy dirty after two days of lorry travel and weeks in tents, to be led by a white-coated manservant into what looked like a typical English drawing room and served tea and macaroons! Phil and I got the giggles, and the staff disapproved of us more than ever. The lush greenness and the mirror-like lake, the lotus flowers, and the kingfishers fishing from the rails of our houseboat, were a perfect finale to our amazing six weeks of high trekking. We met up with Premalia and all travelled back to Delhi by train, arriving with no money left to pay a taxi.

Those weeks remain a high watermark in my travel memories, and thanks to the 400 slides I brought back and the popular lectures they made up, the journey is still vivid and fresh.

It was the last true travelling I was to do, because I was about to lapse into tripperdom – or should it be tripperhood? See the next chapter!

Chapter Fourteen

On Becoming a Tripper

In his new *de Dillon Bouton*
Pa collided with some trippers.
Made them *aussi mort que mouton*
Laid them out as flat as kippers.
What a nuisance trippers are.
We must now repaint the car.

From my childhood. Provenance unknown.

I began becoming a tripper soon after the Zanskar trek. Always before when travelling with my parents, or with friends going off mountaineering with our tents, we had viewed the arrival of coach loads of trippers with a patronising mix of hilarity, pity and distaste. Such an assortment of shapes and sizes! Such awful unsuitable clothes! Poor things, hounded around by their tour guides! How ghastly! Never, never would we sink to such depths!

Oh the arrogance of the young and fit! I am now an addicted tripper. Thanks to the coach and other means of mechanical transport I have been able to travel all over the world. Thanks to tour guides I have seen and learned amazing things. I have been to places I could never have reached on my own. I have travelled sharing rooms and berths with many congenial and interesting people. And still I want more! Happy hours are spent browsing through the travel brochures that pour through my door. Where shall I go next year? North or south? East or west? The world is the oyster of the tourist these days, and by searching out those companies specialising in what is known as 'adventure travel' one can even reach remote wilderness areas.

However when friends say to me 'What a great traveller you are!' they are somewhat mystified when I tell them I am not really a traveller at all. I sit at the feet of the true travel writers, Simon Winchester, Colin Thubron, Rory Maclean, and the intrepid Dervla Murphy among others, and I thank them for the hours of happiness I have had reading their books. To be a real traveller is to spend weeks or months in a country, travelling on foot or by bicycle or local bus, learning as much as possible of the language, befriending and wherever possible staying with local people, even at the risk of developing dysentery or worse! If you have done all that, then you can claim to be a true traveller.

The first time I booked to travel abroad through a company was on a safari trip to Iceland, camping for two nights in each area to walk, and travelling in amazing old Mercedes lorries left behind after the war by the Americans and converted by the Icelanders into incredible vehicles that forded rivers, crossed the sands of the central desert, and tackled the corrugated black lava fields with equal abandon. One was our passenger bus, the other carried the tents and our field kitchen and food. This went on ahead and by the time we arrived big trestle tables had been set up, the cooking was underway, and we ate our meals in the open, then all helped to wash up.

I shall never forget our first night under black lava cliffs where a river of molten rock had flowed down from the Hekla massif many years ago, Landmannalauger, I think it was called. Although it was midsummer the temperature was nearly freezing out of the sun, in the stiff breeze, but the hardy natives told us that we must not miss the experience of bathing in the local hot springs, where the water flowed out from deep down under the lava. I grabbed bathing dress and towel and made my way to the edge of a small deep stream in which several people seemed to be enjoying themselves. As I was struggling to get into my bathing dress modestly under my very inadequate towel a stout German gentleman came along, dropped all his clothes on the bank beside me, and got into the pool stark naked. I dropped my towel and followed him into the water, which was divinely hot and relaxing. Next day we climbed a small mountain above our camp, and came down through a strange landscape of snow patches and steaming fumaroles. It was a good introduction to the unique Iceland experience.

I fell in love with the North on that trip, and a couple of years later found a Scottish company that was offering a cruise round Spitzbergen, or Svalbard as I prefer to call it, run by a Dutch naturalist society, the Plancius of Amsterdam. We flew to Oslo, then on to Tromso, and another 400 miles north to Longyearbyen, where we boarded a small ship aptly and we hoped truthfully named the *Waterproef*. She was an ex-tug, 140 feet long, with just room for twelve crew and twenty-four passengers, and although she rolled horribly she was very seaworthy. Our Dutch captain was highly experienced, and a lover of Svalbard. We also had with us a scientist and lecturer who was known as Ko, and who turned out to be an eminent scientist, Dr Ko de Korte. He had over-wintered on Svalbard, as had our second scientist guide, who had spent time investigating polar bears there. The crew, with one or two exceptions, were all young scientists, geologists, botanists and so on.

For me the expedition was amazing, and I loved every moment of it, though we in fact failed in almost everything we hoped to do and see. The polar bears were absent except for a sighting of one swimming, which looked just like two yellowish chunks of ice moving steadily through the water. One chunk if you looked carefully had a shiny black dot, which was the bear's nose. Their heads and rears are all that show when they swim, which they can do for hours on end. We went to a special place to see walruses, but got a mayday call and had to divert to a kayaker who was in trouble. A helicopter rescued him before we could get there, to the great disappointment of one of our passengers, a photojournalist, who had been getting all excited about the scoop he anticipated making. By the time we got back to the walrus place they were there but it was too dark to photograph them, though they did come curiously round the boat to look at us. And the beach where we were told we would surely see them next day was deserted – all we could see were the grooves in the gravel beach where their two-ton bodies had rested, and some fresh droppings. They were all under the water digging with their great tusks for the shellfish they live on. We went ashore at Smeerenburg, where the stark beach was littered with ruins and remains of the old whaling days, days when these waters teemed with whales, though we saw only two or three during our trip. There were also the sad shallow graves of many men who had died quite unnecessarily of scurvy. Had they only known it, they were surrounded by the edible plants of Arctic sorrel, rich in vitamin C, which could have saved their lives.

The weather had been cold and the sea rough, but there came a glorious day of sunshine when we were landed in our Zodiacs at Austfjordneset, to walk over the tundra and up onto a big glacier. The wardroom of the *Waterproef* was plastered with notices warning us of the dangers of polar bears and giving disturbing instructions about what to do should one come towards us. What you had to do was to walk backwards in the direction of the beach and boats, without hurrying or taking your eyes off the bear, and drop a piece of clothing such as a jacket so that the bear could worry that and give you more time to get away. We were all a little uneasy about this procedure as the shore and tundra was rough and boulder-strewn, and we had visions of falling flat on our backs while trying to remove a piece of clothing while simultaneously walking backwards. We were never allowed to land without at least two men with rifles, who would walk one in front and one behind us. On the beautiful day when we did our walk to the glacier this arrangement went a bit wrong, as we ended up in two groups, a larger one that stayed down on the tundra botanising, and the more energetic who climbed steeply up the ice snout onto the glacier. The tundra in summer is a kaleidoscope of greens and reds and silvery reindeer moss, with saxifrages and many alpines including the yellow Arctic poppy, and we were happily pottering about botanising when one of the ship's crew, who had been with the first group, came dashing down and shouted out that there had been an accident. Theo, one of the student staff who had been appointed to carry a rifle that day, had tripped over it and fallen on the ice, breaking his leg in two places, but luckily avoiding shooting himself in the process. Men were rushing back to the ship – two hours' walk away – to collect a stretcher, and a rescue helicopter had been summoned. The stretcher was needed because the glacier where Theo had fallen was too steep for the helicopter to land, so he would have to be carried up to more level ground. I was by this time on my own, and there was no one with a gun to be seen, so I joined up with another passenger who was also alone, and we walked back to the ship together hoping no bear would choose this time to turn up. Poor Theo was evacuated very efficiently, and we all heaved sighs of relief over a very late supper. I failed to write my diary fully as I kept going to sleep.

The weather turned very rough and even the most hardened of us missed several meals. When it cleared twenty-four hours later we had another shore walk at Sorgfjord, the highlight of which was coming on a ptarmigan family so tame that we could almost stroke them. There was a mother with eight large chicks sunbathing on a rock, their pure white winter feathers still speckled with summer's soft brown. We were told they were one of the few birds that over-winter on Svalbard.

I think it was the night after when the captain called a meeting. He wanted to propose something rather special to us — he described it as 'a little adventurous' — but if any one of us had the slightest doubt or felt it was too risky he would not do it. His proposal was to attempt to circumnavigate Svalbard, a thing he had never done, going right round Nord Austland, the most northerly island of the archipelago and on southeast to the remote Barents and Edge islands. We were all in favour, except for one mystery man, a Brit, I am sorry to say, who had the best cabin on the ship, only emerged to eat, and never went on shore once during the whole trip. However, he was overruled, and as the weather seemed favourable we set off. That night was something I shall never forget. We were passing north of the Seven Islands off Nord Cap, at a latitude of 80.50 north, sailing in an oily smooth sea surrounded by rocky islets. The sun barely dipped below the horizon, and on the other side a full moon rose, creating an amazing blend of light. Ahead there was a strange yellow glow in the sky created by light reflected from the permanent ice pack, and one could dimly see a dark bar, the low shoreline of Storöya Island where we were to land tomorrow. The moonlight made a brilliant path across the mirror surface of the sea, and our constant companions the fulmar petrels flew steadily alongside. None of us went to bed that magical night.

The next morning we were landed by Zodiac on Storöya. Whizzing through ice floes in a Zodiac is one of my favourite things, but getting down into them off the *Waterproef* was a performance. There was just a very basic rope ladder that was thrown over the ship's rail, and climbing down it clad in long boots, waterproof trousers, an enormous Mae West jacket, with two cameras, one hanging on each side, and a pair of binoculars, was tricky, especially as the Zodiac and the ship were both moving with the swell. On Storöya we found a dark shingle beach, a shallow freshwater lagoon with a pair of red-throated divers on it, then an ice cap we were approaching, when we heard a long blast on the ship's siren. This meant *get back on board as soon as possible*. The worst had happened. The wind that had been blowing from the west and holding back the ice pack had now veered round and was beginning to blow the ice towards us. Svalbard is surrounded by pack ice all winter. It was now September, and our small ship had no ice protection whatsoever. There followed some anxious days. It got rough and windy, and soon we had ice floes all round us. I was sharing with a nice Scotswoman, and our two-berth cabin was on the lower deck right forward on the starboard side. Every time we hit an ice floe we felt as if it was coming in onto our pillows. We got to know that when the engine was cut completely and we were just drifting it meant that there were floes all around and the crunching would begin. Next morning we got up to complete silence, to find we were in dense fog, moving at about three miles an hour through dark oily green water. It was uncanny to be moving so silently and sightlessly with only the slopping of the water against our bow and the occasional crunch as we met a small floe. Ko gave us two brilliant lectures that day, while the captain made five attempts to get through the ice in different directions, not helped by Svalbard Radio, which kept announcing that there was no ice where we were. We could not get down the Hinlopen Straights because a strong headwind got up, which eventually blew the fog away but brought more and heavier pack ice. We were not allowed on the bridge – usually a favourite lookout point – because the captain and mate were straining to see oncoming ice floes, though once we were called up on deck to watch a huge iceberg glide by. At last we got clear, the wind dropped, and we were able to backtrack and escape the oncoming ice pack. The first thing we did was to anchor in a sheltered spot for several hours to give the captain some sleep.

The weather at last relented and gave us one more perfect day of trekking. Because of the permafrost, when the snow and ice melts in the summer the water cannot sink down so it forms great shallow pools and lagoons through which one is wading for much of the time. We were landed in a sandy bay from which we climbed up over a headland, picnicked in warm sunshine, then went on down to the far shore where a very curious young reindeer came to investigate us. He went round and round us in circles, and seemed to enjoy being photographed and talked to. The Svalbard reindeer are very small and often more solitary than their bigger European cousins. Meanwhile the *Waterproof* came round the headland to collect us, and we walked several miles in low sunlight along the shore, watching curiously shaped small ice floes drifting in clear blue water and marvelling at the purity of the air and the crystalline clarity of the water, until we met the Zodiacs that had come to pick us up.

I had my sixty-ninth birthday during that trip, and it was Rinie our young Dutch guide's birthday too, so we had 'Happy Birthday' sung to us in Dutch at supper. On our last night there was the captain's dinner with lengthy speeches in various languages. Our trip was considered to have been a failure, but for me it was a marvellous voyage, which confirmed my love of the Arctic.

My eighty-second birthday party was in China, at a Tang dynasty song-and-dance show in Xian. I was on a four-week Silk Road tour via Kashgar and Kyrgysstan to the ancient cities of Bokhara and Samarkand – a journey that needs a book to itself!

All the time I was enjoying being a tripper I was also growing old, and finding that old age has many compensations. Kindly nature attunes us and causes our bodies to tell us in no uncertain words what we can no longer do. The very thought of getting up at 4.00 a.m. to climb a mountain now fills me with horror, but in no way detracts from the pleasure of reliving old climbs. Getting old, I have decided, is all about learning to let go. In return there is time for many things, reading, poetry, walking, just looking at trees and flowers and views, which there was no time for before. And when I look back on these recollections I realise how many valuable things I have left out.

About Men. And Cats. And the Voice

Now that I seem to be gathering up the threads of my memories I must rectify some serious omissions.

Dear men, I owe you a great apology. Any woman's memoirs

should be full of relationships and steamy memories. Mine I fear will disappoint. I like men, have worked more with them than with women, and have had several happy and comfortable relationships that I treasure. Perhaps it was losing two young loves in the war that made me feel that men came and went but music was always there. Perhaps it was because I was the child of a split marriage that whenever I thought seriously of marrying I remembered my parents' misery and dreamed of prison bars. Who knows? Until well into middle-age I dreamed of finding the right man. Sometimes I still do!

Poetry was precious to me all my life, with Victoria Sackville-West's *The Land* my mother's and my lifelong bedside book.

Another of the great pleasures of life for me has been cats, especially in my later years. I believe it was an early monk who wrote:

> For I will consider my cat Jeoffry...
> For God has blest him in the variety of his movements,
> For there is nothing sweeter than his peace when at rest.
> For I am possessed of a cat surpassing in beauty
> From whom I take occasion to bless Almighty God.

The row of little tombstones in the garden grows and each time it is a new heartbreak, but always one starts again with some new enchanter or enchantress.

SINGING

Only after an interval of many years did I realise that the EOG period from 1947 to 1950 was the pivotal time of my life. It was a confused and emotional period full of highs and lows, and it left me with a complete lack of self-confidence. Always before, in my days with the band, I had had the support of Johnnie, who was a sort of Svengali figure, and who always made me believe I could do anything. By the end of 1949 I had lost all hope of ever becoming a great, or even a good, singer. I doubted my voice, my technique, and most of all my talent.

Unfortunately I bottled all this insecurity up and couldn't bring myself to talk about it. I was afraid to invite criticism because I was terrified of what I might hear. I was frozen in a sort of cowardly paralysis.

Now, on looking back and re-reading press notices and letters of appreciation which I had quite forgotten about, I realize that I was not the terrible failure I felt myself to be, indeed I must have had considerable promise. I lately came upon Audrey Christie's note written in July 1947 after my debut in *The Rape of Lucretia*. She wrote:

> "I came out after the first performance to congratulate you, but found you had already flown. In case I don't see you before tonight, I want to send you my very best wishes for your second performance and to tell you how enormously impressed I was by your very charming first performance. I'm afraid it must have been a great ordeal taking on such a difficult part at such short notice and I do think you did it most excellently. Both you and your voice were so pretty, fresh and young, and I overheard several very nice comments. Well done. Audrey Christie."

I think with the wisdom of hindsight that had I made a different decision in 1947 when Mr and Mrs Christie both invited me to come back to Glyndebourne for the 1948 season, and I refused their offer because I wanted to stay with the English Opera Group, the whole course of my life might have been different, although it could not have been more interesting than the path on which I eventually found myself.

Unfortunately it took me several years to realize that Mme de Reusz was not the teacher for me. My diaries of that period are full of "sang badly", "Voice bad", and only very occasionally a tentative "I think I was a bit better today".

The upturn came when, convinced I had something dire wrong with my vocal chords, I went to Ivor Griffiths, the doyen of throat specialists who was in the wings at the Royal Opera House whenever the great and the glorious had voice problems. He gave me a salutary ticking off and told me there was nothing wrong with my vocal chords. 'Go home,' he said. 'Forget all about technique and just sing!' My last singing teacher was another retired Italian tenor who lived in Geneva. And with him I found myself working happily back on the same lines as with Dino Borgioli. I used to save up and go and stay for ten days or so in a very cheap hotel I discovered and have a lesson every day. It was at this time that I think I sang my best opera performances, in roles like Constanze in Mozart's *Il Seraglio* and Fiordiligi in *Cosi fan Tutte* for the Opera Players.

By this stage I had realised that the Royal Opera House, the Metropolitan and the Scala were not for me. There comes a stage in all our careers when we cease to be 'promising' and, unless we are by then at the top, we reach a level plateau where we make our little niche. I was lucky because I had realised way back, when organising the Wigmore Hall lunch-hour concerts, that I enjoyed running things. Also I was developing a great interest in casting young singers and watching them develop. In the early days of Opera Players I sang and sang, but gradually and quite naturally we began putting in other singers, so that eventually I sang only if no one else was available. Our music director Peter Gellhorn said to me one day, 'With this company singers blossom', which gave me enormous pleasure.

Looking back on what I have written about my early days in opera, I feel I may have given the wrong impression of my feelings about Britten's music. Although there is some of it that I personally will never like, much of his work is sheer genius. He set words to music so perfectly that even well known passages such as 'Blow, bugle, blow! Set the wild echoes flying!' that could so easily in song have clashed with one's love of the poem, set by Ben never did. His music matched them perfectly, not just in English, but in some of his early works such as the Michelangelo sonnets in Italian and the French *Les Illuminations*. Much of *Peter Grimes* is pure magic, as is *A Midsummer Night's Dream*. Unfortunately my early experience of his work was with *The Rape of Lucretia* and *Albert Herring*, both of which are in my humble opinion patchy musically, and *The Little Sweep*, which has its best music in the audience songs.

When I was with Ben, I used to get the strange feeling that he was some sort of zombie, through whom music flowed sometimes powerfully for good, sometimes powerfully for evil. At least two people I knew who were sensitive in psychic matters said that they could sense a strong evil presence during performances of certain of his works, in particular *The Turn of the Screw*. I have sometimes wondered if it was an awareness of this that turned him to writing his church operas and much church music in his later life. It was only some years after I had left the EOG that I was able to appreciate the full scale of Ben's genius uninfluenced by his strong personality.

How strange and interesting life is. And now it is time to sum up with a brief account of the spiritual journey, which I believe is what we are all on, whether we like it or not, and to tell about the various teachings that have helped me along my way. The words 'ragbag' and 'hotchpotch' are far too crude for such a treasury. Rather I think of what soprano Margaret Ritchie taught me about learning to sing from many different sources: 'My dear, you pick a flower here and a flower there until you have a perfect bouquet.'

Chapter Fifteen

Faith and the Spiritual Journey

'Imagination is more important than knowledge, for while knowledge points to what there is, imagination points to all there will be.'

Einstein

The last chapter, and much the hardest to write. It's odd that when I reread these memoirs I find that I have written least about that which matters much the most and has been with me all of my long life – a firm belief that I am here on a journey of which this life is only a small part. The very fact of being a living and conscious being is such a great miracle and mystery that for me it presupposes the existence of a supreme spirit who inaugurated what is going on here. Perhaps the reason I have written so little about faith is that I feel strongly that my physical and spiritual life coexist and are part and parcel of a total experience, so that when I write about daily life I am writing about my belief at the same time.

I don't remember at any time having doubted the existence of a supreme spirit. It's the 'How? Why? Where? When?' that has occupied so much of my thinking time, as I am still the same small child who got into trouble in divinity class at school for asking awkward questions. These questionings, and to a lesser extent the problems of the opera company with which I worked for fifty-six years, are the two threads that have formed the warp and weft of my life's tapestry.

It was Buddhism that launched me into spiritual thinking, when my Scottish grandmother, one of the early theosophists, gave me *Esoteric Buddhism* and *Mystic Christianity* to read, and I felt instantly at home

407

and comfortable with them. I still love the Buddhist concept of our Western 'big bang', which for them is a gentler process. According to their teaching we have just left the Kali Yuga, the Fourth Age of iron and darkness and densest matter, near the lowest point of the great Wheel of Life, which was set in motion by the breath of God. They believe that in the beginning nothing existed except the Supreme Being. Then He breathed out life into inert matter and the Wheel of Life began to turn and the process of evolution started. There are seven great ages, the first three being on the way down – the inevitable devolution, as I see it, while pure spirit divided and subdivided itself – bringing into being the Angels and Archangels, and all the heavenly host of our Christianity – until finally the infinite complexity of matter and spirit as we know them now was reached and mankind came on the scene. The Fourth Age is the turning point, though it is said that we are not yet quite at the bottom of the dark times in which we now find ourselves. We will then slowly begin to re-ascend, as God draws in his breath, until we return to the complete purity and oneness from which we came. We all need to make these pictures to express to ourselves the inexpressible, and I like this one, which was derived from my early readings.

By the time I reached my early twenties I was reading avidly, authors varying from Ouspensky and Steiner to Madame Blavatsky, Tagore and Krishna Murti. The next event that influenced my thinking came about by what seems to have been pure chance, and it didn't happen until after the war. I was living in London, but when I went home one weekend my mother told me of a very interesting man who had come to value our house. While he was looking round he noticed the collection of books given me by the friend who had been killed at Arnhem. He remarked on them to my mother, who told him they were mine, whereupon he handed her a piece of paper, which he said might interest me. It contained details of a society called the Order of Hidden Masters, which I joined, and stayed with until its closure years later. The OHM was an anonymous teaching group that sent out lectures to its members. There was no personal contact at any time, though we each had a special teacher with whom we corresponded regularly. The aim of the order was to introduce us to all the great beliefs and philosophies and religions that mankind has created in the search for truth. It was completely unbiased, teaching that all ways to God are equally valuable and to be respected. A principle of the teachings was that science and religion are converging and will ultimately be seen to be one. The OHM taught that the ultimate answer would be found to be of the greatest simplicity – 'as above, so below' they taught us, one great all-pervading spiritual principle-cum-mathematical equation that will make all plain. Stephen Hawking at the end of *A Briefer History of Time* writes:

> If we do discover a complete theory, it should be understandable in broad principle by everyone, not just a few scientists. Then we shall all, philosophers, scientists, and just ordinary people, be able to take part in the discussion of why it is that we and the universe exist. If we find the answer to that, it would be the ultimate triumph of human reason – for then we would know the mind of God.

And here, from a very different approach, is a quotation from 'Hymn to Matter' by that great Jesuit thinker and writer Teilhard de Chardin:

> Blessed be you, mighty matter, irresistible march of evolution, reality ever new-born, you who, by constantly shattering our mental categories, force us to go ever further and further in our pursuit of the truth. Blessed be you, universal matter, unmeasurable time, boundless ether, triple abyss of stars and atoms and generations; you who by overflowing and dissolving our narrow standards of measurement reveal to us the dimensions of God.

I find it very interesting that at this precise time, when scientists are so occupied with the research of dark matter, so many of our best writers, Tolkien and Philip Pullman to mention only two, are writing mind-stretching works of science fiction, and exploring the mysteries of dark matter in their own original and imaginative ways.

It must have been fairly soon after I joined the OHM that I had a strange and frightening experience. Although I used to have a deep fear of black magic and evil psychic forces, I had been dabbling with friends in playing planchette, and reading about candle exercises that could reveal one's past incarnations. I decided to try the candle experiment in my bedroom one night, so I placed a lighted candle in front of my triple mirror on the dressing table and sat down to concentrate and gaze at the flame. The first part, seeing the candle's aura, which is just the rainbow halo around the flame, went all right. The second part, when scenes from past incarnations should appear in the mirror, brought no result. I was reading Joan Grant's book *Winged Pharaoh* at the time, which I found frightening – nevertheless I went to bed and fell deeply asleep. My mother was woken in the middle of the night by a loud crash from my bedroom. She rushed along to see what had happened, and found me standing in the middle of the room shaking with terror, while the central panel of my triple mirror had been lifted from its hinges and crashed facedown on the dressing table. I spent the rest of the night with her, and when we tried to replace the panel into its hinges the next morning we found that it was far too heavy for either of us to lift single-handed. The two outer panels of the triple mirror were still standing in place, and I could not possibly have lifted the large central panel clear of them on my own. Who, or what, had done it? I took this as a very clear message from 'the other side' – wherever that may be – not to dabble in serious matters for which I was in no way prepared.

Years ago when I went to *Fiddler on the Roof* in the West End I was delighted to find that the Fiddler chatted with God all the time in a very homely way, exactly as I do. I have the strong feeling that I am addressing God personally and talking intimately with Him, while at the same time realising that my petty complaints and requests must be being fielded by someone way down in the hierarchy of the heavenly host! I have always felt strongly that I have a 'guardian angel', who has been landed with the task of guiding my very wandering footsteps. He/she acts as an intermediary, and in grey times I imagine reaching up through the clouds to take his/her comforting hand.

This brings me to the puzzling question of sex and the higher beings! To me it seems that the very highest beings must combine within themselves all the attributes of what we call male and female, just as God, the supreme being, does. No need to be two to bring life into being. I came across a teaching somewhere during my OHM studies – I wish I could remember in which belief it originated and am fairly sure it was the Upanishads – that seemed to me an interesting theory. It taught that every soul seed that emanates from the divine originally contained both male and female elements. But at a certain stage came the Fall of Man, the great separation, when Eve sprang from the rib of Adam and their soul seed was split into two parts. Each of us is now either the male or the female part, and that is why throughout history men and women have searched to find their 'better half', that perfect partner, whom we all feel deep down within ourselves exists somewhere for us. Very rarely are the two halves of the same soul seed in incarnation together, and even more rare is it for them to find each other. When they do, we get the great love stories of history, Romeo and Juliet, Héloïse and Abelard, Beatrice and Dante. The teaching goes on that all soul seeds will eventually reunite to make whole and perfect beings. That is, unless someone has become so consistently evil that the tiny spark of divinity in us all, our soul seed, can no longer live with its body, and returns to the divine. That is when we say that so-and-so has lost his soul; and the empty husk of his body will just wither away at death. I like this idea, which implies that there is no eternal fiery furnace or perpetual punishment awaiting the wicked – they just are no more. It does not however help one to understand or accept the unbelievable evil that is in some people. I believe that forces of evil exist here on our planet, where everything material must have its converse, darkness and light, heat and cold, good and bad (this despite many arguments with various Christian Scientist friends!). I also believe that the great wars of the future will be fought in men's minds.

Thinking of the Fall of Man reminds me of a staged performance of *Paradise Lost*, which I saw recently – a brilliant and moving production with a young Adam and Eve played stark naked until after she had eaten the apple. Two angels came to order them out of Paradise, and handed each of them a battered suitcase. In the cases were shoddy modern clothes, which they put on clumsily to hide their newfound shame and embarrassment, before walking slowly away hand-in-hand through the great gates of the Garden into the distance.

I do not come from a church-going family. Nevertheless my mother was one of the most spiritual beings I have known. Every night she knelt by her bed like a little child to say her prayers, but she was a very private person, and church ritual and dogma distressed her. I had not gone to church regularly since my schooldays, but some years after my parents died, when world events were particularly dark and depressing, I suddenly felt that as a believer I must stand up and be counted. I began going to church again, and found no problem in integrating the teachings of Jesus into my mixed bag of beliefs, drawn from many faiths, but all strikingly alike in their basic principles. What matters most is whether one believes in the existence of something greater than oneself or not. And in this context, I must say here and now that I do not believe we are such a deeply irreligious society as many people believe. Many of the young are searching desperately for something they can believe in. Books like *The Da Vinci Code* inspire heated debate among young and old, and few people deny the existence of something great 'out there'. Many of the young have much more open and enquiring minds than they would have had in my young day, and people who would have squirmed with embarrassment or dried up completely not so long ago, are comfortable discussing the existence of some supreme intelligence, even if they find the word 'God' a little inhibiting. The old structures are being broken down, but I believe something very valuable and suited to the age we live in will come from all the lonely personal searches for truth that are in progress in our so-called civilised societies, where the young in particular seem to have nothing that they can cling onto.

It was a long time before I came to believe properly in the power of prayer. I used to feel that I had been born with so much that I had no right to ask for anything more for myself personally. Then there came a time during my mother's illness when I almost reached breaking point and I prayed desperately for help. It came almost at once in the form of a feeling of strength and calm, and since then I have always put serious problems into prayers.

In old age I miss some of my early dreams. The loveliest always involved flying – making the first act of faith and willpower needed to lift one from the ground, flying through the house and round the rooms, and – the final joy – out of an open window and away into the night (it was always night in my outdoor flying dreams). A recurring dream of my youth was that I was flying high in an evening sky at that magical time when the sun has just set, leaving a glow of gold all over the western sky, which turns through blue to purple in the east. The peace and serenity were complete as I flew alone in silence towards the night sky ahead. Suddenly I would be above a hideous dark city with huge viaducts reaching up to draw me down towards streets crowded with traffic and noise. I would fight to stay above it but would inevitably be drawn down into the blackness and turmoil, and would wake up. I have an idea that this dream spoke of my resistance to reincarnating into the dark Fourth Age on planet Earth, and sometimes when driving home late from engagements alone on a dark winter's night and getting lost in a big city – which has happened to me very often – I have felt I was actually living my nightmare, and have taken a firm grip on the steering wheel to master it! Two other recurring dreams that have been laid like ghosts were of falling from a great height, which climbing dealt with, and a terror of appearing in public, which was also quickly routed. Sadly, I no longer dream of flying like a bird; instead I now fly a small aeroplane in my sleep, a tiny sort of one-seater affair in which I can take off and land perfectly, though in real life I have always been rather nervous of flying!

The most profound experience in my spiritual life came some time in my middle years as the result of a terrifying recurring nightmare I had had since childhood. It was as if all the powers of evil, the cruelty of torturers, the horror of inquisitors, the pure malevolence of wickedness, were gathered into one terrible presence that I would wake to find staring at me from the door of my bedroom. It was a faceless, formless being of the blackest darkness in front of which I would start to shrivel up until I felt I was about to be engulfed forever. I would say the Lord's Prayer over and over again, and sign the protective five-pointed star over myself, and gradually the presence would withdraw, leaving me shattered and sleepless. Then one night as the dream was beginning I remember saying to myself, 'Don't be such a worm! Don't allow this Thing to terrorise you! Get up and face it and find out what it is!' The hardest thing I have ever done in my whole life was the effort I made to stand up – mentally – to confront the terror. I did so, and immediately was flooded by an extraordinarily powerful sense of pity for it, which came into me as I remember it through the top of my head. I stretched out my arms towards the dark presence, and as I did so the pity changed to love – such an amazing love, which filled and overflowed me and most certainly came from some source far above myself; and as I moved towards it – there was nothing there. Absolutely nothing. I have never had that nightmare since, and I have never talked about that night to anyone, because the power of the pity and the love that it was given me to experience still moves me to tears. It gave me some inkling of what the angels may suffer as they watch our misdoings here on Earth.

If there is one thing I truly hope, it is that wherever I find myself in the afterlife, there is laughter and wit and jokes! I somehow feel that these have all been written out of our scriptures by men with little sense of humour. After listening to Rabbi Lionel Blue I feel much in sympathy with the Jewish faith, and I feel sure that Jesus and his friends must have met with many funny situations and had some good laughs together during all their adventures. What a pity that they were edited out at some later date! I would have so liked to have met the anonymous seventeenth-century nun who wrote the following prayer – one of my bedside ones:

> Lord, Thou knowest, better than I know myself, that I am growing older and will one day be old.
> Keep me from getting talkative and particularly from the fatal habit of thinking I must say something on every subject and on every occasion.
> Release me from craving to try to straighten out everybody's affairs.
> Make me thoughtful, but not moody; helpful, but not bossy. With my vast store of wisdom it seems a pity not to use it all, but Thou knowest, Lord, that I want a few friends at the end.
> Keep my mind free from the recital of endless details; give me wings to get to the point.
> Seal my lips from my many aches and pains. They are increasing, and my love of rehearsing them is becoming sweeter as the years go by.
> I ask for grace enough to listen to the tale of others' pains. Help me to endure them with patience.
> Teach me the glorious lesson that occasionally it is possible that I might be mistaken.
> Keep me reasonably sweet. I do not want to be a saint, some of them are hard to live with; but a sour old woman is one of the crowning works of the devil.
> Help me to extract all possible fun out of life. There are so many funny things around us and I do not want to miss any of them. Amen.

Many faiths have much fun in them, and I can't resist telling one of my favourite stories because it is an Arab one, and comes from devout Muslim believers whom we in the West tend to identify only with terrorism these days.

Imagine a camel caravan camped in the desert. As the men sit around the fire, a little boy asks his father why camels have such an unorthodox method of reproduction. Well, says the father, it was like this.

When God had finished creating the Earth, he sat back to survey his handiwork, and he was pleased. 'It's beautiful,' he said to himself, as he admired the mountains and seas and the great forests and plains. But after he had been looking for a little while, he began to think that there was something missing. 'It's Life,' he said. 'It needs Life.' So he went back to the drawing board and he created all the living things that are on the Earth, from the birds to the fishes, and from the smallest flea to the greatest whale. And when he was finished he placed them all in their proper places on earth and in the sea and the air. Then he sat back again to contemplate what he had done, and this time he said: 'That's perfect!' But after he had been looking for a time a dreadful thought struck him. 'These creatures I have created are mortal!' he said to himself. 'They will die in time, and I shall have to start all over again. That won't do. They must be able to reproduce themselves.' So he went back to the drawing board for a third time and he designed reproductive organs for every single living creature on the earth. And when he had finished, he summoned all the creatures to come and be given their genitalia. The donkey got there first because he is both greedy and curious, and he chose some organs that were rather too big for him. The creatures came and went all day, and by evening there was no one else waiting, but there was still one pair of reproductive organs left unclaimed on the table. And God said in a terrible voice: 'SOMEONE HASN'T BEEN!' The donkey, who had been watching all day piped up: 'Yes, Lord, it's the camel. He is standing on the edge of the desert with his head in the air snorting and making angry camel noises.' God said, 'Go and fetch him.' So the donkey trotted off, but soon came back alone. 'Lord, he doesn't want to come!' he said. God said, 'Go back and tell him to come at once!' Again the donkey trotted off, and again he came back alone, and said, 'Lord, he said he is not interested and won't come!' God said in his terrible voice, 'Go and order that camel to come at once OR ELSE!' The donkey rushed off and this time he came back with the camel striding along with his head in the air snorting and making angry camel noises. When he reached the table the camel looked down his nose at the pair of organs that were left and said, 'I don't want anything to do with those!' and he turned his back on God and marched off into the desert with his head in the air. And God was so angry that he picked up the pair of organs and threw them after the retreating camel, where they stuck to his backside the wrong way round. And that is how they have been ever since.

I do not think this story is in the Koran! I think I came across it in a book called *The Lost Camels of Tartary* and am most grateful to the author for much gentle pleasure.

I have been thinking – in the shower and out of reach of paper and pencil – about the meaning of the words 'eternity' and 'infinity', and about the extraordinary limitations of the human mind. We live imprisoned within our three dimensions, so everything for us has to be before or after, above or below, and it is impossible to visualise something that has no beginning or end. We crawl along a time tunnel from the past to the future, and know only the present. Our consciousness can function only in one place, though we may be dimly aware that there are other places. Just as I was beginning to feel at home with the Buddhist wheel and a circular pattern for everything, along comes the modern theory that the time-space continuum is somehow flat and in superimposed layers, like those delicious *mille feuilles* pastries. My mind has not yet accommodated itself to that concept. Or to the one that time itself does not move – it is always there, all of it, and it is we who move through it. Try as we will, it is well nigh impossible to visualise something that goes on forever and is everywhere. Even in the short time it has taken to get out of the shower and find a Biro, these thoughts, so lucid when they first came to me, have become muddied. The very act of thinking seems to come between the original meaning and the words to write it down. But whether we like it or not we are part and parcel of eternity and infinity. And I can reach outer space in no time at all – in my mind's eye!

I have tried, wherever possible, to avoid the use of the word 'religion', because it has become sadly divisive. It has been written that 'Religions divide, where spirituality seeks to unite.' The great world faiths, which all originated in pure spirituality, have too often developed into manmade power structures, top-heavy with dogma and riven by ridiculous arguments about trivia. If the angels have managed to retain any sense of humour over the ages, how they must laugh at us – when they are not weeping. As I write, the 200th anniversary of Charles Darwin is being celebrated, and the old bitter argument between creationists and evolutionists has been rekindled. As one who has always believed in the evolutionary scientific approach to creation, and who yet believes in a supreme being, I have sometimes been lost for words to explain my beliefs to creationists. Bishop Tom Butler put it perfectly in a nutshell when, talking on Radio Four recently, he said, 'God created the universe to create itself.'

The great conundrum is how to find for ourselves some sort of a framework to support us on our diverse spiritual journeys, because in this finite and crowded world we all need a firm moral structure if we are not to lapse into total anarchy. We are born with an innate sense of right and wrong, of what is decent and what is not, a sort of natural conscience that only self-violation can override. From whence does this inborn conviction come if not from some far higher source than ourselves? To me it is one of the greatest arguments for the existence of God – that, and the exceeding beauty of the planet we live on, and the great works of art created by man.

True scholars of all schools, religious, scientific and philosophical, will shoot me down in flames for these various rambling thoughts and readings out of which I have constructed my particular frame. It may be only a humble Zimmer, but it has supported me well on the way, and I am still working on it. My great hope is that I shall not be excommunicated from the very pleasant country parish in which I live should any of my neighbours ever come to read these words!

I am lucky to have lived an amazingly rich and interesting life, and my work has enabled me to take part in what must be among the most satisfying of artistic experiences, seeing an opera production through from the audition stage to the eventual performance, as young singers grow from tentative newcomers into a team, and design and costumes all come together, and the music gains power at every rehearsal, until all the diverse elements fuse together to create a powerful whole.

I have touched only on some of the multitude of ideas that have inspired – and beguiled – me during this episode of my spiritual journey. The journey has only just begun, as I count myself a very 'young' soul with everything yet to be untangled and revealed. When atheist friends tease me and tell me I am heading for a bitter disappointment, I remind them that should they be right I would no longer be here to be disappointed. But I hope and believe that dying is going to be the biggest adventure of all. I think of St Francis of Assisi's lovely prayer that begins 'Lord make me an instrument of thy peace' and ends 'for it is in dying that we awaken', thus fulfilling the words of Wordsworth at the beginning of the book, 'Our birth is but a sleep and a forgetting.'

In these dark days of January and February 2009, when our whole world seems likely to collapse around us, the words of that great and wise woman Dame Julian of Norwich ring in my ears, and with her I firmly believe that somehow, sometime, in the end, 'All shall be well, and all shall be well, and all manner of thing will be well.'

Moving On

My dream of perfect dying
Is at the foot of some great mountain
To slip quietly out of my body and to climb
In warm afternoon sunshine
Up through dark forests of pine and larch and fir
Where the air is heavy and hot-scented with resin
Where squirrels dart and black woodpeckers chatter
And reticent small forest flowers hide,
To climb up slowly through the warm sweet air
Little streams filtering through the moss and glittering
On ancient shaggy boulders,
Up and up steeply, alone, without fatigue or fear
Until I come out to the great green Alps
That stretch upwards forever
Where the winds blow keen and icy streams
Run crystal-clear from the high snows above.
Where sounds of distant bells from the far valley
Join comfortable bells of nearby summer cows
Placid, gentle and undemanding

Happily chewing their rich flowery grass
Gentian and primula and woolly edelweiss
While nostril-twitching tang of byre and midden
Reminds me of the gentleness of milk
After stark climbs.
On up and up
Alone, without fatigue, with energy
Tingling throughout my being as I reach
A sudden flash of blue among the stones,
A burning blue set in a silver cushion,
That tiny highest of all plants that gazes
Up to the sky all day and marks the spot
Where grass ends and the foot at last moves up
From the sweet turf to the fresh crunch of snow.
And scrape of boot on rock.
Here crystals sing high songs of violins
And ice adds its own bell-tones clear and hard
The crags boom their deep rocky resonance
And wind shrills its own counterpoint
To the mountain's symphony.
Faster and faster leaving time behind,
Fast and yet sure, breathing deep breaths of purity,
Blue ice once feared now friendly,
Rock curling warm and comfortable under my fingers
The sound of friendly voices gone ahead,
Until at last there close above,
Unattainable yet attained, the summit,
The peak on which I seem to stand on air
Wrapped in the blue space of eternity
And then the last great challenge,
To step fearless and joyful
On into the Unknown.

For SEPN without whom I might never have known the joys of
mountaineering.

Elisabeth Parry, Wanborough, October 2010

419

Appendices

Appendix A: Middle East Tour of 'Thirty Men and a Girl'

During its Middle East tour from November 1943 to August 1944 the Staff Band of the Royal Army Medical Corps gave over 200 official performances, including some 30 for hospital staff and patients, and many other unofficial shows at unexpected halts en route or by special request. The company travelled over 20,000 miles, mainly in a series of decrepit buses and lorries, and visited Egypt, Palestine, Iraq, Persia, Syria and the Canal Zone. Broadcasts were given from five capitals: Cairo, Jerusalem, Baghdad, Teheran and Beirut. Audiences ranged from a handful of white people at an outpost on the oil pipeline to 10,000 at the Alamein Club. The girl is proud to say that she did not miss a show.

Appendix B: The Opera Players, later London Opera Players

During the fifty seasons from 1950 to 2001 the company gave 3,585 performances of thirty-nine different operas, of which twenty-two were standard full-length works, fifteen were one-act chamber operas, and two were specially commissioned works for children.

The company gave employment to:

- 360 singers (soloists, not chorus)
- 22 pianists
- 13 conductors
- 18 directors
- 9 set designers
- 17 costume designers/makers
- 10 wardrobe maintenance assistants
- 8 props and furniture makers
- 32 stage managers, lighting and stage staff
- 7 secretarial assistants
- a large number of orchestral musicians

Appendix C: The Parry Trust and the Welsh National Opera

The first Parry bursary has just been awarded by the WNO to a young Welsh baritone, Gary Griffiths, who is currently studying on the opera course at the Guildhall School of Music and Drama in London. Gary originally trained as an actor. He already has an impressive list of roles performed and concerts given in the USA and in Italy as well as at home. He has appeared in a major role at the Royal Albert Hall, performed with the British Youth Opera, and has recently been selected as a rising star in the BBC *Music Magazine*.

He will make his professional company debut with WNO in the role of Guglielmo in Mozart's *Cosi fan Tutte* in the summer of 2011.

This is exactly the right way to build a young singer's career. Congratulations, WNO and Gary!

Elisabeth Parry, February 2010

Notes

1 QA is short for QAIMNS or army nurse – the grey and red uniforms.
2 The interbred townspeople – not the pure Arab.
3 This is incorrect – there is, or are, about half a dozen trees – when one is being 'shown' Shaibah, the *pièce de résistance* is when one's guide with a historic gesture says 'look' and one sees, by V C Hill of last-war fame, about six straggly tamarisks!
4 Glanmore Spiller, our leading violin – leader of the second violins, BBC Welsh Orchestra, until called up.
5 This fell through, unfortunately.
6 I was able to add later, 'It hasn't!'
7 My mother in her skiing days once showed a bruise to friends for that sum!
8 How he must have been laughing at me – when I got home the aquamarines turned out to be just glass!

Lightning Source UK Ltd.
Milton Keynes UK
UKOW06f0219140815

256868UK00005BA/63/P